DATE			
1-8-97			

THE CIVILIZATION OF THE AMERICAN INDIAN SERIES

The Cheyenne and Arapaho Ordeal

The Cheyenne and Arapaho Ordeal

Reservation and Agency Life in the Indian Territory, 1875–1907

by Donald J. Berthrong

UNIVERSITY OF OKLAHOMA PRESS : NORMAN

By Donald J. Berthrong

(editor, with Odessa Davenport) Daniel Ellis Conner, *Joseph Redde-ford Walker and the Arizona Adventure* (Norman, 1956)
(editor) W. T. Hamilton, *My Sixty Years on the Plains: Trapping, Trading, and Indian Fighting* (Norman, 1960)
The Southern Cheyennes (Norman, 1963)
(editor, with Odessa Davenport) Daniel Ellis Conner, *A Confederate in the Colorado Gold Fields* (Norman, 1970)
The Cheyenne and Arapaho Ordeal: Reservation and Agency Life in the Indian Territory, 1875-1907 (Norman, 1976)

Library of Congress Cataloging in Publication Data

Berthrong, Donald J
    The Cheyenne and Arapaho ordeal.

    (The Civilization of the American Indian series; 136)
    Bibliography: p. 385
    Includes index.
        1. Cheyenne Indians—Government relations.   2. Arapaho In-
dians of North America—Government relations—1869–1934.
I. Title. II. Series. E99.C53B45   323.1'19'7078   75–17795

Foreword

FOR MORE THAN a century the Southern Cheyennes moved freely over the vast reaches of the Great Plains. Their culture was similar to that of other Plains tribes with whom the Cheyennes and their confederates, the Arapahoes, shared a common environment. The Cheyennes provided for most of their wants from the great herds of buffaloes, which until the 1870's seemed inexhaustible. As hunters and warriors the Cheyennes were the peers of the Sioux, Crows, Pawnees, Kiowas, and Comanches and essentially maintained their original ways of life until the Plains environment was changed by whites. Weapons, trade goods, metal artifacts, and liquor they obtained at Bent's Fort, Fort Laramie, and other trading centers did not cause the Cheyennes to abandon their traditional economy or patterns of living.

White settlements west of the Great Plains, however, required links to the East. Inexorably the Santa Fe Trail, the Oregon Trail, the Pike's Peak Road, and, after the Civil War, railroads began to cut through the domains of the Plains Indians. Miners, ranchers, and farmers settled in constantly growing numbers around the edges of the Great Plains, until finally insistent demands arose that the Plains Indians be confined to specific and limited tracts so that whites could utilize productively the range and crop land of the Great Plains. Cheyenne participation in the resistance to the white intrusion upon the Great Plains has been previously described in *The Southern Cheyennes*, to which the reader may also refer for the history and descriptions of Cheyenne culture before 1875.

By the spring of 1875 the Southern Cheyennes and the Arapahoes were restricted to a reservation in western Indian Territory. Their final abode was defined not by a treaty but by an executive order issued in 1869 by President Ulysses S. Grant, which placed the Cheyennes and Arapahoes upon approximately 5 million acres of land south of the Cherokee Outlet, east of the Texas Panhandle, north of the Kiowa, Comanche, and Kiowa-Apache Reservation, and west of the ninety-eighth meridian and the Cimarron River. Three years later more than 760,000 acres were sheared away from the Cheyenne-Arapaho Reservation and were assigned by an unratified agreement to the Wichitas and the Affiliated Bands.

Too few studies in Indian history deal intensively with the reservation period. This book concentrates on the struggle of the Southern Cheyennes to maintain themselves as a people during this period. It was the policy of the United States government to grind the Cheyennes into cultural submission and remold them into replicas of white, Christian farmer-citizens with red skins, and that policy continued for decades after 1907, the terminal date of this volume. Rather than end the book with the formal conclusion of the reservation period, which occurred as a consequence of the congressional ratification in 1891 of the Jerome Commission's Agreement, I continue the narrative through the enactment and application of the 1906 Burke Act to the Cheyennes and Arapahoes. The year 1907, the year of Oklahoma statehood, is, in terms of this study, a peremptory date to conclude it, but until the administration of Indian Commissioner John Collier in the 1930's there is no time that appears to be any less arbitrary.

Research for this volume was undertaken in relatively little-used manuscript and archival sources. Most of these resources are available in the National Archives, the Oklahoma Historical Society, and the Western History Collections of the University of Oklahoma and those of the Kansas Historical Society. Manuscript records have been supplemented with published government documents, eyewitness accounts of participants and observers, and contemporary newspapers. Only a few references to secondary sources are found in my notes, since few scholarly studies have examined in much detail the application of the reservation policy, the Dawes Act, and the Burke Act to Indian tribes. I have, however, included in the bibliography books that emphasize the general formulation and implementation of the Indian policy of the United States government.

Many friends and associates assisted me during the research and writing of this book. At the National Archives, Carmelita Ryan, Jane Smith, Mrs. Sarah Jackson, Robert M. Kvasnicka, and Edward Hill placed at my disposal their invaluable knowledge of the Records of the Bureau of Indian Affairs and the War Department. Mrs. Rella Looney, of the Oklahoma Historical Society, over a period of fifteen years made certain that the records and files of the Indian Archives that pertained to the Southern Cheyennes and Arapahoes were thoroughly examined, and Mrs. Louise Cook guided me through the newspaper collections of the Oklahoma Historical Society. Nyle H. Miller and Robert W. Richmond, of the Kansas Historical Society, brought to my attention historical sources relating to the impact of the Cheyennes and Arapahoes on the citizens of Kansas. The editors of *Arizona and the West* and the *Kansas Quarterly* generously granted me permission to utilize materials published in those journals. My deep gratitude is extended to the librarians and archivists of the University of Oklahoma who labored patiently in my behalf. They include Arrell M. Gibson, Jack M. Haley, Miss Opal Carr, Mrs. Alice M. Timmons, and the late Arthur M. McAnally. Former students Lloyd H. Cornett, Jr., R. David Edmunds, Milton Ream, Terry P. Wilson, and Peter M. Wright contributed both specialized and background information about the Southern Cheyennes and Arapahoes in seminar papers, masters' theses, and research reports. Boyce Timmons and the late Walter S. Campbell introduced me to their Cheyenne and Arapaho friends, thereby furnishing me with insights and knowledge unobtainable in written records. Mrs. Brenda Matthews and Mrs. Doris Collins typed successive drafts of my manuscript with faithful attention to detail. Thavolia E. Glymph rendered valuable assistance by proofreading and checking details throughout the typescript copy of the manuscript. Donald L. Parman, Robert E. May, and Rhio Berthrong read and offered critical evaluations of the final draft, which led to a more accurate and precise version. Errors of fact and other faults within the following pages are, of course, my complete responsibility.

DONALD J. BERTHRONG

Lafayette, Indiana

Contents

	Foreword	*page vii*
I	The Aftermath of War	3
II	The Northern People Come South	27
III	The Beginnings of Agriculture and Education	48
IV	Cattlemen Occupy the Reservation	91
V	Preparations for Allotments	118
VI	The End of the Reservation	148
VII	White Neighbors Arrive	182
VIII	An Indian Policy for New Citizens	209
IX	Allotments and Farming	231
X	The Law of the White Man—The Pressure for Conformity	265
XI	Stagnation and Decay	296
XII	Epilogue	327
	Abbreviations Used in Notes	342
	Notes	343
	Bibliography	385
	Index	391

Illustrations

Three Fingers   *following page* 48
Wolf Robe
Yellow Eyes
Henry Roman Nose
Richard A. Davis and Bull Bear
Whirlwind with wives
Stone Calf and his wife
George Bent and his wife
Left Hand
Sitting Bull
Black Coyote

Willie Burns, Little Bear, Cloud Chief, and
   Little Chief   *following page* 152
Buffalo Meat, Three Fingers, and Wolf Robe
Henry Roman Nose, Yellow Bear, and Lame Man
Southern Cheyenne and Arapaho chiefs gathered for
   a council, 1900
Cheyenne-Arapaho delegation at the Gettysburg
   Battlefield, 1884
Indian and white agency and school personnel
Sam Whitt, John D. Miles, Little Robe, and Ben Clark
John D. Miles

xiii

John H. Seger
Major George W. H. Stouch

Cheyenne-Arapaho Agency at Darlington, 1878   *following page* 256
Cheyenne-Arapaho Agency at Darlington, late
    nineteenth century
Baker's Store and Murray Hotel, Darlington, Indian Territory
Mission building, Darlington, Indian Territory
Seger Indian School
Indian girls entering Seger Indian School
Indian boys cleaning the grounds of the Seger Indian School
John H. Seger supervising a work crew of Indians

Cantonment Indian School   *following page* 328
Young Whirlwind and Little Big Jake with Cheyenne
    students at Carlisle Indian School
Southern Cheyenne Indian Police
Arapaho winter camp
Beef issue, 1889
Southern Cheyenne dancers
Members of the Southern Cheyenne Lance Society
Participants in a peyote ceremony, 1912

Maps

Indian Territory, 1866–1889   *page* 14
Leases on the Cheyenne and Arapaho Reservation   97
Allotments on the Cheyenne and Arapaho Reservation   171

xv

The Cheyenne and Arapaho Ordeal

CHAPTER I

The Aftermath of War

ON THE MORNING of April 27, 1875, Indian Agent John D. Miles assured the Southern Cheyennes and the Arapahoes that they were again at peace. The Red River War, which had begun the year before, was over, and the ringleaders were imprisoned in Florida or were living with the Sioux and Northern Cheyennes. Those Southern Cheyenne bands who had bolted from their reservation were without food, clothing, lodges, ponies, or camp equipment. Agent Miles could not imagine "a more wretched and poverty stricken community." Even the Cheyenne bands led by Old Whirlwind and the Arapahoes who had not joined the fighting were suffering from hunger and privation. So unsettled were conditions on the Southern Cheyenne and Arapaho Reservation that Miles advocated the retention of a strong military detachment near Darlington, the agency headquarters in the Indian Territory, to control "evil-disposed Indians, . . . white horse-thieves and cut-throats." He did not believe that an enlarged Indian police force could "supersede the necessity of military force."[1]

During the spring of 1875 the agency force tried to restore order on the reservation. Educational programs for the children of the tribes had been abandoned, as had small-scale agricultural activities by the more tractable tribal members. Despite the danger of being mistaken for warring bands, Old Whirlwind's Cheyennes and the Arapahoes had hunted buffalo near the reservation's western limits. During the early months of 1875 the hunters found herds of sufficient

3

size to feed their people, but once back at Darlington in their camps the stores of meat were soon exhausted, and they were again dependent upon beef and food supplied by annuities. For the most part the Indians gathered in large camps, where they wasted away from hunger, disease, and lethargy.[2]

Agent Miles recommended that the supply of beef be continued for the fiscal year in 1875–76 in approximately the same quantity as in 1874–75. During the latter year he had received 5,212,659 pounds of beef from 6,839 head of cattle, and he estimated that at least 5 million pounds would be required until July 1, 1876. Superintendent Enoch Hoag, however, reduced Miles's estimate by 500,000 pounds, provided other foods could also be furnished to the Cheyennes and Arapahoes. By midsummer, 1875, there were no cattle on which to subsist the Indians while the warehouses were empty. The fifty acres of corn, squashes, pumpkins, and garden vegetables planted by Indians produced little because of late planting. Again Agent Miles had no choice but to send Cheyenne and Arapaho hunters, accompanied by agency employees and troops, to find buffaloes along the Washita River and in the Texas Panhandle. The hunters brought back to the camps near Darlington about 2,300 hides and enough cured meat to relieve the food crisis.[3]

When government contractors failed to deliver cattle, food, and annuity goods on schedule, Miles was again forced to permit the tribes to hunt on the reservation and in the Cherokee Outlet. It was a matter not only of food but also of health. The camps of the Indians, reportedly "filthy," remained clustered about the agency headquarters waiting for supplies that never arrived. Jason Holloway, the agency physician, reported that he had administered medicine to 962 Indians during the month of August, 1875, and that despite his ministrations four Cheyennes had died in their camps on the night of August 31 from "congestive intermittent fever" and that others were "lying quite low with the disease." He attributed the health problems of the Indians to drinking impure river water, improper diet, lack of salt, and lack of proper exercise. If they were permitted to move onto the Plains, the men would exercise on the hunt, and all the people would be healthier. By mid-September, 1875, only limited supplies of

4

beef were available for issue to the Cheyennes and Arapahoes, and Acting Agent J. A. Covington warned that "it will be impossible to hold the Indians in camp near the Agency without something to subsist them on."[4]

To restore their health and obtain food, the Cheyennes and Arapahoes moved their main villages to Wolf Creek, about twenty-five miles above Fort Supply. About forty-two lodges remained near Darlington, containing the old, weak, and sick and those who did not possess ponies to ride on the hunt. Superintendent Hoag approved of the relocation of the villages because of the excessive illness among the Indians. By November 1 the men had killed enough buffaloes for food but not enough for robes to barter for sugar, coffee, salt, and the other needs of their families. Benjamin Williams, who was supervising the hunting camps, feared trouble between the Indians and white hunters who were slaughtering thousands of buffaloes on the Texas Panhandle. An Arapaho scouting party was fired on by a group of white hunters, who killed a mule on which an Arapaho was riding. The whites fled, anticipating an attack by a larger Indian party in retaliation and leaving behind five worn-out horses, which the Indians delivered to Williams. It was feared by Williams that when the Indians pushed farther west along the South Canadian River and Beaver and Wolf creeks to search for larger buffalo herds trouble would soon develop. To control the Indians while they hunted and to protect them from "bad whites" who were swarming around the camps selling whisky, Williams wanted a military escort of fifteen men and a commissioned officer to stay with each of the hunting villages of the two tribes.[5]

When the Cheyenne and Arapaho hunters were ready to move away from Fort Supply, Agent Miles issued permits to licensed traders to sell the tribes limited quantities of ammunition. Major General John Pope, commanding general of the Department of the Missouri, objected, maintaining that it was dangerous to sell ammunition to the Cheyennes, even for buffalo hunting. Superintendent Hoag reversed Agent Miles's decision, and the Cheyennes and Arapahoes were forced to obtain their cartridges from Kiowa traders who were selling ammunition with the approval of the commanding officer of Fort Sill. Although Hoag and Cyrus Beede, chief clerk of the Central Superintendency, disagreed with General Pope, Beede noted that the general had raised sensitive questions, and, to avoid conflict with the military, hoped that Miles could see the "propriety of withholding these permits for the present."[6]

The Cheyennes and Arapahoes were irritated by General Pope's attitude. So was Agent Miles. He claimed to be unimpressed by "Gen. Pope's bombast" but was willing to accede to the wishes of Superintendent Hoag. The Kiowas and Comanches, Miles pointed out, were as deeply involved in the 1874–75 war as were the Cheyennes, and the former tribes were being supplied with arms and ammunition by Colonel Ranald S. Mackenzie, commandant of Fort Sill. Miles could not understand why the Arapahoes should be placed under such restrictions, since 1,650 Arapahoes had remained near Darlington throughout the conflict. Because Congress appropriated insufficient funds to subsist the Indians at their agency throughout the whole year, Miles thought that the only humane policy was to allow them to hunt during the winter and save the supplies provided by Congress when buffalo herds were too scattered to hunt. Continuing his argument with General Pope, Miles contended that 1,116 of the 1,662 Cheyennes had been declared peaceful by army officers on May 1, 1875. After the conclusion of the campaigns in the winter of 1874–75 and again after the Sand Hill fight, Lieutenant Colonel Thomas H. Neill had failed "to disarm a helpless foe." The same officer, Miles maintained, had invited the Cheyennes who "stampeded" after the Sand Hill fight to surrender under an offer of a general amnesty. That unwise act had resulted in the mixing of the worst "criminals" with the innocent throughout the agency. Miles resented General Pope's implications that he was "robbing his charges and thus driving them from the Agency and reservation in search of food." But he queried, "If Gen. Pope is so full of philanthropy for these Indians and desires to bring to punishment some of these 'thieving agents' why don't he make specific charges and give the Govt. an opportunity to stop us in our thieving careers."[7]

With ammunition secured without their agent's consent, the Cheyennes and Arapahoes remained on Beaver and Wolf creeks until the

6

buffalo herds diminished. General Pope continued to press Miles to assume greater control over the Cheyennes and Arapahoes by calling attention to the unsettled condition of the Sioux north of the Platte River. Superintendent William Nicholson responded to Pope's suggestion that all the Indians of the Central Superintendency be kept away from the Plains, and he ordered them assembled in the immediate vicinity of their agencies. As small parties of Cheyennes and Arapahoes straggled back to Darlington, Miles was told by chiefs that they had secured scarcely enough buffalo meat for their people to eat and too few robes to replace the ponies lost on the hunts and from disease. Knowing that the Indians were short of provisions, Superintendent Nicholson predicted that they would clamor for annuity goods and that only their distribution would hold them near Darlington.[8]

In the spring of 1876, as the army officers continued to denounce Agent Miles, his superiors came to his defense. Commissioner J. Q. Smith explained that although the distribution of food caused some problems starvation was not imminent among the Cheyennes and Arapahoes. Rejecting the War Department's charge that "through the negligence or perverseness of their Agent" the Cheyennes and Arapahoes were starving, Superintendent Nicholson insisted that Miles could not be held responsible for the death of many of the Cheyennes' and Arapahoes' ponies from an epidemic during the winter buffalo hunt. In Nicholson's opinion "a sudden and unlooked for calamity" was "insufficient ground" for an attack on Agent Miles. On April 27, 1876, Miles reported that all the Cheyennes and Arapahoes except twenty-five of the former tribe who remained at Fort Supply because all their ponies had died during the winter, were assembled at Darlington where Miles issued the year's annuity goods in the presence of Major J. K. Mizner, commanding officer of Fort Reno. To supplement the issue, Miles sought permission for a limited number of Cheyennes and Arapahoes to hunt for twenty days so that they could replenish their lodge skins.[9]

General Pope and Superintendent Nicholson approved of Miles's request since the annuity goods contained no material for lodge covering. In no case, the Superintendent specified, should the hunting

7

parties leave the reservation or hunt on the Texas Panhandle. "Whilst I wish to discourage the hunting habits of these Indians," Superintendent Nicholson wrote, "I know that these habits cannot be suddenly changed whilst Buffalo are in the Immediate vicinity of the Agency." Robert Bent, the son of William Bent, former owner of Bent's Fort, was given supervision over the Cheyenne hunters, and four soldiers from Fort Reno were detailed to escort the hunting party. About one-third of the Cheyennes hunted for three weeks, returning to the agency headquarters on July 4, 1876, with an adequate supply of lodge skins but little dried meat. The Arapahoes, who had waited to see whether the Cheyennes were successful, then sent their hunters into the western portion of the reservation.[10]

The War Department and army officers argued that it was the responsibility of the Bureau of Indian Affairs to ration the Indians adequately so that they would remain close to the agency headquarters and nearby Fort Reno. Agent Miles, however, contended that subsistence available from congressional appropriations and annuity funds fell far short of the amounts required to support the Cheyennes and Arapahoes for an entire year. The problem can be illustrated by the difficulties encountered by Miles during the 1875–76 fiscal year. He estimated that approximately 5 million pounds of beef would be required for the year, but only 2,759,400 pounds were authorized for the two tribes, of which 2,091,832 pounds were actually distributed to the Cheyennes and Arapahoes. Contractors habitually misrepresented the amount of edible meat available on the gaunt, tough Texas cattle delivered to the agency. During one six-month period, Miles charged, the cattle received at Darlington averaged only 748 pounds an animal. During the 1875–76 fiscal year, the Cheyennes and Arapahoes received about one-third of the coffee and sugar and one-half of the bacon and flour approved by government officials. With such limited supplies Miles could not possibly appease the appetites of the Cheyennes and Arapahoes. Complaints by Miles did no good. Although the beef contracts had been awarded to reputable cattlemen, the herds driven to the agency "were not fit for beef and yet were 'merchantable,'" causing the Indian agent to plead, "Do give us *one protective* contract." Direct appeals to a beef contractor's representa-

8

tive led to Miles's being told that there were no "fat" cattle in the region available for purchase. To issue some beef to the Indians, Miles borrowed as many cattle as he could during March, 1876, but there were few cattle herds in western Indian Territory, and the agency employee force was too small to make a systematic search.[11]

Undoubtedly stung by criticisms from army officers and knowing that his superiors did not want the Cheyennes and Arapahoes to hunt, Miles decided to assume personal risks to provide the people with food. He knew that at least three cattlemen were ranging herds within a reasonable distance of Darlington. None of the cattlemen would supply Miles with cattle, one fearing that he would find it difficult to obtain payment from the Department of the Interior. Continuing his search, Miles negotiated several verbal agreements with other cattlemen, and, to assure enough beef for issue, he dispatched Deputy Marshal Benjamin Williams to the Cimarron River with a posse "to seize two hundred head of beef cattle from herds" held there. "Don't be uneasy about us," Miles wrote Superintendent Nicholson. "We will see that our Indians do not starve." On April 12, 1876, Deputy Marshal Williams and the posse returned to Darlington, driving in 198 animals, weighing about 137,000 pounds. Although the posse had selected only three- to four-year-old steers, the best animals in the 5,000-head herd, they still averaged less than 700 pounds a steer. Williams' report of his seizure of the cattle should have alerted Miles for trouble. The herd boss told Williams that he had no authority to sell cattle, and "he refused to let the cattle go until he was overpowered." The cattle arrived just in time. Old Whirlwind and his seven hundred people had just returned from an unsuccessful hunt, and they were hungry, as were Little Raven's, Bird Chief's, and Powder Face's Arapahoes. Belatedly Miles asked the Bureau of Indian Affairs to approve of his actions so that he could reimburse the owners for the cattle seized.[12]

Within a few days Miles began looking around for more cattle. The verbal contracts failed, and the new government beef contractor, F. C. Buckley, was not fulfilling his agreement to range herds near enough to Darlington so that Miles could request beef as required. Miles disclaimed any desire to make unreasonable demands on the beef contractors, but he warned Buckley, "I must and will have beef." There were cattle herds ranging in western Indian Territory. Ostensibly the cattle were owned by beef contractors for Indian agencies, but actually they were the property of cattlemen who were hoping to graze their herds on the free grass of Indian land until they could be driven to the Kansas cow towns. Again Miles sent four of his employees to the Cimarron River, but they returned without cattle. The manager of the herd refused to sell steers for the three cents a pound on the hoof offered by Miles, and the four men could not seize the cattle when confronted by thirty Texas cowboys. Miles then requested a military escort from Fort Reno to accompany two agency herders so that between 100 to 125 cattle could be commandeered. If the manager still declined to sell the cattle, Miles informed Mizner that the herds were being held on an Indian reservation contrary to law and were liable to a fine of one dollar for each head held. The fine could be repeated each time a warning was issued.[13]

Major Mizner provided the detail from the Fourth Cavalry stationed at Fort Reno. Lieutenant A. E. Wood and eight men accompanied two agency herders and found a herd within a day's ride of Darlington. When an offer of three cents a pound on the hoof was refused, the lieutenant selected about two hundred of the best cattle and drove them to Darlington. It was estimated by Lieutenant Wood that six to seven thousand cattle were grazing along the Cimarron.[14]

The second seizure of cattle brought prompt and vigorous protests from the cattlemen. On April 25, 1876, Seth Mabry and J. R. Driskell, Texas cattlemen, went to Darlington and claimed that they were the owners of the herds visited by Lieutenant Wood and that E. B. Millett owned the cattle driven off by Ben Williams. Acknowledging that they were technically trespassers, Mabry and Driskell explained that J. M. Daugherty, a beef contractor's agent, had assured them that "if you get into trouble for holding your cattle near the Cheyenne Agency, I will help you out." To Miles they said, "We have had some of your grass . . . & now you have got some of our cattle." They suggested that the cattle be valued at 3 to 3½ cents a pound gross, to be charged against the contracts of the beef contractors and that they would pay 50 to 75 cents a head for grazing their cattle for five months on the Cheyenne-Arapaho Reservation. Miles did not accept the cattlemen's offer and referred the settlement to the Washington office of the Bureau of Indian Affairs.[15]

Major Mizner rather than Agent Miles was censured for the seizure of the cattle. General Pope warned Major Mizner that he had acted improperly and that he was liable for any action that the cattlemen might take to recover their losses. Colonel Mackenzie, sent from Fort Sill to investigate and report on the incident, recommended that the cattlemen be allowed three cents a pound gross for their cattle and that the sum be applied against Buckley's contract. When the report reached the desk of General William T. Sherman in Washington, discussion ended. Sherman believed that Major Mizner was an experienced officer who would not have issued the order to seize the cattle unless it was absolutely necessary. There was, in Sherman's opinion, little for Major Mizner to be concerned about since the cattlemen were on the reservation in violation of Indian treaty rights, and a court would only fine and imprison them for their acts.[16]

Agent Miles and the Indians sought additional sources of funds to subsist the Cheyennes and Arapahoes. On May 17, 1876, Agent Miles permitted Powder Face and his band of Arapahoes to locate on the Chisholm Trail, which ran just east of Darlington; there they could exchange buffalo robes and ponies for cattle. Agency traders also found a means to help. Earlier in the spring of 1876, Lee & Reynolds, the agency traders, had purchased a few buffalo hides from white hunters in the Texas Panhandle. The skins were turned over to Cheyenne women, who cured and tanned them for the traders. Successful in the experiment, the traders sent representatives to Kansas railroad terminals and to the hunting camps, acquiring about five thousand buffalo hides, which were turned over to the women, largely among the Cheyennes. The women received about three dollars in credit at the trader's store for each robe tanned. This meant, Miles reported, an income of fifteen thousand dollars for the purchase of food and other necessities for their families.[17]

Necessity also caused Agent Miles to advance another suggestion to supplement the Indians' income. He offered to accept the responsibility for transporting agency goods and supplies from Wichita,

Kansas, to Darlington with Indian labor for $1.50 for each one hundred pounds. An employee could be made "train boss" to protect the Indians and the property over the 165-mile route. If the government would provide the funds for the purchase of wagons and harnesses, the Indians would have an immediate income and equipment with which to do other work and farming. "The Government is anxious to have the Indians labor," Miles wrote, "& these Indians now make a fair proposition." Superintendent Nicholson doubted the practicality of Miles's idea, since the agent would be responsible for all losses while the goods were in transit. Miles persisted. He was willing to assume all losses for Indian depredations and for negligence by agency employees, but not for losses sustained from storms or floods. If he was made a freight contractor, however, he would willingly assume all liabilities. But "rather than let such a *benefit* slip from these Indians," Miles concluded, "I will take the entire risk, provided no one else will join me, in the venture."[18]

By the late summer of 1876 food supplies at Darlington were alarmingly low. Agent Miles had already borrowed bacon, coffee, and sugar from the Fort Reno commissary, and the arrival of additional food was unlikely. At first he suggested that the Cheyennes and Arapahoes send small hunting parties east of Fort Supply, where considerable numbers of buffalo were grazing. A month later, on September 20, 1876, Miles sought permission for all able-bodied Cheyennes and Arapahoes to hunt through the winter months of 1876–77. Greatly reduced appropriations from Congress, Miles explained, made it "absolutely necessary that the Indians of this Agency engage in the chase for five or six months in order to obtain subsistence to carry them through" the 1876–77 fiscal year. Superintendent Nicholson suggested that the hunt be limited to the period of time necessary for the Indians to kill enough buffaloes for meat to supplement the supplies from governmental sources. The Bureau of Indian Affairs tacitly admitted that the food supply furnished was insufficient when Acting Commissioner S. A. Galpin approved of the extended hunt if the subsistence furnished by the government was inadequate after a 25 per cent increase in flour and beef was added to the Cheyenne and Arapaho issues.[19]

On October 13, 1876, about two-thirds of the Cheyennes and Arapahoes broke their camps near Darlington. They moved slowly toward Fort Supply, setting up their tipis along Wolf Creek, about thirty miles west of the post. At least there were enough buffaloes for meat and robes, for the Indians killed eight hundred animals on one run. The camps, however, would have to be moved because the same herds the Cheyennes and Arapahoes were hunting among were being decimated by white hunters, Osages, Pawnees, Wichitas, and Caddoes. George Bent, who was in charge of the winter camps, frequently reported to Miles. Some of the Indians were handicapped by lack of ponies and had to "hunt the buffalo on foot." (Limpy, a Cheyenne who did not possess a hunting pony, was unable to barter his little daughter's dress, which was decorated with elk teeth, and so he joined the hunt after "borrowing" a horse.) As the buffalo drifted westward, the Indians, especially the Cheyennes, split into small camps scattered along Elk, Medicine Lodge, and Beaver creeks. George Bent explained to Miles, "You know it is best to let them camp in small camps, they can kill more buffalo by doing so." For months the Cheyennes and Arapahoes fed themselves on buffalo meat and supplies obtained from traders who visited their camps in exchange for buffalo robes. "Now we hope," Miles wrote, "that Buffalo in sufficient numbers will be found to keep them on the chase until supplies on hand will be sufficient to feed them humanely during the remainder of the fiscal year." During the winter of 1876–77, the tribes were happy enough and were not too disturbed when they lost some horses to white thieves because the military escort, consisting of one officer and twenty-five men, could not protect the scattered camps.[20]

None of Miles's pleas for more supplies did much good. Instead the Bureau of Indian Affairs informed Miles that he could expect an additional 25 per cent reduction in issue beef. If the minimum weekly ration of four pounds of beef gross for each person was cut to three, Miles asserted that when his accounts were settled he would be "ready of voluntary bankruptcy." Since the cattle used for beef produced only two pounds of edible meat for every four pounds liveweight, any less would keep the "Indians hungry & irritable and our influence for good among them greatly reduced." Despite the successful hunt, the

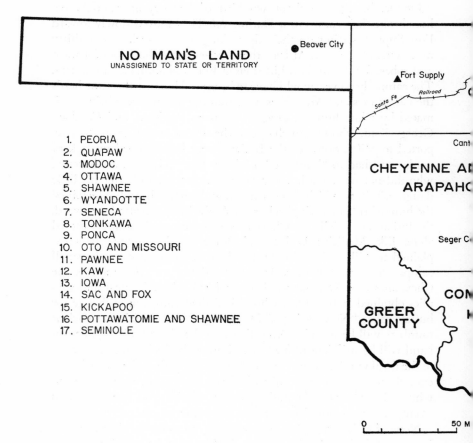

NO MAN'S LAND
UNASSIGNED TO STATE OR TERRITORY

● Beaver City

▲ Fort Supply

Santa Fe   Railroad

Cant

CHEYENNE AI
ARAPAHC

Seger C

1. PEORIA
2. QUAPAW
3. MODOC
4. OTTAWA
5. SHAWNEE
6. WYANDOTTE
7. SENECA
8. TONKAWA
9. PONCA
10. OTO AND MISSOURI
11. PAWNEE
12. KAW
13. IOWA
14. SAC AND FOX
15. KICKAPOO
16. POTTAWATOMIE AND SHAWNEE
17. SEMINOLE

GREER
COUNTY

CON

0   50 M

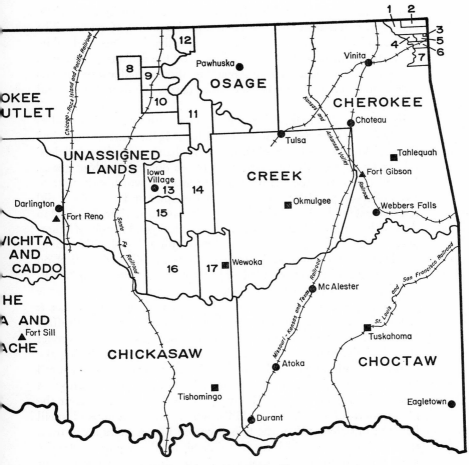

Indian Territory, 1866–1889.

Indians had begun to trickle back toward Darlington by mid-February, 1877, and immediately Miles resumed issuance of rations. The buffaloes had scattered too widely for effective hunting, and white horse thieves increased their depredations on the Indians' pony herds. Even the cavalry detail sent to protect the Indians had lost two horses and a mule to the white renegades from border towns in Kansas and Texas.[21]

Exchanges of buffalo robes for supplies with the Indian traders also worked to the detriment of the Indians. If the Indians furnished the buffalo hides and tanned them, each robe was worth ten traders' tokens, or, supposedly, the equivalent of ten dollars' worth of goods. In trade, however, the ten tokens were actually worth only four to five dollars in goods or money. The Cheyennes and Arapahoes did not understand business affairs based on money and thus preferred to deal with traders' tokens. Miles illustrated the "good supply of ignorance" with which he had to contend by relating that the issuance of goods and other commodities on one day was followed by beef on the next. One old chief complained bitterly that the agent was "cheating them out of one days ration of Beef as we issued flour, sugar & coffee every seven days & Beef one day later making 8 days." Lee & Reynolds, the agency Indian traders, continued to purchase buffalo hides for the women to tan. The ten thousand skins returned as robes furnished the women with "remunerative employment during the summer months and a fund to supply all our ration deficiencies" until October, 1877. Although most of the tribes camped near Darlington during the summer of 1877, hunting parties continued to scour the plains south of the Antelope Hills, where they encountered small herds of buffaloes. Often the kills occurred fifteen miles away from the hunting camps, which made it difficult for the women to dry the meat properly to prevent spoilage. Yet the Indians obtained about one thousand hides for lodges, moccasins, and other uses.[22]

During these times of privation an Indian agent was willing to do many things to obtain more food for the Indians. Before most of the Northern Cheyennes moved to the Indian Territory reservation, Miles took a census of the Southern Cheyennes and Arapahoes. Previously Miles had been reporting the population of the two tribes as 3,503, but on July 14, 1877, he claimed that they totaled 4,065. The enrollment showed that there were 427 Cheyenne families, consisting of 522 men, 820 women, and 957 children, while among the Arapahoes there were 289 families, with 563 men, 553 women, and 650 children. Assigned to the Cheyenne and Arapaho Agency were 2,299 Cheyennes and 1,766 Arapahoes, for a total of 4,065, as of July 14, 1877. Some rise in the numbers can be explained by a return of small groups of Cheyennes who had bolted from the reservation following the 1874–75 conflict and the Sand Hill fight. Undoubtedly, however, Agent Miles was inflating the population to obtain more rations from government sources.[23]

For the third successive year since the wars ended, Miles found it necessary to ask for permission for the Cheyennes and Arapahoes to hunt. By the winter of 1877, however, the buffalo herds on the southern Plains had been so decimated by white hunters that Miles predicted that the Indians would have to move into the Texas Panhandle for a successful hunt. As foreseen, the Indians found few buffaloes within the confines of their reservation and subsisted on the two-week rations issued to them by Agent Miles before departing from Darlington. George Bent reported that he was camping near Fort Supply with his family and finding "nothing but a few old Bulls and not enough to live on." He declined to move farther west if there were no buffaloes, risking the loss of his ponies to white horse thieves who were preying on the Indian camps along Wolf and Beaver creeks.[24]

Even the herds in the Texas Panhandle were few and dispersed. The food issued at Darlington was consumed within three weeks, and soon reports came back to Darlington that many of the hunting parties were starving. Failing to find buffalo for meat, the Indians annoyed settlers on the Panhandle by begging for food. Colonel John P. Hatch of Fort Elliot, Texas, predicted bloodshed if the situation continued, and he asked Miles to recall the Cheyennes and Arapahoes to prevent another Indian war. Miles did what he could for the Indians, some of whom were eating the flesh of dead ponies. He refused to call the people back to the agency since "a very large majority of the 'settlers' in the Pan Handle are 'Buffalo Hunters' well sprinkled with

Horse Thieves, . . . and in my opinion peaceable Indians would have as good a right to secure meat and furs from that district as any one." When reports were authenticated that the Indians were in trouble and lacked subsistence, he authorized Lee & Reynolds to issue four pounds gross of beef for each person for ten days in the hunting camps.[25]

By late December, 1877, the Cheyennes and Arapahoes were demoralized and suffering. Their ponies were too weak to travel, and they saw little reason to return to Darlington where during the past winters they had received inadequate rations at best. J. A. Covington and William Darlington, agency employees, were dispatched by Miles to see what could be done at Camp Supply. They were told to obtain beef from Lee & Reynolds if necessary, but were warned that no further supplies could be issued unless the bands returned to Darlington. If buffalo were still available, the Indians were to be urged to continue the hunt, because the more than 1,674 Northern and Southern Cheyennes and Arapahoes, including school children were rapidly exhausting the agency stores of supplies. Only the Arapahoes under Little Raven and Powder Face agreed to move their bands down to Darlington, although the Northern Cheyennes, led by Hog, Old Crow, Old Bear, and Arapahoe Chief, seemed willing if the Southern Cheyennes would join them. Despite Miles's pressure, many of the Cheyennes thought that they would stay out on the plains and live on whatever buffaloes they could find. Stone Calf, an influential Cheyenne war leader, said that Miles "was hard on him and, . . . there was no grass for his ponies." During January, 1878, the Cheyennes scattered out between the Washita River and the tributaries of the North Canadian River and killed enough buffaloes for food. The conditions were bad enough, however, for some of the Northern Cheyennes led by Old Crow to think about returning to the Pine Ridge Agency, and Miles thought that there was a chance that some were already en route north.[26]

The winter of 1877–78 saw the last tribal buffalo hunt for the Southern Cheyennes and Arapahoes. Only 219 robes were obtained for sale to the traders, and those were mainly secured by Indians "who having plenty of stock, could leave the main body travel quickly, picking up one here and there." Their agent concluded that "with the buffalo gone and their pony herds being constantly decimated by the inroads of horse-thieves, they must soon adopt in all its varieties the way of the white man, by exchanging small ponies, worthless except for riding, for a small number of large animals, horses and mules, suitable for work." In the summer of 1878 chiefs of the tribes attempted to lead their people to the buffalo again but abandoned the idea when scouting parties of young warriors reported that there were few if any buffaloes to hunt. On December 1, 1878, the commissioner of Indian affairs gave a few Cheyennes and Arapahoes permission to hunt. They were provided with rations for four weeks, "which, together with the few buffalo and small game they secured, bridged them over until their return to the agency. It is quite evident now," Agent Miles concluded, "that neither the government nor the Indians can place any reliance upon the supply of buffalo in the future, . . . and ample provision must be made for their subsistence for 365 days." Agent Miles called for an increase of more than two million pounds of beef for issue during the 1879–80 fiscal year to compensate for the lack of buffaloes. The buffaloes were gone, and issues of beef had to take their place.[27]

Not only did the United States government fail to provide food for the Cheyennes and Arapahoes, but also it failed to protect the property of the Indians. Both Agent Miles and Superintendent Nicholson repeatedly called for a sufficient force of civilian law officers or military detachments to check the heavy losses to the Indian pony herds. Occasionally Benjamin Williams, who had been appointed United States deputy marshal in addition to his other agency duties, returned horse thieves to Darlington. Kept under close guard at the Indian agency, they were transported to Wichita, Kansas, for arraignment before a United States commissioner. Usually the alleged horse thieves were turned loose because no funds were available for the agent to send the Indians to Kansas to testify as witnesses against the accused. When Agent Miles solicited the reappointment of Ben Williams as deputy marshal, Superintendent Nicholson supported the request. No United States marshal, Nicholson explained, was ever seen west of the Katy Railroad. He continued, "One of the scourges of the Indian territory is the presence of bad men, some of them refugees from justice, who obtain a livelihood by stealing cattle, herds of horses & other practices which elsewhere are considered crimes." Nicholson indicated that he would apply for six rather than one deputy marshal if he thought the request would be granted. There is no indication that Williams was reappointed.[28]

Unable to evoke an acceptable response for protection from Washington officials, Miles and the Indians turned to other means. Losses from the Cheyenne and Arapaho herds were sufficiently large during the winter of 1876-77 that a reward of five hundred dollars was offered for the arrest or capture of the horse thieves. Big Mouth, an Arapaho chief, lost thirty of his best horses. Stimulated by the reward, Sheriff James S. Weakley, of Russell County, Kansas, informed the Indian agent that he knew where some of the Indian stock had been sold and the names of the men who had driven the horses to Kansas. William Malaley, an agency employee, was sent to search for horse thieves on or near the reservation and was accompanied by a detachment of troops. Riding with the troopers or by himself, Malaley covered more than a thousand miles during a four-month period and managed to apprehend one horse thief and return about one-quarter of the horses lost by the Cheyennes and Arapahoes during the winter of 1876-77. Malaley's prisoner, Joseph Hariman, was captured in early March, 1877. Hariman confessed to his crimes and implicated a number of associates who were holding a large number of Indian ponies in Ellsworth and Russell counties in Kansas. Miles pleaded for sufficient funds to protect the Indian herds and to send the Indians to Kansas to testify against the thieves. "There is," Miles asserted, "a stolen pony in almost every stable from the Cimarron to the Platte."[29]

Although Miles's superiors applauded his success in recovering some of the Indians' stock, they did not allocate additional funds to make his activities more effective. The Indians were vexed and disturbed by the losses of their ponies, which meant wealth and prestige to them. Unless the thieving stopped, Superintendent Nicholson warned, "we shall reap the fruits and wastage of another Indian war." Even though Agent Miles knew exactly where 150 of the best Cheyenne and Arapaho horses were being held in Kansas, his requests failed to bring any response from either Washington bureaucrats or military officers. Infrequently the Indians recovered their own stock. On October 23, 1877, a party of horse thieves raided the herds near the agency, running off forty-two animals from the Arapahoes. A few days later six young Cheyenne hunters recognized some animals as belonging to their Arapaho friends. They jumped the whites, recapturing thirty-eight head. The thieves "stampeded in the direction of the Kansas border." But more frequently the horses and ponies turned up for sale in some Kansas border town. William Malaley, while with the agency wagon train in Wichita, bought a fine white horse for forty dollars and rode it back to Darlington. There, to his sorrow, he learned that it was one of the ponies run off earlier from the herd of an Arapaho chief. He returned the animal to the chief and thus lost about a month's wages.[30]

Another incident disturbed the operations of the Cheyenne and Arapaho Agency during the spring and summer of 1875. After the Red River War, significant numbers of Cheyenne warriors refused to accept the restrictions of reservation life and rode for freedom north of the Platte River to join their kinsmen the Northern Cheyennes and their old allies, the Sioux, led by Crazy Horse. They were joined by a smaller contingent of Southern Cheyennes after the Sand Hill fight. How many fled cannot be determined precisely. Most of the efforts made by the military forces to intercept the fugitives were futile. It was known that they were encamped in a four-hundred-lodge village sixty to seventy miles northwest of the Red Cloud Agency with Northern Cheyennes and Sioux. In mid-July, 1875, John P. C. Shanks, in what was probably an overestimate, listed the number of Cheyennes absent from the Indian Territory reservation as 631. Within a few months, however, some of the Southern Cheyennes began to miss their families and were waiting for an opportunity to return to their homes.[31]

Not only were Southern Cheyennes likely to return to Darlington, but Northern Arapahoes and Cheyennes were also becoming concerned about their safety if they remained with the Sioux. In early October, 1875, the Northern Arapahoes sent a delegation of people headed by Yellow Horse, "a chief of some note, and a fine looking man," to talk with the southern tribal division about the welfare of their people. With a pass from Agent J. J. Saville of the Red Cloud Agency, they traveled uneventfully until they camped one afternoon on a small creek near Buffalo Station on the Kansas Pacific Railroad. Their camp was approached by a detachment of thirty to forty men led by two officers of Company H, Fifth Cavalry. By signs the Arapahoes managed to tell the soldiers that they had a pass from their agent but that the man with the pass was back on the trail bringing in some tired horses. One of the young warriors was sent with a noncommissioned officer, First Sergeant Kirby, to find the pass carrier. Once outside the camp Kirby tried to disarm the young man. Failing to wrestle the gun from the warrior, Kirby shot him, and the Indian died the next day. When they heard the gunshots the cavalrymen charged the Indian camp, but were driven off by the warriors, who then rode hard and fast until they were safely in the Southern Arapaho camps near Camp Supply. Upon the demands of the army, Powder Face, Left Hand, and other chiefs arranged for the surrender of some of the Northern Arapahoes, who finally were locked up in Fort Reno's guardhouses. For almost two months General Pope bickered with Superintendent Hoag about the release of the prisoners. Hoag refused to accept the conditions offered by General Pope and insisted that Agent Saville's pass should have protected Yellow Horse's party unless they had committed some hostile or unlawful act. "If they were guilty, let them be punished if not they should be released," was Hoag's attitude. An investigation by Lieutenant Colonel Eugene A. Carr of the Fifth Cavalry vindicated Kirby and the detachment by establishing that the young warrior had fired at Kirby before Kirby drew his gun. On December 14, 1875, Yellow Horse, seven men, and three women were turned over to Agent Miles. The others of the party, Miles believed, had already returned to the Red Cloud Agency. General Pope did not make any further recommendations or investigations but testily contended that an Indian agent should not give passes to Indians, just as a frontier government should not give passes to whites to roam through Indian reservations.[32]

Until the summer of 1876 the number of returnees and Northern Cheyennes and Arapahoes moving south was fairly small. One party of Cheyennes, consisting of thirty-two men, women, and children arrived at a hunting camp on Beaver Creek on December 8, 1875. They had been refused a pass by Red Cloud Agent Saville, who had told them that they could get through to Indian Territory if they behaved. No more Indians made the journey during the winter of 1875–76, but when war seemed likely north of the Platte River, small parties of Northern Cheyennes began to appear in the southern villages. Skirting the settlements in Kansas, they encountered no trouble on their journey of five or six weeks. They reported that more than one-half of the Northern Cheyennes and a few Arapahoes had joined Crazy Horse and were ready to fight. Probably no more than twenty-five Northern Cheyenne people sought refuge in the Southern Cheyenne camps through the early weeks of May, 1876.[33]

Not all the Indians who moved back and forth between Darlington and the Red Cloud agencies were observed. And for at least two years before 1876 plans were considered to concentrate all the Northern and Southern Cheyenne and Arapaho people on one reservation in Indian Territory. In fact the commissioner of Indian affairs had issued an order for the union of the Cheyennes and Arapahoes, but when no appropriations were provided, transfers could not be undertaken during the 1875–76 fiscal year. With troops in the field against the Sioux and their allies, Miles urged: "Now is certainly a favorable time for the Govt. to require the northern Chey & Arap to come south. Restless members of each tribe & those who may commit crimes will continually give the Govt. trouble in passing to & fro so long as the tribes are permitted to be divided."[34]

As large numbers of northern Indians were shifted to Indian Territory, an impossible burden was placed on the limited food supply at Darlington. When the first group of ninety-seven people arrived from the agencies north of the Platte River, the only instruction received by Agent Miles was to keep records of the amounts of subsistence issued to the northern people so that the cost could be deducted from the appropriations of the Red Cloud Agency. Miles described the group as consisting of "true Northern Cheyennes and Arapahoes," Southern Cheyennes who had fled when pressed by troops during the winter campaign of 1874–75, and others who had stampeded at the time of the Sand Hill fight. The commanding officer of Fort Reno suggested disarming the parties as they came in, but Miles feared that such an action would needlessly alarm the Indians, who appeared quiet and peaceful in the camps.[35]

By late June, 1876, Agent Miles determined more exactly the people who were coming under his jurisdiction. Of the 110 Cheyennes who had arrived from the Red Cloud Agency, 65 were from White Antelope's band, who had escaped the troops during the Red River War campaigns, 24 had fled during the Sand Hill fight, and 21 were Northern Cheyennes. This vanguard indicated that many more were strung out over the trails, hampered by jaded ponies. They also told Miles that he could expect most of the Northern Cheyennes and Arapahoes to transfer to the Darlington Agency because they were only waiting for a few others to make up their minds to do so.[36]

On June 30, 1876, Pawnee, a young Cheyenne warrior from Sand Hill's band, sought out Agent Miles at Darlington. The group, he said, were resting their ponies about thirty-five miles west of Fort Supply after their trek from the Red Cloud Agency. Sand Hill had been influenced to make the two-month trip because the Sioux led by Crazy Horse and the Northern Cheyennes led by Moon Chief were on the warpath and because some of their people who had refused to fight had been killed. Rumors circulating about the Red Cloud Agency worried Sand Hill because it was thought that all Indians friendly to whites would be required to join the army as scouts. Miles believed that Pawnee had been sent in as an emissary to judge how the band would be received because with Sand Hill were men described by Miles as "desperate characters," such as Sand Hill's son, Yellow Horse, who had participated in the attack on the O. F. Short surveying group and had also been involved in the German family murders.[37]

Miles reversed his earlier position and suggested that the incoming parties should be disarmed. After they were intercepted by troops from Fort Supply, the worst offenders should be culled from their midst; otherwise there would be trouble at the agency, where their friends might try to protect the warriors. It was the objective of the Indian agent then to exchange the "criminals" in Sand Hill's band for three Cheyenne prisoners held at Fort Marion, Minimic, Heap of Birds, and Bear Shield. Miles claimed that these men had not been charged with serious crimes and deserved to be freed.[38]

The military did not choose to intercept and disarm Sand Hill's people. On July 10, 1876, the eighty-eight members of the group arrived at Darlington, where they were enrolled, rationed, and sent to the camps of Old Whirlwind and Little Robe. From Sand Hill, Miles learned that he and his people had been at the Red Cloud Agency since their flight on April 6, 1875, from the Cheyenne and Arapaho Agency. The Indian agent at Red Cloud had never asked where the band had come from but had rationed them with the other Indians of his agency. According to Miles the Cheyenne chief said that "he left the Sioux country to get out of the trouble as he & his party did not wish to fight any more—says he has come down here to his home & friends & relatives to remain and be at peace." Two of the warriors Agent Miles wanted to imprison as "murderers," however, remained in the North with Crazy Horse—those being Yellow Horse, Sand Hill's son, and Medicine Man. If Agent Miles could rely on Sand Hill's conversations, he could expect that more of the Southern Cheyennes were en route and that Dull Knife and sixty lodges of Northern Cheyennes were ready to depart from the Red Cloud Agency.[39]

On orders from General Pope late in July, 1876, the military officers at Fort Reno decided to dismount and disarm the returnees as a "matter of safety." When White Antelope's band also arrived at Darlington, Major J. K. Mizner and Colonel Mackenzie supervised the task with Agent Miles's complete co-operation. Together the bands of Sand Hill and White Antelope consisted of sixty-six men, seventy-eight women, and sixty-eight children. Within three days after the bands had arrived, they had conformed to all the conditions imposed upon them by the army officers, and they were transferred to Miles's charge. Colonel Mackenzie thought that the attitude of the Southern Cheyennes and Arapahoes was excellent and that there "was no danger of an outbreak this year, provided they are not absolutely starved into it, or in some other way badly mismanaged."[40]

With three warriors, Dry Hide, Red Cloud, and Howling Eagle, came more news about the situation in the North. They had lost their horses to a party of Utes, except for one, which they alternately rode. At the Battle of the Rose Bud, fought against General Crook, Little Shield, a Southern Cheyenne who had participated in the attack on Short's surveyors and the German family, had been killed. Yellow Horse had come through the fighting unharmed and was remaining in the North. The young men had also heard messengers from Sitting Bull and Crazy Horse relate information about the annihilation of Custer's command. The victorious Sioux and their Cheyenne allies brought to the Red Cloud Agency "sugar, coffee, arms, horses and some scalps around which dances were kept up." Nevertheless, the victory of the Sioux and Cheyennes over Custer did not alter the flow of Cheyennes to the Darlington Agency.[41]

Agent Miles and Major Mizner systematically and easily checked in the new arrivals. Usually a new party was preceded by one or two messengers who appeared at the agency headquarters so that Miles learned of the impending arrival before the military did. To prevent panic or difficulty while the warriors were being disarmed and dismounted, Miles sent a few representatives from the established Southern Cheyenne camps. After the guns and horses were taken from the warriors, they were officially turned over to Agent Miles. Most of the Southern Cheyennes who straggled in and surrendered to the soldiers at Fort Reno arrived in very small groups, usually no more than three or four men accompanied by their wives and children. By April, 1877, few of the Southern Cheyennes who had fled two years earlier had not returned to the Darlington jurisdiction. Agent Miles then was informed that his agency should be prepared to receive fourteen hundred Northern Cheyennes.[42]

CHAPTER II

The Northern People Come South

No one really knew what would happen when the Northern Cheyennes joined their southern kinsmen. Those at the agency and in the superintendent's offices realized that more food would be required and that perhaps the agency staff would have to be enlarged. During 1876 and 1877, when the matter had been discussed in Washington and in Lawrence, Kansas, where the Central Superintendency had its headquarters, no systematic planning had occurred to care for the Northern Cheyennes on the Cheyenne-Arapaho Agency in Indian Territory. Superintendent Nicholson set the tone when he informed Agent Miles that the Northern Cheyennes were to be moved by the military from Red Cloud to Darlington. "Of course," Nicholson confided to Miles, "we are not anxious to have them, but as the Appropriation provides for it, I do not see how we can object," and he ordered Miles to submit an estimate for additional supplies. The Cheyenne-Arapaho agent requested slightly more than 1.6 million pounds of beef and 268, 275 pounds of flour and other commodities to feed the incoming bands.[1]

Lieutenant General Philip H. Sheridan thought that transferring the Northern Cheyennes to Darlington would cause little trouble. He told General William T. Sherman that one officer and twelve men could escort and control them until they reached Indian Territory. No more than fourteen hundred Northern Cheyennes had indicated that they were willing to change reservations, "and if the Commissioner of Indian Affairs will only say the word they shall go quickly and the remainder of the tribe who surrendered to Colonel Miles at Tongue River can be sent by steamboat and rail to the same place." Within the Department of the Missouri there was more apprehension; the officials felt "considerable anxiety lest these Indians upon arriving at the Agency should not be properly subsisted & be thereby induced to return to their old location."[2]

On August 5, 1877, the first large contingent of Northern Cheyennes arrived at Fort Reno escorted by Lieutenant H. W. Lawton of the Fourth Cavalry. The movement of the people took place uneventfully, and Lieutenant Lawton, although handicapped by inadequate transportation of supplies, delivered the Northern Cheyennes nearly three weeks ahead of his estimated travel time. Agent Miles enrolled the Northern Cheyenne bands on the following day. They contained 190 families consisting of 235 men, 312 women, and 386 children, over whom Miles assumed jurisdiction on August 7. Only 3 Arapaho men and 1 woman arrived with the northern people. During the fall of 1877 a few more of the Northern Cheyennes arrived, and by Miles's figures 943 Indians had been added to the Cheyenne-Arapaho Reservation.[3]

Tensions developed quickly between the Northern Cheyennes and Agent Miles. In addition, bickering and belittling of each other's valor began between young southern and young northern warriors. When rations were issued on August 8, 1877, Miles attempted to distribute the food to families, but the chiefs and warriors objected. They forced the families to pile the commodities together, and "when again in bulk they first took the lions share and then distributed the balance among the people. In order to prevent a repetition of this sharp practice," Miles declared, "I shall resort to such measures as may seem proper and prudent. These Northern folks have much to learn to be up with our folks and yet I trust our leaven will prevail." From his past experience with the Southern Cheyennes, Miles had learned that there was some "squirming" by the chiefs and warriors when they were displaced from controlling the distribution of food. He defended the distribution of food to families because "it goes into the mouths of all alike." Temporarily, however, Miles realized that because of an understaffed agency force he would be forced to use the old bulk plan, thus losing in "one week what we have gained in

28

one year, . . . yet men cannot perform impossibilities." By September 1, 1877, the Northern Cheyennes, Miles later reported, had accepted his system of issuing rations to families "quietly and gracefully," and he anticipated no further objections from the chiefs and warriors.[4]

Miles's optimism faded quickly as complaints from the Northern Cheyennes and some Southern Cheyennes began to mount. Flour was in short supply at Darlington, and to compensate the superintendent temporarily permitted Agent Miles to issue more beef. The regular issue of beef, however, contained only three pounds of beef liveweight for each family member a week. When resumed, the regular beef issue brought loud complaints from the Northern Cheyennes and the more turbulent people among the southern bands. Superintendent Nicholson faced the issue squarely in a letter to the commissioner:

The truth is the ration prescribed by you is not sufficient to satisfy them, except where they are able to add thereto by hunting or when they are able to make something extra by tanning buffalo robes or hides furnished them . . . by the Traders. At this season they can obtain no extras in this way—they depend entirely upon the ration. They are hungry and ill-humored.

Fresh from the northern conflicts with troops and with a very limited military force in Indian Territory, the Northern Cheyennes were confident "in their own ability to cope with the Government," which forboded trouble. To alleviate Miles's problems, Nicholson suggested that the beef ration at Darlington be increased by 25 per cent and that the garrison at Fort Reno be reinforced from troops at Fort Sill, since "the Cheyennes are much more likely to give trouble than any other South Western Indians."[5]

The Northern Cheyennes complained bitterly to Lieutenant Lawton, the man who had escorted them from the Red Cloud Agency. During early September, 1877, while visiting at Fort Reno, Lawton found that the Northern Cheyennes were camping some distance from the agency headquarters, which they refused to visit. From Major Mizner and Mr. Rowland, the latter having accompanied the Indians from Red Cloud, Lawton learned that the Northern Cheyennes had not been issued full rations for weeks. No flour or corn had been included in their rations, and no other commodities were substituted in lieu of these foods. Unless the Northern Cheyennes were provided with more substantial rations, Rowland was certain that the young men among them would steal horses and return to the Red Cloud Agency. Standing Elk and Living Bear, important Northern Cheyenne chiefs, told Lawton that the rations received by them were insufficient to prevent starvation and that many of their women and children were sick from want of food.[6]

On September 30, 1877, Lieutenant Lawton was ordered to Fort Reno to investigate and report on the condition of the Northern Cheyennes. In the week that followed he had ample opportunity to witness the issuance of food and to council with the leaders from the northern bands. Dull Knife, Wild Hog, and Standing Elk spoke for their people. Dull Knife, especially, was conciliatory. He assured Lawton that the Northern Cheyennes remembered the promises they had made to remain peaceful and stay with their southern kinsmen. Wild Hog and other leaders nevertheless complained that they had received no corn, hard bread, hominy, rice, beans, or salt, while the sugar and coffee issues lasted only three days instead of seven as intended. Many of the beefs issued by the agent were small, some were lame, and others looked as if they had been "starved to death." Part of the problem, Lawton believed, lay in the manner in which Miles issued beef to the Indians. A band with as many as fifty people or more would receive one animal, which might be small or underweight. No beef would be butchered to make up the shortage to that band, while another band might receive as much as 150 pounds more meat from a larger animal. Although Miles knew that the Indians were not receiving enough to eat, there was nothing he could do because he was following the rations prescribed by the commissioner of Indian affairs. Lawton also visited the principal Northern Cheyenne encampment, about twelve miles above the agency on the North Canadian River. The bands had put up their lodges on a hill overlooking the river, which provided them with water, and an adequate wood supply was close at hand. Yet many of the people were sick, suffering principally from "malarial complaints," for which the agency physician dispensed quinine. Since the doctor did not visit the camp and most of the Northern Cheyennes were unwilling to make the twenty-four-mile trip to Darlington for each dosage of medicine, Lieutenant Lawton estimated that at least 150 people were ill with fevers and other ailments.[7]

When Lawton's reports were made known to Miles, the Indian agent rejected the lieutenant's conclusions. He claimed that the Indians did not find him personally unsatisfactory and that the northern bands voiced nothing more than "general complaints which is common to the Indians who received his subsistence from the Govt." Miles noted that he had been authorized to issue 25 per cent more beef during the month of October, 1877, and that he was confident that "there has been no suffering among them for want of food though they would and could have eaten twice as much of the small Rations regular, had it been issued to them." When Lawton continued to criticize and challenge the integrity of Miles's administration at Darlington, the Indian agent indicated that he would be pleased to have an official investigation based on Lieutenant Lawton's allegations.[8]

While the Northern Cheyennes were still grumbling about short rations, Miles applied additional pressure upon them. He wanted the Northern Cheyennes to send their children to the agency school as did some of their southern friends. Standing Elk, Broken Cup, and Living Bear agreed to Miles's request, but Dull Knife and Wild Hog declined. When Lieutenant Lawton was on his tour of inspection, Dull Knife declared they would eventually send their children to school if the bands decided that they would remain at the Darlington Agency. After the agent threatened to cut off their rations, Dull Knife and Wild Hog reluctantly pledged support to the schools. While Miles was claiming that "there never was since my connection at this Agency a better state of harmony and feeling among the tribes and different bands," Colonel Mackenzie at Fort Sill and General Pope at Fort Leavenworth were warning that, unless the Indians were better fed, there was the constant danger of an outbreak. Miles apparently placed too much reliance on the fact that he had succeeded in obtaining a fair representation of Northern Cheyenne children in the agency school, which meant to the agent that they were interested in "remaining here and behaving well."[9]

Miles survived the criticism of the army officers and others who wanted him replaced. Philip McCusker, a part-time Indian trader who occasionally served as an Indian interpreter for the army, charged Miles with dishonesty and collusion to defraud the Indians. According to McCusker, Miles was a part owner of the Indian trading company on the Cheyenne-Arapaho Reservation. There were supposed to be two firms at Darlington, but actually there was only one, and without competition Miles's partners charged Indians three times the price of goods sold to whites. Favorites of Miles were given preferential treatment. For example, George Bent was allowed to serve not only as agency interpreter but also as an employee of Lee & Reynolds at a salary of one hundred dollars a month. McCusker also claimed that Miles issued Bent two head of beef a week and twenty to twenty-five pounds of beef a day at the agency butcher shop. According to McCusker, Miles was well aware of the liquor trade with the Indians, and he permitted to graze on the reservation a large herd of cattle in which he had a personal interest.[10]

It is evident from Miles's reports that he had little admiration for the Northern Cheyennes who chafed under his administration. The northerners, Miles wrote, "do not hesitate to make unreasonable demands" and "will require time, firm and just treatment, to win their confidence, and when this is gained, I shall expect progress." After a year at the Darlington Agency the Northern Cheyennes had failed to settle down and begin to plant crops as they had promised. Their refusal led Miles to conclude, "It may become necessary in the future to compel what, so far, we have been unable to effect by kindness and appeal to their better natures." With some of the Northern Cheyennes, however, Miles did not have the opportunity to use the force he implied was necessary because he was jolted by the news that some of them had left the reservation.[11]

Four days before the Northern Cheyennes' flight Miles knew that at least some of the bands were unhappy enough to risk leaving. Four "foolish young men" had left, the signal for Major Mizner to send out a patrol from Fort Reno to watch the Northern Cheyenne camp. At the same time Miles called the northern bands to Darlington for a head count, but they refused to come to the agency headquarters. The leaders and chiefs admitted to Miles's messengers that a small group of about twenty-four men were ready to move, but at the moment they were hunting deer on the Salt Plains, evidently to feed their people during the hard ride northward, when they would have little time to hunt. At Darlington several Northern Cheyenne chiefs explained to Miles that the bands would not set up their tipis near Darlington because the people feared "something bad" would happen. Major Mizner, who was with Miles at the council, assured them that he would control his troops and that Miles only wanted to take a head count. Mizner gave the chiefs a deadline of nightfall on September 7, 1878, to move to agency headquarters. The Northern Cheyennes ignored the deadline.

Agent Miles was awakened at three o'clock on the morning of September 10 by the captain of the Indian police and by American Horse, a chief of the Northern Cheyennes who had separated the eight lodges of his family and relatives from the main village. They told Miles that most of the disaffected Northern Cheyennes had left behind their lodges but had stolen camp equipment from those who were unwilling to ride with them. Major Mizner sent out his cavalry with fifteen Indian police to act as scouts and trailers. After a hasty check Miles estimated the fugitives at 353 people—92 men, 120 women, 69 boys, and 72 girls. A day later Miles reduced the number of those who had fled and sent a list of the names of 85 adult males to Commissioner E. A. Hayt. They were led, Miles thought, by Dull Knife, Wild Hog, Little Wolf, Crow Indian, Chewing Gum, Old Bear, Squaw, Black Horse, Day, and Red Blanket. Those who fled, Miles reported, were Northern Cheyennes, and they were neither assisted nor encouraged by the Southern Cheyennes.[12]

The pursuing military detachments and Indian police caught up with the Northern Cheyennes on September 13, 1878, fifty miles northwest of Camp Supply, while they were camped on a tributary of the Cimarron River. The followers of Dull Knife and Wild Hog fought off the soldiers, killing three troopers and Chalk, an Arapaho scout, and wounding three other cavalrymen. The officers had asked the Cheyennes to surrender before the fighting began, but the Indians refused. The soldiers and Indians abandoned the fight as darkness fell. The next day the warriors returned to resume the fray and found the soldiers en route to Camp Supply because of lack of water. Captain Joseph Rendlebrock, who had two troops of the Fourth Cavalry and Indian police with him, explained that his command had been surrounded by about 130 warriors in the hills near the Cimarron River while the women and children continued their flight.[18]

General Sheridan's reaction to the Northern Cheyennes' flight was simple and direct. It had been caused by "insufficient food and irregularity in its supply," a condition common to many reservations and agencies. If those fleeing north were allowed to succeed, other Plains Indians would interpret the army's inability to contain the Northern Cheyennes as a sign of weakness, thus jeopardizing peace on the Plains and the success of the reservation system. Sheridan therefore ordered General Crook "to spare no measures . . . to kill or capture the band of Cheyennes on the way north."[14]

Information coming from army sources was critical of the Bureau of Indian Affairs and its employees. Amos Chapman, an old scout serving as an interpreter at Camp Supply, witnessed the declining quality and quantity of the food issued to the Northern Cheyennes and the Indians' growing restlessness. He first saw the Northern Cheyennes in July, 1877, he recalled, while they were still moving toward Darlington with Lieutenant Lawton. They initially were pleased with the country and particularly pleased with the army rations supplied by Lieutenant Lawton and asked Chapman whether the food to be supplied at Darlington would be similar. In November, 1877, Chapman witnessed a food issue, and Old Crow's wife brought Chapman her share to show him how little it was compared with the army ration. She claimed that the food lasted only three days and that by that time the Northern and Southern Cheyennes could not find enough buffalo herds to sustain them for six months of the year as they had before. Standing Elk, Wild Hog, and Dull Knife all told Chapman, after an unsuccessful buffalo hunt as far as the Staked

34

Plains in the Texas Panhandle, that they did not want to return to Darlington, where they would be starved on rations that amounted to only one-half those furnished by the army. Chapman had two more opportunities to visit the Northern Cheyennes in April and July, 1878. On July 23, 1878, the Indians at the Darlington Agency were issued beef and corn meal but no flour, sugar, or coffee. The Northern Cheyennes told him that they had decided to leave Indian Territory for their old ranges above the Platte River. Ben Clark, who served at Fort Reno in a capacity similar to Chapman's, related much the same intelligence. Old Crow and others told him that they were given insufficient food, that there were no buffalo to hunt, and that their people were sick.[15]

Although irritated by the army's criticism, Miles did not immediately reply. When an article in the *New York Times* appeared on October 15, 1878, charging that the Northern Cheyennes left the reservation because of short rations and that "they satisfied their hunger with diseased horse flesh," Miles was instructed by William M. Leeds, the acting commissioner of Indian affairs, to answer the accusation. Miles began his defense by mentioning that most of the information in the *Times* article came from an officer stationed at Fort Dodge, Kansas, who was not in a position to know from personal observation the conditions at the Darlington Agency. Other information came from Amos Chapman, who had little to do with the reservation Indians except to bargain with their women for purposes of prostitution. Miles denied that the Northern Cheyennes or any other Indians at his agency were forced to eat "decayed or any other kind of horse meat." The Northern Cheyennes were issued the same food as the other Indians on the reservation, a ration of three pounds of beef and other foods for each individual each week. When other commodities were lacking, Miles contended that he increased the amount of beef issued, but he admitted that the rations authorized for distribution at Darlington were less than those specified in the Northern Cheyennes' treaty of September 26, 1876. Miles insisted that the spirit of the 1876 treaty was not being ignored since items not furnished to him were substituted for by issuance of other commodities. The government ration, Miles commented, was sufficient for

35

Indian families because each ration was the same whether for adults or children, but Indians had the habit of consuming their beef, coffee, and sugar within three or four days and then subsisting on flour, corn meal, and other small rations until the next issue. Rations were on occasion withheld from the Northern Cheyennes, he admitted, but always in compliance with general policies approved by Washington to force them to place their children in school or to contribute to their self-sufficiency through the growing of food crops. Whenever food was withheld, he treated the Northern Cheyennes precisely similar to the Southern Cheyennes.

The Northern Cheyennes, Miles countered, contributed to their own problems. They absolutely refused to "touch a plow or handle a hoe" in spite of their treaty which required them to make efforts toward self-sufficiency. None of the chiefs who departed on September 9 had signed the 1876 treaty, and one of them said that he had come to Indian Territory under great pressure and then only on a trial basis. In summary, Miles maintained that the Northern Cheyennes demanded the issuance of their rations in bulk, refused to work, and made themselves objectionable to the Southern Cheyennes; thus they were forced to camp apart from the Southerners' villages, and trustworthy Southern Cheyennes repeated the visitors' boast that they could cut their way back north any time they chose. They had never been disarmed as claimed and possessed over one hundred Springfield carbines taken at the Custer fight. Miles denied that he furnished the Indians with guns superior to those of the United States Army. Previous cases of fraud at other agencies, Miles concluded, made it impossible for an Indian agent to prove his honesty, but he would welcome a thorough investigation of his conduct.[16]

One factor that also caused Northern Cheyenne unhappiness was not emphasized by Miles while he was defending himself. He could not check the rising number of deaths among the Northern Cheyennes. Miles was not responsible for those deaths because in 1877 he had been denied permission to build a hospital at the agency or to expand the number of employees caring for the health of the Cheyenne people. Commissioner J. Q. Smith told Miles that since all funds for the employee force at the agency had been exhausted, he must reduce the existing and already overworked staff or find other sources of money before a hospital could be established. Also, medical supplies periodically failed to reach the agency on schedule. A report on the deaths among the Northern Cheyennes, undoubtedly only an incomplete listing, after they had been at the Darlington Agency for a little more than two years reveals that ninety-four people had succumbed to diseases. Miles noted that sixteen men, twenty-six women, and forty-four children had died, the adults usually dying from dysentery, chills, and fevers, and the children for the most part dying shortly after birth. This led Miles to recommend "that the ordeal of acclimation for a northern Indian to this climate is severe there can be no question, as has been abundantly verified in the transfer of other tribes to this country; and such a policy is wrong and should be abandoned."[17]

Dull Knife's attempt to fight his way through to his old home did not deter the transferring of another Northern Cheyenne band to the Indian Territory reservation. Early in December 1878, 186 people consisting of the bands led by Little Chief, Crazy Mule, Ridge Bear, Iron Shirt, and Black Bear arrived at Darlington from Sidney Barracks. They joined the more than 640 Northern Cheyennes who chose not to ride with Dull Knife. The late arrivals did not lessen Miles's problems; they had hardly been disarmed and rationed when they demanded to be sent back north as soon as possible because they did not like the southern reservation.[18]

Little Chief spoke freely to Major Mizner of Fort Reno through Ben Clarke, the post interpreter. He and his people had been happy living in the region of the Black Hills where there were still plenty of buffalo to hunt and deer whose skins provided clothing for the people. After surrendering to General Nelson A. Miles at Fort Peck, Montana Territory, Little Chief's people had been ordered by General Sheridan to move to Indian Territory, where they had heard that the country was unhealthy, and many of their people had died. Little Chief hoped that eventually his people would be given land on the Tongue River or Musselshell River because he knew that gold prospectors were taking over their old ranges around the Black Hills. Like Dull Knife and Wild Hog, Little Chief objected to sending his children to school, explaining to Major Mizner that "the Spirit above did not intend for our children to learn to read and write—he gave the white people the desire to read, write, farm and to live as white people live." Obviously Agent Miles's idea of placing the thirty school-aged children of Little Chief's band in a new building, "thereby gaining perfect control" over them, was going to run into difficulty. Still, Little Chief emphasized that he did not want trouble and that on their way down to Indian Territory, he said, his people had not even killed a "pig or chicken of the white man." Dull Knife, Little Chief contended, was wrong in going north without permission.[19]

By March, 1879, Little Chief's complaints were so vigorous that Agent Miles feared another break similar to Dull Knife's. Little Chief was described by C. E. Campbell, the acting agent in Miles's absence, as sincere in his desire to leave the Darlington Agency and as a brave and able leader "recognized as the superior of all others." Nothing pleased Little Chief. The southern lands did not belong to his people, the school children did not get enough to eat, the rations lasted only two days, his guns should not have been taken from him because he now had to kill the issue cattle with axes, the beef made his people sick, and there was not enough game to live on. Generals Nelson A. Miles and George Crook had promised him that he could return North if he did not like his new home, and he was only waiting word from the army officers before setting out on the return journey. In Lawrence, Kansas, Miles was worried because he knew that Little Chief had never been satisfied with life in Indian Territory. He asked the commissioner of Indian affairs what policy should be pursued with Little Chief's bands if the alleged promises had actually been made to them by N. A. Miles and Crook. Agent Miles could also have added that the Southern and Northern Cheyennes continued to bicker among themselves. The southerners did not want a single warrior of Dull Knife's band to be returned to Darlington. The chiefs insisted that if the northerners returned, sooner or later they would "breed trouble" and end the friendly relations existing between whites and the Southern Cheyennes. Even Stone Calf, one of the bitterest Southern Cheyenne chiefs, refused consistently to support Little Chief in his complaints.[20]

Little Chief caused concern among the agency and military officers. When Dull Knife's threats had been ignored, his people had broken loose, and no one wanted a repetition of that incident. Major Mizner warned his superiors that Little Chief would not farm, send his children to school, or accept the orders of Agent Miles. If the children of Little Chief's bands were seized or forcibly placed in school, the likelihood of an outbreak would be increased. The Northern Cheyennes, the Major believed, had been at the Darlington Agency too short a time to be coerced by "any extreme or radical measures," and he suggested that new procedures and policies be introduced gradually. On March 13, 1879, Little Chief, with Iron Shirt and Ridge Bear, visited the agency headquarters and protested that he did not want to be considered as hostile to the government. The Southern and Northern Cheyennes had been counciling and "making medicine" for about a week, and it was likely that the southerners' more moderate attitudes were influencing the northerners. Little Chief, however, did not abandon his position that Generals Miles and Crook had promised him that he would be able to return to the North. Since he and his people were going to be at Darlington for only a short time, there was little reason to place their children in school.[21]

At first General Pope was willing to temporize with the Northern Cheyennes. He told Major Mizner to use all of his influence to deter Agent Miles from forcing the children of the northern bands into the agency schools. To render the warriors less formidable, General Pope suggested that the rifles and carbines they possessed be traded for smooth-bore Harper's Ferry muskets, which he said were good enough for Indian hunters. Soon, however, Pope began to advocate a harder line toward the Northern Cheyennes. First he deployed fifteen companies of infantry and cavalry to reinforce the garrisons of Fort Reno and Fort Supply and Cantonment. To General Sheridan he complained that he could not act without a request from Agent Miles, even though he believed that the Northern Cheyennes were about to break loose at any moment, thus endangering the whole Kansas frontier. "I have never," he wrote to Sheridan, "concurred in the policy of re-enforcing the Indians in Indian Territory by these bands of wild Indians from the North, so lately hostile and who come

to this region with promises unfulfilled and engagements not kept."
Finally General Pope sought to have all adult male Northern Chey-
ennes imprisoned to prevent a tragedy similar to that surrounding
Dull Knife's flight.[22]

While General Pope was worrying about an outbreak, Agent Miles
began to seek the release of seven Northern Cheyenne prisoners held
in the Dodge City, Kansas, jail. Wild Hog, Old Crow, Big Head,
Left Hand, Porcupine, Noisy Walker, and Blacksmith (the last was
also known as Buffalo Cow with Calf) were charged, along with
Dull Knife and 150 male Northern Cheyenne Indians, with the first
degree murder of Washington O'Conner on September 17, 1878, in
Meade County, Kansas. Miles visited Topeka and Dodge City to
guarantee that the prisoners would receive a fair trial, taking with
him Almerin Gillett, a Wichita lawyer. It appeared that none of the
seven being held for trial were directly involved in the killings on the
Kansas frontier. It had been Little Wolf's warriors, covering the
retreat of the others, principally the women and children, who had
killed the whites. When Miles visited the Northern Cheyennes in
their cells, he found all of them in fairly good spirits except Wild
Hog, and even he gained hope during his talk with Miles. All claimed
that if they were freed they would "plant corn" and "chop wood."
They still preferred the northern hunting ranges to Indian Territory,
but Miles said they pledged to "give us all their children in school."
Miles did effect the release of the prisoners' women and children, who
were returned to Darlington under military escort in early March.
While in Kansas, Miles sought a change of venue so that the Indians
would not face a prejudiced jury composed of Kansas frontier
settlers.[23]

In trying to free the imprisoned Cheyennes, Agent Miles received
the co-operation of his superiors and army officers. Commissioner
Hayt contended that the Northern Cheyennes had already been sufficiently punished by the military forces during and after their incar-
ceration at Camp Robinson, Nebraska. General Crook and other
officers conceded that Old Crow and his people had not been involved
in the "massacres committed by the Cheyennes." Old Crow was
released and escorted back to Darlington by Amos Chapman on

July 4, 1879, while the other six prisoners were transferred to Lawrence, Kansas, to stand trial. Immediately Old Crow "exerted a good influence over other Northern Cheyennes and advised them to drop every chief and leader who opposes the wishes of the Govt."[24]

Wild Hog and the five other Northern Cheyennes charged with murders of Kansas frontiersmen were freed after a trial in Lawrence, Kansas. Represented by J. G. Mohler, a lawyer of considerable reputation in Kansas, the Indians gained their freedom on October 13, 1879, when the prosecuting attorney decided not to press charges against the six Northern Cheyenne defendants. On October 27, 1879, Wild Hog, Noisy Walker, Left Hand, Blacksmith, and two other men were returned to the charge of Agent Miles, who wrote that he was uncertain what influence they would have on the other Northern Cheyennes still at his agency.[25]

During the spring of 1879 the Northern Cheyennes did not seem likely to break away from Darlington as had Dull Knife six months earlier. Little Chief repeatedly requested that he and some of his headmen be taken to Washington to confer with officials to clarify the status of his people. Miles continued to press the Northern Cheyennes to place their children in school and accept the same agency policies as were applied to the Southern Cheyennes, but he temporarily abandoned his efforts to gather their children in school by using troops. Heber M. Creel, a Seventh Cavalry officer detailed to learn the Northern Cheyennes' language but more importantly to report their moods to the army, noted that "threats only tend to make them stubborn—they are not frightened into anything." Although Little Chief continued to plead that he wanted to return to the Tongue River area as promised earlier, Ridge Bear and Crazy Mules, two influential Northern Cheyennes, requested that ground be broken for them so that they could plant crops and gardens. Lieutenant Creel doubted any breakout would occur in 1879 unless the Northerners were "forced to it." They knew that Little Wolf had surrendered to Lieutenant Clark on March 25, 1879, while en route to Fort Keogh, and the Northern Cheyennes were watching what disposition the army would make of Little Wolf and his band.[26]

In an effort to persuade Washington officials to support his policies,

Miles outlined what he was doing at Darlington. A school had been completed for the Northern Cheyenne children at Caddo Springs, some three miles north of the agency headquarters, but the chiefs still refused to place their children in it. Use of military force or the withholding of rations to accomplish his objective seemed unwise to Miles at the time. He believed that all of the Northern Cheyennes should be gathered together in one place, either at Darlington or some reservation in the North. Chiefs of the Northern Cheyenne assumed that Little Wolf and the women and children who were scattered among the Sioux would neither be forced nor would willingly agree to be sent to Darlington. For Little Chief and his people, however, Miles thought that the "ordeal of acclimation" had passed.[27]

To settle the issues faced by Miles and the grievances of the Northern Cheyennes, Little Chief and five of his fellow Northern Cheyenne chiefs arrived in Washington in mid-May, 1879. They met with the commissioner of Indian affairs and the secretary of the interior and called upon President Hayes. Little was settled in Washington. Officials promised Little Chief that either all the Northern Cheyennes would be assembled at Darlington or he and his bands would be permitted to move back to their old homes on the Northern Plains. The chiefs could do little but accept the decision of the secretary of the interior, but still they indicated a clear preference for the original homeland. Miles knew the conference was unsatisfactory, for he explained later, "Divided as they are, there will always be an excuse for passing back and forth, and so long as one Northern Cheyenne is permitted to remain north, there will be discontent among those here, and, as a result, an obstruction to their progress here." Miles could also have added that if the Northern Cheyennes were not compelled to accept his policies, the Southern Cheyennes would not alter their way of life.[28]

Although Little Chief stated that he would not lead his people away from Darlington, he also said he would continue his appeals to Washington. He and his people were disappointed and continued to grumble. Major Mizner, understanding their attitude, sought and received reinforcements for the Fort Reno garrison. Little Chief, in response, conceded that a flight would be foolish, but Major Mizner reminded the chief that some of his people had expressed themselves so vigorously that there was a chance some would break away regardless of the wishes of the chiefs and most of their people. When Agent Miles had a chance to assess the attitude of Little Chief, he remarked that the northern leader seemed well disposed. The young warriors were behaving better, and, to build good will among them, he invited Black Wolf with his wife and young child to dine with him at Darlington.[29]

Antagonisms continued between the northerners and the southerners. The former were suspected of stealing the Southern Cheyenne and Arapaho horses and hiding them for a break away from Darlington. Miles thought that some Northern Cheyennes might be incorporated into the agency Indian police to prevent "horse stealing, and many little domestic broils." Consequently, five warriors, four from Little Chief's bands and one who had come to Darlington with Dull Knife, were selected to serve as Indian police. The warriors, Miles optimistically felt, could be relied on to carry out any duty required of any soldier.[30]

Washington officials did not comprehend the problems faced by Miles. If he applied coercion to the Indians, they would bolt from the reservation; if he did not, they would ignore his policies and instructions. To compound his difficulties, the Indian office reduced the weekly beef ration from three to two pounds on September 1, 1879. Miles immediately appealed the order on behalf of the Northern and Southern Cheyennes. Little Chief simply told his agent that he could not live on two pounds of beef a week. Miles agreed with him and informed the commissioner of Indian affairs that the lesser amount would not "sustain life" and would drive the Indians from the agency in search of game which would lead to trouble with border settlers. After visiting the Indian camps, Miles was even more emphatic than before. An issue of two pounds of beef each week would mean "hunger and suffering" to Indian people who only a few years before had depended on buffalo and game to supplement the government issues of food. As yet the Southern Cheyennes and Arapahoes and their northern kinsmen had found no industry to substitute for the meat and robes taken on their hunts. Dry weather had destroyed the crops of the Indian farmers, only twenty Indians could be employed in cutting hay, a few more could be employed as wood cutters for the agency fuel supply, and those engaged in transportation of supplies were still paying for their wagons and equipment. Few Indians, Miles insisted, could support themselves without considerable assistance from the government.[31]

Southern Cheyennes let Miles know that they also were displeased with the reduced rations. At Cantonment about 150 lodges of Southern Cheyennes led by Stone Calf, Minimic, and White Horse and 70 lodges of Southern Arapahoes under Little Raven began to discuss obtaining food outside of the reservation. Their reckless talk disturbed Colonel Dodge, who reported that "they say they had better be killed than starved to death." Dodge's interpreter, Amos Chapman, predicted "widespread trouble" unless more food was soon issued to the Indians.[32]

Little Chief, now more determined not to remain at Darlington, used every argument and opportunity to make his dissatisfaction known to Agent Miles. He and two of his fellow chiefs, Iron Shirt and Black Wolf, sought the assistance of General Nelson A. Miles to have them transferred to the Assiniboine Agency. General Miles agreed with the Northern Cheyenne leaders that the southern climate was unhealthy for them, endorsing their request with the statement that it was "humane and just and wise to allow them to return North." Little Chief did not want his children in the white man's schools, and he did not want their wagons, commenting to Miles, "My lodge poles are my wagons." Here the Southern Cheyennes taunted him and treated him badly. Up North, Little Chief knew life would be better. There he and his people lived on buffalo "and ate all day until night, Got up the next morning and went to eating again. No one died up North. We die on account of eating poor beef. It gives no strength." The Southern Cheyennes, Little Chief told Agent Miles, could become farmers as the government desired, but "it is no use for the Govt. to make roads for me. I am no fool and can make my own road."[33]

Conditions at Darlington changed little during the summer of 1880. At times the lack of food caused the warriors to defy their

44

agent and the military officers. The young men among the Northern Cheyennes were earnestly talking of war, trading for good ponies, and disposing of their personal property not needed to fight their way North. Fearing that the Northern Cheyennes would steal their horses, the Southern Cheyennes and Arapahoes guarded their herds night and day. One day Hippy, a young Southern Cheyenne man, wanted more beef to feed his hungry family. Having missed his issue of beef the preceding week, he climbed into the issue corral to obtain another steer, which he claimed was rightfully his. Miles ordered the warrior out of the corral, but when Miles and his office force attempted to leave the issue lot and ride back to the agency office, two young Southern Cheyennes, Bull Coming Up and Little Coyote, beat Miles's team over their heads with quirts. Farther down the road their fellow warriors drew themselves up into a line so that Miles could not reach his office. Unarmed, Miles had no alternative but to give the young Cheyenne his extra beef. The Indian police accompanying Agent Miles were ordered to arrest the three young men, but the policemen declined because they knew that warriors "would die fighting before they would be arrested." Major Randall led two troops of cavalry from Fort Reno to rescue Miles, but it was too late to take the culprits. The young men were stripped to fight, and they were backed by four hundred Cheyenne warriors fully armed and ready to aid their friends. If any attempt had been made to arrest the three warriors, the whole agency force and the cavalry would have been "massacred." Finally the chiefs persuaded the young men to go to the agency. There Miles delivered a lecture about the issue regulations. Nothing further was expected to come of the confrontation, but Miles pointed out that the Indians knew they could not be controlled by the troops unless they were divided among themselves.[34]

Little changed during the remainder of Little Chief's stay at Darlington. Miles tried to enforce regulations and enroll the Northern Cheyenne children in school, and the leaders of the northerners evaded Miles's request. As long as Little Wolf's band was not brought to Darlington, the others would not respond to governmental policies and regulations. Among themselves the Northern Cheyennes differed

45

on where they wanted their reservation in the North; some wanted land on the Powder River, others on the Yellowstone, and a third contingent favored lands more to the east. Finally the commissioner of Indian affairs, realizing that the Northern Cheyennes would never settle down in Indian Territory, asked Miles to determine where they would accept a reservation. Although Little Chief preferred being located at the Crow Agency at the mouth of the Rosebud on the Yellowstone River, it was decided to shift him and his band to the Pine Ridge Agency.[35]

Once the reservation was selected, the commissioner had to decide who would be permitted to leave Indian Territory. Crazy Mule and Ridge Bear had separated their families from Little Chief's camp and were willing to remain at Darlington. They were growing vegetables, freighting, and their children were in school. Remnants of those who came with Dull Knife and Standing Elk, however, demanded to leave with Little Chief. They were denied this when it was decided that only those people who came with Little Chief would make the journey to Pine Ridge. Finally, on October 6, 1881, Little Chief's people were provided with two months' rations, their pro rata share of the annuity goods, and a cavalry escort. According to Miles's count about 235 individuals were listed for the exodus, including 35 very young children born in Indian Territory. When the party reached Pine Ridge, however, it was found that 82 others had secretly and without authority joined Little Chief. This meant that over 300 Northern Cheyennes had departed from Indian Territory.[36]

Agent Miles's problems with the Northern Cheyennes were not yet over, however. After Little Chief's departure, 684 Northern Cheyennes still remained at Darlington to upset the operation of the agency. It took Congress two years to appropriate funds for the complete removal of the northerners, which was finally done in 1883 when five thousand dollars was set aside. During the summer of 1883, Agent Miles began sorting out the Northern Cheyennes and Arapahoes who did not want to remain at Darlington. At first the chiefs, such as Standing Elk, Wild Hog, Porcupine, Old Crow, and Ridge Bear, forced all of their people to declare their intent to move back to the North, and at that time Miles estimated that 450 individuals, including 14 Northern Arapahoes, would leave Indian Territory. Then the number slowly declined despite Miles's edict that those who remained would have to "settle down to business." On July 19, 1883, 405 Indians were supplied with rations for their journey and a military escort. Within a few days, however, about 60 of the group had returned to Darlington and told O. J. Woodward, the acting agent, that they did not want to go to Pine Ridge because they had been forced to enroll for the removal by the chiefs. Most of those who left the removal party stated that they had intermarried with the Southern Cheyennes and did not want to leave their wives or husbands and families. Agent Miles viewed the departure of the Northern Cheyenne contingent as a blessing which "removed all serious disturbing elements, and the way is open for advancement, that could not be accomplished in the presence of the Northern Cheyennes."[37]

If Miles's figures are correct, not all of the Northern Cheyennes ever returned to their northern home. About 340 Northern Cheyennes remained to mix with the southerners and add to the Indians administered to by Agent Miles and his successors. After the departure of the last removal party, Acting Agent Woodward claimed that 6,014 people were still within the jurisdiction of the Southern Cheyenne and Arapaho Agency, a figure much too high but probably used to increase the rations distributed to the Indians from governmental funds. Agent Miles later reported that only 48 people returned to Darlington from the removal party. If Miles was more accurate than the acting agent, the number of Northern Cheyennes who remained in Indian Territory was about 330.[38]

CHAPTER III

The Beginnings of
Agriculture and Education

THE NORTHERN CHEYENNES were frequently blamed for the lack of progress toward self-sufficiency by the Southern Cheyennes and Arapahoes. Their presence did cause some tensions and resistance to governmental policy, but few of the Southern Cheyennes and Arapahoes were willing to farm, send their children to the reservation schools, become Christians, or work as white men as long as they could retain even a portion of their original way of life. Only when the buffalo had virtually disappeared on the southern Plains would the warriors and hunters consider another manner of supplementing the weekly rations and annuity goods. The regimentation required to produce crops sufficient to serve as a substitute for the buffalo meat and the cash derived from buffalo robes was entirely foreign to the culture of the Plains Indians. Yet officials concerned with the welfare of the Indian believed that nothing less than a complete revolution in the economy and society of the Plains Indians was necessary. The formulators of governmental policy were committed to changing the Indian from a hunting to an agricultural economy.

It seemed simple enough to persuade an Indian man to exchange his gun and hunting pony for a plow and a draft horse. The idea was to begin with a vegetable garden and a few acres of corn for each family and to educate the Indian youngsters in reading, writing, and arithmetic. Indian boys would be taught the use of agricultural implements, while the girls would acquire skills to care for a frame house instead of a lodge. Missionaries and agents gradually would

Three Fingers, Southern Cheyenne chief. *Courtesy Western History Collections, University of Oklahoma Library.*

Wolf Robe, Southern Cheyenne chief. *Courtesy Western History Collections, University of Oklahoma Library.*

Yellow Eyes, Southern Cheyenne head man and Dog Soldier leader. *Courtesy Western History Collections, University of Oklahoma Library.*

Henry Roman Nose, Southern Cheyenne chief and graduate of the Carlisle Indian School. *Courtesy Western History Collections, University of Oklahoma Library.*

Richard A. Davis (left), Southern Cheyenne, a graduate of Carlisle Indian
School and the first tribal member to be an assistant farmer for the
Cheyenne-Arapaho Reservation, with Bull Bear (right), a Southern Chey-
enne chief. *Courtesy Field Museum of Natural History.*

Whirlwind, Southern Cheyenne chief, with wives. *Courtesy Western History Collections, University of Oklahoma Library.*

Stone Calf, Southern Cheyenne chief, and his wife. *Courtesy Western History Collections, University of Oklahoma Library.*

George Bent, son of William Bent, interpreter and employee of the Cheyenne-Arapaho Agency, with Magpie, his wife. *Courtesy Western History Collections, University of Oklahoma Library.*

Left Hand, Southern Arapaho chief. *Courtesy Western History Collections, University of Oklahoma Library.*

Sitting Bull, leader of the Ghost Dance among the Southern Arapahoes. *Courtesy Western History Collections, University of Oklahoma Library.*

Black Coyote, Southern Arapaho, captain of the Cheyenne-Arapaho Reservation Indian Police and leader of the Ghost Dance among his people. Watonga, Oklahoma, is named for him after his tribal name, Watan-gaa. *Courtesy Western History Collections, University of Oklahoma.*

inculcate the beliefs of Christianity, replacing the supernaturalism and ceremonies that diverted the Indian from accumulation of goods and the means of self-sufficiency. Eventually the Indian would become the replica of a white farmer. He would in time grow his own food, own his farm, educate his children, attend a Christian church, and blend into the stream of American civilization. Assimilation within a generation was the goal, but generations would lapse before white officials and churchmen would realize that the goal was unattainable.

The 1874–75 conflict meant that previous agricultural pursuits were virtually abandoned. Agent Miles noted that during this fiscal year only two mixed-blood and three full-blood Arapahoes occupied and cultivated separate tracts from the agency fields on which they had located permanent homes. Ten other Arapahoes were working on five-acre fields included within the agency farm. To expand the amount of land available for Indian farming, Miles suggested the allocation of two thousand dollars for the breaking of five hundred acres of prairie sod. The plowed land could then be divided into lots ranging from five to fifteen acres on which he could place "families who desire to *settle down* & go to work." Indian ponies were too small and weak to be used for "sod busting," and none of the Indians owned a set of harnesses to use for plowing. Without assistance the Indians could not be expected to do more than grow thirty or forty bushels of sod corn during the next year. Agent Miles insisted, unrealistically perhaps, that 75 per cent of the Cheyennes and Arapahoes were willing to farm during the 1876 season if the government would only furnish them plows, harnesses, hoes, and other agricultural implements.[1]

In his campaign for more government funds, Agent Miles interpreted the Cheyenne and Arapaho agricultural enterprises in their most favorable light. He was, of course, under some pressure to do so. By threatening to withhold rations from able-bodied men who refused to go to work, Congress had included in the 1875 Indian Appropriation Act a clause which required that Indians contribute to their own support by manual labor. Miles told his superiors that the "attitude of these Indians as to manual labor is steadily improving," and he pointed to a "number of hopeful converts who have raised some

57

fifty acres of corn, melons, squashes, and a variety of garden vegetables," despite a cold, wet spring that made it necessary to replant
the gardens and fields. Those Indians who enjoyed some success
with their crops and gardens were, according to Miles, "loud in their
promises of what they intended doing when the 'grass grows again.' "²

Agent Miles had far too little assistance and funds with which to
encourage the Indians in their first farming attempts. Only one
employee during 1876 was designated as a farmer, and he was
primarily responsible for the agency farm which provided hay for
the headquarter's horses and food for the staff and their families.
During the harvesting season the farmer was assisted by John H.
Seger for a month and a half, while Big Back, a Cheyenne, and Fat
Bull, an Arapaho, were employed as herders to watch the agency
milk and beef cattle. After all expenses had been met for annuity
goods specified under the 1867 Medicine Lodge Treaty, Miles had a
balance of only $217.50 which he suggested be spent for young heifers
and milk cows to be distributed among the Indians engaged in
farming. Miles could not expend even that small amount because
congressional authorization for its use had lapsed, and then it had
been frozen in the treasury by a ruling of the attorney general.³

Agent Miles grossly exaggerated the Cheyennes' and Arapahoes'
inclination toward farming. He wrote to a Cherokee leader, Joshua
Ross, that four hundred Cheyennes and Arapahoes had engaged in
farming to some extent during 1876 and that 75 per cent of the tribes
would have grown some of their food if only the government had
furnished the required farming implements. The Indian agent
claimed that he had seen Cheyennes "with axes and knives cutting
and digging up sod, preparing ground for a small patch of vegetables
& corn and after being thus prepared have planted and cultivated it
with their fingers." If Congress, Miles argued, would only appropriate
what "is actually *due them* and *necessary* to place them in a condition
to *help themselves*, they will soon step into the scale of independence
& self reliance that is now enjoyed by others of their race who have
been more favored."⁴

Some of the Cheyennes and Arapahoes did respond to their agent's
entreaties to turn to agriculture. There were Cheyennes motivated

58

enough to use axes, sticks, and their hands while preparing the ground, planting, and cultivating their garden patches when they were unable to obtain plows or hoes. Miles had received enough funds to break seventy-five acres of land for each tribe; tribal members were assigned from one to five acres of plowed land. Generally corn, potatoes, and garden vegetables were planted with seeds furnished at government expense from Benjamin Coates, a Philadelphia Quaker, and through bartering with their neighbors the Caddoes.

The Arapahoes were more willing than the Cheyennes to spend time in their fields. The chiefs of the tribe exhorted the members to follow their example, and Miles mentioned that Little Raven, Left Hand, Yellow Horse, Row-of-Lodges, and other prominent men were beginning to farm. Arapahoes also planted 110 acres of corn and vegetables along the North Canadian River in addition to the land Miles broke for them. Two Arapaho mixed bloods, John and Robert Poisal, had enclosed a 75-acre farm about two miles east of Darlington on which they cultivated corn for their cash crop and vegetables. Powder Face, an Arapaho chief, sold buffalo robes for one hundred dollars, using the money to purchase cattle from George Washington, the Caddo chief. Other Arapahoes followed their chief's example, giving Miles hope that this would lead the owners to care for the animals properly. If the Indians paid for the cattle with their own funds, the agent hoped the herds would be appreciated more and have "a decided tendency in localizing and teaching the principle of respecting the rights of individual property." Miles also noted a change in some of the young warriors who were hired as herders for the one thousand cattle kept on hand at the agency for beef issues. Since Miles had only enough money to employ one herder from each tribe, the chiefs furnished six additional young men from each tribe to ride herd each night during the entire month of July. The young warriors took their turns cheerfully, and Miles wrote, "I only need to say that these same young men, who I now intrust with the herd, four years ago would maliciously proceed to our agency herd, without leave or license, and shoot down a few fat beeves, help themselves to a few choice cuts, and ride off to camp, defiant of our protests and efforts to protect the property."[5]

Government rations and the food grown were still far from sufficient to prevent hunger among the tribesmen. A young Cheyenne man killed a cow belonging to another, claiming that his family could not maintain themselves on the meat allotted to them by the government. Miles agreed with the man when he was brought into the agent's Darlington office by Little Robe and Big Horse for trial. The accused pleaded that he thought he was killing one of Big Horse's cattle and that he did not want to be known as a thief. Miles did not name the young man, who claimed that he had no ammunition with which to hunt for his family, who needed something to eat. If the beef ration was not increased, Miles predicted that the incident would be repeated. In dismissing the case, Miles did not imprison the man but took from him his only horse, which was sold to pay for the cow.[6]

Miles believed that, as the buffalo hunts became less successful, the Cheyennes and Arapahoes would turn to agriculture or stock raising. The Central Superintendency staff who were members of the Society of Friends supported Miles's assertions when they forwarded the agent's estimates for funds required to start the Indians on farms. Superintendent Nicholson inquired if the construction of ten houses at the cost of $209.22 each would not strengthen the Indians' "determination to be loyal to the Government" and encourage them "to give hearty support" to Miles. The agent used the funds provided by Superintendent Nicholson to break more land, some two hundred acres, which the Indians plowed "with a determination that will convince the most skeptical that they are in earnest and willing to work for themselves when an opportunity is given them." If the 1877 season were favorable and the crops successful, Miles thought a "new stimulus will be added to their efforts in the future." All the available seeds were distributed to aspiring Indian farmers, who, finding that there were not enough plows for each individual, used them in turn until the whole band had been served. Major Mizner of Fort Reno also presented five plows, obtained from the sale of ponies, to the Indians. To ensure an equitable division of rations, Miles installed individual rations, which he claimed were received joyously. Members of the agency staff, Miles wrote, were "doubly paid for our extra work above the usual method of issue" by seeing "the expression of delight on the faces of the old 'thrown away' women as they lugged off an equal portion with those usually more favored." There were a few chiefs and warriors who were disappointed in not "receiving the Lion's share as usual but no notice was taken of their effort and the distribution went quietly on."[7]

Despite Miles's claims of the Indians' willingness to work, agricultural productivity increased but slowly on the reservation. After the first surge of enthusiasm, the Indians grew tired of plowing and breaking new land; therefore, Miles decreed that he would only break more sod for the Indians equal to the acreage they broke for themselves. Since both tribes brought only 123 new acres into cultivation, the increase in cropland was small during 1877. Yet the moderate yield of corn and vegetables changed some of the Indians' attitudes. The Arapaho chief Left Hand complained undoubtedly more for his women than for himself when he told his agent, "I have worked hard all summer breaking ground, building fence, planting and cultivating corn, melons & c., and now lazy Indians hang around my camp and eat me poor."[8]

With agriculture only a limited success among the Cheyennes and Arapahoes, Miles began to look for other means to introduce the Indians to gainful employment. Miles was convinced that "these people can better turn their attention to grazing than to farming extensively." He therefore sought authorization to purchase more than 400 young heifers to be distributed among Indians who would care for them. By late June, 1877, Miles was permitted to purchase 325 head of cattle at a total cost of $2,698.25. They were divided equally among the two tribes into small herds and assigned to "deserving Indians" who were working for the Cheyenne-Arapaho Transportation Company, a recently formed enterprise that moved supplies from Wichita, Kansas, to Darlington.[9]

John H. Seger, who was supervising the Cheyenne-Arapaho Manual Training and Labor School, also began to emphasize animal husbandry among the schoolboys. A considerable portion of his students' time was spent in the fields of the school farm cultivating more than one hundred acres of corn and ten acres of vegetables. The 1876 crop resulted in a profit of more than one thousand dollars which

Seger used to establish a foundation herd for the school farm. The next year a little more land was worked, and seventy-five tons of hay were cut by Seger and his boys. The profit from the crops was again turned into cattle. The two crops allowed Seger to build a herd of 171 cattle and also 40 swine, all of which were owned jointly by the youngsters in school. Two of the older boys, Dan Tucker and Ah-tuck, were employed by Agent Miles to herd the cattle.[10]

Another of Miles's suggestions also provided work and income for the Indians on the reservation. In 1876 the Indian agent had recommended employing Cheyennes and Arapahoes as teamsters and freighters to haul goods from the rail terminal at Wichita, Kansas, to Darlington. At first the idea was thought impractical, but an amendment to the 1877 Indian Appropriation Act enabled Miles to purchase wagons, harness, and other equipment enabling the Indians to transport goods and supplies to various Indian agencies. Congress also provided that warehouses could be maintained and storekeepers and other employees engaged to facilitate the shipment of supplies. With permission, Miles formed the Cheyenne-Arapaho Transportation Company and bought forty wagons and eighty sets of double harness, which were assigned to individual Cheyennes and Arapahoes. The Indians paid for the wagons and harness from their labor in freighting the supplies to Darlington at the rate of $1.50 a hundredweight. The Transportation Company, supervised by J. A. Covington and William E. Malaley, made its first trip to Wichita in September, 1877. The sixty Indian freighters camped near the edge of Wichita, traded robes for articles desired by their women and families, loaded the wagons, and departed without an incident of drunkenness or disorder.[11]

Commissioner Hayt congratulated Agent Miles on the successful transportation of agency goods with Indian labor. Miles had established the first agency transportation company within the Indian service, but it was not without its problems. Bad weather during the winter season prevented a steady utilization of the Indian trains, and more wagons had to be obtained to replace those damaged and to provide greater freighting capacity. Once the wagons were paid for by Indian labor, Miles had to arrange for the teamsters to be paid in cash. Ed Fenlon, who held the freighting contract between Wichita and Darlington, did not like the Indians' competition and forwarded supplies from Wichita immediately to prevent them from accumulating for the Indian trains. Miles requested that a larger warehouse be obtained in Wichita so that the goods could be held for the Indians. By July, 1879, the Indians had ninety-five wagons operating between Wichita and Darlington from which they received an income to supplement the rations and annuities, and the government saved between fifty and seventy-five cents a hundredweight for goods sent to the Cheyenne and Arapaho Reservation. More Indian men evidently were willing to labor as freighters than as farmers and thereby learn how to care for property and equipment and use their income for the purchase of food and other necessities.[12]

Only a small minority of the Cheyennes and Arapahoes worked as freighters or in their fields. The others continued to draw their rations and annuities whenever issued. The Indian men accepted the annuities, and the women received the weekly rations of food. Miles described the issue days:

Every week there is a long line of them awaiting their turn to be supplied. They also are cheerful and merry. . . . While these people are not to be looked upon as paupers by any man, yet this method of furnishing them with food must be more or less demoralizing, and there should be some limit carefully devised to have them produce sufficient for their own support, the rations to the men to be contingent upon their working.

Working meant primarily agricultural activities, and it was the policy of the Office of Indian Affairs "to encourage and enforce regular labor among the Indians." Commissioner Hayt elaborated that "it is the earnest desire of this office that the Indians should be induced to engage in agricultural pursuits to as great an extent as is possible." As long as the Cheyennes and Arapahoes remained in their large camps near Darlington and were issued rations without working, many would never undertake agricultural or other kinds of labor.[13]

Miles had made some progress in breaking the authority of the chiefs and warriors by installing a system of distributing rations to individuals rather than to the leaders of the bands and camps. Still, most of the Indians lived in large camps, where they shared food and continued their traditional modes of living. In mid-March, 1878, Miles called a meeting of the chiefs and men of the tribes and told them that they should begin doing something for themselves. The Indian leaders asked Miles how they could begin to farm without implements, tools, and seeds. The Indians had a point. The agricultural implements ordered the preceding year had not arrived at Darlington in time for the 1878 planting season. Such delays were common in succeeding years.

To break up the large camps, Miles advocated settling Indians in smaller villages twenty to twenty-five miles from Darlington along the fertile river and creek bottomland. This meant that more land must be broken, and Miles's request for 350 additional acres was granted by Secretary of the Interior Carl Schurz. To prevent inter-tribal jealousy, Miles also requested that an additional farmer be authorized for the reservation so that each tribe could have one man to instruct them in farming techniques. Again approval was granted, contingent upon sufficient funds in the Bureau of Indian Affairs. Throughout the crucial planting season of 1878, however, Miles continued to operate with only one farmer and one assistant farmer. With the additional land broken in 1878, the Cheyennes and Arapahoes planted 1,064 acres. Miles commented that more would have been cultivated if the implements ordered had arrived on time.

When the crops were harvested, the Cheyennes' fields yielded far less than those cultivated by the Arapahoes. The latter produced, according to Miles, 9,600 bushels of corn and 360 bushels of potatoes, while the Cheyennes harvested 2,400 bushels of corn and 120 bushels of potatoes. J. A. Covington, who served as both farmer and supervisor of the Transportation Company, reported that the Indians were also successful in raising radishes, turnips, tomatoes, peas, cucumbers, squashes, and cabbages in their garden patches, but, because the vegetables were often eaten before maturity, it was difficult to estimate the quantities grown.[14]

Climatic conditions intervened in 1879 to lower the yield of the Indians' field crops. The spring rains were sufficient to produce vegetables, especially potatoes, and the yield more than doubled over that of the previous year. Corn production, however, declined slightly, and the numbers of new acres placed in cultivation were few because the ground was too dry and hard to break. Basing his estimates on observation, Miles claimed that grains would fail once every four years. It would be better, in his opinion, to break up the old bands and large encampments so that the Indians could turn their attention to smaller, individual gardens. To accomplish this scattering of the Indians, Miles urged them to select their farms and begin breaking land in tracts of two to one hundred acres. About 175 Indians designated the lands they wanted, and 40 of them fenced and cultivated their fields. Miles's program took effect as far away as Cantonment. There the Indians chose their lands along the creek bottoms, forcing Colonel Richard I. Dodge, commanding officer at the post, to pay for every log and pole needed by his garrison. The colonel complained that woodcutting parties from his post were being hampered by Indians who were in possession of "quasi-warrants" issued by Agent Miles. Yellow Bear, an Arapaho chief of some note, presented Colonel Dodge with a bill for the logs cut on his claim. Miles continued to advise the Cheyennes and Arapahoes to devote more time and money to acquiring cattle. He maintained that the reservation was "naturally a good grazing country, and cattle reared on this range do not require the preparation of forage or grain for winter use."[15]

Miles hoped to use the school herd managed by John Seger as an example of the practicality of converting the Cheyennes and Arapahoes to stock raising. Schoolboys could also be trained in the management of cattle, and when they had completed their courses, they would take with them their rightful proportion of the herd as their "beginning" in self-sufficiency. Initially the school herd was approved by Washington officials, and Secretary of the Interior Schurz authorized the purchase of 400 head of stock at a cost of $3,200.00. The calves also produced by the herd were retained, and A. E. Reynolds, the post trader at Fort Supply, donated seven blooded bulls to improve or maintain the quality of the beef cattle collected by Miles. By the late summer of 1879, Miles estimated the market value of the herd at $9,181.40, which represented about 973 head of cattle.[16]

No sooner was the school herd of significant size and firmly established than the commissioner of Indian affairs ordered it distributed among the Indians. By retaining the herd's natural increase and purchasing young heifers over a five-year period, Miles and Seger had more than fifteen hundred head of cattle in the "mission herd," as it was called. "Among so many Indians," Miles protested, "the *pro rata* share is so small that but little incentive is presented in the issue of three or four cattle to properly care for them." The animals would be sold or would be eaten when subsistence rations ran short during the year. Still, Miles maintained that the experiment with the mission herd demonstrated the "benefits to be derived from stock raising and the advantages to be gained by inducing these people to interest themselves in this pursuit."[17]

Miles's prediction that the cattle would soon disappear after issuance to the Indians largely came true. He reported, upon request of the secretary of the interior, that some of the Arapaho chiefs added the animals to their herds, of which they held a fair number before the distribution. A few of the Arapaho schoolboys sold their cattle for cash so that they would have the means to attend Carlisle Institute. One youngster, who owned seventy-three head, sold all but eighteen. Miles doubted that the schooling to be received would be more valuable than the cattle; the youth's "desire to go to school was stronger than his desire of gain and it would have been foolish to have entered school leaving the original number to care of friends—but it is doubtful if the advantages of school will repay the sacrifice made." Among the Cheyennes it was a different story. They usually sold, gambled off, or used the cattle as presents in place of ponies, or they killed them for a feast. Since the numbers of cattle owned by each family were so few—generally only three head—the Cheyennes could not anticipate future gain, and, to rid themselves of "non-paying trouble," they "sold, killed and otherwise got rid of what seemed only a nuisance." To have a significant impact upon the tribes, Miles estimated that the herd should have been allowed to develop until it contained fifteen thousand head. Then each schoolboy's and schoolgirl's share would have been about thirty animals when they left school. Unless the herd was kept intact and not issued yearly, he predicted, the Indians would simply "hold a feast when occasion arises."[18]

Dry weather continued during the 1880 growing season, which meant no increase in agricultural activity among the Cheyennes. Also it was apparent that the Cheyenne men preferred almost any kind of labor to that of working in the fields with the women. They desired employment far beyond the limited funds provided for the agency. When manual labor was required to build a large brick warehouse, the men volunteered to haul stone, make brick, burn lime, and do whatever the building supervisor asked. So avidly did the Cheyennes seek employment that each project had to be visited each day to determine that none but authorized laborers were working. A few young men, Miles wrote, would always "go to work in the brick yard and elsewhere without the knowledge of this office, and subsequently claim payment for the labor with a pertinacity which could not be resisted." Agency work supervisors reported that the young Indian's initial enthusiasm for work was greater than his discipline for sustained labor. Although the man would tire quickly of the tasks he was assigned, he would later renew his efforts, and each period of activity would be longer. Miles thought that young Indians eventually would work continuously and would "feel lost when not at work."[19]

The number of Indians owning freight wagons soon exceeded the number required to transport goods and supplies to Darlington. Nevertheless, Miles continued to seek authority to buy more wagons for the Cheyennes and Arapahoes every year. He hoped to increase the number of wagons and teams from seventy-four to at least one hundred vehicles with the capability of moving 200,000 pounds of freight in one train. Wrote Miles, "The mere occupation of these Indians with profit will prove a great factor in their civilization besides providing them with some income to supplement Government issue." The agency office was besieged by Indians who wanted wagons assigned to them because, Miles concluded, freighting was the great success in employment thus far found for the Cheyennes and Arapahoes. After the wagons were paid for from earnings of the Indians working as freighters or teamsters, however, there were few funds to employ them for cash wages. Even after the supply was adequate to meet the agency's transportation needs, Miles sought still more wagons, claiming that the system begun at his agency and now widely copied by others was only another means of paying for the transportation of Indian goods. What Miles overlooked was the disappointment of the Indian not selected to freight between Darlington and Wichita once his wagon was paid for. The wagon then fell into disuse and the Indian returned to inactivity.[20]

Faced with the government policy of changing Indians into farmers, Miles found various reasons to explain why the Cheyennes and Arapahoes did not work in their fields more productively and consistently. He claimed, rather ineffectively, that some of the Indians knew that Congress had not confirmed title to the 1869 presidential proclamation reservation. In 1880 he stated that if the title to their reservation was confirmed "a great number can be easily induced to locate and cultivate the ground." Powder Face, Left Hand, Yellow Bear, Curley, and other Arapaho chiefs, rather than turning their attention to farming, were developing respectable-sized herds of cattle by protecting the cattle issued to them by the Indian Office funds and by breeding the cows to the blooded bulls furnished by A. E. Reynolds, the Fort Supply post trader. It was claimed in 1880 that the Indians owned about three thousand head of cattle, some of which were protected with registered brands.[21]

The most persistent factor in explaining the lack of agricultural progress, however, was the climate of the Southern Plains. Even when the Indian men put aside their disdain for farm work, their labor was not likely to be productive because of the sparse rainfall during the growing season. The corn planted during these years did not mature rapidly enough for harvesting and the green fields of April and May produced nothing more than a few cornstalks and blades for fodder by June. The early rainfall induced the Arapahoes, especially, to plow and plant, but their work was unproductive. Even the agency farm, supervised by the Darlington staff and consisting of ninety acres of corn and thirty-nine of millet, met the same fate as the Indians' fields. The crops planted by schoolboys at the two reservations' manual-training schools also failed because of the dry weather, which lasted until mid-June, 1881. Miles again stated that the climate of the Southern Plains could not be relied upon for agricultural purposes, although he accepted the belief of the age that plowing the fields and planting trees and orchards would attract moisture and rain. Irrigation, Miles also thought, could not be adopted for the Cheyenne-Arapaho Reservation because of an insufficient water supply in the rivers and streams, the nature of the terrain, and the type of soil—a "high, level, sandy loam with little or no clay subsoil"—to hold the irrigation water. When the Cheyennes made little pretense of opening farms and gardens, Miles explained that the attitude of the "incorrigible Northern Cheyennes" had influenced their southern kinsmen to such an extent that they refused to farm.[22]

When Joshua Ross, the president of the International Fair Association, Muskogee, Indian Territory, invited a delegation of Arapahoes to exhibit their farm products, Miles declined the invitation. He explained that the Arapahoes had no funds to make the trip, that they had no "farm products to take with them to place on exhibition and that they are *close run* for the necessaries of life." He added that Left Hand, Big Mouth, Cut Finger, Bear Robe, and White Buffalo wanted to attend the Muskogee fair, if their transportation and food costs could be provided for them, to "learn more of the methods and practices adopted by your people who have made such great progress in civilization."

The only significant source of income for the two tribes came from transporting their supplies from Arkansas City, Kansas, a railroad terminal closer to Darlington than to Wichita. Those Cheyennes and Arapahoes who could not acquire wagons came close to starvation. About four hundred people whose camps were near Cantonment and who were led by Powder Face and Black Coyote of the Arapahoes, as well as Little Chief, Little Robe, and Little Big Jake of the Cheyennes joined the village of the Kiowas' Buffalo Medicine Man on the North Fork of the Red River. Powder Face and Black Coyote sought the assistance of the Kiowa agent to obtain food, but the Cheyennes were too stubborn and proud to make a similar request even to feed their families. The Kiowa, Cheyenne, and Arapaho warriors hunted for the buffaloes needed to begin the ceremony of the Kiowa medicine man and after several weeks killed a bull and a cow, but the four-day ceremony failed to bring back the buffaloes. Little Chief and his northerners led the exodus from the encampment and departed "in disgust with the Kiowas."[23]

With agricultural production inconsequential and government rations too few for more than a marginal diet, the Cheyennes and Arapahoes continued to seek alternative employment. It was estimated that congressional appropriations were about 40 per cent too low to issue the Indians full rations during the forthcoming year. The Indians sought to purchase wagons from freighting wages in preference to waiting for the wagons issued from annuity funds, since the latter always arrived too late in the season to be used to transport supplies to Darlington. By the summer of 1881, Miles had assembled a pool of about 135 wagons which could transport about 400,000 pounds of freight in one trip from Arkansas City to the agency headquarters. Since government freight was insufficient to utilize the full capacity of the Indians' wagons, goods for the Fort Reno and Indian traders were usually included in the cargoes. A wagon with a full load could hold 2,000 to 3,000 pounds of freight, which meant that the Indians could pay for each wagon and harness, at a cost of $103, in one trip to the rail terminal. Those Indians who wanted wagons but could not obtain them occasionally labored at the agency and schools chopping wood, making bricks, and putting up hay. More Indians, however, merely existed on government rations and annuities because of the scarcity of funds for Indian employment and the failure of crops on Indian farms.[24]

When, early in 1882, transfer of the San Carlos and Mescalero Apaches to southwestern Indian Territory was being considered, Miles supplied his superiors with a fair estimate of the agricultural potential of the region. He thought that the Kiowa-Comanche Agency and his agency could easily assimilate ten thousand more Indians, if they were properly located. The terrain was high, rolling prairie with narrow wooded valleys along the streams. Hardwood was scarce, but some cottonwoods skirted the streams, and the stream valleys where the productive land lay. The Washita, Cache Creek, North Canadian, South Canadian, and Cimarron valleys were ranked by Miles in order of soil fertility, but even then Miles recommended that the farms in the valleys be joined to large tracts of lands in the higher ground for grazing purposes. If the Indians were allowed to develop stock raising and farms together, Miles could see no reason why "industrious people may not prosper and eventually become self-supporting." He warned the commissioner of Indian affairs that the Indian farms must be carefully located and that even a *"white man* would 'starve to death' if placed on 160 acres or even a section of the high lands in this country." Miles's advice would be forgotten a decade later, when the Cheyennes and Arapahoes were allotted land under the Dawes Act and received only one-quarter sections, which frequently were unusable as farms.[25]

By 1882, after seven years of near failure to introduce farming to Cheyennes and Arapahoes, Miles and his staff realized that the usual cycle of plowing, planting, and cultivation of crops would have to be changed. Finally it was learned that fields plowed in the early winter, allowing the spring rains to accumulate in the soil, and then packed down before corn was seeded were the only areas on which the grain matured. Spring plowing followed by planting and cultivation would not work in western Indian Territory. The Indian agents, who came from the Old Northwest, as did most of their staff, finally had learned that soil moisture had to be conserved carefully.[26]

The new knowledge came too late to avert a food crisis on the reservation in 1882. It also may have come too late to persuade the Cheyennes and Arapahoes to drop their prejudices against farming after a succession of crop failures. The Indians' crops were scarcely in the ground when Commissioner Hiram Price ordered Agent Miles to reduce the beef issue by one-third for the remainder of the fiscal year. For the Indians the following winter was the worst yet for finding means to supplement governmental issues because there was little freighting or other employment available. Miles judged it his duty to warn Major George M. Randall, the commanding officer of Fort Reno, that trouble was likely to occur. He reported that the regular ration, as Major Randall knew, was "barely sufficient to keep soul and body together and to reduce this allowance one third would be a national cruelty and a challenge for war or starvation." Miles wired Commissioner Price that slashing the beef ration to two pounds a

71

week "cannot be made at this time without suffering to the Indians and probably trouble in the near future. Indians will not submit to an enrollment for beef on the basis of two pounds gross, nor can they live on such ration."[27]

After Miles's initial flurry of telegrams, he provided the commissioner with fuller details about why the ration of beef should not be reduced. "All sober, thinking, well-disposed Indians," Miles wrote, "expressed themselves as anxious to conform to all the possible requirements of the Government but that they could not subsist and live on a less ration than they have been receiving," while the less friendly were emphatic that "they *would not* submit." Miles offered five reasons why the ration should not be reduced: (1) at that time of the year there was the least consumable meat on the cattle, (2) Indian ponies were too weak from winter grazing to be used in pulling freight wagons, (3) there was little wild game left in the region, (4) crops had been a total failure on the reservation in 1881, and (5) a reduction in beef issues would decrease by $150 a week the sale of cattle hides to Indian traders. Further, Miles argued, if beef was reduced, other commodities would have to be increased, and they also would not last until the beginning of the new fiscal year. Commissioner Price rejected the agent's pleas. "There is no treaty," the commissioner responded, "with your Indians to supply them with full rations and Congress had failed to appropriate sufficient for that purpose, hence my instructions in letter of fifteenth must be obeyed." Helplessly, Miles asked Major Randall, "What can we do further?"[28]

Miles was incensed and did what he could to head off disaster. In his view the Indians were working when they could. They had, for example, during the past year transported two million pounds of freight to the agency and had chopped five hundred cords of wood for fuel, and they could hardly be blamed for the crop failures during ten successive seasons. Miles also tried to enlist the support of Senator Preston B. Plumb of Kansas. He informed Plumb that unless the usual level of rations was continued the Indians would raid the cattle herds held on the Cherokee Outlet. Miles asserted that his people could not live on less and that it "would be easier and cheaper to prevent trouble, than to suppress it when once inaugurated. The facts are all before the Commissioner."[29]

The Indians, as Miles predicted, refused to enroll for the reduced beef ration. The only solution that Miles could achieve was to have the Indians accept the regular amount of meat, but for a ten-day rather than a seven-day period. In the presence of Major Randall the Indians accepted Miles's proposal, reserving their "strong talk" for later. The Northern Cheyennes, as Miles expected, were the most adamant. In council they proclaimed to Miles, "We are going to starve here, and wish to start on our journey north according to promises made in Washington and we want to go now."[30]

When Senator Plumb inquired about the operation of the agency and the beef deficiency, Agent Miles responded with a long and bitter letter. The shortage of beef was caused when Congress in the 1881–82 fiscal budget restored to the War Department the funds previously allocated for the subsistence of the Indians in Indian Territory during May and June, 1881. Miles charged that the government was not fulfilling its obligations under the 1867 Medicine Lodge Treaty. To date, Miles wrote, he had been permitted to spend only $165.50 for two corn planters and two mowers while the treaty had specified that $20,000.00 could have been used to purchase agricultural machinery and equipment for the Cheyennes and Arapahoes. He never had available the full amount of the "civilization" fund for the payment of agency employees, and the $14,000.00 treaty provision for clothing was insufficient for 6,220 Indians, especially when the goods furnished were of "shoddy" material. To use the treaty funds effectively, Miles had already persuaded the Indians to delete trinkets, strouding for blankets, and tobacco from the list of goods furnished under the treaty obligations.

Miles was particularly critical of the governmental policy to turn the Cheyennes and Arapahoes into farmers. It was hopeless, he wrote, to attempt to confine these Indians to agricultural activities, especially when white men with all of their education and agricultural skills would starve in an effort to produce a livelihood in western Indian Territory by relying on grain crops alone. Miles argued that, because the reservation was primarily grazing country, pastoral pursuits must

73

be relied upon if the Indians were to become self-supporting. The Indians, the agent believed, could become herders and stock raisers in a short period of time, while "at farming he makes slow progress even under favorable circumstances. While in this country to have his efforts prove unfruitful 3 years out of 4 will prove disastrous to our farm efforts." He agreed that farms or allotments in severalty along the streams might be the means of breaking up the Indians' camps and tying them to dispersed farms, but he urged that large grazing areas contiguous to the allotments or farm should always be reserved for the Indians' use.

The orders of the Washington office to break up the mission herd ruined a means of bringing the Cheyennes and Arapahoes to a self-supporting status. Miles claimed that the Indian Office thought "something rotten" was occurring because the herd was growing rapidly. He was directed to issue the fifteen hundred animals worth twenty thousand dollars to camp Indians, but it would have been better to simply herd the cattle into the slaughter pen and butcher them for the benefit of the tribes. Not only would the school herd in time have provided the Indians with an income, but educationally it was also important. The schoolboys could have been trained in stock raising and ranching, and their parents could have seen the results of the youths' stay in school when they brought a small herd back with them to the camps. The accumulation of property in the form of cattle was something the Indian could see and appreciate, while the advantages of a literary education were not very apparent. Despite his loss in a "knock-down" fight with the Washington office over the herd, Miles advocated the re-establishment of an even larger herd on the reservation under the control of an agent who should be given broad discretionary powers in its management. If the herd did not prosper, Miles said his superiors should "decapitate him."

In 1882, Miles insisted that the Cheyennes and Arapahoes needed substantial support from the government. He found as many alternate jobs for the Indians as funds and opportunities permitted. They hauled freight to Darlington and Fort Reno, cut hay, and chopped wood, but the income realized did not offset the reduction in congressional appropriations for food. Although Agent Miles disliked

74

feeding "lazy Indians as bad as any one can," he concluded that reduction in rations would bring trouble and raids for cattle by the Cheyennes and Arapahoes.[31]

Miles claimed he had somehow to find about forty thousand pounds of beef a week in addition to the authorized issue to keep the Indians from starving. Cheyenne and Arapaho chiefs representing all of the bands appeared at Miles's Darlington office and told the agent that they were "destitute of beef and must have it." Miles wrote to Major Randall early in April, 1882:

These people cannot live on [83,000 pounds of beef], and unless a deficiency of about forty thousand pounds per week is furnished from some source regularly and promptly actual hunger will drive them to deeds of violence. . . . Hunger drives civilized men to deeds of violence. What may we expect here surrounded by six thousand savages. Can you not touch the heart of some one in authority who will appreciate the situation?

In the hope of borrowing cattle from herds grazing in the Cherokee Outlet and from government beef contractors, Miles sent out representatives so that the Indians could be subsisted until the new fiscal year began on July 1. The Cheyennes and Arapahoes were saved from privation when Major Randall provided some beef from his reserve supply and Congress passed an emergency appropriation of fifty thousand dollars to buy cattle for the Indians on the reservations of southwestern Indian Territory.[32]

The congressional emergency appropriation did not last for the remainder of the 1881–82 fiscal year. On June 23, 1882, the commissioner of Indian affairs ordered Miles to reduce the beef issue to eighty thousand pounds a week. Disgruntled and hungry chiefs again began another round of councils with their agent. In the councils Cheyenne chiefs Whirlwind, Big Horse, Big Man, Red Wolf, Strong Bow, and White Shield and Arapaho chiefs Powder Face, Left Hand, Big Mouth, Medicine Pipe, and Sitting Bull recommended that annuity funds due under the Medicine Lodge Treaty be expended only for beef and the support of the agency schools. Such items as blankets, cotton goods, clothing, trinkets, hardware, bacon, baking powder, beans, and corn should be stricken from the annuity list.

The amount saved, estimated by Miles at more than thirty-four thousand dollars, should be used to buy more beef for the tribes. Miles's anxiety and the Indians' hunger were shortly relieved when the slash in issue beef was restored.[33]

The fluctuations in the amounts of beef issued angered the Indians and worried Miles. The Indian agent began to look for a means to assure a sufficient and constant supply of beef for the Cheyennes and Arapahoes. Probably at the suggestion of their agent the Cheyenne and Arapaho chiefs asked that cattle herds of white ranchers be located at "remote points" on the reservation upon which a reasonable rent in cattle could be levied. The Cheyennes and Arapahoes knew that Agent Hunt of the Kiowa-Comanche Reservation was receiving a tax from the cattle herds feeding on the grass of the reservation that bordered theirs on the south. Miles admitted that, while this proposal did not have the sanction of law, "there could certainly be no wrong committed but an advantage derived."[34]

As Miles continued to press his arguments, he presented four reasons why rangeland on the reservation should be rented to cattle-men. If the Cherokees could rent their lands in the Outlet, why could not the Cheyennes and Arapahoes have the same privilege? Either money or cattle from the rented lands would eliminate the uncertainty of irregular beef rations. Cattle drifted onto the reservation from the Cherokee Outlet and the Texas Panhandle. Since military patrols could not prevent unauthorized cattle from grazing on the reservation, why should not the tribes benefit from the inevitable use of their rangeland? Lastly, Miles had already identified cattlemen who would pay for grazing privileges with cattle.[35]

Commissioner of Indian Affairs Price, supported by Secretary of the Interior Henry M. Teller, quickly rejected Miles's proposals. Price asserted that it was the Indian Office's policy to discourage occupancy of Indian lands by whites and to encourage the Indians to provide their own subsistence. The support Miles's scheme received from army officers also irritated the commissioner. General Pope's endorsement of Major Randall's telegram which upheld the Indian agent noted that permitting cattlemen to occupy the Cheyenne-Arapaho Reservation and contribute beef to alleviate the hunger of the Indians "would cure a trouble which may soon be past dealing with except by war." Price's reply revealed the early bureaucratic rigidity of the Indian Office as he testily wrote, "it is not probable that threats or unfavorable comments from other parties will change the practice of the Indian Bureau."[36]

Not only was Miles denied permission to rent, lease, or issue permits for the use of the grassland, but he was ordered to clear the reservation of all cattle not owned by Indians. Only cattle owned by whites who had intermarried with Cheyennes and Arapahoes that were "actually and bonafide their own" were exempted from the order. Consequently, Miles faced the 1882–83 fiscal year in no better shape than before. He would be limited to 125,000 pounds of beef liveweight for each weekly issue to the Cheyennes and Arapahoes, and he also knew that when funds ran short in the Department of Interior another reduction in the beef issue would follow. No advances against future deliveries would be permitted, and any additional requisitions for more beef would be rejected by the Bureau of Indian Affairs. Secretary of the Interior Henry M. Teller recognized the insufficiency of congressional appropriations when in February, 1883, he approved the use of thirty-four thousand dollars for the purchase of stock cattle. The money normally would have been used for the purchase of clothing and annuity goods, but the secretary thought that two superior objectives could be served by diverting the funds for the purchase of cattle. Since the reservation was admirably adapted to grazing, the Cheyennes and Arapahoes could be taught to care for cattle herds, and at the "same time the cattle enable the Department to relieve any distress for food which cannot be otherwise met."[37]

Cheyenne and Arapaho farms did not thrive much better in 1882 than in the past. Indian farmers abandoned their fields in April, which was dry and windy. June brought more moisture, prompting hopeful statements from Miles about a good corn crop and above-average yields in other grains. Then three weeks of heavy rain and two severe storms in July turned Miles's optimism to pessimism. The oat and millet crops were beaten to the ground and were a total loss, while the young orchard planted by Miles at the agency was destroyed. Few of the Indians enlarged their fields. Instead, they devoted more of their

77

time to tending the small herds because the agent convinced them that stock raising was more profitable than trying to grow crops.[38]

Paralleling the program to teach adult males agricultural techniques was an educational curriculum that would instruct Indian youths in self-sufficiency. Education was regarded as a "fundamental and indispensable factor" in leading the Indians, who were wards of the nation, toward a civilized life. Congress was urged by the Board of Indian Commissioners in 1875 to establish a "common school system" as a part of the nation's Indian policy. Not only was Indian education based on "simple justice and duty," but, it was argued, progress for the Indians "consists not so much in feeding or governing the *adults* as in educating the *children*."[39]

Until the winter of 1875–76, there was no reservation school for the Southern Cheyennes and Arapahoes. The only instruction carried on before that time was in a mission school maintained by the Society of Friends, attended by few more than fifty Arapaho boys and girls. Even before the school building was ready, John Seger was working with the mission schoolboys in a forty-acre plot of corn. Illness of the contractor, William Darlington, delayed the completion of the structure until December, 1875. As the building was being readied for use, Arapaho chiefs promised that one to two hundred of their children would attend; the Cheyennes were far less co-operative. Seger agreed to a contract to educate and board between sixty and one hundred pupils for $6.50 for each pupil a month. Miles estimated that, once the school opened, it would cost the government, excluding the students' share of annuities and rations, from $3,000.00 to $5,000.00 for the remainder of the 1875–76 fiscal year.[40]

Fewer children than the chiefs had promised became Seger's pupils. On January 1, 1876, only eleven Cheyenne and nineteen Arapaho boys and nine Cheyenne and twenty-four Arapaho girls were enrolled in the first class. Cheyenne chiefs White Shield, Big Horse, and Bull Bear brought their youngsters to Seger. Bull Bear, a noted war chief of the Dog Soldiers, explained that he had raised his other sons to be warriors but that his nine-year-old boy he gave "to Washington to educate." Another unnamed Cheyenne was willing to forget his hatred toward the whites, telling Agent Miles, "The Whites killed my father and mother at Sand Creek and last summer took my only brother and sent him away from us. My heart had felt bad towards whites many years but today I have thrown that feeling all away. Take my child as proof of my sincerity."[41]

As the term progressed, more pupils left their lodges for the school-room. When the first term of the school ended on June 1, 1876, the enrollment had risen to 112 pupils, consisting of 33 Cheyennes, 78 Arapahoes, and 1 Apache. By the terms of his contract Seger and his teachers were required to provide an "ordinary English education," instruction in agriculture for the boys, and instruction in domestic arts for the girls. Although the children were taught reading, writing, and arithmetic, Seger instituted a program that fitted the school's description as a "manual training and labor school." Seger was not furnished with a farmer to supervise the school farm, but he and the larger boys plowed, planted, and cultivated 110 acres of land for corn and vegetables. They cut, chopped, and hauled wood for the school and the agency and fed and cared for the school and agency herds. For their work the boys received one-half of the profits from the crops and herds.[42]

When the new school year began in September, 1877, the class-rooms and dormitories were filled to capacity with 113 pupils. The curriculum and work programs that Seger had devised were not altered significantly except to add a beginning course in teaching the pupils to count money. Agent Miles agreed completely with Seger in the manner of running a school for Indian children. He asserted that "mere literary education, without the more important element of industry, is but time poorly spent." Great emphasis was placed on the "industrial education" of the boys as they were taken into the fields to tend the school crops, learn to butcher and cut meat, bake bread, feed and water cattle and hogs, mend shoes and harnesses, milk cows, and cut and store hay for agency and school animals. From the sale of surplus grains, vegetables, and hay Seger purchased additional stock to form the nucleus of the mission herd.[43]

The school served functions other than educational and vocational ends. When the Northern Cheyennes arrived at Darlington in August, 1877, Agent Miles immediately brought pressure to bear upon the chiefs to place their children in school. Standing Elk, Broken Cup, and Living Bear agreed, but Dull Knife and Wild Hog demurred. By November 23, Miles had secured a fair representation of Northern Cheyenne children, who served in effect as hostages to ensure the good behavior and co-operation of their parents and bands. The school was also expected to destroy the children's interest in and adherence to Indian culture. One astute and perceptive observer noted:

In changing the name and dress, and cropping the hair (which with many is a sign of mourning) it seems to be the intention to obliterate as far as possible the child's identification with parentage and history. This would be most repugnant to us if we were subjected to it, and I am quite sure the Indians are not indifferent to it.

If "pride of family and history" was emphasized during the education of children, he added, Indian parents would no longer feel that they gave their children away to the government when they entered the white man's schools.[44]

No appreciable change occurred in the curriculum or programs of the school during its early years. The building that housed the school was composed of a central hall of two stories flanked with wings two and three stories high. An inspection in 1878 commended Miles and Seger for their educational program. The industrial training the students received was "noteworthy for its success," and Inspector John McNeil reported that Seger "inspires the Indian youth of both sexes with the idea of property as well as a desire for its acquisition. . . . The school herd is a model idea well worth of imitation." Only about 10 per cent of the children on the reservation could be instructed in the school at one time, even though the capacity of the dormitories had been increased to accommodate 135 pupils. For the schools to have much significance for the Cheyennes and Arapahoes, Agent Miles did not want the children taught "statistical knowledge" but rather hoped that they would be instructed in the "duties of life which will devolve upon them as men and women." And, of course, more children would have to be brought into classrooms and work programs.[45]

Not all of the earliest education for the Southern Cheyennes took place at the reservation boarding school. The warriors who had been judged leaders of the 1874–75 war and sent to Fort Marion, Florida, received instruction while in prison. Some of the youngest of the group were transferred to Captain Richard Pratt's school at Carlisle Barracks, Pennsylvania, when it opened in 1878. A few others continued their education at Hampton Institute in Virginia. Fifteen of the warriors and chiefs, however, returned to Darlington late in April, 1878. Howling Wolf, one of the returnees, persuaded twenty-one young Cheyennes to cut their hair and adopt white clothes. Their number was too small to have much impact on the whole tribe, but for a period of time they worked industriously cutting and chopping wood for use at Fort Reno. Only one of the young men from Fort Marion returned immediately to the customs of his people. He participated in the 1878 Cheyennes' Sun Dance, endured the torture, and explained his action by saying that he was fulfilling a vow he made when he was sent as a prisoner to Fort Marion. Major Mizner noted that, while the returned prisoners wanted to continue to live as they had at Fort Marion, reservation conditions probably would cause them to revert to camp life since there was little opportunity to use the knowledge they had gained, with little work, no houses, and limited clothing available.[46]

To provide educational facilities for more children, Miles requested that another school be constructed for the reservation. The two tribes bickered over the one school, and, because the Arapahoes sent greater numbers of pupils to it, the Cheyennes viewed it as the Arapaho school and were reluctant to send their children to it. More Indians were willing to send their youngsters to school if the government would fulfill its promise of providing one teacher for every thirty students. Education was now compulsory, and, in any event, Miles noted, "it is conceded by all that the only way to civilize the Indian is to educate them and give them a thorough industrial training." The new school buildings were at Caddo Springs, about one mile north of Darlington. It was there that the Cheyennes sent their children. Thereafter the Arapahoes dominated the school at Darlington, while the Caddo Springs school was looked upon by the Cheyennes as theirs.

The additional facilities, completed in August, 1879, meant that there were places for about 375 pupils in the two reservation boarding schools. By Miles's estimate about one-quarter of the school-aged children of the two tribes would have an opportunity to be educated.[47]

Miles's drive to increase the number of Cheyenne pupils generally succeeded. Little Robe, who lived near Cantonment and who had formerly prevented his people from sending pupils to the Darlington school, promptly sent his band's quota to Caddo Springs. With the Indian children in school, Miles believed that his control over the parents was greater than it would be with troops. As he wrote earlier, not only did the children learn the patterns of civilized life but the families of school children tended to settle down and undertake some activities for self-support. Miles stated that he had yet to see the first Indian "give the Government trouble when his child is in school." Not all the Cheyennes were co-operative, however. Little Chief of the Northern Cheyennes, while conferring with the secretary of the Interior in Washington, claimed that his people were exempt from the ruling that required children to attend school. To the commissioner of Indian affairs Miles complained that Little Chief "reviles those who have their children in school and unless . . . his influence [is checked] the Northern Cheyenne children would be withdrawn by their parents." When the commissioner limited the exemption to Little Chief's family, the stubborn leader retorted to his agent, "All of my band were not required to put their children in school. That this only meant my family is a lie." Consequently, the number of children in Little Chief's band was unusually high because other northerners placed their children in his camp to be covered by Little Chief's exemption.[48]

In the fall of 1879 information was received at Darlington that the Cheyennes and Arapahoes could send twenty-five children to Carlisle Institute. At the off-reservation boarding school they would join the younger Cheyenne warriors who had followed Captain Pratt to the Pennsylvania school. Miles asserted that the tribes could have furnished one hundred pupils for Captain Pratt's school. He added that, when there were enough schools for the education of all Indian children on and off the reservation, "we may expect to see a radical change from ignorance and superstition, idleness and vagrancy to intelligence and propriety." But the education of the Indian must be more than intellectual training because, if the students do "not understand how to break the land and plow the corn or how to keep the house and cook the victuals, the effort at permanent civilization will amount to but little and the expenditures will have been in vain." Teachers of Indian children must be not only competent in the class-room but sensitive and acceptable to their pupils. The agent had witnessed instructors who were successful and experienced in the eastern states fail on his reservation because they could not make the students feel that "someone loved them."[49]

Cheyennes who had been reluctant to put their children in the reservation boarding schools eagerly presented their children to the Indian agent so that they could be sent to Carlisle. Cheyenne chiefs who had placed their children in the Darlington and Caddo Springs schools also saw their children leave for Carlisle. Bull Bear, Big Horse, and Heap-of-Birds of the Cheyennes represented their tribe's leadership, while Arapaho chief Left Hand's son Grant and Little Raven's daughter Anna were among the eighteen Cheyenne and ten Arapaho boys and girls who departed from Darlington on October 9, 1879. The quota was exceeded when Acting Agent Campbell found it impossible to deny three Cheyenne men the right to send their boys to Carlisle. Pawnee Man, called by the acting agent one of the most progressive Cheyennes, brought his son Dick to Campbell, "fully clothed and prepared for school." He had purchased the clothing with money he had earned chopping wood. Gentle Horse, a brother of Black Kettle who had followed Pawnee Man's example, also was successful in having his son sent off with his friends. In addition, Antelope, one of the former Fort Marion prisoners who was serving as an agency Indian policeman, smuggled his son Lincoln aboard the wagon train as it departed from Darlington.[50]

The enthusiasm of the Cheyennes and Arapahoes for the Carlisle school did not diminish quickly. Agent Miles suggested that he be permitted to select twenty-five additional pupils for Captain Pratt's institution. Hardly a day passed without an Indian requesting that his child be among those sent to Carlisle. To gain additional support,

83

Miles suggested that a few of the Cheyenne and Arapaho chiefs be allowed to visit Carlisle. When the new pupils were added to the Cheyenne and Arapaho youths already attending Carlisle, 50 per cent had previously attended reservation schools, 66 per cent were children of Cheyenne and Arapaho chiefs and head men, and 10 per cent were mixed-blood children of the two tribes. After Miles had received permission to escort twenty-five children and four chiefs from the tribes to the eastern school, he recommended that two young men from the "soldier element" be allowed to accompany their chiefs. Miles wrote to Commissioner R. E. Trowbridge that they possessed influence "vastly greater among the younger part of the tribes than that of most noted chiefs. . . . with this class once interested in the work of education and progress, fully one-half of the obstacles we now contend with, would be overcome."[51]

In 1880 more Cheyennes and Arapahoes permitted their children to attend school than ever before. Each of the two reservation boarding schools had an average attendance of 150 pupils, and there were 62 boys and girls at Carlisle Institute. Agent Miles tried to increase the effectiveness of the schools' curriculum by improving the quality and quantity of teaching and support personnel. He wanted a total of fourteen employees, including a superintendent and four teachers for each school. While the budget suggested by Miles came to only $565 a month while the school was in session and $225 during the summer vacation period, even such a modest request could not be immediately granted. He also hoped to bring more discipline to the schools by adding military uniforms for the boys, cutting their hair, and introducing them to infantry marching drills and calisthenics modeled upon Carlisle's program to counteract the childrens' unfettered camp life."[52]

Within five years education was having some results on the lives of the Cheyennes and Arapahoes, especially among the younger people. In 1881 the number of students enrolled at the reservation boarding schools declined from 300 to 250, but the number attending Carlisle rose from 62 to 70. Twelve other Cheyenne and Arapaho youngsters were receiving instruction in other eastern schools, including Hampton Institute. Despite the growth of facilities and greater use of nonreservation boarding schools, only 27 per cent of the children of the two tribes were in school, and the vast majority were still in the camps, where they were untouched by the white man's learning. A few Carlisle and Hampton students were beginning to return to the Darlington Agency. For the most part the first group had been prisoners at Fort Marion whose training had been continued at Carlisle and at Hampton Institute. Miles reported that they comprised a majority of the Indian employees at the agency and were good workers. Henry Roman Nose, who had learned tinsmithing, was at work in the agency shop. Making Medicine, now named David Pendleton, was preaching the Gospel in Cheyenne. Of him Miles said, "A better Christian man we do not find." Pendleton had been trained for three years by the Reverend J. B. Wickes of the Episcopal Church at Paris Hill, New York. Upon returning to the reservation on June 14, 1881, Pendleton refused to participate in the Sun Dance or other ceremonies with his people. Two days after his return he conducted a funeral service for a son of Big Horse, using Episcopal rites. According to Miles, the returned students from Carlisle, Hampton, and the reservation schools are "going to kill much of the 'Indian' in the Indians of this agency in due time." Initially the policy of using Carlisle and Hampton "to furnish native teachers in all the civilized pursuits" appeared to be working satisfactorily.

A problem, however, was already arising on the reservation that would become more troublesome in the future. John Seger returned from an extended vacation and found a number of the older Arapaho schoolboys living in tribal camps. To a considerable extent they had "resumed their former habits of camp life, and instead of being clothed in citizen's dress, had cast it aside and were wearing blankets, and were not putting to use the knowledge and skills they had acquired" while in the Arapaho Manual Labor and Boarding School. Because the amount of employment at the agency was too limited, only seven Indian youths were working as apprentices in shops and offices, and agricultural endeavors could not keep all the schoolboys busy when they had completed the units of education offered at the boarding school.[53]

In September, 1881, another educational facility opened at Darlington. More than a year earlier the Board of Mennonite Missions had requested permission to begin missionary activities on the Cheyenne-Arapaho Reservation. The Reverend S. S. Haury had been nominated as the first Mennonite missionary who would take the Christian message to the Arapahoes. The board mentioned that Mr. Haury would work not only among the school children but with adults as well. A farm would be opened near the agency to support the costs of the missionary and educational work. Agent Miles's endorsement of the Mennonite request brought quick approval from the Office of Indian Affairs, and a class of seventeen Arapaho children began instruction under the supervision of the Mennonites.[54]

In 1882 the two reservation boarding schools and the Mennonite mission school enrolled only 227 pupils. Regardless of where the boys and girls attended school, the program was similar. The young men seemed to enjoy the work in the fields but found other chores less pleasant. The girls were taught "all kinds of house work, sewing, mending, washing, cooking and it is notable in camp that when school girls have returned to live the lodge is kept in much better condition, many little changes and comforts are introduced, and the cooking is better, all traceable to the knowledge and influence of the school girl." Even the limited exposure to white attitudes in the school seemed to make some impression on the young women. Agent Miles noted that "we have frequent applications at our houses and particularly at our schools by young girls for protection telling us they have been 'sold' to some man whom they despise and who had an old wife or two and they would rather die than live with him."[55]

On July 10, 1882, eighteen youths who had completed their three-year course of instruction at Carlisle returned to Darlington. They were replaced by fourteen boys and fifteen girls from the two tribes, and Miles recommended that they remain at the Pennsylvania school for five years. The longer period, Miles thought, would prepare them "in their studies and character . . . to be better able to meet and withstand the unwholesome camp influences which are brought to bear upon their return home." By the time the students were sent to Carlisle, they were usually able to read and write and were beyond the first rules of arithmetic. They had not been trained in any craft or skill, but they did know how to work as a result of their activities in the school fields or housekeeping chores at the schools. Wherever possible, Agent Miles saw that the Carlisle boys were given jobs in the agency shops and that the girls went to work in the schools as assistants to the matrons in the kitchen or sewing rooms.

During the summer of 1882, Mr. Haury, as an experiment, placed fifteen Arapaho boys in farm homes near Halstead, Kansas. It was assumed that the boys would learn more in the Mennonite homes and on their farms than in the reservation boarding schools. The Mennonites agreed to continue the education of the young men, and Miles suggested that the program be enlarged to include older girls who could cook and help during the harvest season. The Indian agent suggested that a fund be established to place hundreds of Indian youths in farm homes where they could come in "contact with our civilization, in order that they may know better what it is, and adapt themselves, so that they may apply it in their every-day lives."[56]

John H. Seger, who had been associated with the Arapaho Boarding School since its opening in 1876, resigned in March, 1882, because his salary had been reduced as superintendent of the school from seventy-five dollars to sixty dollars a month. Possessing two trades, Seger declared that he owed it to his family to work where he could support them better. Not only had Seger gained the respect of the Indians because of his sensible programs as superintendent of the school, but he had worked with the adult Indians, persuading them to buy mules, larger horses, and household furniture and to learn simple farming activities. During the latter period of his service, Seger supervised the construction of a brick kiln, and he had hoped to be able to teach the Indians bricklaying so that they could build themselves permanent homes. D. B. Hirshler replaced Seger, and the educational programs instituted by Seger soon began to decline because the new superintendent lacked the Indians' confidence.[57]

In December, 1882, a fourth school was opened on the Cheyenne-Arapaho Reservation. Only twenty-five students were enrolled in the new school, which utilized the old army post at Cantonment. Mr. Haury shifted from Darlington to Cantonment to supervise the new school, and he took with him the same educational curriculum that had been established at the other reservation schools. He found that the Cheyennes did not want their children to attend the same schools as those of the Arapaho children. Immediately Mr. Haury, with the aid of some of the older boys, opened a fifteen-acre farm, taking special care "to have the work done slowly and thoroughly, thus insuring the acquisition of systematic knowledge on the part of the boys." The Reverend H. Voth replaced Haury at Darlington, continuing the instruction of the Arapaho children in the rudiments of the English language, with limited results. Younger children readily acquired the ability to speak English, but the older pupils were beginning to resist because of the ridicule they faced from their parents and their peers who were not attending the schools.[58]

In 1883, Commissioner Price criticized the agricultural and manual-training programs of the Cheyenne and Arapaho boarding schools. Despite Miles's constant insistence that those parts of the youngsters' education had been emphasized, a routine inspection, Price claimed, revealed that the manual education of the boys and girls was lagging behind programs on other reservations. Price labeled this deficiency a "radical mistake." Price wrote:

The girls in your two schools *must* be taught cooking, washing, ironing, sewing, the making as well as the repair of garments, everything which pertains to good house-wifery, including bread making and dairy work. No matter what school exercises have to be sacrificed, this kind of training must be given. . . . I am aware that it is more trouble to get work done this way, and that your larger girls have been sent to Carlisle but I know from observation in other Indian schools that *it can be done.*

Price also insisted that the industrial training for boys was inadequate. The whole school herd should be entirely cared for by the boys, who should also raise the feed and cut all the hay needed for the animals. Price also suggested that the size of the school farm should be increased. In the school shops boys should be taught the use of simple tools and be given sufficient instructions so that they could repair broken furniture and assist in the repair of school buildings. In concluding his strictures to Miles, Commissioner Price demanded: "Their hands should have more training than their heads. Half the time spent in work would not be too large a proportion."[59]

By the summer of 1883, the second large contingent of Carlisle students was scheduled to return to the reservation. The twenty-one young people had completed three years of instruction, but Commissioner Price recommended that they remain at Carlisle for two more years. He pointed out that they had "just learned how to speak, how to think, and how to work, and are now ready to get the most possible benefit out of all the advantages that Carlisle can offer." Price requested that parental permission be obtained for the pupils to remain at Carlisle, and he asked Miles to explain to the parents that if the students remained they would show "the same love of their children which makes them long for their return." Most of the parents wanted their children back with them on the reservation, and only a few were willing for their children to continue their schooling. But all agreed to allow their children to stay at Carlisle if they could come home if they became ill. This was the Indian way of saying that the pupil should be dismissed from school if a real need existed or if the student wanted no more education. Such students as Cleaver Warden and Leonard Tyler remained at Carlisle for the additional two years. Also in 1883 seven Cheyenne and Arapaho boys and girls were transferred from the reservation schools to the West Branch, Iowa, Indian Training School.[60]

The problems encountered by returned students are typified by Harvey White Shield's efforts to use his education and commitment to Christianity. After his return to the reservation he preached the Gospel to the Cheyennes, and he pleaded to Agent Miles, "I want very much to work some place. . . . If you put me to work in your office as a clerk and copy some thing every day, or help to work at some place [I can] . . . earn a living for my people. . . . Please give me work to do." The experience of White Shield was so common on other reservations that congressmen questioned the wisdom of continuing education among Indians. Five years later White Shield was still seeking an opportunity to use his education and his interest in the ministry. He decided against joining the Army Indian Scouts and considered moving from his home on Kingfisher Creek to either Washita or Cantonment. At the latter place, he thought, he could both preach and teach in the Cantonment school. He wrote to Mr. Voth at Darlington that

you have convince me to devote my service in the Lords and I too have been made to feel after earnest prayer for light and guidance that there was a work than cannot be done by any other but that work alone is to be done by myself which the Lord had laid before me that there is a place in the vineyards of the Lord where I must bring the sheaves to the house every morning for several days past the familiar text comes in my mind thus, "The harvest truly is plenteous but the laborers are few."[61]

CHAPTER IV

Cattlemen Occupy the Reservation

AGENT MILES WAS convinced by the early 1880's that the Cheyennes and Arapahoes would never become farmers. Another occupation would have to be found if the tribes were ever to become self-sufficient, and stock raising seemed to be the most logical of all alternatives. The climate, lack of sufficient agricultural implements, Indian resistance to agricultural labor, and inadequate instructional staff to assist the Indians in farming had led to repeated crop failures. The Cheyennes in particular refused to engage in farming, not because of "any dislike or carelessness on their part, but rather [because of] past experience, their previous attempts having proven almost total failures." Some of the Cheyennes, reported Miles, had accumulated small herds and were "as careful as a white man would be. Many have a few head, which will in a few years increase, and if properly managed convince them that it is far better to let their cattle graze on the lands they possess than to kill and eat them, with no provision for the future." The Cheyennes' aversion to farming did not mean they were lazy. Their agent described them as "industrious and energetic," searching for employment as "laborers or as teamsters, or anything that will bring them a return in cash." Miles could have added that employment opportunities were extremely limited and that there were too few funds from government sources to employ even the younger educated Indians. Restrictions of money available to pay agency employees in the 1882–83 budget forced Miles to discontinue Indian labor on the agency farm. Those dismissed began renting the land for one-third of the crops.

The Arapahoes were more advanced in stock raising and farming than were the Cheyennes. Arapaho leaders had settled in the rich bottomlands of the North and South Canadian rivers within ten to fifty miles of Darlington. By 1883, Powder Face, Left Hand, and other chiefs had gathered herds of cattle of improved stock to which they gave great care and attention, and their example was followed by other younger members of the tribe. Around the Arapaho camps there were corn fields in the bottomlands, as well as vegetable gardens, the produce of which was sold to Fort Reno and in Darlington. As stock raising and farming increased, the Indians gradually settled down. They were still camp Indians, Miles explained, but increasingly they used bedsteads, tables, stoves, and other household conveniences. Some were abandoning their tipis for abodes consisting of wooden floors and house frames over which they stretched canvas.[1]

Miles continued to work toward occupation of the reservation by cattlemen despite his rebuff from the Washington office during the summer of 1882. By December of that year he was ready to call a council of Cheyenne and Arapaho chiefs and representatives of the range-cattle industry. Two to three hundred Cheyennes and Arapahoes assembled at Darlington on December 12, 1882. Miles had also invited some cattlemen to come to the agency headquarters so that they could witness the proceedings and agree to the terms of any arrangement that might occur. The Indian agent prepared carefully for the council. He, agency employees, Indian traders, intermarried whites, and mixed bloods talked to the tribal chiefs and distributed money provided by the cattlemen to persuade them to sign the document granting grazing privileges for about 2.4 million acres of the reservation. George Bent, Robert Bent, and Ben Clark importuned the Cheyennes, while John Poisal, Jack Fitzpatrick, and Mary Keith worked among the Arapahoes with funds undoubtedly provided by interested cattlemen. Later the cattlemen denied before a United States Senate committee that any money had been used to influence the Indians. George Bent has been singled out by present-day Cheyennes as the man who most profited from the leasing agreement. He was accused of collecting and keeping the rental money, of receiving a valuable gold watch, and of appropriating for his own use many cattle abandoned by the cattlemen.[2]

In council the Cheyennes and Arapahoes agreed to allow cattle to graze on all of the reservation between the two Canadian rivers and west of a line running between Cottonwood Grove and the Wichita Reservation. It was stipulated that the cattlemen should be charged two cents an acre annually for a period of not less than five nor more than ten years for tracts twenty to thirty miles square. The agreement, it was estimated, would give each member of the two tribes an annual income of ten dollars. Payment for the grazing privileges were to be made semiannually. Half was to be paid in breeding stock and half in money, the money to be spent for the benefit of the tribes, as approved by the commissioner of Indian affairs. The seventeen Cheyenne and nine Arapaho chiefs who signed the council report represented, in Miles's view, about nineteen-twentieths of the Indians, while Ed Fenlon, one of the successful cattlemen gaining grazing rights, asserted that 97 per cent of the tribal members were represented at the council.[3]

Even before the council was held, substantial cattle herds were using the rangeland on the reservation. The Standard Cattle Company informed Secretary of War Robert T. Lincoln on December 15, 1882, that its representatives had occupied some of the reservation by the consent of "friendly and well-disposed Indians." Rumors had come to its attention, however, "that our tenure there is not secure and that we are liable to be ordered out at any time and to our great inconvenience and loss." By late 1882 the Dickey Brothers, a second cattle outfit, were running 22,500 cattle on the southern portion of the Cherokee Outlet. They were paying the Cherokee Nation grass money and also gave Little Robe's and Cohoe's Cheyenne bands from $350 to $500 a month in cash and cattle to allow some of their cattle on the Cheyenne-Arapaho Reservation. A third and more troublesome occupant was B. H. Campbell, of Wichita, Kansas, who was running about 3,000 head by an agreement with a mixed blood without the consent of the tribal council. Undoubtedly there were other cattle on the reservation because Agent Miles reported in the spring of

1883 an estimated 51,200 cattle grazing on Texas Panhandle and Cherokee Outlet ranges adjacent to the Cheyenne-Arapaho lands. Cattle from those herds drifted onto the reservation without the tribes' permission.[4]

Within a month after the council Miles submitted "leases" to the commissioner of Indian affairs for the secretary of the interior's approval. The tracts varied in size from 575,000 acres for Hampton B. Denman, of Washington, D.C., to 138,000 acres for James S. Morrison, of Darlington, who had married a daughter of Big Mouth, an influential Arapaho chief. Morrison applied for his range in the name of his two mixed-blood children, whom he was educating and raising in the white culture. In all Miles forwarded seven agreements to Washington covering 3,177,880 acres, leaving 1,170,432 acres free for the occupation of the confederated tribes. There was insufficient land to satisfy all those requesting ranges within the reservation.[5]

Immediately both cattlemen who were included in the list to receive grazing privileges and those who were not began to complain. Robert D. Hunter, a successful applicant, disliked the fact that Ed Fenlon, H. D. Denman, and others were given priorities in choosing land, claiming that Miles's allocations of rangeland were unfair. Miles was alerted to trouble when representatives of cattle corporations called on him at Darlington, implying that their friends in Washington would "block the game" unless Miles worked out suitable agreements for them with the Indians. John Volz, a government beef contractor who held two to three thousand head west of Cantonment, unsuccessfully pleaded his case to Secretary of Interior Henry M. Teller and Commissioner Price. Of all the dissatisfied cattlemen B. H. Campbell was the most difficult for Miles and his superiors to handle. The Wichita operator mustered the support of several Republican politicians in his behalf, and yet he obtained none of the Cheyenne-Arapaho land because Secretary Teller refused to interfere in Miles's decisions. Campbell did, however, obtain permission to use temporarily the grass of the Oklahoma country for two thousand cattle.[6]

For three months the agreements sent to Washington by Miles were not acted upon. The Indian agent did, however, before the official decision by Secretary of the Interior Henry M. Teller, learn through "private though reliable information" that the secretary would not approve "leases" officially but that cattlemen making satisfactory arrangements with the Cheyennes and Arapahoes would not "be interfered with" and would receive "protection." On April 25, 1883, in response to a letter from Ed Fenlon, Secretary Teller established the basic policy for the agreements between cattlemen and the Cheyennes and Arapahoes. Fenlon requested that his agreement "be formally approved, if deemed necessary," that he be placed in possession of the tract designated, and that the Indian agent be empowered to remove intruders from his range. With utmost care not to give Fenlon or others any title or interest in Cheyenne-Arapaho lands, Teller stated that he would not decide what authority either the Department of the Interior or the Indians possessed to make such an agreement because "it is not the present policy of the Department to affirmatively recognize any agreement or leases."[7]

Secretary Teller required that the agreement be approved by tribal authority with all tribesmen sharing in the income. He also stipulated that the terms of the agreement be fair and reasonable and that the cattlemen utilize Indian herders working under the management of skilled employees. No disreputable persons could be employed within the reservation's limits, and no permanent improvements were to be placed upon the assigned ranges. At any time that the Indians became dissatisfied or if improper and lawless persons were employed within the reservation's boundaries, the Department of the Interior could exercise its supervisory authority "to the extent of removing all occupants from the Territory without reference to such lease or agreement on such notice as shall be right and proper under the circumstances." About all the secretary conceded to the agreement holders was that they would be protected on their ranges from intruders who held no agreements with the Indians.[8]

In his view Secretary Teller granted the cattlemen grazing permits and nothing else. He did not intend to give cattlemen any interest in the lands of the Cheyenne-Arapaho Reservation, explaining later, "The privilege to graze cattle is but a license and not a lease. It conveys no interest in the land occupied." The secretary of the interior continued: "It is true that Indians did attempt to make leases for a fixed period during which the parties would, if the power existed, have all the rights of leases but doubting the power to make as well as the policy of such leasing, I declined to approve the same as a lease, but did treat them as amounting to a license to be revoked by the Indians at will."[9]

Interested cattlemen were aware that the Fenlon letter gave them little security on the Cheyenne-Arapaho ranges. As a result an attorney for R. D. Hunter and A. G. Evans sought to obtain an "unqualified endorsement" from Teller for his clients' agreements. Teller firmly refused to alter his decision and suggested only that the agreements be deposited in the Indian Office in case of controversy over their terms with the Indians or the Interior Department. The secretary also applied the same policy when cattlemen wanted to lease Uintah and Southern Ute lands in Colorado. Teller wrote, "I said very plainly in the letter to Fenlon that the Dept. would do nothing to recognize such leases in Indian Ty." A similar policy was continued in the spring of 1885, when Grover Cleveland's administration was asked to approve leases for the Kiowa, Comanche, and Wichita Agency. Cleveland's Secretary of the Interior Lucius Q. C. Lamar adhered to Teller's policy and insisted that cattlemen possessed no rights under the "pretended agreement." Naturally cattlemen did not like Teller's decision, and they understood that they assumed risks when they placed herds on the Cheyenne-Arapaho Reservation.[10]

On May 22, 1883, Agent Miles began notifying the cattlemen that they could start stocking their ranges. Only two of the seven original agreement holders actually occupied their portion of the Cheyenne-Arapaho Reservation, and the others transferred their licenses to other cattlemen or cattle corporations. Miles also warned trespassers with herds on the reservation to remove them. He sent William F. Darlington, a trusted agency employee, with forty Indian police to arrest all persons found on the reservation without proper authorization. When the ranges were fully stocked in 1885, an estimated 220,000 animals were grazing on the Cheyenne-Arapaho Reservation.[11]

When on June 20, 1883, the licensees made their first semiannual payment of $31,178 to the Cheyennes and Arapahoes, problems arose. An earlier partial payment of $6,500 had been made on April 30, 1883,

to the chiefs' council, but the money was placed in the Emporia
(Kansas) National Bank so that a larger amount could be accumulated before the actual distribution occurred. Not all the tribesmen
were willing to accept their portion of the grass money. Three powerful Cheyenne chiefs, Little Robe, Stone Calf, and White Shield,
among others living near Cantonment, refused to share in the distri-
butions. Most of the tribesmen, however, accepted their money and
used it wisely, buying needed food and winter clothing. Although
Miles minimized the size of the dissenting bands and insisted that
they had been represented during the councils of December 1, 1882,
and January 13, 1883, the resisting Cheyennes complained to Colonel
J. H. Potter, commanding officer of Fort Supply, that they had never
signed the agreements and that they were being crowded off their

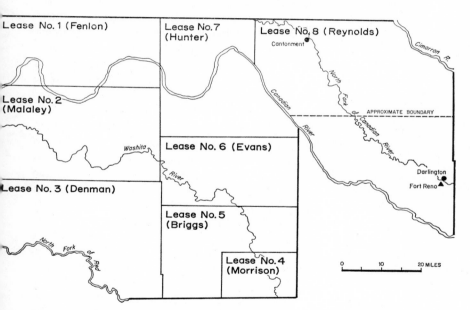

Leases on the Cheyenne and Arapaho Reservation. The southern and
southeastern boundaries of Lease No. 8 are close approximations of the
actual boundaries.

97

lands. Beginning in the summer of 1883 the bands living around Cantonment became the center of Indian resistance to Miles's licensing program. The dissenting bands, numbering about seven hundred persons, substantially exceeded Miles's estimate that they represented only 5 per cent of the tribes.[12]

Miles maintained that the problems with the dissenting bands resulted from the influence of Amos Chapman, W. W. Wells, and Wesley Warren (the last a black man)—all married to Cheyenne women. These men served as intermediaries for cattlemen such as the Dickey brothers, who wanted more range within the Cheyenne-Arapaho Reservation. Miles should have ignored the pressures to license more of the reservation, on October 15, 1883, but he set aside 714,249 acres for George E. Reynolds, which meant that the Cheyennes and Arapahoes were restricted to a mere 426,202 acres of their 4,294,412-acre reservation. More importantly, the new agreement covered the part of the reservation upon which the Cantonment bands had their camps. To make the agreement appear valid, Miles obtained the consent of ten Cheyenne and Arapaho chiefs and head men, but none of the signatories to the second ratifying council were the leaders from around Cantonment.[13]

Miles's licensing program received criticism for reasons other than those levied by the Indians. The agreements with the seven-man syndicate were "surrounded by many circumstances," according to one newspaper account. Teller's role in the licenses was viewed as arbitrary and inconsistent and should be investigated to determine the legality and motives of his action. Robert S. Gardner, an Indian inspector from the Department of the Interior, focused more directly on the Indian agent. He believed that the annual rent of two cents an acre was only a "small moiety" of what the ranges were worth. A year later on the floor of Congress a claim was made that the Cheyenne-Arapaho range was worth annually eight to twelve cents an acre, while Secretary Teller thought the cattlemen would "readily consent to double or treble" the rent paid in the original agreement. Grass money, Gardner also thought, encouraged the reservation Indians in "Idleness and Dependency" while they waited for the cash payments. The number of Indians transporting supplies from Caldwell, Kansas, Gardner reported, had sharply declined from the time when freighting had supported one hundred teamsters and their families.[14]

On March 31, 1884, as criticisms mounted and difficulties began to appear between the Indians and the cattlemen, Miles resigned as Indian agent for the Cheyenne-Arapaho Reservation. During his twelve years as Indian agent Miles had inaugurated many innovations in the administration of an Indian reservation. He had issued rations to heads of families instead of to chiefs, transported agency freight by means of Indian-owned wagons and Indian teamsters, used Indians to carry mail, persuaded Indian boarding-school pupils to invest their money in cattle, and placed pupils on farms and among white families. One of Miles's supporters, James E. Rhoads, a representative of the Society of Friends on the Board of Indian Commissioners, lauded Miles's system of granting grazing priviliges on the reservation to cattlemen. If the Indians had invested only one-half of the payments from the cattlemen in cattle, Rhoads maintained, in ten years the Cheyennes and Arapahoes would have sufficient cattle for their own support and could fully utilize their lands. "If any one can devise a better plan than this," Rhoads concluded, "they may criticize him when they could do no better." Earlier, however, Miles had implicitly promised that if the renting of the grasslands on the reservation did not work he would resign. The system was in trouble because of Indian dissent, and he resigned.[15]

Miles's successor, D. B. Dyer, witnessed the full disruption of the cattle-grazing policy. Despite previous experience as an Indian agent among the Modocs, Dyer was unable to check the rising tensions as the months passed. The new Cheyenne-Arapaho agent was a brusque and stubborn man who expected his smallest wish to be granted immediately by his charges; the Cheyennes would make no such capitulation to any man. Miles's program, in Dyer's estimation, had made little impact on the lives of the Cheyennes and Arapahoes. "I have here," Dyer wrote to Commissioner Price, "as poor and ignorant [a] class of people as it has been my lot to meet. They are not only hungry for the lack of wholesome food but they are in need of clothing." Because they were hungry, the tribesmen had begun raiding the herds of the lessees, who, in response, demanded that the new Indian agent protect their herds. As the turmoil increased, the number of pupils in the schools declined, the power of the soldier societies rose, and the warrior faction continued to make attendance of the "medicine dances" compulsory. The Dog Soldiers were particularly adamant that all Cheyennes attend the annual Sun Dance.[16]

Since Miles's program of developing Indian-owned cattle herds had not succeeded, Dyer quickly shifted his attention to agriculture. He called a council to meet at Darlington, where the more tractable members of the tribes made their customary promise to go to work in the fields if the government would assist them. From the Indian Office, Dyer sought fifty plows, work teams, and barbed wire to protect the Indians' crops from cattle. The Indian agent reminded Ed Fenlon of their agreement in Caldwell, Kansas, that Fenlon's cattle company would aid the Cheyennes and Arapahoes by breaking new land and enclosing it with fences. To another owner of cattle on the reservation Dyer mentioned that the Indians now decided to take their payments in cash rather than in cattle.[17]

Within a month after his arrival at Darlington, Dyer learned how tense the Indians were when a serious situation developed at Cantonment. A cattle trail ran close to the abandoned post, which Mennonite missionaries had converted into a subagency and school for Cheyenne and Arapaho children. Little Robe, Stone Calf, White Shield, Big Horse, and other Cheyenne chiefs and Powder Face and Black Coyote of the Arapahoes had established their camps in the vicinity. On May 4, 1884, a Texan, E. M. Horton, was trailing four hundred ponies through from Texas to Kansas. Warned that the normal crossing of the North Canadian River was impassable, Horton turned off the trail and drove his horses toward the camp of Running Buffalo, an influential member of the Cheyenne Dog Soldiers. The warrior tried to turn the herd away from his camp, where his family maintained a small garden patch, and probably tried to levy the usual tax upon the herd. Horton would have none of that. Running Buffalo fired his pistol into the herd to stampede them and apparently threatened Horton. After Horton shot Running Buffalo's horse, the bullet also hitting the Indian, either Horton or one of his herders finished off the murder by shooting Running Buffalo twice more. Realizing that he was in serious trouble, Horton proceeded to Cantonment, where he placed himself and his men under the protection of Reverend S. S. Haury, the Mennonite missionary. Haury put the Texans in the old stone-walled bakery and drove the horses into a corral. The Cheyenne and Arapaho men living near Cantonment surrounded the bakery, demanding either that the missionary surrender Horton to them or that Horton give Running Buffalo's family and friends enough horses as a gift to pay for the taking of the warrior's life.

Haury telegraphed to Darlington for help. The next day a detachment of cavalry from Fort Reno and eight Indian policemen arrived. With neither Horton nor the horses in their hands, the Cheyennes were in an ugly mood. The presence of the cavalry, the Indian police, Amos Chapman, William T. Darlington, and Haury, however, calmed the Cheyennes. Finally, Left Hand Bull, who was making the decisions for the Dog Soldier friends of Running Buffalo, accepted one-half of Horton's horses to settle the matter. Whether Horton gave up the horses freely, as the Cheyennes later claimed, or whether he gave them to the Indians as the only way he could save his life and those of his men cannot be determined. Horton and one of his employees were then escorted to Fort Reno and from there to Kansas. About a month later Agent Dyer implemented Secretary of the Interior Teller's demand that the horses which Horton had distributed among the Cheyennes be sent to Darlington. The horses were surrendered and were returned to Horton.

The incident at Cantonment upset Agent Dyer. He named Little Robe and Stone Calf as leaders of "outlaw" bands living in the vicinity of Cantonment. He described the old scout, Amos Chapman, who was married to a daughter of Stone Calf, as a dangerous man who enjoyed the complete confidence of the Cantonment bands. Wesley Warren, the agent thought, also exercised an unwholesome influence among the Indians. Chapman and Warren were the intermediaries for cattlemen from the Cherokee Outlet who, for private payments to the Cantonment bands, ran their herds on the reservation without obtaining a license from the governing body of the federated tribes. They also backed the Cheyennes' insistence that the tribe be given one-half of Horton's horse herd. Dyer maintained that the Horton affair took place because neither he nor the commanding officer at Fort Reno had the "power to round up a few worthless Indians."

With tensions at Cantonment eased a little, Agent Dyer called a council with Stone Calf, Little Robe, and their people. Claiming to be the leader of the Cantonment bands, Stone Calf acted as their spokesman. Confronting Dyer, the chief stated that his people would not respect the agent's authority and would not obey his orders. Not only would Stone Calf and his people kill cattle for food and depredate as they chose but also they would invite other bands to join them in their resistance to Dyer and the occupation of the reservation by cattlemen. Ending his speech, Stone Calf told the Indian agent that he and his warriors "did not propose to let any one open up new farms or adopt the ways of white men." Dyer came away from the Cantonment meeting determined to break the power of the dissidents, and he asked that one thousand troops be stationed on the Cheyenne-Arapaho Reservation to carry out Bureau of Indian Affairs policies.[18]

Cheyenne soldier societies maintained pressure on their people to retain control of the reservation and preserve their old way of life. In this period of reservation life the Arapahoes recognized the power of the Indian police, while the Cheyennes clung to their soldier societies to maintain tribal discipline. Students such as White Buffalo, upon returning from Carlisle to the reservation, were shamed and abused by Mad Wolf, a "Captain of the Dog Soldiers," for working in the agency sheet-metal shop. Just as important was the fact that the agency had insufficient positions in which to employ all the returning students, who quickly reverted to the traditional camp life. Dyer stated that, in reality, the only way to control the soldier societies was to disarm the tribesmen. Otherwise his Indian police were powerless, and, in any event, the police would not fight their own kinsmen and warrior friends.[19]

Early in December, 1884, a delegation of Cheyenne and Arapaho chiefs met with Secretary Teller and voiced their objections to the leasing of their reservation to cattlemen. Powder Face of the Arapahoes spoke first and told the secretary that he had come to Washington because "I am getting scared." He was concerned because the vast herds of cattle and the great numbers of people tending them were interfering with the Indians' use of their lands. Powder Face complained that "my horses and cattle are lost" among the lessees' cattle and that his people were having the same experience. The chief urged, "Agent Miles and all of them come around my agency, and from Texas they come. . . . I want them to go away and the white people and Texans to go away." Whirlwind of the Cheyennes generally supported Powder Face. So many people were using the reservation, Whirlwind maintained, that he felt that the boundaries of the reservation were meaningless. His people were being surrounded by "big herds of cattle and it was almost impossible to keep them out." Although Agent Dyer accused the soldier societies of being the main disruptive groups on the reservation, Powder Face, Whirlwind, and their fellow chiefs plainly were dissatisfied with the results of the leasing policy initiated by former Agent Miles.[20]

On December 19, 1884, Dyer testified before a Senate committee investigating conditions among the tribes in Indian Territory and amplified the opinions he had expressed previously in correspondence to the Indian Office. Basically, he stated, it was impossible for him to control the soldier societies, and Dyer singled out the Dog Soldiers as the most troublesome of the warrior groups. Almost every adult male Indian on the reservation was armed with the newest-model rifles and pistols, which were easily obtained from the merchants of Caldwell, Kansas. The Indian police were powerless to arrest or disarm the turbulent warriors because the latter would surely be supported by their fellow soldier-society comrades. Money from the cattle licenses averaged about $6.25 per capita, which was insufficient to prevent hunger among the tribes. Nevertheless, the vast majority of the Cheyennes and Arapahoes refused to farm, and those who attempted to fence their land or garden patches were forced by the Dog Soldiers to abandon their crops and attend tribal ceremonies held during the critical late spring months of the agricultural season.[21]

In principle Dyer supported Miles's licensing policy. He contended that if the Cheyenne warrior societies were controlled, the amount of money derived from the grazing permits could be increased. He did not believe that any of the Indians were "unduly influenced" when they signed the agreements. Secretary Teller essentially agreed with Dyer's recommendations by suggesting that those tribesmen who wanted to break away from the old tribal customs should be protected by United States troops from the "threats and lawless acts and depredations of the 'dog soldiers,' a reckless, vicious class, who refuse to work or allow others to do so."[22]

After Dyer returned to Darlington, the Indians became more amenable to his policies. Rumors passed around the reservation that more troops were on their way to Fort Reno, and this information had a quieting effect on the warrior societies. If the troops did not arrive, however, the Indian agent asserted, "we will go back to something most likely worse than former times." To John D. C. Atkins, the new Indian commissioner, Dyer renewed his campaign for additional military support and co-operation. "As long as the bad element of the tribes feels that it can do its pleasure and go unpunished," wrote Dyer, "we certainly cannot hope for much steady progress." The "bad elements" were, of course, the soldier societies led by the Dog Soldiers. They destroyed fences, kept their children out of school, burned the ranges, plundered the cattle herds (including those of the government), and threatened death to those who refused to terminate their farming.[23]

Agent Dyer was never able to fully convince either the Indians or the Indian Office of the soundness of his ideas. He knew that the program to turn the Indians into stock raisers was not working because the cattle issued to them from money derived from the grazing permits were eaten by the Indians. To give him better control over the tribes, he also thought that it would be better to concentrate their camps within a fifteen-mile radius of Darlington, but he never had the force with which to compel them to do so. He also tried unsuccessfully to persuade the government to give greater assistance to Indian youths when they had completed their term in the schools. He argued to the commissioner of Indian affairs that it did not make sense to spend one thousand dollars on Indian pupils for their education and then abandon them by refusing additional support to help them establish their homes and farms. To instruct the camp Indians in working in the fields, Dyer wanted the funds for the agency staff increased by 50 per cent. "Ignorant, blanket Indians," in Dyer's view, could not be expected to saw logs; build houses; repair wagons, plows, and agricultural equipment; or break and fence their own land.

Throughout his tenure as agent Dyer was never able to control the Cheyenne soldier societies. According to Dyer, they ruled "with an iron hand, and their will, right or wrong is absolute." Even Indian policemen, such as Pawnee Man, were not immune from their control. Pawnee Man was an honest, energetic, brave young warrior who for several years had cultivated ten to fifteen acres of corn near Darlington. Dyer encouraged him to cut enough posts to enclose forty acres at Caddo Springs, where the Cheyenne Boarding School was located. Pawnee Man cut the fence posts on the promise by Dyer that he would have the land plowed, furnish the seed corn and fence wire, and assist him in every way to grow his first year's crop. The Dog Soldiers visited Pawnee Man and told him not to have the land plowed or to accept the fence wire because if he began his farm, all his horses would be killed. "But the question is," Dyer asked of the commissioner, "do you propose to let the Dog Soldier element rule the business of this Agency—or will you whip them into obedience to your wishes."[24]

When the troops requested by Dyer failed to appear by the spring of 1885, the Cheyenne warriors resumed their disruptive tactics in full force. They again killed cattle as they had during the winter of 1884–85, when the agency beef contractor estimated that he alone had lost about five hundred head. Seth Mabry, another of the cattlemen, judged that "renegade Indians" killed cattle valued at one hundred thousand dollars during the year before the herds were removed. When confronted by Dyer, some of the reservation leaders promised to control their young men, but others stated that they would kill cattle "when and where they pleased." Animosity also persisted between the Cheyennes and Arapahoes—an unpleasantness that had begun a decade earlier, when the Arapahoes generally refused to follow the Cheyennes during the Red River War of 1874–75. Even Little Raven, a respected Arapaho chief, was not immune to Cheyenne reprisals, as he learned when Left Hand Bull killed six of the chief's ponies. Horse Back, an Arapaho living twenty miles east of Cantonment, had fenced in a bit of land, and Left Hand Bull cut the fence wire and pulled up the fence posts. As discipline continued to disintegrate on the reservation, the Arapahoes joined "heartily in the plundering of whitemen's herds of cattle." To cover their rustling, the Indians destroyed the bones and hides, and, for every Indian who was apprehended killing a cow, thousands were never caught. While visiting the agency office in early May, 1885, Stone Calf and Little Robe made it clear that they were spoiling for trouble. They and their warriors talked of forcing all Cheyennes to attend the "medicine-making" ceremonies scheduled for late May. The chiefs contemptuously stated that the few troops garrisoning Fort Reno and Fort Supply could never control them.[25]

In early June, 1885, the Cantonment bands made good their threat to cause trouble. First, Flying Hawk, a Cheyenne, had an argument with Haury because he wanted to withdraw his children from the Mennonite school. When Haury objected, Flying Hawk, urged on by Bear Robe, walked up and down with gun in hand in front of the missionary's residence, threatening to shoot the minister before sundown. On the following day Bear Robe—also known as Thomas Carlisle because he was a former student at Carlisle Institute—joined a party of Cheyennes led by Stone Calf and Little Man in rounding up a trail herd on the Caldwell Road. Before the Cheyennes were through, they had also destroyed fences erected by the licensees to separate the various ranges on the reservation. Dyer wrote to the commanding officer at Fort Reno, "The situation in that section [near Cantonment] grows more serious from day to day and it will result in the loss of lives of good innocent whites if allowed to go unchecked."[26]

On June 15, 1885, three companies of the Fifth Cavalry rode into Fort Reno as an advance party to reinforce the post's garrison. The Cheyenne Dog Soldiers remained unimpressed and continued to round up the tribesmen for the medicine ceremonies, concentrating particularly on those tribal members who had begun to farm. They were further emboldened by medicine men who were proclaiming the power to "spoil the Whiteman's Guns." By mid-June six more companies of the Fifth Cavalry were enroute to Fort Reno to join the garrison and the regiment's advance party. As the additional troops appeared, Colonel Edwin V. Sumner took charge of Fort Reno, and the reservation quieted down. In mid-June the Indians were gathered about eight miles from Darlington at the "medicine camp." Nervous, Agent Dyer requested that Colonel Sumner detail ten troopers to patrol and protect the agency and its employees, since the Indians "were preparing their weapons for service."[27]

Little Raven and other Arapaho leaders, however, thought there was little danger. Stone Calf's Cheyennes, who were displeased by Haury's fencing of six thousand acres for his mission herd, did no more than object that there were already too many fences in their country. Colonel J. H. Potter, the commandant at Fort Supply, also found that the telegraph line between Cantonment and Fort Reno had not been cut by Bear Robe as suspected. Rather, a party of whites needing wood to cook their food had dismantled the line (later Colonel Potter used unburned parts of the telegraph poles to cook his coffee while en route to Cantonment). According to Potter, the basic dissatisfaction around the Mennonite mission at Cantonment resulted when George E. Reynolds was granted his grazing rights. Agents Miles and Dyer naturally had tried to protect Reynolds' investment by requesting that the tribesmen move to Darlington, where they had already concentrated a greater portion of the two tribes. The Cantonment bands maintained that they wanted to remain where they were, begin farming, and not move to Darlington, where they would only loaf around the agency's headquarters.[28]

Private feuds also disturbed the reservation. Colonel Sumner arrested Roman Nose, called by Agent Dyer "a half Cheyenne and Sioux" who "is known to be one of the worst sneaking thieves and villains in the Cheyenne tribe." Until his arrest, Roman Nose enjoyed a reputation among the Cheyennes as a powerful medicine man, but his debauches, threats to others while drunk, and thievery brought him into ill repute. As a result his fellow tribesmen were not unhappy when he was sent to prison. Not all the circumstances of Roman Nose's arrest are known, but Stone Calf vindicated the medicine man by accusing Ben Clark and his friends of shooting into Roman Nose's lodge, killing a little girl instead of Roman Nose. After his arrest Roman Nose was transferred to and held for a year in confinement at Fort Leavenworth, Kansas, before it was decided to prosecute him in the federal courts for his attack on Ben Clark and for other alleged crimes.[29]

The turmoil on the reservation eventually brought investigators to Darlington. Frank C. Armstrong, an Indian inspector, was the first to reach the agency, arriving on July 5, 1885. He immediately began a series of interviews with the Cheyennes and Arapahoes and submitted recommendations to Secretary of the Interior Lamar. The inspector recommended that the soldier bands supply the Indian police and scouts for Fort Reno and that army personnel train them in their duties. Despite the amenability of the Arapahoes to the cattle-grazing permits, virtually all the Cheyenne leaders—even those who had signed the original agreements, such as Whirlwind, Little Big Jake, Howling Wolf, and Big Horse—now demanded that the cattlemen remove their herds from the reservation. Since Miles had persuaded the Indians to accept the licenses, assuring them that the agreements could be revoked at any time, Armstrong suggested that the arrangements be terminated quickly so that the cattlemen could shift their stock to other ranges. The low rental fees for the Cheyenne-Arapaho lands for two and one-half years, Armstrong claimed, would partly compensate the cattlemen for losses they might sustain from the termination of the licenses. Finally, the Indian inspector described Darlington as a "white town on an Indian reservation," where far too many unauthorized whites interfered in the lives of the Indians, and he recommended that the whites be ejected from the reservation.

Armstrong's views were closely followed by President Cleveland and his cabinet officers when they tried to restore order on the Cheyenne-Arapaho Reservation. Although the Indian inspector praised the efforts of Agent Dyer, he stated that the agent could no longer effectively carry out his duties because of his conflict with the Cheyennes. Without an adequate military force to control the Indians, Dyer, in Armstrong's opinion, was all but helpless to prevent the troubles that arose on the reservation.[30]

News that the Cheyennes were unhappy spread into southwestern Kansas, and, when three or four persons were reported to have been killed at Fargo Wells, Kansas, thousands of settlers abandoned their homes, crops, and livestock, fleeing to nearby towns for protection from anticipated raids. Kansas frontiersmen had felt the sting of Cheyenne wrath in 1868, and vivid memories still remained of Dull Knife's dash to freedom in 1878 and of the fierce warriors who had once ruled the Central Plains. Kansas politicians demanded that their people be protected and remained wary of the situation. Although Kansans remained nervous until mid-July, 1885, Governor John A. Martin determined that cowboys, working for cattlemen who found farmers interfering with ranching activities, had spread the rumors that the Cheyennes were off their reservation. "If anybody was killed at Fargo Wells,"[31] wrote Governor Martin's informant, "it was in a drunken row among the cowboys."

Generals Philip H. Sheridan and Nelson A. Miles were ordered to Darlington to look into the causes of the Cheyennes' complaints. On July 17, 1885, two days after his arrival at the agency headquarters, Sheridan gathered the leaders of the dissident Cheyennes at Darlington to hear them out. Stone Calf, the leading Cheyenne chief at Cantonment, presented the case for his people. The Indians maintained that Running Buffalo, shot by Horton at Cantonment, had committed no wrong and Indians disclaimed any knowledge of the murder of a white man at Robert Bent's ranch. The chief indignantly denied that the Cheyennes wanted trouble with the whites or that his young warriors were preparing to attack the frontier settlements. He demanded that George and Robert Bent, Ben Clark, Ed Geary (Edmund Guerrier), and all others co-operating with the cattlemen be removed from the reservation, along with Agent Dyer. In particular Stone Calf condemned George Bent, who, the chief alleged, had told the Cheyennes and Arapahoes in the winter of 1882–83 that they could not be given their usual rations if they did not sign the agreements and accept the money derived from the grazing permits. George Bent had enraged Stone Calf by threatening to lead the troops when they arrived to punish the Cheyennes. Even after the agreements were completed, Stone Calf said, the pressure had continued, and many of the Indians accepted the grass money because they "were scared," even though they had never signed the documents.

The Cheyennes, though a frustrated people, still had their pride. They were beset with many worries but were not too cowed to present them forcefully to General Sheridan. His band, Stone Calf told General Sheridan, had lost 210 ponies to white horse thieves during the seven years they had lived at Cantonment. They were concerned about rumors that a railroad would be built through their reservation and about their lack of full understanding of the boundaries of their land. They also did not know what was their just due in terms of rations and annuities, and they grumbled that even the cattle issued to them were yearlings and two-year-olds, which appeared "sickly and poor as though they were not fit to eat." Stone Calf ended by demanding that the cattlemen be removed from his reservation.[32]

Other Cheyenne chiefs supported Stone Calf's allegations. Little Robe, White Horse, White Shield, Spotted Horse, Hawk, and Little Magpie wanted the cattle to leave because of the problems that had arisen since the winter of 1884–85. They claimed that they had lost horses and cattle to whites, through either thievery or absorption into the licensees' herds. On July 19, Sheridan called together the representatives of those Cheyennes who had signed the original licensing agreements. Whirlwind spoke first, claiming that, although his people had initially refused to sign the papers, they finally agreed to the terms proposed by the cattlemen and Agent Miles because the latter and George Bent "told us to do so." Although he was a leader among the more amenable bands of Cheyennes, Whirlwind now wanted the cattlemen ejected because all the Cheyennes deeply resented constantly being accused of crimes that they had not committed.

The spokesmen for the Cheyennes continuously alluded to their understanding that, if they were imposed upon by the cattlemen in any way, the licenses would be revoked. Little Medicine maintained that the cattlemen had enclosed far more land than the Cheyennes and Arapahoes had consented to in January, 1883. This charge had validity, especially after George E. Reynolds occupied his tract and insisted that the Cantonment bands be shifted from the lands he rented. Even Powder Face, a chief of the Arapahoes since 1869, agreed with Stone Calf and Little Robe that it was unjust for them to be moved from the camps they had selected and occupied since 1875. The Arapahoes, however, did not support all the Cheyennes' demands and complaints, desiring only to farm and live peacefully according to the wishes of the government.[33]

Sensing that their investments and cheap land were in jeopardy, the cattlemen began presenting their case to Washington officials. R. D. Hunter, writing to Secretary of the Interior Lamar, stressed the fact that during the three or four years that cattlemen had utilized the ranges in Indian Territory the Indians' income had increased by about $330,000. The "leases," according to Hunter, had been "negotiated and consumated openly, fairly and with the full concurrence of the Indians," who were treated justly, protected from the intrusion of whisky peddlers, taught how to work cattle, and "educated" not to steal the property of others. The cattlemen, Hunter stated, had invested $24,000,000 in stock for the "leased" ranges in Indian Territory. Hunter denied that the troubles on the Cheyenne-Arapaho Reservation had grown out of the "leasing of their lands, nor are the cattlemen in any way responsible for them." Abram S. Hewitt, who had no personal observations to offer about conditions on the reservation, emphasized that if his corporation was evicted additional losses would be sustained by the investors. He claimed that the Cheyenne and Arapaho Cattle Company's $500,000 investment had already shrunk by one-third because of severe winters and the consequent lack of natural increase of the herds.[34]

At Darlington, Ed Fenlon argued for the cattlemen's point of view before Sheridan and his fellow investigators. He insisted that the cattlemen were blameless in the troubles plaguing the reservation and that he, like the other cattlemen, had given his employees strict orders to avoid any conflict with the Indians. "The four or five Chiefs who decline to accept their lease money," Fenlon testified, "are the worst Indians in the tribe" and added that they were the same leaders who constantly caused problems for their agent and for the government. In Fenlon's view the accusation that the cattlemen had robbed the Indians was groundless because "the Indians have no property worth mentioning, no improvements on their land, no cattle." All of the conflict, he claimed, resulted from the fact that, before the "leases" were obtained, "squawmen," acting through a few chiefs, held cattle for outside parties who paid those chiefs more money than they could have obtained under the leasing arrangements that benefited the whole of the tribes. Concluding his testimony, Fenlon complained that he and his associates were being condemned on evidence provided by the "vilest class of white men and Indians." He also stated that the two tribes were being controlled by an "aggressive minority composed of a few chiefs and their dog soldiers" and that he could prove that some bands of the Cheyennes had lived "for months on our leases without any means of subsistence other than that derived from killing our cattle."[35]

During the investigations hints arose that herds owned by army officers had contributed to the unrest on the reservation. It was charged by the Wichita *Eagle* that Colonel Potter, Captain J. M. Lee, and Colonel Michael Sheridan had invested in herds that grazed on the ranges around Cantonment before the agreements of January and October, 1883. It was insinuated that the army officers utilized the same means as Dickey Brothers and Lee & Reynolds to run their cattle on the reservation by using Amos Chapman and others to make payments to Little Robe, Stone Calf, and the leaders who later dissented to the licensing arrangements completed by Agent Miles.[36]

Information from Agent Dyer, Indian Inspector Armstrong, and testimony before the Senate committee provided enough information to enable President Cleveland to act. Before he could remove the cattlemen, Cleveland had to deal with their contention that the agreements were in essence leases that gave them vested rights in the ranges of the Cheyenne-Arapaho Reservation. Attorney General Augustus H. Garland found nothing in the decisions of the Supreme Court or the United States statutes to justify the cattlemen's contention that they were privileged to remain on the reservation regardless of the Indians' desires. In the opinion of Garland, Sections 2116 and 2117 of the *United States Revised Statutes* could be a basis for an order to remove the cattlemen from the reservation. Even if the secretary of the interior or the president had signed the agreements, the alleged leases would not have any standing in a court of law. Although Section 2117 exempted licensed users of Indian land from penalties imposed by other statutory provisions, the attorney general concluded that the section in question did not validate the leases, and it did not vest the supposed lessee with any legal right to remain in the Cheyenne-Arapaho Country.[37]

On July 23, 1885, President Cleveland took action and ordered the Cheyenne-Arapaho Reservation cleared of the licensees' cattle within forty days. Announcement of the presidential order "fell like a thunderbolt upon the grass lease men of this reservation." Appreciative of the political influence of the cattlemen and their supporters, the President on July 25 sought Sheridan's opinion whether the Cheyennes and Arapahoes would consent to a later removal date. The order was not altered because Inspector Armstrong maintained that forty days was sufficient time for the cattlemen to shift their herds; otherwise the cattlemen would remain on the reservation until the following spring.[38]

As Cleveland undoubtedly expected, his order brought a series of vigorous protests from the cattlemen. By letters, through the newspapers of Kansas and Missouri, and in a memorial to President Cleveland, the ranchers insisted that there were insufficient empty ranges at that time of the year to which they could shift their cattle. They would have no alternative but to dump their herds on the market for whatever price they could obtain and suffer substantial losses. Moving their 250,000 cattle from the Cheyenne-Arapaho Reservation would require a work force of more than one thousand cowboys and five thousand horses, and they could not be assembled in a period of only forty days. Sheridan also was held accountable for the eviction order. Seth Mabry, one of the ranchers on the reservation, maintained that the general had ignored the Arapahoes and 90 per cent of the Cheyennes who wanted the cattlemen to remain. One cattleman commented that Sheridan was "a pretty good soldier," but he was "never accused of being a statesman."[39]

Before and after the removal order Cleveland was urged to evict the cattlemen. T. A. Bland, editor of the *Council Fire*, a reform journal interested in Indian affairs, and Edward M. McCook, a controversial former Colorado territorial governor, were especially antagonistic to the cattlemen. McCook wrote:

These men [the cattlemen] are apparently representatives of great and official influence, and seem to have behind them an autocratic element, mysterious as it is powerful, which banishes from the fair land they now hold, every American citizen who is not with or of them. As trespassers, their representatives to your Department, are not the prayers of the weak appealing, for your protection, but the demand of the strong, who, from ripe experience, evidently believe that the future and the past will be the same.

After President Cleveland ordered the cattlemen off the Cheyenne-Arapaho Reservation, he received the plaudits of farmers, village merchants, and small ranchers who had experienced the competitive impact of large cattle corporations benefiting from the cheap rented land on Indian reservations.[40]

After working with the Cheyennes for more than a week, General Sheridan believed that there would be no more trouble on the reservation. He assured Governor John A. Martin of Kansas that there would be no hostilities in the southwestern portion of his state. The problems had arisen from oppression of the Indians and bad control over them. "When I leave here," Sheridan assured Martin, "the people of Kansas may gather their crops and sleep peacefully at night."[41]

To President Cleveland, Sheridan wrote a fuller report, in which he explained that the Cheyennes and Arapahoes were split into three factions: those who sustained the licensing policy of Agent Miles, those who had signed the agreements to gain the favor of Miles, and those who had opposed and obstructed the licensing policy. Pressure from Miles, from whites legally and illegally on the reservation, and from many mixed bloods who co-operated with Miles had convinced the more pliable Indians to sign the agreements. Sheridan admitted that he could neither prove nor disprove Miles's contention that 95 per cent of the tribesmen approved the licenses. Far too many whites, however, had access to the reservation. Sheridan estimated that 200 men, described by the general as "loose white population who follow the cattlemen," roamed over the reservation at will. In addition, 160 cowboys employed by the cattle companies, 70 agency employees, 55 Fort Reno employees, and 21 "squawmen" lived on the Indian lands. Although Running Buffalo's death was unrelated to the licensing problems, resistance to the cattlemen became more intense thereafter, especially among the Cheyenne warriors who resented Agent Dyer's efforts to concentrate the tribes within easy reach of the agency headquarters.

It was clear to General Sheridan that Dyer had to be replaced because he lacked the patience and tact needed to deal with the Indians. His coercive tactics had caused the Cheyennes in particular to become absolutely hostile to him and his policies, even though most of the agent's efforts were not implementations of the license agreements. As a result, on July 22, 1885, Secretary of the Interior Lamar informed Dyer that by order of President Cleveland he was suspended as Indian agent and that the reservation was temporarily placed under military control. While Sheridan was at Fort Reno, the Cheyennes began to settle down, allowing a new reservation census to be taken. The new enrollment established that there were about 1,300 Arapahoes and 2,169 Cheyennes, compared to the 1874 count which placed 2,366 Arapahoes and 3,905 Cheyennes under the care of the Darlington Agency. The presidential order removing the cattle-men and the news that Captain Jesse M. Lee of the Ninth Infantry would replace Dyer as Indian agent ended the threat of violence. The Indians were satisfied that President Cleveland would treat them "justly and firmly."[42]

Captain Lee's first duty as Indian agent was to enforce President Cleveland's removal order. Where Dyer had often been denied adequate support by military officers, Lee was assured sufficient troops to accomplish his task. Early in August, 1885, President Cleveland "flatly but courteously refused" to alter his decision when a delegation of cattlemen headed by Seth Mabry visited him in Washington. Although the cattlemen complained that they would lose about one dollar on each of the 210,000 cattle evicted from the reservation, they began telegraphing their representatives to begin preparations to shift the herds. After it became generally understood that the President would not extend the September 4, 1885 deadline, cowboys began spreading rumors that they were going to burn the ranch houses, corrals, and other improvements placed on the tracts by their employers. Captain Lee immediately requested the commanding officers of Forts Reno, Supply, and Elliott to send details of troops to visit the various ranch headquarters. The presence of the soldiers, it was hoped, would deter lawlessness by the cowboys and conflict with the Indians.[43]

Most of the cattlemen endeavored to comply with President Cleveland's proclamation. The first cattle outfits to remove their herds completely were Dickey Brothers and Hunter and Evans, but even they encountered difficulties. The warriors led by Stone Calf, Little Robe, and Spotted Horse stampeded the Hunter and Evans herds, and the officer in charge of the military detachment at the Mennonite mission arrested thirteen Indians. After Dyer had left the agency, he singled out those chiefs "as outlaws of the worst stamp, each is guilty of more than enough crimes to hang him." The example made of the guilty warriors caused others to desist from similar attempts. Although some of the cattlemen found empty ranges in other portions of the Great Plains from Texas to Montana, others simply dumped their herds in the vacant and unassigned lands of central Indian Territory. On September 4, 1885, the deadline for the herds' removal, about fifty thousand head still remained on the reservation, and Agent Lee used troops to maintain pressure on the delinquent cattle outfits. Finally, on November 6, 1885, Lee reported that all of the licensees' herds were off the reservation.[44]

The episode of the cattlemen was ended. Despite its brevity, the two and one-half years that the range-cattle industry had occupied the reservation revealed that the power of the traditional social and political organizations of the Cheyennes and Arapahoes was not yet completely eroded away. When the crisis reached its peak, the warrior societies and the chiefs whom they supported were able to enforce their will against the Indian agent, the mixed bloods, and those of their fellow tribesmen who had succumbed to white institutions. They could demand that the tribes attend their traditional ceremonies and defy the Indian agent who was supported by the Indian police and military forces of the United States. General Sheridan found their grievances plausible, and he in essence agreed with the dissident Cheyennes. Yet the eviction of the cattlemen probably weakened the hold of the Cheyennes and Arapahoes on their land. If the cattlemen had been left undisturbed on the reservation, the application of the Dawes Act of 1887 to the reservation might have been delayed longer.

CHAPTER V

Preparations for Allotments

THE CATTLEMEN and cowboys were gone. But soon another and more serious threat to the lands of the Cheyennes and Arapahoes appeared. For decades reformers and Bureau of Indian Affairs personnel had insisted that the communal reservation lands of the western Indians should be divided and allotted to individual Indians so that all the Indians could be assigned agricultural or grazing tracts. As early as 1854 a Sioux agent's comment summed up the attitude of reformers when he wrote, "The common field is the seat of barbarism; the separate farm the door to civilization."[1]

Allotting land to Indians by treaties began in 1854. For twenty-five years allotments to Indians were presented as the solution to the "Indian problem." Toward the end of the 1870's the Board of Indian Commissioners restated the Sioux agent's judgment by insisting that the Indians "should be taught . . . the advantage of individual owner-ship of property, and should be given land in severalty, . . . and . . . the title should be inalienable from the family of the holder for at least two or three generations." Five years later bills containing the ideas of the commissioners of Indian affairs in the mid-1880's were being urged forward in the committees and on the floor of Congress. Allotments, or land in fee simple, and citizenship for Indians were usually combined in the suggested legislation. The early congressional bills treated Indian rights too generously, and they met defeat in Congress.

Finally in 1886–87 the right factors were present for the passage of an Indian allotment act. Senator Henry L. Dawes of Massachusetts, working closely with Alfred Riggs of the American Board of Commissioners for Foreign Missions, E. Whittlesey of the Board of Indian Commissioners, and Charles C. Painter of the Indian Rights Association, prepared the final bill. The measure, sponsored in Congress by Senator Dawes, appealed not only to eastern philanthropists and reformers but also to western senators and congressmen representing land-hungry farmers and ranchers. It was easy to see that if the Indians were allotted land and were made citizens of the United States then the surplus lands of the western reservations could be opened for white settlement. Few heeded Colorado Republican Senator Henry M. Teller's warning that Indians would not benefit from allotments until they had made "considerable progress in civilization."[2]

The Dawes Act, or the General Allotment Act, of 1887 gave discretionary power to the president of the United States to make reservation Indians landowners and citizens. The amount of land to be allotted Indians varied from 160 acres for heads of families to 40 acres for infants. In those areas where reservations contained only grazing or dry lands, the size of the allotments could be doubled. Land allotted to individual Indians was inalienable for twenty-five years, and all allottees were subject to the laws of the state or territory of their residence. Each reservation's surplus land, after allotments had been assigned, was to be available for sale to whites in one-quarter sections, the proceeds of the sales to be held in the United States Treasury for the benefit and use of the tribesmen. Those tribal members who had already separated themselves from their reservation and people and who had "adopted the habits of civilized life" were immediately declared citizens.[3]

As the allotment system was being discussed in Congress from 1884 onward, it became the duty of the Cheyenne and Arapaho Indian agents to prepare their charges for assumption of land ownership and citizenship. There never was any question that the allotment system would be applied to the Cheyenne and Arapaho lands, and from 1879 pressures mounted to open Indian Territory to white settlement. David L. Payne and other leaders of the Boomer movement periodically led their followers into the Unassigned Land of central Indian Territory, only to be evicted by troops and courts. The Boomers soon won considerable support from powerful congressmen, and if there was a legal way by which white settlers could be placed upon Indian land, it would be done. Consequently, time, land hunger, and the Dawes Act would eventually cause the opening of the Cheyenne-Arapaho Reservation.[4]

For about four months Captain Lee as Indian agent could do little for the Cheyennes and Arapahoes because he was very busy supervising the removal of the cattlemen. The Indians were not now fretting about the cattle and fences on their reservation, but their earlier concerns had caused them to neglect their crops and gardens and withdraw their children from the reservation schools. The Indians no longer received the grass money, which had amounted to about one-third of what their ranges were really worth; they suffered from a reduction in rations by 25 per cent, and they received far less than predicted from the grain crop. Former Agent Dyer had estimated that ten thousand bushels of corn and wheat would be harvested on the reservation from Indian fields during the later summer and early fall of 1885, but only about one thousand bushels of grain matured. Even if the wheat had survived, there was no threshing machine on the reservation to prepare it for market.[5]

Agent Lee tried to obtain a threshing machine at a cost of eight hundred dollars for the Indian farmers. He recommended that a steam-driven rig, complete with a stacker and all fixtures, be acquired. It would be moved from place to place on the reservation as needed. The commissioner of Indian affairs denied Lee's request and pointed to an earlier letter to Indian agents. The department, the commissioner ruled, would not approve the purchase of labor-saving machines for Indians, in this case a threshing machine, but "estimates for flails" would receive favorable attention. Caustically, Lee commented, "I am not aware that the present head of the Bureau entertains favorably a plan to render industry among these Indians most difficult."[6]

Once Lee had carefully considered the condition of the Indians, he began to change the policies of his predecessors. To prevent the Cheyennes and Arapahoes from interfering with the operations of the cattle outfits, about seven-eighths of the tribes had been assembled near Darlington, and only the Cantonment bands remained any distance from the agency headquarters. After inspecting the reservation, Agent Lee recommended shifting one to two hundred Indian families to the Washita River. The tract, known as the Washita Lease, contained more than three hundred thousand acres of land, enclosed by a good, solid four-wire fence and was "the most beautiful country for agriculture and grazing" that Lee had seen in the West. When the Indian colonists were selected, Miles suggested that John H. Seger be appointed to supervise the relocation of the Indians.[7]

Additional clusters of Indians were to be sent out from Darlington to settle on the reservation's more fertile and better-watered lands. Lee anticipated that one E. Cratzer could take charge of 100 families on the South Canadian River, eighteen miles from Darlington; Haury could supervise 200 families centered at Cantonment and scattered up and down the North Canadian for twenty-five miles; and L. Sleeper, the agency farmer, could care for 75 families on Salt Creek, forty-five miles northwest of the agency headquarters. Near Darlington, Lee hoped to appoint an additional farmer who could assist the remaining 125 families and the intermarried whites, some of whom had begun to farm east of the agency during Miles's administration. After the Indian Office had approved Lee's plan, the relocations began.[8]

By the spring of 1886 the dispersal was underway. On the Washita, Seger, with about one hundred families, led by Bob Tail and Little Medicine, began breaking land and planting crops. Seger's settlement of Cheyennes and Arapahoes would be known as Colony. It was not easy to lead Indians who resisted farm labor, but Seger had the confidence of the Indians, who had known him for more than a decade. Modern Cheyennes still remember Seger appreciatively because "he ate with them and he smoked with them and he went in sweat hut with them. He was just like one of the Indians—Cheyenne." Their work, which Seger directed from a log cabin for eight years before a house was constructed for him, was often interrupted by visits from the Kiowas. The Kiowas, Cheyennes, and Arapahoes often gambled and loafed together. Bob Tail and Little Medicine kept their promises to Agent Lee and led their people in starting farms at Seger's

Colony. They were advised by Lee to "cut off all things that keep you and your people from getting ahead. Hold fast to the good road. Stick to that colony, learn all you can about work. That way you will help your children and your people and Washington will help you. Listen to all Mr. Seger tells you."[9]

Other settlements established by Lee were less successful than Seger's. Some of the farmers, such as Seth Clover, who headed the group on the North Canadian around Robert Bent's ranch, were political patronage appointees whom the Indian office insisted be continued on the agency's payroll despite their ineffectiveness. In the opinion of the agency physician, Clover, nearly seventy years old and afflicted with epilepsy, would never be fit for duty. Robert Bent assisted Clover as much as he could, but the agricultural work languished because of the lack of implements, seeds, and money to break a sizable tract of land for corn and wheat. Big Head, a Cheyenne who was establishing a farm near Bent's Ranch, was entrusted with all the equipment and seeds Lee could spare. The people were to share one harrow, a cultivator, one and one-half bushels of seed corn, and sixteen packages of garden seeds. The Indians were urged to break their own land and were assured that, although they would not be paid for their labor, they would be given special consideration and assistance later when funds became available.[10]

By the time Lee had assumed his duties as Indian agent, some mixed bloods, such as John Poisal, and intermarried whites had well-established farms east of the agency in the Unassigned Lands (also known as the Oklahoma Country). In 1876, Benjamin F. Keith, Peter Shields, and Herman Hauser had been permitted by Miles to make their homes east of the reservation boundary line under the assumption that their farms would be included within the reservation when the eastern boundary line was properly surveyed. The three whites were married to Arapaho women, and they were joined by George H. Johnson, who had a Cheyenne wife, and nine full-blood Arapahoes and Lame Bull, a Cheyenne. The intermarried whites in particular had built up large farms and ran herds numbering hundreds of cattle. They had invested hard work to sustain themselves and their Indian families, employing white men to help manage their crops and animals. Lee wanted to move all of the group back to the reservation, but they refused, and the commissioner's office was uncertain about the status of their claims to the unassigned lands.[11]

A larger problem, however, faced Agent Lee. It was caused by the July 23, 1885 presidential proclamation which not only evicted the cattlemen but ordered the removal of "all unauthorized persons" from the Cheyenne-Arapaho Reservation. Men such as Keith, Shields, Hauser, and Morrison were of little concern to Lee because they worked their farms and supported their families. To expand their operations, Keith and the others employed whites and blacks on short- and long-term bases for a share of the crops grown. The laborers in turn lived with Indian women, but they did not have the stability of the older intermarried whites and sometimes left behind mixed-blood children for others to care for. Lee believed that the whites and intermarried men made some contribution to the reservation by bringing land into cultivation, freighting goods from Kansas when the Indians' enthusiasm for work declined, and furnishing many of the teams used by Indian freighters. Lee felt that he had two alternatives to follow: either clear the reservation of all whites or allow those to remain who did not impair the progress of the Indians. Lee sought clarification of the proclamation from the Indian Office.[12]

Agent Lee was not the first agent to face this problem on the Cheyenne-Arapaho Reservation. Miles had written long and bitter denunciations against white men who bought Indian women from their parents or who used them as prostitutes. Soldiers and employees at the military posts gave Miles the most cause for complaint when he tried unsuccessfully to restrict the frequency of intermarriage. "New cases," Miles wrote, as the Indian Office delayed replying to his query, "are daily occurring of illegal marriages, being nothing more or less than barefaced prostitution and the only result is to foist a number of half-breed bastards on the Government for support." Even if the intermarriage was performed according to law, the man usually looked upon the union as binding only as long as he remained in Indian country.[13]

Miles's most vehement letters followed when he learned of the death of Ute Woman. Miles conceded that prostitution by Indian women was so common that it did not need much discussion, but he did want authority to protect Indian women if possible. Ute Woman had been captured by the Arapahoes during their wars against the Utes in Colorado. She was kept by the Arapahoes in their camps for years and then sold to Scabby, a Cheyenne. After Scabby died, his wife, Yellow Woman, took Ute Woman to Cantonment, where she was offered to soldiers. On one particular night, Elk Horns, a Cheyenne, induced a large number of soldiers to have sexual intercourse with Ute Woman for as little as fifty cents a man. Elk Horn kept Ute Woman available for the soldiers from sundown to sunrise and collected a large sum of money for his pimping. After her return to an Indian camp near Cantonment, Ute Woman hemorrhaged and died several days later. The Indians believed that her death was the result of "excessive sexual intercourse."[14]

Perhaps Ute Woman's death triggered Miles's attempt to rid the reservation of undesirable white men. On February 9, 1880, Miles ordered his Indian police to round up all white men found on the reservation without a pass. Sixty-four were found, thirty-five were ordered to leave the reservation within a month, and twenty-five were given twenty-four hours to leave. Throughout the reservation only eleven whites were found to be married by either law or Indian custom to Indian women. Except for Wesley Warren, a black man who was married to a Cheyenne woman and lived at Cantonment, the other ten were judged by Miles to be competent to support their families, and Miles, of course, did not try to drive them off. Undoubtedly there were others, particularly white Indian scouts, post traders' employees, and others living at Fort Reno, Fort Supply, and at Cantonment whom Miles did not mention.[15]

When a soldier stationed at Cantonment requested authority to marry an Indian woman, Miles objected. He pointed out that "such marriages are no benefit to the Indians, generally speaking, and are often subversive of morality both to Indians and soldiers." Miles knew that many such marriages had occurred and that when the soldier's term of enlistment expired, he left the country, leaving behind illegitimate children whose livelihood must come from public funds. Normally, a white man who purchased an Indian woman did not view the arrangement as a valid marriage. The man regarded the union as binding as long as it served his personal needs and he could enjoy the privilege of securing property in Indian country. The result, according to Miles, was mixed-blood paupers to be clothed and fed at government expense and a ruined, helpless Indian woman. Such a man, Miles said, customarily "jumped the country," entered white society, and married again.[16]

Some of the white men were particularly difficult to handle because of their influence among the Indians. One such case was Robert L. Arbuthnot, whom Agent Lee encountered when he was trying to rid the reservation of disreputable whites. In May, 1885, Arbuthnot attempted to lead a delegation of Cheyennes and Arapahoes to Washington without Dyer's permission. None of the Indians had passes, and they were returned to Darlington. Arbuthnot continued on to Washington, where he sent letters back to his Indian friends asking them to send him money, claiming that he was in a position to help them with their affairs in Washington. Though known to the agents as a notorious debaucher of Indian women, he was nevertheless considered by some Indians as their best friend. His letters trying to destroy the Indians' confidence in Agent Lee prompted that official to complain that "the majority here are responding so nobly to efforts in their behalf . . . [it] is nothing less than a crime that any one should seek to promote dissatisfaction and retard their progress."[17]

To reduce the ease with which non-Indians could enter the reservation, Lee posted a notice on December 17, 1885, that required all persons not of Indian descent to register at the agency headquarters. After December 26 all non-Indians who remained on the reservation for more than twenty-four hours were required to obtain a permit from the Indian agent. About a month later Lee completed his census of whites and blacks who were living and working among the Cheyennes and Arapahoes (the census did not include agency personnel or the employees at Fort Reno). But there were twenty-four non-Indians living with Indian women—twenty whites, three blacks, and one man of black and Indian ancestry. Only six of the men were married by white man's law, and all but three of the men had children by their Indian wives. Some of the men objected to Lee's recommendation that they marry according to law because, they said, their women might not understand or would refuse to participate in the white marriage ceremony. Thirty-six other non-Indians were working for Indians or for traders or were simply listed as temporary residents on the reservation.

Lee puzzled where the line should be drawn to cut down white access to the Indian reservation. Some of the intermarried whites and mixed bloods insisted that they needed white laborers for their farming and ranching operations. Indians were still viewed as "unskilled and unreliable" and therefore nonprofitable to employ. Rules designed by Agent Lee provided in essence that any non-Indian had to be employed for a stated period of time by some person with a right to live among the Indians, be of good moral character, and depart from the reservation upon the discretion of the Indian agent. Such a person signed a statement that he would not marry an Indian woman without the consent of the Indian agent and that he would not attempt to alienate his employer's crops, stock, or other property.

While Lee tried to reduce the number of laborers working on the reservation, he aimed more directly at the intermarriage of Indian women and non-Indian men. Occasionally, he said, marriages were successful and productive, but most of the time the non-Indian husband simply adopted Indian camp life and lived off his wife's relatives. Lee claimed that the average "squawman" did not elevate the Indians but rather "descended" to their level and their way of life. The agent also argued that a white man should never be permitted to acquire land in his own name and should never accumulate more holdings than would normally devolve upon his wife so that he and his children would not share in a tribe's right to the land. This would prevent, according to Lee, "any white man, however, low and discreditable" from coming to the reservation, marrying an Indian woman, and thereby acquiring a right to 320 acres of land.[18]

After receiving approval of his plan from the Indian Office, Lee set out to remove the "squawmen" from the reservation if they did not marry their Indian women. He planned to give them thirty days' notice, and, if they disobeyed the regulations, he would expel them. Also, by rigidly controlling employment of whites, he hoped "to rid this reservation . . . of tramps who come and go in astonishing numbers. . . . I shall make the 'round up' in about thirty days if not sooner," he wrote to a fellow Indian agent, "and shall endeavor to follow it up by periodical arrest and expulsion of all unauthorized" to be on the reservation. With authority from Washington, Lee proceeded to prohibit non-Indians from marrying full-blood Indian women according to Indian custom. He also sharply restricted "outside labor" on the reservation. No white laborer could remain on the reservation for longer than six months, marry without permission from the Indian Office, effect a permanent abode, or obtain lien on his employer's property. To employ workers the individual was required to have more than sixty acres under cultivation, or, if engaged in stock raising, he must have employed an Indian herder before a second could be employed. "All shiftless and indolent characters," Lee warned, "must leave this reservation. Any white or colored person found loafing around Indian camps, or who may be engaged in gambling with Indians will be arrested and removed."[19]

Factionalism within the Cheyennes continued to plague the tribe during Lee's administration. As usual, the Arapahoes gave the agent little trouble because their chiefs, such as Powder Face (who would die in February, 1886), Left Hand, and Tall Bear, remained amenable to governmental policies. The Cheyennes were another matter. At the first tribal council held by Lee, Stone Calf dominated the scene when Cheyenne chiefs were called upon to speak in behalf of their people. Stone Calf belligerently called for better rations, including more beef and other commodities, such as sugar, coffee, rice, dried apples, and fruits. He demanded that his rations be issued at Cantonment, where he and Little Robe lived, that white men break the sod for his people's gardens and farms, that a reservation boarding school be built at Cantonment for his children, and that whites stop killing the game and cutting down trees.

Once Stone Calf had spoken, no other Cheyenne leader would contradict him, not out of fear but because Indian custom held that the first spokesman should be supported. To find out what the other Cheyenne chiefs thought, Lee met privately with Little Big Jake, Little Medicine, Cut Nose, Howling Wolf, White Antelope, and

127

Red Wolf. Together they condemned Stone Calf and Little Robe for retarding the progress of their people, for not freighting goods from Kansas, and for failing to send their children to school. Plows, corn planters, and mowing machines were desired by these chiefs, who wanted to co-operate with their Indian agent. The reservation years had by now driven a deep wedge between the traditionalist and assimilationist factions of the Cheyennes.[20]

Stone Calf, the most stubborn of the Cheyenne chiefs, died in early November, 1885. After Little Robe led the Cheyenne Cantonment bands to the Washita River to bury their chief, Lee tried to replace Stone Calf with White Horse, a more pliable leader. Through Haury, White Horse was told that the Indian agent wanted him "to be a leader among the Cheyennes at Cantonment in all things" and to assist in keeping "everything right." Lee encouraged White Horse to adopt the white man's ways. He pointed out to the new chief that he had sent a white farmer to help them in their fields and two men to break some land for them. Not enough money was available to help all the Indians, Lee admitted, but he asked the chief not to become discouraged and to place children in school so that their parents could be rationed at Cantonment, as Stone Calf had asked. "I cannot look into a man's thought," Lee wrote White Horse, "and tell what he thinks, but I ask you not to listen to any talk that gives a man two hearts. I want to tell you the best thing is to hold fast to the Government, never let go of what Washington says."[21]

Working patiently with those Cheyennes and Arapahoes at Cantonment who seemed willing to begin tilling the soil, Lee tried to domesticate the bands. Some of the Cheyennes responded to Lee's encouragements and did what work they could without adequate implements or work teams. Roman Nose, Thunder, Black Wolf, Strong Bow, Dead Man's Foot, and Flying Hawk opened a few acres of land, a gesture that brought from Lee the promise of breaking and stirring plows, harness for their teams, cultivators, and corn planters when the next shipment of implements arrived at Darlington. When Flying Hawk complained that he did not have wire to enclose his field or enough assistance to learn how to plant his field, Lee replied that shortages of funds limited services. Only five white men were provided by the government to teach the Indians agriculture, and they could not remain in any one camp for long. After showing the Indians what to do, the farmers had to move on to other camps and leave the Indians to work for themselves. Not only were there not enough farmers, but Lee admitted that he could not send horses or mules to help the Indians break their sod.[22]

Some of the Cantonment chiefs refused to follow the suggestions of their agent. The old way of life was still too attractive, and living off the cattle herds moving through the reservation was too tempting. Texas drovers made matters even easier for the Cheyennes when they refused to follow the established cattle trails and let their herds wander in search of good grass. On the trails and off, Cheyennes, led by Little Robe, Mad Wolf, and Bear Shield began taking beef by force and "by hostile threats, drawing rifles and pistols, rounding up herds and enforcing their demands." Others simply crossed into the Cherokee Outlet and helped themselves to cattle when they were hungry. Lee insisted, however, that the troublemakers were limited to fifteen to twenty lodges of people, who could be controlled by a troop of cavalry if it would patrol the cattle trails in the western portion of the reservation. Most of the Indians at Cantonment, Lee informed the patrol leader, "are well-disposed and . . . they need quite as much protection in their rights as white men with their passing herds." Toward the end of August, 1886, Lee believed that because most of the herds had passed for the season, the trouble had subsided enough to withdraw the cavalry patrol.[23]

Agent Lee found out that it was difficult if not impossible to protect the rights and property of the Indians. With warmer weather coming in the spring of 1886, Lee warned his superiors, white thieves would again begin preying on the Indians' stock. How could an Indian work his fields when his last pony was run off by white renegades? Lee knew of instances where Indians engaged in freighting or farming were "literally robbed of their last team of horses. These same Indians or some of them are now borrowing or hiring horses to help them in their industry. Last fall an old Indian and his squaw having lost by theft it is believed—all his horses, put in his wheat by dragging a brush over the ground." Thieves did come, and the ponies disappeared

129

into Kansas, Texas, and the Chickasaw Nation, leading Lee to comment that "not [in] one case in ten are their wrongs redressed or protection assured them" through the courts of the white man.[24]

Horse thieves were indiscriminate in their raidings, preying on the strong and influential and the weak and helpless alike. Cloud Chief, one of the more important Cheyenne leaders, had recently opened a farm and raised a good crop. While he was farming, white horse thieves stole several of his ponies. From the money his crop brought, he purchased several more animals and freighted goods to Darlington from Kansas. After two trips, however, one of his workhorses was stolen. Undaunted, Cloud Chief borrowed another team from friends and continued freighting as long as there was grass for the horses. Another example cited by Lee was the story of Lame Antelope, an older, crippled Indian, who, during the winter of 1885-86, selected his farm, built a comfortable house with logs he cut and hauled himself, and moved in with his family. His earthly possessions consisted of the house and two ponies. By putting up hay for his ponies, Lame Antelope got them through the winter and by spring was ready to plow. Before he could break the land, however, a horse thief ran off the Indian's best pony, which Lee thought "is now probably frisking around in some enlightened community and Lame Antelope is still struggling to become civilized." In two years the Indians lost more than two hundred of their best horses, causing the Indians, as Lee said, to view "the majesty of the law . . . a complete farce, an absolute nullity so far as any protection the law gives him in these matters." He added, "If any white community were preyed upon as these Indians, such community would take matters in its own hands and make short work of the miscreants."[25]

Despite their frustrations the Cheyennes and Arapahoes responded to Lee's urgings. More of their men went to work at farming than had ever done so before, using the inadequate supply of farming equipment to its fullest extent, even dragging plows that had not been used for years to stir the broken sod. Lee kept insisting that the Indians needed better equipment with which to work. He recommended the purchase of four seed drills for wheat so that the Indians would not have to broadcast the seeds in the high winds typical on the Plains. The Indians had raised more than two thousand bushels of wheat during the 1884–85 season, and, if the rainfall was sufficient, Lee thought, more acreage could be planted in that grain. Under Lee's leadership even some of the minor chiefs such as Wolf Robe went to work, and he was credited with having "the best looking corn field at this Agency owned and tended by an Indian."[26]

Hopeful as he was, Lee admitted that it was too early to notice much progress toward "civilization." The amount of land under cultivation by Indians on the reservation had almost doubled from the 1884–85 season. The willingness of the Indians to work amazed Lee, and he wished that the "Indian haters" could see them building fences, plowing, planting, sowing seed, and engaging in all varieties of farm work. He believed that the dictim, "If no man works, neither shall he eat," should be changed to, "If a man does work he must eat."[27]

Near the beginning of his tenure as agent, Lee had thought that many of the Cheyennes and Arapahoes would profit from being given patents and having land assigned to them in severalty. His opinion changed radically after he became better acquainted with the tribes and discovered that most of the Indians were still unprepared to become landowners. Even if the allotments were made inalienable by an act of Congress, the law could be repealed or changed, leaving the "Indians entirely dispossessed and left to the charity bestowed upon helpless vagrancy." He glumly predicted that border whites, coming among the Indians with Bibles and land patents in hand, would lead to their "absolute dispersion and ultimate extermination." Lee did not "expect these Indians, who but a few years ago were classed as the 'wildest,' transformed . . . into fullfledged civilized beings." He did not want them ground down as slaves or broken of every vestige of manhood by physical force, and he hoped that Washington officials would realize that "kindness, firmness, and justice reach the bulk of mankind, be they Indian or white."[28]

Lee, who had become thoroughly familiar with the Cheyennes and Arapahoes, was replaced by Gilbert B. Williams, a civilian, on September 16, 1886. Williams was a mediocre man with little imagination or energy. During his tenure of office among the Indians at Darlington, he constantly magnified his accomplishments and slavishly followed the policies of the Indian Office. He was particularly misleading when he discussed the degree to which the Cheyennes and Arapahoes were progressing toward self-sufficiency in order that it would appear that the Indians were ready to assume control of their own land and become citizens.[29] Agent Williams made a few minor modifications in policies after assuming his new post. He made it possible for Indians to break their own land and receive three dollars for each acre plowed, the proceeds to be spent in acquiring more agricultural implements or farm animals. After much indecision the group of intermarried men and mixed bloods who had located farms east of the agency headquarters were permitted to remain and continue their improvements, but John Poisal was denied permission to hire two white men to assist in his farming operations.[30]

Williams tried to continue Captain Lee's program of scattering the Indians more widely over the reservation by making more arable land available. It was his hope to locate each Indian family on 320 acres of land, thus increasing the Indians' sense of "individuality and self-reliance. Chieftainship is thus crushed and the dance drum is never heard in the farming districts." By 1887 five farming districts were operating, of which John H. Seger's was the most successful.[31]

When Williams learned that an Indian was likely to begin working the land, he encouraged him with promises of assistance. Bull Telling Tales, a Cheyenne living near Cantonment, received a letter from his agent urging him to "raise a good crop this summer so I can say to the Big Chief at Washington that you are on the right road, and this will make his heart glad." If Bull Telling Tales broke some land and planted a crop, Williams promised, he would receive a cow and a calf. The Cheyenne, however, was not ready to settle down. He asked to move to the South Canadian River and have his place near Cantonment turned over to another Indian. The only thing Williams could do was urge him to report to the farmer in the other district and go to work, which Bull Telling Tales was unwilling to do.[32]

One possible effect of dispersing the Indians on the reservation was trouble with cattlemen driving their herds from Texas to Kansas. Red Moon, a Cheyenne chief, had established his camp near the westernmost cattle trail to place a "tax" on the cattle moving through the reservation. The agent wanted the trail herds confined to the authorized trails, especially near Cantonment, so that the Indians with gardens and farms would not be disturbed. He asked for additional troops to patrol the cattle trails so that the Indians could levy their tribute from the cattlemen.[33]

Agents Lee's and Williams' efforts to scatter the Cheyennes and Arapahoes gradually diminished the influence of their traditional chiefs, especially among the Cheyennes. Young Whirlwind, who had replaced Stone Calf, Wolf Face, White Antelope, Red Wolf, Little Chief, and Burnt-All-Over admitted that they were disturbed by what they heard about the Dawes Act and that they lost control of their bands when the people lived on farms rather than in the old camps. All but Little Chief did nothing to support themselves, and as a group they wanted to go to Washington to talk. Although they had collected some money to live on, they still needed rail fare, and the Indian agent dissuaded them from making the expensive trip. The Indian agent thought, however, that a council in Washington might settle the Cheyennes. If a meeting could not be arranged, it would be helpful if the commissioner of Indian affairs would write a letter to the Cheyennes assuring them that their rights would be protected by the government.[34]

In his first annual report Williams wrote glowingly of the accomplishments of the Cheyennes and Arapahoes. Despite dry weather and the failure of the corn, wheat, and oat crops, the Indians were still opening more land and had 2,500 acres under cultivation. The well-cultivated fields, the agent wrote, were enclosed with substantial fences, and neatly whitewashed houses proved that the Indians had made remarkable progress. The Indian farms were not "truck patches." They ranged from five acres cultivated by the beginning agriculturalist to one hundred for the more experienced farmers. On the reservation seventeen homes had been finished for the Indians, and seventy more were under construction. The Indians were required to haul logs to the sawmill and the lumber to the location of their houses, which were no mansions but the simplest kind of frame houses, made of cottonwood lumber and covered with building paper.

Most Indians, however, still found their lodges more comfortable and durable.[35]

When the Indians tired of farm work, they held their dances or visited with neighboring tribes, particularly the Kiowas and Comanches. Seger Colony, about twenty miles north of the Kiowa, Comanche, Wichita reservations, was a convenient place for the tribes to get together, dance, visit, and gamble. In the early summer the Kiowas went to the Cheyenne-Arapaho lands or invited their neighbors to join them for the annual Sun Dance. The agents tried with little success to limit the visits to two or three days; the Indians usually maintained their ceremonial camps for two weeks or more. Such activities, of course, took the Indians from their farms and gardens and allowed their stock to wander free. On one occasion Williams asked the Kiowa, Comanche, and Wichita agent to jail all "his Indians" found on the Kiowa Reservation, but where could one find a jail large enough to hold several hundred Indians?[36]

Despite the lack of adequate rainfall for three out of four years and low prices for grain on the reservation, Agent Williams insisted that more Indians were turning to farming. Corn grown by Indians was selling at Darlington for 30 cents a bushel. When Williams offered the Cantonment bands 56 cents a bushel for corn if they would transport it to Darlington, they refused and demanded one dollar a bushel. To this demand Williams replied, "It would take two years of universal failure of crops to put corn at $1.00 per bushel." The Indians replied that they would rather keep it for five years than sell it for less. During his second year as agent Williams reported that the Indians were farming 3,375 acres, compared with 2,550 the preceding year. More farms and homes were being established throughout the ten farming districts organized on the reservation, the largest of which was around Cantonment, with 106 farms and 755 acres under cultivation. By Williams' report of 424 Indian farms in 1888, those Indians working the land were cultivating a little less than 8 acres each. Thus, since there were 3,202 Indians on the reservation in 1888, only about 20 per cent of the adult Indians were engaged in farming. Even the 20 per cent figure is suspiciously high, because Williams was constantly emphasizing his success to make his record appear attractive to his superiors.[37]

The year 1888 was nevertheless a successful crop year on the reservation. Agent Williams requested authority to decrease the oats and corn purchased through contract from an outside source by 25 per cent so that he could buy the Indians' surplus grains from them. If the government was trying to encourage agriculture, it would be wise to delay buying any grain from contractors until after the Indians' surpluses had been determined, thus assuring a local market for their crops. No railroads were yet available to make it feasible to ship grain from the reservation. Even Williams realized that one good year did not make agricultural enterprises successful among the Indians. He came to the conclusion, as had other agents before him, that the country was better adapted to stock raising. He commented in 1888, "The soil is good; in the river bottoms excellent; but the usually dry summer months are very discouraging."[38]

During the early months of 1889, Williams spent most of his time trying to protect the reservation from intruders. White Shield reported that cattle were constantly drifting in from the Texas Panhandle, and Williams sought their removal. He was also concerned about the anticipated opening of the Oklahoma Country, which would bring white settlers to the eastern boundary of the Cheyenne-Arapaho Reservation. He ordered William T. Darlington, captain of the agency's Indian police, to use his force to patrol the eastern boundary of the reservation. Williams, however, did not have to concern himself too long with those problems; he was replaced on May 1, 1889, by Charles F. Ashley.[39]

An investigation of Williams had led to his removal. While he appeared competent enough to manage the agency office, it was claimed that he did not "devote that intelligent and effective supervision over the Indians and the agency employees" to assure successful instruction of the Indians in agricultural activities. Rumors of "unchastity" and "financial jobbery" could not be traced to any responsible source by the investigators. Perhaps Williams should have been given better farmers to instruct the Indians; at best they were a pretty indifferent lot. One lacked the ability to work with the Indians, another had no energy, another had little experience at farming. Only Seger was effective with the Indians, and he was lauded for his "untiring energy and industry and strict integrity." He was "an effective manager of Indians, and through kindly treatment, exemplary life, good tact and encouragement, is inducing the Indians to engage in peaceful pursuits and agriculture." Of the 429 Indians at Colony, 75 were actually growing crops. More could have been accomplished by Seger if he had been furnished implements with which to assist the Indians.[40]

Charles F. Ashley, the new agent, was beset with a host of administrative problems as he assumed his duties at Darlington. He wanted to cancel the delivery of a steam thresher waiting at the Santa Fe warehouse in Oklahoma Station. He maintained that the Indians at Seger Colony did not need it and that it was too expensive to operate. The farmers helping the Indians needed to be replaced. Ashley pointed to John F. Black, who the agent said had nothing to recommend him except the backing of the powerful congressman from Illinois, Joseph G. Cannon. None of the work teams at the agency was fit for plowing and thus had to be replaced immediately. Even the moralistic regulations of the Indian Office handicapped him. Washington bureaucrats demanded that George Bent, who had served for eighteen years as interpreter at Darlington, be dismissed for excessive drinking. Ashley objected, saying that Bent's knowledge of the Indians and his extensive personal acquaintance with individual tribal members made him indispensable. Ashley temporarily retained him.[41]

It was clear that the condition of the Cheyennes and Arapahoes had deteriorated during Williams' administration. The reservation schools, other than those run by the Mennonites, were operating far below their normal enrollment. Throughout the farming districts fields once cultivated by Indians were abandoned, and Ashley found that he could consolidate three of the smaller districts into one and still cover the Indians' needs. Traditionalists still controlled many of the bands. Those led in former times by Stone Calf and Little Robe were now led by Young Whirlwind, Little Big Jake, Little Medicine, and Howling Wolf, who were described by Ashley as the key chiefs opposing the government's program. He called them "the non-progressive Indians, . . . turbulent, untractable, worthless; they will not listen to reason, and pay but little attention to advice given to them by the agent." They and their followers were still pressuring the former school children to return to camp life. The Cheyenne chiefs demanded food for feasts from the agent, and if the demands were denied, they became "threatening and insolent." On one occasion when they were not given permission to leave the reservation and were restrained by troops from Fort Reno and the Indian police, they became ugly and sullen. "It may yet be necessary," Ashley warned, "to use the strong arm of the Government in a most emphatic manner with these Indians."

Still, Ashley found some optimistic signs. When a railroad came nearer to Darlington, the Indians would have the means to ship their grain surpluses to markets, and when the local white population increased in Oklahoma Territory, they would also purchase the Indians' corn, wheat, and oats. Most of the Indians on the reservation opposed the allotting of their lands, but with time, the Indian agent thought, he could lead them to a more favorable attitude toward taking their land in severalty.[42]

When Ashley described the beef issue at Darlington, he betrayed many of the common prejudices held toward the Indians. Indians were notified of the forthcoming beef issue, and the cattle were driven into a corral with a chute. The name of the leader of the issue band was called, and the animal was turned loose on the prairie to be shot by a "buck" and butchered by a "squaw." As the beef was hacked into portions for five or six families (a total of about twenty-five persons), the women wrangled over the choice portions of the carcass. The method of butchering cattle by the Indians, wrote Ashley, "necessarily stimulates the brutal instincts, and correspondingly deadened the finer sensibilities." The Indians demanded that they continue to slaughter their own meat and retain the hides, because to have only the meat distributed among them would deprive them of more than five thousand dollars they could obtain from the traders for the hides. The older people did not want the method changed because it reminded them of the old buffalo hunts. But the only change Ashley recommended was that the public should not be allowed to witness the shooting and butchering of the beef.[43]

The Cheyennes and Arapahoes were troubled people. They were deeply disturbed by the coming of whites to the eastern part of the reservation and by the inroads made on their traditional way of life by government policies. The old people and leaders decried the chiefs' loss of power, young men and women educated in the schools found few outlets for their new skills and knowledge, and, with a few exceptions, most families lived near the point of privation. It is not surprising that when the Cheyennes and Arapahoes learned that they would lose their precious land they sought the solace of a new Indian religion. Since the late 1870's in varying degrees the Indians of the mountains, plateaus, and Northern plains had come to listen to the message of Wovoka, the Paiute religious leader who preached the message that the Indians would one day again control their lands. The buffalo would return and the good, satisfying old way of life would again be possible. By the late summer of 1890 the Ghost Dance as taught by Wovoka had come to the Southern Cheyennes and Arapahoes and found adherents.

Information reached the Southern Plains during the fall and winter of 1889–90 that "Christ was located about two hundred miles north" of the Shoshoni Agency in Wyoming. Certain prominent medicine men in their visions held conversations with Christ, who said that his coming would benefit only the Indians. "Whites were to be removed from the country, the buffalo would come back and the Indians restored to their original status." The Arapahoes, a more religious people than the Cheyennes, manifested a particular interest in the reports from their northern friends. They raised enough money to send two of their leaders, Black Coyote and Washee, the former a lieutenant and the latter a sergeant in the Indian police, to the Shoshoni Agency in search of Christ. The emmissaries did not see Christ, but they confirmed his existence in conversations with other Indians, undoubtedly with the Northern Arapahoes, who shared a reservation with the Shoshonis.

After Black Coyote and Washee returned to Darlington, all work on the reservation ceased. Carefully the Arapahoes made their Ghost Dance shirts, gathered in camps once more, danced, sang, and were exhorted by their priests. Unlike the other Indian ceremonies, all drums, rattles, and musical instruments were prohibited because "Christ did not like so much noise." During the ceremony "an Indian would exhort for awhile, the excitement growing more and more intense as he told them what Christ was going to do for them, until finally hundreds of them would rise from the ground, commence circling around singing and crying until they were apparently exhausted." Others tried to follow Black Coyote and Washee to the north, but Agent Ashley denied them permission. Somehow the Cheyennes and Arapahoes learned that Christ had written to the Great Father in Washington that in two years all whites must be expelled from Indian country or be destroyed. The Cheyennes and Arapahoes decided to remain quietly on their reservation for that period of time.

Ashley thought that if conflict broke out in the north over the Ghost Dance it was possible that as many as two hundred of the "wild Cheyennes" would try to ride to the sides of their friends. The remaining Cheyennes and all the Arapahoes, Ashley felt certain, would remain "loyal and true to the Government." Although the followers of the Ghost Dance withdrew their children from the schools so that the families would be united if trouble came, the "progressive" elements of the tribes assured Ashley that there would be no outbreak or serious trouble on the Cheyenne-Arapaho Reservation. Excitement over the Ghost Dance diminished quickly, according to Ashley, but the dances still attracted many Indians well into 1892.[44]

Rather than give proper emphasis to the influence of the Ghost Dance, Ashley explained the sudden decline in agricultural activities as being a result of the prevailing cycle of dry weather. No rain fell during May and June of 1890, causing nearly a total failure of corn and a maturing of only about one-half of the oat crop. Ashley came to realize that wheat was a safer crop for the region, but in 1890 it was grown only by the Indians working with John Seger. Still, the Indians sold more than eleven thousand bushels of grain to dealers and traders in the nearby towns of Oklahoma Territory and freighted in from the railroad to Darlington 1,800,000 out of a total of 3,000,000 pounds of agency supplies. For their labor and wagons and teams the Indians received more than seven thousand dollars.[45]

During the 1880's education of young Cheyennes and Arapahoes was sporadic and generally ineffective. The school population was substantially larger than in the preceding decade, but almost any displeasure on the part of the Indians led to a withdrawal of children from school. The safest procedure was to send the children to non-reservation schools, where they would be farther from the turmoils and conflicts of their people. In October, 1884, Agent Dyer reported that he had sent thirty-six Cheyenne and three Arapaho youths to Chilocco, an Indian school in Chilocco, Indian Territory, and fifty-four Cheyenne and twenty Arapaho students to Haskell Institute, in Lawrence, Kansas, leaving only sixty pupils in the Arapaho and twenty in the Cheyenne reservation boarding schools. When the argument between the Indians and the cattlemen became heated during the winter of 1884–85, the leadership of the tribes threatened a boycott of the schools unless they were permitted to visit Washington to make their grievances known.[46]

The assertion that the Indians placed their children in school either to be rid of them or to please the agent does injustice to the parents. They, like all human beings, loved their children and felt responsible for their welfare. Powder Face, whose son was at Carlisle, heard that the boy was sick and wanted Captain Pratt to send him home. The chief was so concerned that he purchased new clothing for himself so that he could make the trip to Pennsylvania to bring his son back with him to Indian Territory. Clarence, the chief explained, had never been strong after being thrown from a horse. Although Captain Pratt assured Powder Face that Clarence was well, the concerned father wrote: "When I heard my son was sick I was half scared—if you let my son come home I will pay his fare—I love my son better than all my property and I want to see him pretty bad. . . . I send you Five Dollars to give to my son."[47]

The Mennonites were fairly successful in their efforts to work with Indian children. They maintained schools at Darlington for the Arapahoes and at Cantonment for the Cheyennes. In the mid-1880's they continued to send some of their pupils to live in the Mennonite settlements centered around Halstead, Kansas. There the youths attended either the public or the Mennonite schools, where they continued their education while working on farms. The Mennonites hoped to prepare the Indian youths as "teachers and workers" for the mission school. They recognized that, although the youths might not be as well prepared academically as teachers from the East, they would have the advantage of knowing the special needs of their people. Several of the pupils reported back to the Reverend Mr. Voth at Darlington about their experiences in Kansas. Henry Miles wrote to him: "I have been all through with threshing. Now we work in the fields. I harrow. I not forget all you told me about Jesus. I pray to him every night make us walk good way." Henry had been placed in a school where he studied arithmetic, worked in the "Third Reader," read gospel stories, learned geography, and practiced writing. On weekends Henry and his friends attended Mennonite prayer meetings and Sunday school because "we like to walk on the good road."[48]

One of the older students who was enrolled in a Mennonite college happily reported that he was making good progress. Josiah Kelly was learning more "about Jesus, you know when I was at Darlington sometimes I ashamed to pray but now I don't have shame to pray and talk English." During the year in Kansas, Josiah remained content and looked forward to returning to his people to "help my uncle plant corn and other kind of plants such as potatoes." He enclosed four dollars for his mother and asked Voth to read the letter to her: "Now I send you $4 which you want but do not play with cards with this money it is the worse thing to play cards with money. Our father Jesus did not say in the bible or I never heard that we should play cards with money but we must not do this."[49]

Adult Indians were also instructed by the Mennonites in farming and housekeeping. The Reverend Mr. Haury at Cantonment commented that, though it was commonly maintained that "these Indians were too filthy to live and enjoy good health in houses," the families who occupied houses around Cantonment seemed "to abandon their filth more or less by occupying houses, and their health increases." As others noted, Haury said that the Arapahoes were more successful in growing crops than were the Cheyennes. Both tribes began in the spring with three to fifteen acres of corn for each farmer, but, when the time came to cultivate the grain, the Cheyennes abandoned their fields to "make medicine." The result was predictable: the Cheyennes did not harvest more than one bushel of corn an acre.[50]

By 1886 even the recalcitrant bands of Stone Calf and Little Robe had sent some of their children to school. They were the very last to give their children to the agents for education. Although other missionaries were at work among the Cheyennes and Arapahoes, the Mennonites made the largest impact because they worked with the Indians in their fields. Captain Lee, while serving as agent, did not anticipate any rapid conversion of the Cheyennes and Arapahoes to Christianity, explaining:

They worship the Great Spirit, pray to him in sickness, and thank him for the few blessings they enjoy. Much of their faith is the same as ours, but it will be generations before they can understand the efficacy of infant baptism, or comprehend the Trinity, the miracles, the inspiration of the Scriptures, and other mysteries connected with the Christian religion. To many of their minds these things are as incomprehensible as their religious observances are to us.[51]

Generally, those trying to educate the Cheyennes and Arapahoes were critical of the nonreservation schools, particularly Carlisle. Dyer insisted that the final test of an Indian's education must be his ability to earn a living and that therefore "book study" was secondary. "The folly of making booklearning superior to industrial knowledge is reflected here as clearly as if it were in a mirror," he wrote. He insisted that the Indians must be trained in reservation manual-labor schools and that "any other courses of education given to these 'blanket Indians' will be a curse to them." If they were educated, the younger people were ridiculed by their elders and the traditionalists, whose influence upon the children was substantial. When parents visited the students too frequently or when the students were allowed to return to the camps during the holidays or vacation periods, the pupils' progress toward the goal of self-sufficiency was retarded.[52]

The inappropriateness of education at Carlisle or other nonreservation schools seemed apparent to Williams when he reviewed the record of students returning to the reservation from Captain Pratt's school. One hundred and eighty students had undertaken studies at Carlisle, and three female pupils had matriculated at Lincoln Institute in Pennsylvania. One hundred and twenty of the students were males, and sixty-three were females. In the spring of 1887, twenty-five of the students had died, seventy-six were on the reservation, and the others were either at Carlisle or other nonreservation schools. At the time of Williams' report, thirty-one males and fifteen females had returned to camp life, abandoning what they had learned in school. Twelve of the young men were employed as army scouts, three were employed at the agency, and one was working for a trader. Of the girls, three were lawfully married and on farms with their husbands, and three still adhered to civilized life, although they were unemployed and living with their parents. The agency did not provide suitable employment for the returned students, and they were averse to working on farms since many of the boys had learned specific crafts in the schools. Occasionally some of the youths had been employed in the agency shops, but they gradually dropped their work. By 1887 only one remained employed at his craft in Darlington.

The record led Williams to conclude that the reservation school rather than Carlisle prepared the young people for productive lives on the reservation. "The broken tongue in reservation schools is considered sufficient to prepare an Indian for a farmer or an ordinary mechanic," Williams asserted. He considered it preferable to educate Indian youths in reservation schools among their own people where the parents could observe the development of their offspring. He claimed that he had little difficulty in persuading a young man from a reservation boarding school to settle down on a tract of land and open a farm. Williams, however, overlooked several factors. From the outset Carlisle selected its students from the families of the chiefs and leaders. These proud people would not accept manual or common farm labor under the most favorable conditions because of their heritage and status. (There was one notable exception, Grant Left Hand, the Arapaho chief's son. He was employed for some years at a trader's store in Darlington after his return from Carlisle.) The agent also

143

ignored the possibility of continuing the Indian youths' training on the reservation and at the agency headquarters by removing the political hacks who had been placed on the payroll by influential politicians for patronage reasons. The government made little effort to find suitable employment for the returned students and thereby gave them no alternative but to return to the camps of their parents.[53]

School and missionary activity at Cantonment suffered when the Mennonite missionary Haury resigned. Without knowing the circumstances prompting his resignation, Agent Williams wrote that "every Indian who has come under your beneficence sincerely mourns your departure." The Cantonment bands felt differently. When rumors persisted that the missionary had been involved with school-girls at Cantonment, Agent Williams and an Indian inspector finally went to Cantonment and found the charges only too true. A council of chiefs at Cantonment declared that they wanted no more men like Haury sent among their people. Although the Indians did not "entertain the highest sentiment regarding chastity," said Williams, they would use the incident to hinder the agent's efforts to place the children in school. The Cheyennes especially grasped "every excuse for withholding their children; for two years past they have given as a reason that the buildings were old, damp and unhealthful but as soon as a new building was erected they would fill it."[54]

One former student referred to Haury's example when he refused to marry a girl after she became pregnant. The Reverend Mr. Voth claimed that Johnny Williams was the cause of Jeannie Arrow's pregnancy, and at first the youth agreed to marry the girl, explaining that "my father and Arrow were very anxious to us marry each other." But Jeannie had confided to him that another young man "had done it to her." "It would not be right," Johnny argued, "for me to marry the girl while the baby belongs to another person and let me have the baby in my care. . . . I would not do it." When Johnny was reprimanded by Voth for his untrustworthiness, the young man wrote to Voth: "You Mennonites ought to think and *must think* before you say anything to others. You ought to think of the people that use to act as if they were very good people & yet they had done the very, very same thing." In justifying Johnny's refusal to marry Jeannie,

Williams said that the girl had had sexual relations with a number of his acquaintances and that when she came back to Cantonment she proclaimed that "she is not ashamed & would go without a husband." Concluding his letter to Voth, Johnny wrote: "If you don't believe me, its all the same to me. Hoping you will not bother me any more about this."[55]

Not all the returned students caused concern. Leonard Tyler and Jennie Black, full-blood Cheyennes, had been educated at Carlisle and Haskell Institutes and were married by Voth in September, 1889. Agent Williams claimed that it was the first such marriage performed on the reservation. The ceremony was attended by many of the "progressive" Cheyenne chiefs, such as Cloud Chief, Wolf Chief, Buffalo Chief, Sleeping Wolf, Cedar Tree, and Spotted Wolf and their wives. These young people were ignoring the prejudice and ridicule of their people, and the agent wanted to help them. Agent Ashley recommended that Tyler be given an appointment as an assistant industrial teacher and his wife be appointed a steamstress at the Cheyenne boarding school.[56]

After more than a decade of persuasion had failed, Agent Ashley decided to use other means to fill the reservation boarding schools. In 1889 he decided to withhold rations from those families who refused to place their children in schools. Of course, the number of school children on the reservation still exceeded the capacity of the schools, but the agent was expected to fill every available space. When the edict went into effect, Young Whirlwind, a Dog Soldier chief, sent Pawnee Man into the commissary building at Darlington to seize food for all the Cheyennes who had been denied rations. Entering the building, Pawnee Man drove the employees and Indians out by threatening them with a cocked rifle. Ashley, with some Indian police, arrested Pawnee Man. The Dog Soldier explained that he meant no offense to the government or to the agent since it was the customary way for Cheyennes to control the actions of their people through the force and authority of the Dog Soldiers. Lacking the support of his fellow warriors, Pawnee Man placed his daughter in school the next morning, and the charges against him were dropped. Certainly the strength of the soldier societies had declined rapidly, and they could no longer thwart the programs of the Indian agent as they had done in the early and mid-1880's.[57]

Although the traditionalists' power had diminished, this did not mean that they would co-operate entirely with governmental programs. The "Court of Indian Offences" was established on the reservation on January 1, 1889, but was not activated until the following summer. Agent Ashley appointed two Cheyennes, Pawnee Man and Wolf Face, and an Arapaho, White Snake, to serve as judges. The Cheyennes balked at efforts to use the court to curtail the practice of multiple wives, the purchase of women, and the distribution of property upon the death of an Indian. Continuation of the court on the Cheyenne-Arapaho Reservation seemed pointless to Ashley because traditionalists would not control their own people or work toward change in tribal customs. He hoped that at some future date students educated at Carlisle and Haskell could be appointed to the court, but in 1890 the younger men did not "have the courage to authoritatively oppose the customs of their people."[58]

Although the Cheyennes and Arapahoes were unprepared for citizenship and allotments, the Dawes Act would soon be applied to them. Only 84 families occupied houses, and only 274 families lived on individual tracts of land. An estimated 20 per cent of the Cheyennes and Arapahoes were engaged in any work related to agriculture, and those who were farming cultivated a little less than eight acres each. Most of the tribesmen indicated that they had no desire to change their way of life—at least not until the expiration of the Treaty of Medicine Lodge in 1897. "Labor," explained their agent, "is foreign to their nature; by most it is considered degrading. The Arapahoes are by far more the most industrious and are proportionately despised by the Cheyennes. A few of them work at such industry as the agent is able to furnish, but seldom continue at it longer than a few weeks or months, when they get tired and quit." Although the country of the Cheyennes and Arapahoes was well adapted for ranching, what Ashley called their "insatiate greed" for meat had in the past prevented the development of cattle herds of sufficient size to contribute significantly to their food needs. Only 25 per cent of the Indians wore white man's clothing, and only one out of six could speak or understand enough English for ordinary conversations. Even among those who could speak English, only about one-quarter had had more than a few years of schooling. But forces were in motion that would shortly involve the tribes in a cession agreement with the federal government.[59]

CHAPTER VI

The End of the Reservation

In 1889 various factors combined to lead toward the application of the Dawes Act to the Cheyenne-Arapaho Reservation: the Indian Office and Congress were driving toward the goal of making citizens of reservation Indians, western farmers and ranchers were looking longingly at Indian land as the last major unsettled area, on the public domain fertile land was becoming scarce, and private individuals were hoping to divert to their pockets a portion of the funds paid to the Indians for ceding their lands.

Two years after the passage of the Dawes Act a group of former agents for the Cheyennes and Arapahoes and attorneys joined forces to obtain a portion of the funds paid to tribes when the cession agreement occurred. Former Agent D. B. Williams, working for a Wichita, Kansas, lawyer named McMecham, appeared at Darlington and conferred with a few chiefs of the two tribes. Later in the spring of 1889 former Agent Dyer went to the agency and rekindled the Indians' interest in their Medicine Lodge Treaty reservation, which they had never formally ceded to the United States. Finally, in mid-May, 1889, former Agent John D. Miles and Samuel J. Crawford also went to Darlington, where they convinced John H. Seger and the Reverend Mr. Voth that the Cheyennes and Arapahoes had a legitimate claim to the tribes' former reservation, most of which lay in the Cherokee Outlet.[1]

No formal tribal council was called by the conspirators. Instead, a few educated members of the tribes and a faction of chiefs led by

Little Chief of the Cheyennes and Left Hand of the Arapahoes were taken to Oklahoma City. On May 23 and 24, 1889, Crawford, Miles, J. P. Henderson, and Matt Reynolds entertained the chiefs of the two tribes and their interpreters and began to work out the details of the contract. Miles denied to a reporter that he was anything more than an observer and asserted that he was interested only in seeing that the Indians "had a fair and full expression of their wishes and to hear their statements as to their claim to the Cherokee Outlet." The chiefs mainly discussed their desire to negotiate with the government for a cession of the Cherokee Outlet, but they also seemed willing to sell a portion of the reservation they were occupying. Before the meetings disbanded, the Indians and lawyers had agreed to a contract specifying that the latter would arrange for the sale of the Outlet lands to the government for $1.25 an acre. This would include the Cherokees' share, which was placed at 47 cents an acre. For their services the attorneys would receive 10 per cent of the sum obtained from the government. The preliminary contract was submitted to the commissioner of Indian affairs who in turn, on June 15, 1889, forwarded it to the secretary of the interior.[2]

The final agreement was signed on August 20, 1889, in Arkansas City, Kansas. Finalized before Judge Cassius G. Foster, the agreement between the chiefs and attorneys stipulated that the latter would be compensated for any money received from the government for the lands of the Cherokee Outlet, the 1869 Presidential Proclamation reservation, or any other funds obtained by the tribes when the sale of the reservations was consummated. Taking no chance that the Indians would understand the document's significance, the attorneys arranged for Leonard Tyler to read only the first few vague sentences of the agreement, while the other key interpreters were drunk, a fact still remembered by living Cheyennes. To assure the complete co-operation of the interpreters and the educated members of the tribes, the lawyers explained that they would receive their fees when Congress approved the cession agreement. The contract, which received the approval of Secretary of the Interior John W. Noble, claimed that eight Cheyenne and four Arapaho leaders had been duly appointed to negotiate the contract with Crawford, Reynolds, Miles, and Dyer.[3]

The mechanism for completing the cession agreement had already been constructed by Congress. By the Springer Amendment to the Indian Bill of 1889 the president was authorized not only to open the Oklahoma Country to settlement but also to appoint a three-man commission to negotiate with the tribes in western Indian Territory for their lands. As the reservation cession agreements were completed, the lands would be added to the newly created Oklahoma Territory. The commission, known as the Cherokee, or Jerome, Commission, was composed of Chairman David H. Jerome, former governor of Michigan, Warren G. Sayre, of Indiana, and Alfred M. Wilson, of Arkansas. They were ready to come to the Cheyenne-Arapaho Reservation after arranging for an agreement with the Sac, Fox, Potawatomi, Shawnee, and Iowa Indians for their surplus lands.[4]

When the Jerome Commission arrived at Darlington on July 7, 1890, another group of Indians lost their lands. All the necessary conditions were present: the tribes had been divided into contending factions, key chiefs had been deceived by their supposed friends, the Indian policy of allotment required implementation, land-hungry whites were waiting for the reservation to be opened for settlement, and easy money was waiting for white spoilsmen. Agent Ashley assembled the full tribal councils to meet the commissioners. Chairman Jerome opened the first meeting by appealing to the Indians' self-interest. The Cheyennes and Arapahoes knew that the buffalo and game were gone, he said, but they still had hopes that the animals would return as Wovoka had told them. The white man lived differently and understood that the Indian "must live by growing something out of the ground or else he will starve."[5]

From the outset the commissioners used threats and promises to influence the Cheyennes and Arapahoes. They were limited by instructions received from Secretary Noble, who had told Chairman Jerome, "Be careful not to give too much" for the Cheyenne-Arapaho Reservation. Noble pointed out that the confederated tribes did not have a good claim either to the lands given to the Wichitas and Affiliated Bands or to the Cherokee Outlet. Chairman Jerome was also informed that it was preferable to gain the consent for the cession from three-fourths of the adult males as required under the 1867

Medicine Lodge Treaty, but if that was not possible, to "close with [a] majority if you cannot get more." According to the law of the land, Jerome explained, if the Indians did not fully utilize their reservations, they could be required to take allotments and sell the remaining lands. The President did not desire to seize the reservation as empowered by the Dawes Act, but Jerome was unsure of the Cheyennes' and Arapahoes' fate if the commissioners were unsuccessful in their quest for an agreement. To quiet the Indians' fear, Commissioner Sayre promised that every tribal member would select his allotment before "any white man comes at all." If the agreement was reached, Sayre promised, "there will be more money paid every year than is now paid to the Cheyennes and Arapahoes."[6]

Traditionalist chiefs of the Cheyennes forcefully replied to the commissioners that they did not want to sell any portion of their lands. Old Crow, speaking for the Cheyennes living on the Washita River, said:

The Great Spirit gave the Indians all this country and never tell them that they should sell it. . . . See, I am poor. I have no money; I don't want money; money doesn't do an Indian any good. Here is my wealth [pointing to the ground]. Here is all the wealth I want—the only money I know how to keep.

Young Whirlwind brusquely told the commissioners to tell the President that the tribes did not want to sell their land. After Chairman Jerome asked the interpreters whether the Indians understood the issue and tried to keep the discussion focused on the president's power to take the land, Young Whirlwind commanded the interpreter, "That is all, cut it off." The talks continued with Left Hand and Tall Bear of the Arapahoes and Cloud Chief and Elk Tongue (also called Pushing Bear) trying to change the tone of the meeting by asking for a little time to consider the problems of their people.[7]

While the chiefs met with their bands, Miles attempted to present the contract with the Cheyennes and Arapahoes that allowed attorneys to represent them in discussions about the Cherokee Outlet. Miles had prevailed upon Left Hand to present the document to Chairman Jerome, but Wolf Face, one of the Cheyennes present at the first meetings in Oklahoma City, objected angrily to what Miles and Left Hand were doing. In future years the validity of the document would be denied by the Cheyennes and Arapahoes. Jerome, however, cut the exchange short by ruling that the contract was not relevant to the business of allotting the present reservation.[8]

Responding to a request by the chiefs for presentation of a full explanation of the government's offer, Commissioner Sayre made the initial proposal. The Cheyennes and Arapahoes were to accept the 1869 Presidential Proclamation reservation, relinquish all rights to other lands, and approve a cession of land which in 1872 had placed the Wichitas and Affiliated Bands on a tract of their current reservation. From the reservation the government would also need lands for educational, military, missionary, and agency activities. Each Cheyenne and Arapaho would receive either 80 acres of farmland or 160 acres of grazing land. If families so desired, their allotments could be selected so that a family of five could take their lands in a block. Sayre assured his Indian listeners that many families could group together and "take lands that join and make one great ranch and live there just as you please." Those people who had made improvements on a tract would not be required to move to another location. The government pledged to continue the annuity money due the tribes under the 1867 Medicine Lodge Treaty until 1897 and to pay the tribes $1.5 million for surplus lands. One-third of the purchase price would be distributed among the tribes on a per capita basis, while $1 million would be deposited in the United States Treasury, bearing 4 per cent interest for the benefit of the Cheyennes and Arapahoes. If the tribes accepted these terms, Sayre temptingly maintained, they would be "the richest people on earth; no entire white people will have the home and money the Cheyennes and Arapahoes will have."

Immediately after Sayre's presentation Old Crow and Chairman Jerome engaged in a bitter debate. The Cheyenne chief insisted that his people did not want their reservation cut up into farms and that, if individual leaders violated the wish of the majority of chiefs and tribesmen, "we will punish them." Jerome angrily reminded Old Crow that the Dawes Act could be imposed on them without their

Left to right: Willie Burns as a child, Little Bear, Cloud Chief, and Little Chief, Cheyenne chiefs. *Courtesy Western History Collections, University of Oklahoma Library.*

Left to right: Buffalo Meat, Three Fingers, and Wolf Robe, Southern
Cheyenne chiefs, at Ben Beveridge's house in Washington, D.C. *Courtesy
Western History Collections, University of Oklahoma Library.*

Left to right: Henry Roman Nose and Yellow Bear, Southern Cheyenne chiefs, and Lame Man or Cohoe, Southern Cheyenne artist. *Courtesy Western History Collections, University of Oklahoma Library.*

Left, Southern Cheyenne and Arapaho chiefs gathered for a council in the summer of 1900. Included in the group are Henry Roman Nose, Magpie, Yellow Bear, Three Fingers, Bull Bear, and Cometsevah. *Courtesy Western History Collections, University of Oklahoma Library.*

Below, a Cheyenne-Arapaho delegation at the Gettysburg Battlefield on November 28, 1884, en route to the Carlisle Indian School. Included in the group are Black Wolf, Whirlwind, and Little Big Jake, Southern Cheyenne chiefs, and Left Hand and Powder Face, Southern Arapaho chiefs. *Courtesy Oklahoma Historical Society.*

Indian and white agency and school personnel. Agent John D. Miles is at the left behind the chair. The second person to his right is Leonard Tyler who worked in the agency office before becoming the leader of the peyote ceremony, and the fourth person to the right of Miles is Robert Burns, long a trusted clerk and interpreter for various Indian agents. *Courtesy Western History Collections, University of Oklahoma Library.*

Sam Whitt as a boy, John D. Miles, Indian agent, Little Robe, Southern Cheyenne chief, and Ben Clark, army scout and interpreter. *Courtesy Oklahoma Historical Society.*

Above left, John D. Miles, Indian agent. *Courtesy Oklahoma Historical Society.*

Above, John H. Seger, agency employee, school superintendent, and founder of the Cheyenne-Arapaho settlement at Colony, Oklahoma Territory, where a school was established. *Courtesy Oklahoma Historical Society.*

Left, Major George W. H. Stouch, acting Indian agent. *Courtesy Oklahoma Historical Society.*

consent and that the United States Army was available to enforce the law. Old Crow was not afraid: "Now I am going to speak my mind to you if I am killed for it. . . . We have been robbed of our land and the worth of our land ever since the white man came into the country and they ought to be full of it." Little Big Jake, Spotted Horse, Young Whirlwind, Wolf Face, and Little Medicine, all influential Cheyenne chiefs and band leaders, supported Old Crow's brave stand. Backed by Mad Wolf and Howling Wolf, leaders of warrior societies, Young Whirlwind summed up the attitude of those who refused to sell the reservation: "We look upon this land as a home and our mother and we don't expect to sell it."

As the councils entered their fourth day, it was evident that Old Crow and his followers were in no mood to compromise. Money did not tempt Old Crow; he kept insisting that the "land and the streams of water that run through it—that is all the wealth that I want." When Chairman Jerome sought the opinion of the Arapahoes, it was apparent that they wanted to bargain for more favorable terms from the government. The venerable and respected Left Hand of the Arapahoes did not want the issues to be pushed too fast upon his people. In the same vein Row-of-Lodges commented, "When a white man or any Indian makes a trade, he wanted a little time to think and when a man buys a horse he wants to look it all over whether it is all right or not and so it is about our lands."

On July 11, Left Hand presented the Arapahoes' counterproposal. The Arapaho chief suggested that each person of the tribes be allotted 160 acres of land, the remainder to be sold for $1.45 an acre. Left Hand's plan was supported by a number of Arapaho speakers, but only four Cheyennes dared as yet to differ with the stance taken by Old Crow. Now it was the commissioner's turn to ask for more time, and he warned the chiefs that they "must not expect too much of the Commission to agree to all that you want."

When the councils reconvened, Chairman Jerome assented to only one of Left Hand's stipulations. Each person could receive 160 acres of land. But the commissioners stated that not more than 80 acres should be classed as farm- or cropland. Since the government had already paid other Indians over $2 million for the reservation's lands,

Jerome maintained that $1.5 million was the maximum sum that the President and Congress would allow. Commissioner Sayre played upon the credulity of the Indians by pointing out that each Indian could expect more than $500 for the surplus lands. There was, of course, no intention to disburse the whole $1.5 million among the tribesmen; yet, Sayre continued: "If you had five hundred dollars in silver you could not carry it home in your pockets. You would have to carry it home in your saddle bags."

The Cheyennes for the most part remained obdurate. White Shield and his warrior leaders Sergeant Meat and Little Man from Cantonment wanted no part in the discussions. They recalled that General Sheridan, when he had met with them in 1885, had told them to keep control of their reservation at all costs. It was becoming obvious that, if the commissioners were to succeed, they would have to persuade the Arapahoes and a minority of Cheyennes to cede their lands. Even compliant Cheyenne chiefs like Cloud Chief and White Antelope, whose father had died at Sand Creek, insisted that Left Hand's terms were the only conditions for an agreement. These chiefs led by Left Hand and Cloud Chief implied that the government should treat them well because they had farmed, sent their children to school, and had lived peacefully since 1869.

Impatiently Commissioner Jerome pressed for an agreement. He could not give the Indians more than $1.5 million because Congress had placed that limit on him. Further, he argued, he had already exceeded the congressional limit of $1.25 an acre when the $1.05 paid to the Creeks was added to the sum of $1.5 million he was offering to the Cheyennes and Arapahoes. At this point two young, educated men entered the discussion. Cleaver Warden and Leonard Tyler, representing the educated Arapahoes and Cheyennes respectively, wanted more money than Jerome was willing to concede. When the chairman of the commission could not make even these men back down, he testily remarked that there were two ways to break the stalemate: "settle with us [or] settle under the law." Then, hoping to influence some of the wavering Indians, Jerome pointed out that his plan offered the Cheyennes and Arapahoes more than three times the amount of land provided under the Dawes Act and the maximum amount of money that Congress would appropriate to compensate the Indians for their surplus lands.

As the councils dragged on, the Indians became restive. When a shortage of beef was interpreted by them as an indication that the commissioners were not powerful men, a hasty telegram to Washington brought not only more beef but authority for Agent Ashley to issue the tribesmen whatever it would take to keep the Indians in conference with the commissioners. The issue of the lawyers' contract also delayed the proceedings. It became clear that, although the chiefs had signed the document, it was their understanding that Miles and his cohorts would be involved in negotiations only for the old reservations and the Cherokee Outlet. That had been the interpretation of Leonard Tyler and the chiefs who had signed the document in Arkansas City.[9]

Left Hand and Cloud Chief wrung one more small concession from the commissioners. Although they failed to increase the sum to $2 million, as had been suggested by Leonard Tyler, they did increase to 5 per cent the interest to be paid on the money to be deposited in the treasury. After twelve days of talking, Left Hand and Cloud Chief accepted the crucial points of the commissioners' offer. They were willing to accept 160 acres of land for each person, half in crop and half in grazing land, and $1.5 million for the surplus lands, $500,000 of which was to be distributed immediately after congressional approval of the agreement on a per capita basis and the remainder was to be deposited in the treasury at 5 per cent interest. But then Left Hand changed his mind somewhat. He wanted all the allotments to be either in cropland or in grazing land so that his people could select their allotments in blocks and not be forced to take portions of their lands at different sites. Further, Left Hand did not want the $500,000 to be distributed under the supervision of the secretary of the interior. Undoubtedly merchants and traders had influenced the chief so as to make their sales of goods a little easier in satisfying their customers' tastes.

Again Chairman Jerome's temper rose. He had already prepared a document based on Left Hand's and Cloud Chief's previous concessions. To the Arapaho chief the chairman complained: "Now the trouble is that you are listening to some one else. . . . I believe that Left Hand is an honest man but he bends his ear to some one else, he listens to bad advice." No, Left Hand replied, he was listening to the young, educated men who wanted more money and land in blocks. When the day ended, only one detail remained unsettled. The Indians still wanted the per capita payment paid directly to the Indians without the secretary of the interior supervising its expenditure.

On July 21 one last try was made by the commissioners to reach a complete agreement, but before discussions could begin, a group of Arapaho Indian scouts left the meeting place. Left Hand was startled: "I have been chief among my people and have always been looked upon as chief and this is the first time that they have ever surprised me by turning away from me." When Cloud Chief restated his adherence to Left Hand's modifications, the commissioners present, Jerome and Sayre, knew that no agreement was possible at that time between the Cheyennes and Arapahoes and the government. Secretary Noble had assured them that the terms offered the Indians were liberal and need not be increased. "Do not worry with them or their lawyers much longer," the secretary advised the commissioners. "It is not worth while." The commissioners indicated their willingness to remain at Darlington for a few more days if the Indians changed their minds. Nothing happened, and the commission departed for Washington and waited for cooler weather before returning to the Southern Plains.[10]

On October 7, 1890, the full commission resumed its talks with the Cheyennes and Arapahoes. One obstacle to the talks had been removed. Chairman Jerome had demanded that the Crawford group of lawyers be eliminated from the councils because the lawyers' contract had been "utterly repudiated by Cheyennes [and] . . . the Arapahoes also disclaim it, particularly as to all outside Cherokee Outlet." Secretary Noble was embarrassed to ask the lawyers to withdraw because of his "personal consideration" for Matt Reynolds, but the secretary believed that he "must act" to complete the cession agreement. The lawyers did relinquish all claim for fees relating to the 1869 Presidential Proclamation reservation but not to fees for the services concerned with the Cherokee Outlet. Secretary Noble suggested that ultimately the lawyers' fees could be determined by the amount of money paid to the tribes for their rights to the Cherokee Outlet. Old Crow, Young Whirlwind, Little Medicine, and Little Big Jake boycotted the early sessions, making it easy for the commissioners to deal with the "progressive" Cheyennes and Arapahoes. In the interim the tribal factions had not altered. Paul Boynton, an educated Arapaho-Cheyenne acting as interpreter for Left Hand, patiently related the terms offered by the commissioners. Only with much difficulty did the chief finally understand that the government was offering about fifty cents an acre for the surplus lands. On October 10, once Left Hand understood, he appeared willing to accept the government's proposition.[11]

When the concluding speeches of the Indians were made on October 13, it was clear from Left Hand's remarks that most of the tribesmen still opposed the sale of their reservation. After the last of the oratory, Chairman Jerome proposed that Left Hand, the oldest chief present, should be the agreement's first signator. As he approached the table to make his mark on the document, almost apologizing for causing the lengthy bargaining, the Arapaho chief said, "I have asked the commission and their friends here how I was going to live and I have asked a few questions concerning parts of the treaty and now I have found out that I understand every part of it and I am willing to sign now." In accepting the agreement, Left Hand defied rumors that the first signer would be killed, and he acted, said Agent Ashley, "for the best interests of his people."[12]

Even after the chiefs who had negotiated the agreement had signed, the signatures of 75 per cent of the tribes' adult males were required before the document could be submitted for congressional approval. The commissioners remained at Darlington, assisting Agent Ashley in obtaining the signatures. Colonel James F. Wade, of Fort Reno, was asked to persuade young warriors and army scouts to sign the agreement, but many of them refused. Captain Tall Bull, a Cheyenne of the agency Indian police refused to affix his mark, and the commissioners tried to have him dismissed from the post, but Ashley retained Tall Bull despite orders from Washington. Cloud Chief, White Antelope, and Starving Elk initiated the move against Tall Bull, but when the Indian police captain did not obstruct the gathering of signatures, Ashley saw no reason to dismiss him. To increase the list of signers, women were permitted to add their names. Commissioner Jerome maintained that the women could properly sign if they were signing for deceased spouses as heads of families. But the women's names would not be counted among those needed for submission of the document to Congress. When the commissioners left Darlington in late October, 1890, they reported that 422 members of the tribes had approved the agreement.

Former Agent Miles and others interested in the contract also helped Agent Ashley gather signatures. Young, educated members of the tribes, mixed bloods, and intermarried whites helped Miles and his friends, and were promised money when the agreement was ratified. Michael Balenti, an old employee of the post traders, and his mixed-blood wife, Belle, fed Indians at his home following Jerome's request that he use his influence in behalf of the agreement. Balenti spent about $250 on his activities, but when time for the settlement came, "George [Gilbert] D. Williams, Ex-Indian Agent, . . . put his hand in his vest pocket and handed me a roll of bills . . . it amounted to Two hundred Dollars." In addition Crawford prevailed upon Paul Boynton to work among the Arapahoes. Boynton's mother was a Cheyenne, and his father was White-Eyed Antelope, an Arapaho chief. Boynton asked for $500 for his work, but on October 5, 1891, Agent Ashley called Paul into his office and informed him that D. B. Dyer wanted to see him in the next office. There Dyer counted out $150 for Boynton, who objected that the amount was less than that agreed upon. The former agent shrugged off Paul's objection, saying that he had "others to pay." The others included George Bent, Jesse Bent, Leonard Tyler, and Cleaver Warden. The four later denied that they had received money, but C. C. Painter, of the Indian Rights Association, claimed that George Bent had received at least $500 and the others had received lesser amounts.[13]

Agent Ashley pressed every possible group of adult males to obtain the necessary number of signatures. Amos Chapman was asked to use his influence among the Cheyenne and Arapaho scouts at Fort Supply to get their marks and names on the document. Chapman was informed that, if the Indians did not sign the document, the Dawes Act would be applied to them without their consent, they would receive less land, and their claims to the reservation would meet opposition in Congress and the courts.[14]

Not until November 13 did Ashley believe that 75 per cent of the adult males had signed the document. Under the terms of the 1867 Medicine Lodge Treaty that percentage of signatures was required if any subsequent land cession was made. The agreement negotiated in 1890 did just that. Consequently, Ashley offered 464 signatures or marks of Cheyenne and Arapaho men, reasoning that there were 1,585 males among the two tribes, of whom only 618 were adults. It is still charged among living Cheyennes and Arapahoes that Agent Ashley included 42 minors and 100 women among the agreement's signators. Ashley conveniently juggled the number of males in the two tribes around so that, by his reckoning, 967 of them had not yet reached the age of twenty-one. It is very unlikely, however, that almost 2,000 of the slightly more than 3,200 people of the two tribes were younger than twenty-one. The declining birth rate of the tribes because of malnutrition and venereal disease and the high incidence of tuberculosis and other diseases during the decades before 1890 indicate that Ashley's figures have little credibility. It is likely that Ashley knew that he should have submitted 680 signatures but that they were simply not available. He merely did the best he could, and never was challenged by government officials to justify his calculations.[15]

On January 29, 1891, however, a delegation of Cheyenne chiefs protested the validity of the cession agreement. Old Crow, Young Whirlwind, Little Big Jake, White Horse, White Shield, Red Moon, and Wolf Face went to Darlington, where they contested the sale of the reservation and the manner in which the councils had been held. They contended that not even a majority of the men had signed the papers and that the attorneys during the proceedings and afterward had acted without their consent. Their protests were, of course, ignored; white settlers needed more land in Oklahoma Territory.[16]

When the Cheyenne and Arapaho cession agreement was approved by Congress on March 3, 1891, the congressional act followed the terms of the conferences held at Darlington. The Cheyennes and

Arapahoes ceded all their lands except those that would become their allotments from the 1869 Presidential Proclamation reservation. The government excluded certain lands from allotment for school, military, missionary, and other purposes but stipulated that if the Indians had made improvements within sections sixteen and thirty-six of each township, which were reserved for school purposes, the government would compensate itself elsewhere for those acreages. The whole reservation was classified as agricultural and grazing land, and each allottee was to receive 160 acres of land, consisting of 80 acres of cropland and a similar amount of grazing land. All tribal members eighteen years of age or older could select their own land, while land for minors would be selected by the children's parents. Within ninety days after the approval of the agreement, the Indians were required to select their allotments; if they did not, the lands could be selected for them by the allotting agents. All allotments were protected from alienation as provided in the Dawes Act for a period of twenty-five years, at which time a title in fee simple would be issued to the allottee or his heirs.

For their surplus lands the Cheyennes and Arapahoes received $1.5 million. Sixty days after Congress approved the agreement $250,000 would be distributed among the tribesmen on a per capita basis; later a like sum would also be disbursed, but with the supervision of the secretary of the interior. One million dollars would be deposited in the United States Treasury, to bear 5 per cent interest annually, the interest to be divided each year among the tribes in a per capita payment. Annuities due under the 1867 Medicine Lodge Treaty were not disturbed, and Congress appropriated $15,000 for surveying the reservation and making the allotments. Congress also paid the Choctaws and Chickasaws $2,991,450 for their rights to the Cheyenne and Arapaho Reservation—which accounts for the Jerome Commission's reluctance to raise the amount of money paid to the Cheyennes and Arapahoes.[17]

An accurate census and allotment roll was necessary before the funds could be distributed or the lands assigned. Tribal members who were living on March 3, 1891, children born by April 19, 1891, and adopted members of the tribes were qualified for allotments. When the enrollment began on April 25, 1891, the traditionalists led by Old Crow and Young Whirlwind tried to have the reservation divided into two portions so that they could occupy the western part as an undivided reservation. At first they refused to enroll, but, when faced with the loss of rations and annuities, some of them began placing their names on the census roll. It was difficult for Agent Ashley and his assistants to group the Cheyennes and Arapahoes by families because the Indians, as in the past, when rations and annuities were to be issued, loaned their children to other families to increase the size of the family so that they could gain more of whatever was being distributed. Chiefs from the Washita and Cantonment districts refused to assist Ashley, and he was forced to rely on leaders and head men residing near Darlington. Finally a roll was completed on May 26, 1891. Three weeks later the Indians began receiving the first installment of $250,000 due them for their surplus lands.

After June 19, 1891, Cheyennes and Arapahoes began driving away from Darlington loaded down with silver dollars. Many of them immediately made their way into the towns of Oklahoma Territory along the eastern border of the reservation, where they purchased draft animals, harness, wagons, saddles, blankets, and household items. Seeing what the money could buy, the followers of the traditionalist chiefs began adding their families to the census roll. Some parents produced children not previously included on the tribal rolls to avoid sending them to school. But the same parents re-enrolled those children so that the families would share fully in the cession payment.[18]

The Cheyennes and Arapahoes hoped that the chief allotting agent would be someone who knew them and whom they trusted. Cloud Chief, Left Hand, and four other chiefs visited Ashley at Darlington and suggested that William F. Darlington, who had accompanied his father to the reservation in 1869, receive the appointment. He did not. By mid-May, 1891, Marine D. Tackett, the chief allotting agent and his crews were ready to take to the field to survey the Indians' allotments. Their work was delayed because the first cash payment to the Indians was slow in arriving at Darlington. Until the money was received, the Cheyennes and Arapahoes refused to select their lands and wandered away from Darlington back to their camps. Cloud Chief assured M. D. Tackett, who was waiting impatiently to begin work, that there would be no trouble once the money was available. Tackett considered beginning his work at once, but Indian Inspector W. W. Junkin and Ashley persuaded him to wait so that the Indians would have no grievances.[19]

Rather than giving the Indians the entire sum due, the officials doled out the first payment in $50,000 installments. With that sum in the hands of the Indians, Tackett tried to get their consent to designating their allotments. Cloud Chief refused:

We do but one thing at a time and the commissioners with who we made the treaty told us we should have our money first, when the balance of the money is paid we will then determine about the land. Our people are waiting. We have had no talk about the land & will not until all who are willing to take [payments] under the treaty get their money. Then we will determine where in the reservation we will settle.[20]

In retaliation for the delays in the payments the Cheyennes and Arapahoes dawdled in taking their lands. Only after $150,000 had been paid did Cloud Chief and his followers begin to permit their people to choose their allotments. From July 18 to September 30, 1891, when the funds appropriated by Congress had been exhausted, the Cheyennes and Arapahoes slowly took their lands. Tackett estimated at the later date that there were still about fourteen hundred Indians who had not been assigned their plots. The recalcitrant bands under Old Crow, Young Whirlwind, Red Moon, and White Shield retreated to the western portion of the reservation, refusing to accept either their money or their lands. White settlers in Oklahoma Territory waited impatiently for the completion of the allotments, since the reservation could not be opened for settlement until the process was completed. One newspaper editor, learning that the Indians were dying off, commented, "A dead Indian does not require 160 acres of land nor does it take so long to allot him."[21]

The press of Oklahoma Territory watched and reported carefully the allotting procedure. Although it was difficult to transport the silver dollars to Darlington from St. Louis, that was the only currency

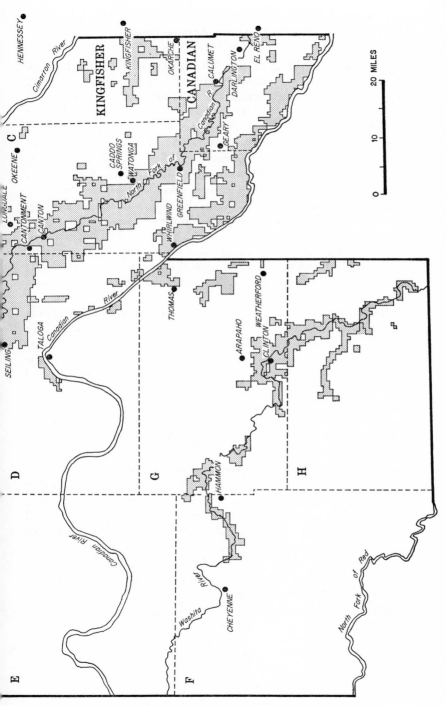

Allotments on the Cheyenne and Arapaho Reservation.

the Indians were willing to take. The money delighted the Indians. One Indian family with three or four children was observed leaving the agency with about a thousand dollars in silver spread out on an old blanket in the bottom of their wagon, "the squaw and papooses playing with the bright coins." The editor of the Kingfisher *Free Press* assured his readers after a conversation with Fenton Antelope, a twenty-year-old Cheyenne educated at Haskell, that there would be no trouble once the money was paid to the Indians. Some delays occurred because the Indians did not understand that their old gardens and farms had been located on the section lines, and they objected when their allotment had to conform to the regular survey lines. Most of the early allotments were taken in the Canadian and Washita River valleys and along Deer Creek. But Chief Allotting Agent Tackett and the press thought that the Indians were being treated too generously, since each family was receiving far more land than it could possibly use.[22]

Even before Tackett's crews were in the field, citizens of Oklahoma Territory were demanding that the reservation be opened no later than October 1, 1891. At a mass meeting held in El Reno resolutions were passed calling for the earliest possible opening date for the reservation so that white settlers could select their homesteads, build their homes, and plant their crops by March, 1892. The gathering also wanted those reservations available for settlement to be opened simultaneously so that the eastern areas of Oklahoma Territory would not receive the bulk of the new population. It was believed that, unless some such procedure was established, speculators could buy up land and sell it later to disappointed homeseekers for large profits.[23]

Territorial Governor A. J. Seay also supported the early opening of the Cheyenne-Arapaho Reservation. He contended that, unless the lands were available for settlement in the spring of 1892, "it will mean great hardship, destitution, sickness and death among hundreds of settlers," whose numbers were rapidly increasing along the borders of the reservation. Agent Ashley denied the governor's allegation and emphasized the need for the Indians to receive their lands before the country was opened to settlement.[24]

When the allotting crews ceased work, merchants and real-estate promoters in El Reno and Kingfisher chafed at the delay. It was claimed that they and their fellow citizens were willing to pay the salaries of new allotting crews if Congress did not. Otherwise, it was feared, such towns as Guthrie and Oklahoma City situated on the Santa Fe Railroad would predominate in territorial politics and would enjoy a more rapid population growth than other cities in the new territory. Yet such favoritism was not reflected in the statehood convention held in Oklahoma City on December 15, 1891, which called for Congress to pass a deficiency appropriation so that the Cheyenne-Arapaho Reservation could be opened in time for the settlers to plant a spring crop in 1892.[25]

Commissioner of Indian Affairs Thomas Morgan invited a delegation of Cheyenne and Arapaho chiefs to Washington in December, 1891. His purpose was to talk the chiefs into persuading their people to speed up the selection of their allotments, using as bait the $250,000 installment still due the tribes. Commissioner Morgan had heard that the Indians were buying old carriages, wagons, and "broken down" horses and mules from "unscrupulous and intriguing traders." Some of the information came from Kingfisher businessmen, who did not appreciate that fact that El Reno was receiving most of the business— E. F. Mitchell, of El Reno, had reportedly sold thirty thousand dollars' worth of horses and mules to the Indians. A Kingfisher newspaper claimed, "It is quite probable that the Indians have paid the amount named for the horses and mules, but it would be no doubt, much nearer the truth to say that they had paid thirty thousand dollars for about fifteen thousand dollars worth of horses and mules." It was also reported to the office of the secretary of the interior by Governor G. W. Steele of Oklahoma Territory that the Cheyennes and Arapahoes were "being cheated outrageously in the purchase of horses and mules and other supplies." Cloud Chief, Little Chief, Left Hand, and Row-of-Lodges, however, tried to dispel the commissioner's apprehensions, especially since Mitchell was traveling with the party.

Mitchell had already sold a large number of animals to the Indians and was probably looking for additional profits when more money became available. Cloud Chief maintained that he had personally inspected many of the wagons and animals and had also made many of the arrangements for the sales. Commissioner Morgan, who was eager for the opening to take place quickly, did not press the matter beyond warning the delegates that "there are a great many very mean white men that will cheat the Indian if they can." Concluding his meeting with the delegation, Commissioner Morgan assured them that the secretary of the interior had approved the distribution of the second $250,000, and the chiefs went home to await the second series of payments, which began in the spring of 1892.[26]

Early in 1892, Congress provided more money for surveying and allotting the reservation. To speed up the process a suggestion had been made that the allotting crews and supervisors should be citizens of Oklahoma Territory. Agent Ashley, Indian Inspector Junkin, and Chief Allotting Agent Tackett defeated the move because they felt that Tackett's men could complete the assignment more rapidly than new inexperienced crews and "with better satisfaction to the Indians."[27]

While the allotting crews were waiting to return to work, more Cheyennes and Arapahoes were added to the final tribal roll. Cloud Chief and Left Hand proved to Agent Ashley's satisfaction that a number of men and women had returned to the reservation to accept the money and allotments due them under the 1891 agreement. Some, such as Sharp Nose Woman, the mother of Robert Burns, had lived in the north for more than twenty years. After her husband had been killed at Sand Creek in 1864, Sharp Nose Woman had married either a Northern Cheyenne or an Arapaho man named Rock or Stone, with whom she lived until 1884. Since Rock had "thrown Sharp Nose Woman and her children away," there was no reason for her to remain in the north away from her son and relatives. A few other people who had been living among the Kiowas and thirteen children born between April 24 and June 18, 1891, were also added to the roll.

One of the twenty-four names added to the roll was Kiowa Dutch, for whom Agent Ashley made a special plea. Kiowa Dutch had been captured by the Kiowas and sold to the Bent family as a slave. He had resided among the Cheyennes for thirty-five years, had received his share of the annuities and goods since the Medicine Lodge Treaty, and had signed the original roll and agreement in 1891. Despite all this, neither the Cheyennes nor the Arapahoes were willing to approve the man as an allottee. Ashley believed that Kiowa Dutch was a member of the Cheyennes, even though he was not recognized by the tribe, and he recommended that his name be allowed to remain on the allotment roll. On March 23, 1892, the commissioner of Indian affairs, approved all the Indian agent's recommendations.[28]

Secretary of the Interior Noble exerted pressure on those Cheyennes and Arapahoes who were refusing to accept their allotments. He sent notices to them stating that they had until February 22, 1892, to take their land, after which time he would have their allotments selected for them. He said that they must accept their share of the payment or the money would be placed in the United States Treasury and that it would be difficult for them to obtain their funds at a later date. So that their fellow tribesmen would add to the pressure, Noble also threatened to withhold the second $250,000 until all allotments were completed. He instructed Ashley to see that the tribes understood the notice, but he also said that he was not going to "cut them off from selections, even after the 22nd of February." He hoped to see the reservation ready for white settlement by April 1, 1892, because, "Unless this land is opened early settlers may lose their crops for this year."[29]

On February 8, 1892, Tackett and his crews resumed the allotment of fourteen hundred Cheyennes and Arapahoes who had not yet been assigned land. They first worked in the Cantonment District, where the Indians had previously refused to take allotments. They next moved to the upper Washita River, where they remained until the allotments were completed on March 29, 1892. When they had finished, Tackett and his men had assigned 3,329 allotments to the Cheyennes and Arapahoes. Of the 4,294,415 acres of the reservation the Cheyennes and Arapahoes retained 529,692 acres, while 231,828 were reserved for school or educational purposes and 32,343 were set aside for military reservations. Slightly more than 3.5 million acres were available for homesteaders.[30]

The allotting agent faced some difficult problems, not all of which were resolved to the benefit of the Indians. In 1885, John H. Seger had led a group of Cheyennes and Arapahoes to the Washita River on the southern boundary of the reservation. There he had assisted some of the people in selecting desirable lands upon which they subsequently built homes. As a result of a survey made in 1883, because Caddoes and other tribes objected to the location of a cattleman's range when the reservation was rented, it was found that the settlement was within the boundary of the Cheyenne-Arapaho Reservation. The official survey in 1891, however, proved that some of Seger's colonists were living on the lands of the Wichita and Affiliated Bands. By the time the error was discovered, the good land had already been taken, and some "progressive and desirable" Indians were some distance away. C. C. Painter, of the Indian Rights Association, charged that, when the Indians finally examined their allotments, they found them on a barren, infertile tract. Seger's plea to the "heart [rather] than . . . the head to get justice for the Indians" was ignored by Indian Commissioner Morgan.[31]

A. L. McPherson, one of the allotting agents, also tried to assist Seger's colonists. He stated that no Caddoes or Wichitas were settled close to the line and that they did not intend to use the land for agricultural purposes. There was no good reason for "disturbing these Indians especially since Article 4 of the 1891 agreement provided that the Indians could remain on tracts they had cultivated and improved." McPherson asked the commissioner of Indian affairs to give the question his immediate attention so that "these poor fellows" could be given all possible assistance. Nevertheless, some of the people whom Seger had assisted were denied permission to retain their farms and were moved to inferior allotments.[32]

A similar problem also arose involving some mixed bloods and intermarried whites who had settled east of the reservation in Oklahoma Country. Under the Treaty of Medicine Lodge any member of the tribes who was a head of a family could select 320 acres for farming purposes on the reservation. There was again some uncertainty about the actual location of the reservation boundary line. In 1876, John D. Miles, then Indian agent, had supervised the lands selected by three intermarried whites, Herman Hauser, Benjamin F. Keith, and Peter Shields, near the eastern boundary of the reservation. During the controversy over removing the cattlemen in 1885, these

176

men were ordered to shift their farms back to the reservation by Secretary of the Interior Lamar, but the order was reversed nine months later. Thus, when the boundaries of the reservation were finally fixed, all three farms were still within the Unassigned Lands. Before the region was opened for settlement on April 22, 1889, the whites knew that their choice farms were in jeopardy because the newcomers would quickly file claims on the improved and fertile lands. Hauser, an old enlisted soldier, wrote to his former army officers seeking help. As the natural guardian of six mixed-blood children, Hauser said, he had worked hard to develop two quarter sections of land. From 1876 to 1889 no question had been raised about Hauser and the other families living off the reservation. "I have been warned," Hauser wrote to Colonel J. J. Coppinger, "by well-meaning friends that I must lose no time in making my claim to these improvements as otherwise I would lose them. . . . As I understand it, relief now lies in the hands of the President of the United States, and as delay means ruin, I am bold enough, Colonel, to ask you if you cannot help me." John Poisal, a mixed blood, the Keiths, and the Shieldses were in the same condition as Hauser.

At first Secretary Noble protected the four farmers from the claims of other homesteaders. He ruled that the head of the family and his wife could each file for 160 acres of land under the Homestead and Dawes acts. The wives' portions of the farms were treated as allotments. Although the secretary of the interior signed the needed documents, the patents were never delivered to the Indian wives. Then the Indian wives and their children also applied for allotments on the Cheyenne-Arapaho Reservation. The question arose whether or not they would be allowed to retain their interest in the Oklahoma Country farms and still qualify for additional allotments.[33]

Samuel J. Crawford began pressing Washington officials to allow the families to claim both their farms and allotments on the reservation. The Kansas lawyer, who had offices in Washington, claimed that his clients, Mrs. Hauser and her six children, had "by error or oversight been denied and deprived of their right" to select allotments. As members of the Cheyenne tribe they could not be denied their allotments any more than they could be denied the right to share in

177

the funds available from the sale of the surplus lands of the reservation. To cover all possible future claims, Crawford submitted a
complete list of the Hauser, Shields, and Keith families and called
particular attention to the fact that Louise and Annie Hauser and
Peter Shields had had their names struck from the allotment roll.
After quoting Article 3 of the 1891 agreement, which specifically gave
all Cheyennes and Arapahoes the right to allotments, Crawford
argued, "If this does not give these people the right to select or have
selected for them each 160 acres of land, then language it seems to me
has no meaning and human reason is a mith [sic]."[34]

Crawford won the first round of the struggle in Washington. Assistant Secretary of the Interior G. W. Shields recommended that, since
preliminary, adverse judgments had already been rendered in the
courts against the allotments of the Indian wives and their children in
Oklahoma Territory, it might be wise to reserve lands for them on
the reservation. Allotments were rapidly being completed, and the
reservation would soon be opened to settlement. There was a possibility that the Indian families would be without any land on which
to make their homes if the unfavorable decisions against them continued. In making his recommendation, Shields concluded that, if
the lands reserved for the Indian families were not needed, they
could always be opened for settlement at a later date.[35]

For a time the farms appeared to be safe from conflicting claims.
Thomas H. Carter, commissioner of the General Land Office, informed the commissioner of Indian affairs on March 23, 1892, that a
claimant's request for the allotment of a minor heir of Herman
Hauser had been rejected. This decision was followed on April 10,
1892, by Secretary Noble's judgment that the Shieldses, Keiths, and
Hausers should be settled on their farms under the Dawes Act. He
did not, however, agree that the tribal members should also be given
allotments on the tribes' former reservation because, in Noble's opinion, "one home was all that was contemplated by Congress."[36]

Despite the favorable decisions in Washington, the Shieldses,
Keiths, and Hausers still faced the loss of their farms. James Mills, a
white man looking for improved land, took possession of the Keiths'
farm. Mills told Charles Keith that if he went to the farm for any

purpose "there would be one less Keith in the world." The United States attorney for Oklahoma Territory refused to intervene in the dispute, and Agent Ashley looked about for a means to avoid costly litigation. Another interloper, William Adams, tried to gain possession of the personal property and the lands of the Hauser family. Hauser had died in December, 1891, leaving William Biggert, an employee of a Fort Reno post trader, as his executor. Adams claimed that when he worked for Hauser as a hired hand he had an informal agreement with Hauser to care for the latter's stock, consisting of fifty head of cattle and horses and forty hogs for one-half interest in the animals. Only after considerable difficulty was Adams foiled in his efforts to take possession of the Hauser homestead and the allotments of the widow, Amy Hauser, and her children. For several years Ashley and his successors were able to keep the Indian families on their farms east of the old reservation line.[37]

For two years the families had no more problems. Then in 1893 for some reason Major A. E. Woodson, who succeeded Ashley, reopened the issues. Woodson reasoned that Mrs. Hauser had taken two allotments, one under the Dawes Act and one under the 1891 agreement. Perhaps Agent Woodson became irritated with Mrs. Hauser when she refused to sell her Dawes Act allotment for three hundred dollars in cash and another nine hundred to be deposited in a bank, to be expended upon improving an allotment on the old reservation. Mrs. Hauser, the Indian agent reported, wanted the whole price in cash. This arrangement he refused to approve since "she would make no good use of the money—but divide it with the hungry horde that are prompting her to make such demand."[38]

Rumors circulated that Woodson was trying to force the Hausers, Keiths, and Shieldses to abandon their farms east of El Reno. Immediately four white claimants appeared and took possession of the families' improvements and wheat crops. Keith, who had fought hard for his land, complained to the commissioner of Indian affairs that Agent Woodson was "incompetent to fill the position" of Indian agent because of his long army experience and because he was "so cross and crabbed, that the Indians are afraid to go near him." Woodson, however, persisted in his effort to force the families to abandon their farms and accept the allotments set aside for them on the reservation. The land to which Woodson wanted them to move was described by Keith as "on a high dry ridge, without water, timber or improvements of any kind. We do not like to be humiliated further by going to the Agent, nor do we wish to take the law in our own hands."[39]

Before Keith's letter arrived in Washington, Secretary of the Interior Hoke Smith overruled the decisions of his predecessors. Since the Keith, Shields, and Hauser families had been allowed land under the 1891 agreement, they were precluded from receiving lands under the Dawes Act. Secretary Smith rejected the arguments of the families' lawyer that they were entitled to lands under both the 1891 agreement and the Dawes Act. The intent of the acts, in Smith's mind, was to give the Indians only one home on a tract of land, by which action they could dissolve their tribal relationships and become "civilized" citizens of the United States. The secretary could have added that these families were at least as civilized as the new settlers who had flooded into Oklahoma Territory. Smith's decision turned on the fact that the lands under the 1891 Agreement had been patented whereas under the Dawes Act the patents to the farms were still retained in Washington. Once lands were patented, Smith held, they passed from the control of the Department of Interior other than for trust purposes.[40]

Mrs. Mary E. Keith, the wife of Benjamin Keith, appealed the secretary's decision. Since January 21, 1895, she protested to the Indian agent, John Baldwin and James Mills had been in possession of her land, and they were living in her house with their families. They were benefiting from a farm that was enclosed by a good fence and contained more than fifty acres of wheat. She pleaded:

It would be a hardship to compel me to surrender the home where I have lived over twenty years, cultivate and improve it and commence anew upon a tract of new, unproductive land among the sand-hills of Kingfisher County. . . . It is over thirty-five miles from my present home; it is cut up with a small creek and several ravines and but a small portion of it [is] fit for cultivation.[41]

Eleven months later Secretary Smith reversed his decision as it applied to Mrs. Keith. She was allowed to retain her lands in Canadian County provided her husband would join her in signing a reconveyance to the government for her allotment reserved under the 1891 agreement. All other members of the families, however, were forced to accept allotments assigned to them on the Cheyenne-Arapaho Reservation, much to their economic detriment.[42]

As the time to open the reservation approached, the chiefs tried to delay the influx of settlers. On April 4, 1892, Cloud Chief, Left Hand, and Row-of-Lodges protested that not all the conditions of the cession agreement had been met. They reminded Ashley that some of the Indians had received neither their share of the cash payments nor the interest due them from the one million dollars on deposit in the United States Treasury. More importantly, they also pointed out, fifty to sixty Indians had died before the allotments were assigned. Those Indians, the chiefs asserted, had selected their lands, but the tracts had not been allotted because congressional appropriations for surveying the reservation had been exhausted. If their lands were not restored to the roll, their heirs would suffer considerable loss.[43]

Pressures had risen too high for the opening of the reservation to be delayed. On April 8, 1892, therefore, E. F. Weigel, special inspector of the Department of Interior, received final instructions to open the Cheyenne and Arapaho Reservation at twelve o'clock noon, April 19, 1892. Of the millions of acres once controlled by the tribes, they now retained only 529,692 acres. Even that small remnant would in another ten years begin to slip away from their possession because of the acts of Congress and the greed of land-hungry farmers and landjobbers.[44]

CHAPTER VII

White Neighbors Arrive

AT HIGH NOON on April 19, 1892, between twenty-five and thirty-thousand settlers made a run into the Cheyenne-Arapaho Reservation, and immediately began a new era for the Cheyennes and Arapahoes. The tribesmen had long been in contact with white men but never as neighbors and never in such overwhelming numbers. Within a few hours the Cheyennes and Arapahoes became a minority, constituting about 10 per cent of the population among the farmers, small ranchers, and inhabitants of the small towns in the six counties that had formerly constituted the Cheyenne-Arapaho Reservation. As citizens of the United States and Oklahoma Territory the Indians in theory possessed all the rights and privileges of citizenship with their lands and property protected from alienation under the terms of the Dawes Act and other legislation. In practice, however, it was difficult to guard the Indians against the prejudices and the avariciousness of the new residents and officials of the Cheyenne-Arapaho country.[1]

Agent Ashley succeeded in preventing conflict between the settlers and the Indians during the land run. He advised the tribes just before the opening of the lands to go to their allotments and warn off whites who might attempt to establish claims on their land. According to Agent Ashley's instructions, if whites appeared on an Indian allotment, the Cheyennes and Arapahoes were to assist them in finding unallotted land and to help them as much as possible. The Indian agent also attempted unsuccessfully to have Territorial Governor

Abraham J. Seay appoint "two intelligent and competent Indians" as county officers to ease the frictions between the two groups. To further reduce likely troubles with the homeseekers, the chiefs and head men gathered most of their people in two large camps so that the young men of the tribes could better be controlled. Food was distributed throughout the tribes so that hunger would not cause additional discontent, especially among the Cheyennes, who believed that "the sale of the surplus lands . . . was not authorized by a majority of their people." To assure sufficient rations, Commissioner T. J. Morgan and Secretary of the Interior Noble sought a supplementary appropriation from Congress for the Cheyennes and Arapahoes because their 1892–93 allocation had been reduced from $125,000 to $60,000. It had been anticipated that the Indians would reserve sufficient funds to meet their needs from the interest payment on the tribal reserve in the United States Treasury. Secretary Noble called the reduction a "serious mistake" and obtained an additional $50,000 to maintain an adequate food supply for the Cheyennes and Arapahoes.[2]

The Cheyennes and Arapahoes did not remain entirely in the large camps when the settlers came pouring into their former reservation. Some stayed on their allotments in small camps to participate in Ghost Dances. The leader of the Ghost Dance, Sitting Bull (a Northern Arapaho also known as Scabby Bull), had gained a large following among his southern kinsmen, among whom was Left Hand, one of the Arapahoes' most influential chiefs. Although the Ghost Dance ceremonies did not threaten the settlers with violence and the Arapahoes tried to hold their dances secretly, the new residents knew full well when they occurred, and they were a little restive about the Indians' belief that they would be restored to control of the earth when Wovoka appeared. Of greater immediate concern, however, were the threats of conflict in the western portion of the land under the jurisdiction of the agency.[3]

Red Moon, White Shield, and Spotted Horse and their bands had bitterly opposed the sale of the reservation in 1890. Within two weeks after the opening of the reservation, garbled reports reached Agent Ashley and Governor Seay that Red Moon and White Shield, leading one hundred warriors, had informed the settlers of County F that they had three days to leave their claims. The officers of County F panicked, as did Governor Seay, who requested that troops be sent immediately into the western counties to protect the lives and property of the settlers. The governor even visited Darlington on May 6 with what he considered proof that White Shield and Red Moon were at the county seat of County F with two hundred warriors. He asked that a "company of soldiers . . . be sent at once to prevent a possible massacre of whites." Agent Ashley knew that Governor Seay's information was misleading because the bands of the two chiefs consisted of no more than forty-six males fifteen years of age or over and that the entire population of the bands, including women and children, did not exceed two hundred.[4]

The Cheyennes of the western bands were not guiltless. They were using the same threats to intimidate the settlers that they had used on the cattlemen when they exacted tribute on the cattle herds moving to Kansas in the 1870's and 1880's. When the allotting agents appeared in 1891 to assign allotments, the dissident Cheyennes ran the agents off, and they thought that the same bluff would work on the settlers. At worst, commented Amos Chapman, the old army scout who was married to one of Stone Calf's daughters, though Red Moon and White Shield were "somewhat bad," they harbored thoughts of deeds they dared not do. They tried to intimidate the settlers, but there was no real danger in the western counties.[5]

Probably the source of the rumors was the movement of the bands from their allotments near present Hammon, Oklahoma, toward Cantonment to receive the second payment of money due from the sale of the reservation. Without hesitation Red Moon, White Shield, Spotted Horse, and Elk River agreed to go to Darlington for a conference with Agent Ashley and Colonel Wade, the commanding officer of Fort Reno. During the council the four chiefs denied completely the allegations made by the officers of County F and Governor Seay. Instead they placed the blame entirely on the county officials, who, they maintained, created the rumors so that the Indians would be removed from their allotments, making them available for settlers. Once Ashley heard the accounts of the chiefs, he charged that the officers disseminated the scare stories "for improper purposes," and he added that, if the officers persisted in such irresponsible conduct, they were "unfit persons to hold any office" under the governor's control.[6]

Once convinced that there was no real threat of violence on the part of the Indians, Ashley countered with his own accusations. The new settlers, he protested, "have stolen the Indian's fence posts, wire, burned and shot through his teepee, abused and misrepresented him, and, in one instance when the husband was not home attempted to assault his wife." Civil officers closed their eyes to the settlers' depredations on Indian property, Ashley maintained, and if the depredations continued, he believed, they would "result in retaliation and consequent disaster to the Indians," a result he was trying to avoid. Governor Seay acknowledged little except to admit that apparently the Cheyennes and Arapahoes had abandoned "going on the war path." He hoped, however, to promote "good understanding and good feeling" between the Indians and their new neighbors so that both groups could "enjoy without disruption or fear all the rights guaranteed to them by the laws of Congress and the Territory."[7]

Fear and tension persisted in the two westernmost counties of the Cheyenne-Arapaho country. On November 20, 1893, a Texas cowboy, Tom O'Hara, alias Red Tom, followed Wolf Hair from the town of Cheyenne for about a mile and shot him dead. When Wolf Hair's friends among Red Moon's and Spotted Horse's bands heard of the "unprovoked murder," they vowed to avenge the young man's death. Agent A. E. Woodson, who had succeeded Ashley as acting Indian agent at Darlington, pleaded with Red Moon and Spotted Horse to prevent their people from committing any unlawful acts. He urged them not to try to "get possession of this man," but to "wait patiently and let the law take its course; you may rest assured that every effort will be made to bring this man to a speedy trial and just punishment." The Cheyennes remained quiet and even obeyed Woodson's admonition not to kill the settlers' horses and cattle in retaliation for the murder of Wolf Hair.[8]

A coroner's jury quickly indicted Tom O'Hara for first-degree murder, but four months elapsed before an assistant United States attorney recommended that the cowboy be tried before a local court.

As the months dragged on, O'Hara's friends began to make efforts to free him from jail. A judge from a neighboring county was prevailed upon to issue a writ of habeas corpus, and only with difficulty did Agent Woodson prevent the release of the man. When it became apparent that public prosecutors would do little to obtain a conviction of O'Hara, the Cheyennes and Arapahoes raised money to obtain additional legal counsel for the trial. To assure some fairness and to remove the trial from an area dominated by cattlemen and cowboys, a change of venue was obtained, and O'Hara was tried in Canadian County. When the case went to trial in December, 1894, an all-white jury heard the evidence, deliberated for two days, and returned a verdict of not guilty. The decision to free O'Hara was greeted with derision by a Cheyenne newspaper editor, who called the verdict a "farce."[9]

While O'Hara was still in jail awaiting trial, another shooting took place in County F. W. S. Breeding and T. S. Carter, two white men who had moved into the county from Texas, rode into Chief Hill's camp, threw a rope around the neck of an unbranded pony, and began to lead it away. When Chief Hill objected and tried to remove the rope, Breeding drew his six-shooter and at point-blank range shot the Cheyenne twice through the right lung. Desperately wounded, Chief Hill managed to stagger to his lodge, get his Winchester, and kill Breeding. Believing that he was still in danger, Chief Hill then turned on Carter and fired one more round, which broke the latter's arm. Three shots in all were fired by Chief Hill, shots that killed one and seriously wounded the second of the white thieves. Carter fled, carrying the news to the white community. Soon a large number of mounted, well-armed men were searching the countryside for Indians. An Indian policeman sent by John H. Seger from Colony was intercepted by fifty to sixty white men. They probably would have killed the policeman if he had not been carrying letters from the sheriff of Roger Mills County to Agent Woodson.[10]

The small Indian camps in Roger Mills County were in turmoil, particularly the camp of Big White Man, in which Chief Hill lived. The settlers in the county were not content with information that Chief Hill was expected to die, and they organized to take matters into their own hands. A news release of Carter's version of the shooting only heightened the anger of the settlers. The blame was placed on Chief Hill, who, it was claimed, threw a cartridge into his Winchester before Breeding had drawn his gun. Rather than three shots, Carter asserted, many shots were fired, which led the white mob to conclude that more than one Indian was involved in the shooting. Bands of armed men began prowling through the western counties, and some of them rode directly to Big White Man's camp and demanded that the Indian who had killed Breeding and wounded Carter be surrendered to them.[11]

The territorial press blew the shooting into a series of bushwacking fights between the Indians and cowboys. According to the newspapers' version, twenty-eight Indians and fourteen soldiers and settlers had been killed before sheriff's posses from counties G and H had surrounded the Indians on the upper Washita. Trouble had been brewing for some time in the western counties, newspapers commented, because white men had been pasturing cattle on Indian allotments contrary to the wishes of the Indians. For their part the Indians had been raiding the cattlemen's herds, and one such raid had occurred the night before the fighting erupted. The fighting had ended, and the troops who had been rushed from Fort Reno had the Indians under control.[12]

Despite the presence of a deputy United States marshal, a justice of the peace, and a detachment of cavalry, eighty white men forced the law officers to seize Roman Nose and Thunder as "hostages." Only with difficulty did the officers maintain the prisoners in their custody, and the mob reluctantly dispersed when the officer in charge of the cavalry told the whites that if they wanted trouble "they could not start it too quick to suit him." Chief Hill was not arrested at the camp because of his critical wounds, and he denied that any other men were present in the camp when Breeding and Carter arrived. Fearing for their safety, the Indians in Big White Man's camp moved farther down the Washita River to live with Young Whirlwind's people, temporarily abandoning their allotments.

The Texans who had settled Roger Mills County had no love for the Indians. One former resident of the county stated that his neighbors would "like no better fun than the job of killing those d——— Indians." It was common knowledge that a rancher in the western counties would "buy a pony and steal four." In addition, a cattleman was overheard remarking when Prairie Chief's sister died, "Another Indian dead; I wish they were all dead."[13]

To protect the lives of Roman Nose and Thunder, Captain George K. Hunter, with a cavalry detachment, escorted the two men to Fort Reno to await trial. An indictment for manslaughter returned against the two Indians by a grand jury, despite the absence of any evidence that they were in the vicinity of Chief Hill's camp when the shooting occurred, gave substance to Agent Woodson's fears that it would be impossible to obtain a fair trial in either Roger Mills or Custer counties. Woodson watched carefully the events related to the imprisonment of the two Indians and personally gave the necessary bond of five hundred dollars to free the men before the trial took place. He also arranged for the men to appear in court and provided that they would be defended by a competent attorney and that the friends of Roman Nose and Thunder from the Red Moon District could be present in court on November 14, 1894, when the trial began. Both Roman Nose and Thunder were declared not guilty, and they returned to their people. Finally, in late April, 1895, the case against Chief Hill was dismissed. The trouble arose, in the opinion of the judge, because of "encroachments of white men and was not premeditated by the Indians."[14]

Prejudice against the Indians in western Oklahoma Territory was also manifested when Cosah Red Lodge was accused of rape. Early in June, 1895, an elderly white woman was assaulted by an Indian outside the town of Arapaho. By June 11, 1895, Red Lodge was under arrest and confined to save him from irate citizens, who were offering sixty-five dollars and a pony if the young man was turned over to them. Although Woodson assumed that Red Lodge was guilty of the crime, he nevertheless ordered Richard Davis, a full-blood Cheyenne Agency farmer and a Carlisle graduate, to arrange for counsel to defend the young Cheyenne. Through Davis, Woodson warned the young men in the district that they "cannot be too careful in their intercourse with whites," because offenses "of this character will set all the white people . . . against them and result in bad feeling on their part and great injury to the Indians."[15]

There was a baseball game in Arapaho one afternoon, and the sheriff of County G wanted to watch the local athletes play ball. Since Arapaho was without a jail, the sheriff took Red Lodge with him to the ball game. There he deputized a number of men to guard and protect the prisoner, but the crowd was ready to kill Red Lodge on the spot. As the mob surged toward him, Red Lodge jumped from the buggy in which he was being held and motioned for the deputies to shoot him. Red Lodge, who could not speak or understand English, acted out the role of a warrior. He pointed to his chest and head and by signs told the whites to kill him. When the sheriff emptied his six-shooter at Red Lodge but missed, cowboys swinging their lariats tried to capture Red Lodge as he ran toward the oncoming crowd. Finally someone managed to shoot Red Lodge in the abdomen, and the mob began beating and stabbing him into insensibility and left him for dead.

George Coleman, one of the agency farmers, examined Red Lodge, found him still alive, and took him to a physician in Arapaho. To be shielded from additional maltreatment, Red Lodge was placed in the custody of Captain J. C. Mackay, who had brought his troop of cavalry to Arapaho to safeguard other Indians from the whites. All of this was needless, because upon investigation and the testimony of six Cheyennes who knew both men, it was learned that Little Man, not Red Lodge, was the rapist. Little Man was not to be found, and the woman admitted that she had been mistaken in identifying Red Lodge as her assailant. At the trial six other Indians and four whites from Watonga testified in Red Lodge's behalf, saying that he was in Watonga when the woman was assaulted, and he was declared innocent by the jury.[16]

Not all Indians accused of crimes were innocent. Howling Wolf, a Cheyenne, was found guilty of raping a young woman near Watonga in mid-April, 1893. After Howling Wolf's arrest, he was placed in jail in Watonga, but it was found necessary to send him to Kingfisher with an escort of fifteen men. Even in Kingfisher, W. M. Pulling, the issue clerk at Cantonment, feared for Howling Wolf's life because five men, probably the girl's relatives, had trailed the party to that city vowing to lynch the Indian if possible. Howling Wolf escaped from jail and hid among his relatives and friends, who defied the Blaine County sheriff when he tried to seize the fugitive. Agent Woodson finally arranged for Howling Wolf to stand trial. He was convicted and, after serving a short term, reported back to Cantonment, where he said that he regretted his crime and promised to settle down on his allotment.[17]

The property of the Cheyennes and Arapahoes was in jeopardy from their white neighbors. Short of cash and stock for their own agricultural activities, whites looked upon the Indians' possessions as a means of supplementing their resources. In the eastern counties of the Cheyenne-Arapaho country a territorial herd law required each landowner or farmer to fence in his cattle, swine, and horses. It was easy for a white to seize an Indian's animals as strays, holding them until the Indian could informally redeem them without going to court. If the Indian had no money, the animals were usually appropriated for the use of the white neighbor or sold for what they would bring in a nearby town. Without much effect Agent Woodson appealed for legal assistance so that the Cheyennes and Arapahoes would not be robbed of their property. The cases involving the appropriation of Indian property were so numerous that Woodson could not even list them all in his correspondence to the Indian Office. Even George Bent had some of his property seized and sold by a merchant for an alleged debt; the only assistance the Indian agent could offer Bent was a letter threatening the merchant with a law suit if restitution was not made.[18]

To emphasize the problems of the Cheyennes and Arapahoes, Agent Woodson forwarded to the Indian Office a letter of complaint written by a Cheyenne woman. Mrs. Mollie Short Teeth, who lived near Kingfisher, was trying to help some of her friends because the Indian policeman of the district, a man described by her as "only good to eat and sleep, he go nowhere, looks after nothing," was of no help to the Indians. A Mr. Bannerd seized twelve ponies belonging to White Bear and High Wolf because they could not satisfy the man's demands for fifty cents a head for alleged damages to his crops.

Since the two men had no money, Mrs. Short Teeth offered Bannerd $1.50 in cash and one of her hogs, which, upon inspection, he refused to accept. "Please Agent," wrote Mrs. Short Teeth, "see what you can do for these men; they are willing to pay but they have nothing to pay *now*." Woodson's accompanying letter to the commissioner of Indian affairs emphasized that the Indians without money or means to defend themselves in the local courts frequently gave or sold away their other animals to satisfy claims for damages assessed by farmers. In addition to the seizure of stock, Woodson wrote, tools, farming implements, saddles, and other personal property were stolen by whites who had no respect for an Indian or his property.[19]

Even if an offending white was brought to court, there was little chance that an all-white jury would render a verdict favorable to an Indian. Wrote Agent Woodson:

The poor Indians, ignorant of their rights under the law in many instances quietly submit to . . . imposition rather than attempt to defend themselves or their property. Such people dare not trespass on the rights of white persons for fear of speedy punishment; but [the whites] . . . have no such fear in plundering Indian houses, and frequently do so with impunity.

An appeal to the United States attorney was usually a futile attempt to remedy wrongs against Indians because he was almost always too busy with other and, to him, more important matters.[20]

Failing to arouse much sympathy or assistance from his superiors in Washington or from federal officials in Oklahoma Territory, Woodson appealed to the Indians' fellow white citizens. When Pawnee Man, a former Dog Soldier leader who had previously farmed a patch of ground on the agency reserve, moved to his own allotment, Woodson wrote a letter of introduction for Pawnee Man to his neighbors so that he "might show the people of his neighborhood the kind of man he is. I hope they will all treat him kindly and protect him in his rights as a citizen." The agent also gave White Buffalo, an Arapaho, a letter when he could not gain the effective use of his allotment because whites were grazing cattle on his land. They were apprised that "the rights of this Indian are the same as white citizens, and they must respect them . . . [and] when stock trespasses upon

191

his allotments that he is privileged under the law to take up the same and hold it for such damages as it may commit, or as strays." Finally Woodson did receive some assistance from the United States attorney when whites were illegally stripping Indian allotments of timber. But before the crimes were stopped, walnut, hickory, and cedar logs had been shipped through El Reno in railroad carload lots.[21]

Whites employed ingenious methods in fleecing the Indians of their money and property. Man-on-a-Cloud, a Cheyenne living near Watonga, made a trip away from the agency and left his wagon with a liveryman in the town for safekeeping. The liveryman used the wagon for his business during the Indian's absence, but when Man-on-a-Cloud returned the businessman demanded an exorbitant fee for caring for the wagon. When the Cheyenne could not pay, the liveryman obtained a chattel mortgage on the wagon and immediately threatened foreclosure. Pressure from the agency, however, delayed the proceedings in the county court until an agreement was reached between the two parties.

Even Indian policemen performing their duties were not immune from scheming whites. Black Man, a Cheyenne serving as a policeman at Watonga, was ordered to remove a flock of sheep that were illegally grazing on some Indian allotments. One of the sheep was accidentally killed during the removal, and Black Man took the carcass home. Although the owner had been previously ordered to remove his sheep by the county judge, he received two of Black Man's horses as compensation for his loss. Black Man eventually recovered one of his ponies.[22]

There is substantial evidence that Agent Woodson was not really being candid when in his 1895 report he maintained that the situation was improving. The Cheyennes and Arapahoes, he asserted, were "no longer at the mercy of unscrupulous and designing individuals who once fattened and grew rich on the spoils of traffic with them, while they are fast imbibing a knowledge that renders them able to drive a shrewd bargain and to obtain full value of their merchandise." Well after he made his report Woodson continued to complain that whites were stealing Indians' timber, farming tools, and implements. The crops and gardens of Indian farmers were frequently destroyed by stray stock owned by whites. Even if the guilty parties were brought to trial, Woodson wrote later, "the penalties imposed have been extremely light, and in many instances, conviction before juries insensible to the rights of the Indians has failed." Although a number of Indians testified in a case, the cumulative evidence rarely offset the statements of a single white man. "To steal from the Indians or the Government," Woodson told the commissioner of Indian affairs, "does not impress such unscrupulous persons as being a serious offence, and with them it is seemingly considered cause for self-congratulation when they can do so with impunity."[23]

Another form of economic harassment endured by the Indians during their early years of citizenship was illegal taxation of their personal property. By law not only were allotments exempt from taxation but so was personal property that had been acquired from money derived from the federal government or from trust funds. The whites coming to Oklahoma Territory were poor and struggling to start their new farms or ranches. Such impoverished people paid few taxes, and local officials, after the opening of the reservation, sought means to add as much of the Indians' property to the tax roles as possible. Immediately after the organization of Canadian County, which contained Darlington and many of the better farms owned by mixed bloods, county officials threatened to tax all the personal property of the Cheyennes and Arapahoes within the county. Agent Ashley warned the county officers that practically all the Indians' property was purchased with restricted or trust funds and therefore was not subject to local or state taxes. He refused to allow the county commissioners access to the agency records, but, he reported to the commissioner of Indian affairs, "Most of the prosperous Indians have been assessed with a view of testing the matter in the courts."[24]

For five years after the opening of the reservation the Indian agents tried with little success to keep Indian property acquired with federal funds off the local tax roles. Despite assurances from the Indian Office that all allotted land and all improvements on that land or cattle, horses, and personal property purchased with annuities or interest money or from rental money for the allotments were exempt, the assurances did little good. Only property purchased or acquired

193

by the labor of the Indians themselves was taxable. The laws of Oklahoma Territory, however, made no distinction among those who owned personal property, and county officials were determined that the Indians should bear some of the costs of local and territorial government.[25]

An opinion by Oklahoma Territorial Attorney General Charles Brown in 1893 heartened local tax collectors. He gave the broadest possible construction to the fact that the Indians had taken their allotments and were citizens of the United States and Oklahoma Territory. Since they were subject to the laws of the federal and territorial governments, the Cheyennes and Arapahoes were "taxable the same as whites, except that their lands are inalienable, and are not subject to taxation for a period of twenty-five years." Newspaper editors, reflecting the attitude of other whites, happily expanded the list of Indian taxable property to include the buildings on the allotments and the Indians' personal property. A letter from the secretary of the interior to the territorial governor of Oklahoma requesting that Indian trust property be stricken from the tax rolls, so that the Indians would not be disturbed in their efforts "to get a fair start upon their individual allotments," was ignored. Attorney General Brown believed that it was the whites who needed considerate treatment. The settlers saw Indian families with five times as much land as they owned also receiving money for their lands, sharing in annuities and rations, and profiting from the "benefits of civil government without burdens."[26]

County officers followed the opinions of territorial rather than federal officials. Counties with substantial numbers of Indian allottees residing within their jurisdiction entered government property issued to Indians on their assessment rolls. When Woodson heard that stoves, fencing, farm implements, and other articles issued by the government to the Cheyennes and Arapahoes were to be taxed in Kingfisher County, he asked that the commissioner of Indian affairs intervene through the United States attorney to prevent the forcible collection of the illegal taxes. Despite the warnings from Agent Woodson, counties such as Canadian kept Indian personal property on the delinquent tax list. Most of the Indians against whom the delinquent taxes were lodged owned nothing more than two ponies worth no more than forty dollars. The Indian agent protested that the collection of the delinquent 1893 taxes would be a "gross injustice" and that the amount realized if the collection was enforced would be less than the expenses incurred.[27]

As the Cheyennes and Arapahoes continued to pay their illegal taxes, some of the tribesmen remembered the exemptions promised by the commissioners while the 1891 agreement was being discussed. Few of the Indians did what one tribal member did when he chased a county assessor from his allotment, preventing the official from gathering a list of his personal property. Most of the Indians, however, were too ill-informed to understand their rights, and they paid taxes even though federal laws specified otherwise. Little was done on behalf of the Indians, although Woodson had obtained a promise from an assistant to the United States attorney that he would personally take charge of the court cases. Woodson, after two years of futile arguments, thought that it was "high time" that something be done, especially in County G, where tension between the Indians and settlers was already great. Illegal taxation would, Woodson maintained, increase the Indians' bitterness toward the whites.[28]

When taxes in County G appeared inevitable, Woodson made an effort to have the Indian property assessed properly. He instructed the agency farmer in Arapaho to see that Indian ponies would not be listed at more than five to ten dollars a head, which represented their market value. After obtaining the tax roll for the county, Woodson discovered that "all the horses found in one camp have been assessed as belonging to one individual, when as a matter of fact, they belong to half a dozen or more." Such a listing would make the tax easier to collect and also mean the loss of horses to many individuals if the person assessed could not pay the tax levied. Agent Woodson also complained about the assessment of the poll tax against each adult Indian male despite the fact that many of the Indians did not vote in local elections and were often prohibited from exercising the franchise by local officials.[29]

Although the Cheyennes and Arapahoes objected to taxation in any form, they were still paying taxes and were threatened with seizure of property to pay the delinquent judgments against them. As late as 1896, Woodson was still struggling with county officials to make local tax assessment conform to federal law. To protect the Indians, Woodson attempted in the spring of 1896 to assemble a comprehensive list of all personal property owned by the Cheyennes and Arapahoes. Spotted Horse, Elk River, and others from the western Red Moon District traveled all the way to Darlington to object to Woodson that they feared such a listing would be the basis for additional taxes. Practically all the Indians could not understand why they should be taxed at all when the Jerome Commission had promised them exemption for the twenty-five-year trust period.[30]

In the spring of 1896 the value of Woodson's inventory of Indian property became apparent. When Ed Guerrier, a Cheyenne mixed blood, and John Otterby, an educated full blood, were assessed for all of their personal property by Canadian County officials, the Indian agent was able to inform United States Attorney Caleb R. Brooks that the animals, implements, and household equipment of the two Indians were improperly assessed. Guerrier's personal property was valued at $925. This valuation included thirty-five horses, eighty head of cattle, farming implements, a wagon, and household furniture worth five dollars. Even the wealthier Cheyennes were not overburdened with worldly goods.

The Indian agent asked United States Attorney Brooks to represent the Indians in court so that the issue could finally be settled. To assist in the case against the county officials, Woodson sought tax lists from Indians who could speak English and testify in their own behalf and who were certain that the assessments against their personal property were illegal. As a result of Woodson's long fight and conscientious supervision some county officials came to realize that they should obey federal law regarding the taxing of Indian property. Still, counties with a significant Indian population continued to urge that Indians be taxed for needed revenue. "Either the United States should pay taxes on Indian lands, or a law should be passed compelling the Indian to cultivate or lose a portion of each allotment, and in either case the land should be taxed," ran an editorial in a Blaine County newspaper. Seven years after Woodson began his fight, another Indian agent was informed that the United States attorney for Oklahoma Territory was instructed to enjoin all efforts to tax the personal property of Indians that had been acquired through the aid of the federal government. Because of taxation the Cheyennes and Arapahoes looked on citizenship as a detriment that carried no appreciable benefit for them because they were unable to exercise a citizen's normal rights or privileges.[31]

Settlers also strongly resented the ownership of good agricultural land by the Cheyennes and Arapahoes. Most whites believed that the Indians had been given the best lands on the reservation and that they had been forced to make their claims on less desirable tracts. Some of the more aggressive newcomers who had not found suitable land during the run threatened to take their land where they chose: "We hereby give notice that thirteen of us are going to move on this creek [near Cloud Chief] at once in spite of hell and high water. The Last Thirteen Home Seekers, August 9th, '92 A.D." Territorial officials like Governor Seay implicitly supported these people when they contended, as did Seay, that "the Indians have taken the very cream of the Cheyenne and Arapaho lands, some heads of families controlling as much as 8 or ten quarters." From his personal observation, Seay maintained, no Indian actually cultivated more than ten acres and generally that two sections of land was more than cultivated by a whole village of Indians. Seay also maintained that the fertile land should be in the hands of white farmers who could put it into cultivation through a system of leases. He urged that the federal government adopt a "broad, liberal policy" of leasing that would be fair to the Indians and profitable to white farmers.[32]

It was already possible for settlers to lease Indian allotments when they arrived in the Cheyenne-Arapaho Country. In 1891 Congress had passed a statute that permitted non-Indians to lease allotments for a period of three years. During that time the Indians received lease payments, and the lessees were required to improve the allotments with buildings, fences, and wells and to break the land and place it in crops. It was assumed that the leases would provide immediate cash income for the Indians and that the allotments would be improved by the lessees so that the Indians could utilize them at a later date when their agricultural skills were more fully developed. What was not anticipated by those who passed the act was that the lessees would come to believe that they had a vested interest in the land superior to that of the allottees and that they would eventually demand legislation that would permit alienation of the allotments despite the Dawes Act, which guaranteed a twenty-five-year trust period for all Indian allotments.[33]

During 1892 very few leases were completed for Cheyenne and Arapaho allotments. Many of the first settlers planted their crops after their claims were established and then returned to Kansas, Texas, or other states to wait for harvest time before building their homes. Those who remained found that the leasing law and regulations demanded more than the land was worth. Three years, the prospective lessees objected, were too short a time for them to recover the investment made in buildings and improving the land. Agent Ashley therefore recommended that the statute be amended, extending the leasing period from three to five years. A few whites were willing to take a chance on leasing Indian allotments. For example, the allotments of Tom White Shirt's wife and two children were fortunately located so that two men were willing to sign a lease, during which time they would enclose the land with a solid fence, build a four-room house, construct stables and a shed, and plant an orchard of at least two hundred fruit trees. Upon the expiration of the lease the improvements would remain, and in the interim White Shirt would receive one-third of the crops grown. The lease, however, was not approved because it did not contain a clause limiting the period of occupation by the lessees.[34]

When Captain A. E. Woodson became acting Indian agent in 1893, it was evident that the leasing system must be changed to be successful. He agreed with his predecessor that three years was too short a leasing period to be profitable to the lessees. Most of the Cheyennes and Arapahoes were unable to put their allotments into cultivation because they lacked the means to break the land; thus it would remain in a "wild state" for years unless it was tilled by the white settlers. The older Indians, in Woodson's opinion, would never become farmers. Improvements made on Indian allotments would, however, benefit the younger Cheyennes and Arapahoes who, it was hoped, would eventually settle down on farms. Woodson suggested that the settlers work through their congressional territorial delegate to obtain a more effective leasing law.[35]

Woodson hoped that the appointment of three young Haskell and Carlisle graduates to work as farmers among the Cheyennes would ease the misunderstandings that were arising between their people and the white farmers. At first Woodson thought that educated Indians would serve their fellow tribesmen better than whites employed as additional farmers because the whites drew their "pay and frittered away their time." Within a month the Indian agent had changed his mind. He admitted that while Andrew Tasso, William Fletcher, and Leonard Tyler, the three Indians selected for the experiment, were competent to manage small farms themselves, they did not have sufficient experience or knowledge to serve as intermediaries between the Indian and the lessees. They lacked the "good judgment, tact and business capacity to adjust such matters to the end that the Indians may not be unjustly dealt with, and that legal complications may be avoided if possible."[36]

As a result it fell to Agent Woodson to protect the Indians as best he could. The Cheyennes and Arapahoes were not ready to assume the responsibility of caring for their economic interests, and almost daily they came to him with tales of white men's "imposition and injustice." Whites took particular advantage of the Indians when they dealt directly with them on leasing matters without the assistance of the agent. The settlers assumed that, since the Indians were citizens, the regulations of the Bureau of Indian Affairs were not applicable. In that manner "many improper and irresponsible persons" moved onto the allotments and did not pay the Indians the amounts of money specified in the informal and unapproved leasing contracts.[37]

Seldom could a Cheyenne or an Arapaho protect himself from the sharp business practices of whites. Even Paul Boynton, who had received as much education as the Indian schools on and off the reservation provided, lost money to whites. He was allowed to make a lease with E. F. Mitchell, the trader who had profited handsomely by selling horses and mules to the Indians, for an annual rental of fifty-five dollars and a good fence to be placed on his allotment. Mitchell never gave Boynton a copy of the lease, and he "went busted." The lease and Mitchell's business at Darlington were sold to another Indian trader, Gustav Thelen, who tore down the fence, transferring the wire and posts to other property he owned. Although Boynton argued that the fence was his, Thelen claimed it was his because he had paid Mitchell for it. When Boynton finally obtained a copy of the informal lease, he found that the fence was not included among the terms. Boynton complained to Agent Woodson: "I have been deceived as to the terms of the contract. I fully understood that the fence was to be my property. I now want to get possession of my allotment." Since the lease of the allotment had not been approved by the Bureau of Indian Affairs, Boynton regained control of his land, but the fence was gone and nothing could be done about it.[38]

Wherever possible, whites avoided signing formal leases, which required the approval of the Washington office. They could obtain the allotments for less from the Indians informally, although they were subject to removal from the allotment at any time. A Kingfisher newspaper editor, J. V. Admire, had a different point of view about the informal leases. He agreed that the leases signed without the approval of the Indian Bureau were illegal, but the Indians, he wrote, "have no idea of the solemnity of a contract, and will repudiate it the moment they think it is in their interest to do so." He hoped that some way could be found to cut through the red tape so that the large body of land owned by the Indians could be brought into cultivation.[39]

Agent Woodson kept pushing for a more viable leasing law. He tried to interest Dennis T. Flynn, the Oklahoma territorial congressional delegate, in his ideas, which he maintained would help both the Indians and the whites. In three years the annuities due from the Medicine Lodge Treaty would end, and without additional income the Indians would "become paupers dependent largely upon the several counties where they are located." He suggested that the allotments not used by Indian families be leased for a period up to ten years for one-third of the crops raised and improvements upon the land. The crop payment could be turned into cash to support the family, and the improvements could be used by the children when they were ready to establish their own homes. The plan would net the counties of Oklahoma Territory more population and greater revenue, with which schools, roads, and bridges could be constructed. Woodson also called the tribes' chiefs to Darlington, where he explained to them the necessity of leasing much of their unused lands. The Indians surrounded by white farmers would learn by example how to farm, and a child would "grow up under the influences of civilization and, in a comparatively few years, the principal distinction would be his color."[40]

Woodson's plan to improve the conditions of the Cheyennes and Arapahoes also called for an expenditure of a portion of their permanent fund of one million dollars in the United States Treasury. After they had selected one of the family's allotments to live on while leasing the others, Woodson would distribute the funds among the people so that they could build houses, buildings, and fences. Captain J. M. Lee, the former agent who was an observer at the council, agreed that rigid supervision of the money was necessary. Otherwise "the unwary Indian would become the victim of every unscrupulous and designing white man in that region."

To push his plan along, Woodson escorted a delegation of Cheyenne and Arapaho chiefs to Washington. The Cheyennes, Young Whirlwind stated there, would lease their land but did not favor withdrawing any portion of their permanent fund from the Treasury. Left Hand thought that it might be wise to consider the use of the permanent fund especially for the benefit of the young people because they lacked money to make a start in life. The chiefs of both tribes insisted that their people did not have enough to eat when they were engaged in the heavy labor of farming. Young Whirlwind told Indian Commissioner D. M. Browning, "When a young man works in the forenoon very hard and goes home he finds nothing to eat, he rests and goes out without anything to eat, you cannot expect him to work as much as if he had something to eat to refresh him."[41]

Before going to Washington with the chiefs, Agent Woodson had hoped to use a new leasing law passed by Congress to the advantage of the Cheyennes and Arapahoes. He estimated that 2,000 of the 3,293 allotments were available for leases, which, to be acceptable, must contain some permanent, tangible benefits to the Indians. Woodson prepared a schedule of prices for the leasing of allotments, which received the approval of the secretary of the interior. For the best agricultural land within twenty-five miles of a railroad each quarter section would cost the lessee four hundred dollars in cash or improvements, and the lessee would also be required to break one hundred acres of each allotment during a five-year period of time. Less desirable cropland would cost 10 to 50 per cent less, while grazing land would cost only 60 per cent of the best land, and the lease would not require that any land was to be broken.[42]

As the number of leases increased, Agent Woodson began enforcing the terms of the agreements more rigidly upon the whites and Indians alike. If the lessee did nothing to improve the allotment or break the land, he was removed as fast as Woodson could bring action. If an Indian was trying to exploit a white, the latter was protected in his rights as provided in the leasing contract. Walking-in-the-Middle, a Cheyenne woman, leased her allotment and a portion of her children's to Joseph Feinagle, described by Woodson as a "hard-working German." After the lease had been agreed to and the first payment made, James Frost, a troublesome Ute Indian, moved in with Walking-in-the-Middle and tried to evict Feinagle from the allotments so that he could, as Woodson reported, "rent the land which Feinagle had broken and fenced for some more money, which he is ready to spend as it comes into his wife's hands." Woodson wanted the assistant United States attorney to inform the Indian that the lessee "had rights that he cannot abridge or take away, and he should be compelled to respect them." Frost countered with some accusations of his own. He charged that Feinagle was subleasing to another man and that he had broken less land than agreed to, had not built the fence, and had removed a house from the allotments without the permission of his wife. Feinagle stayed on the land, and two years later Frost stole two horses and a pistol from an agency policeman and fled.[43]

Unfortunately, the changes in leasing policy did not bring many benefits to the Indians. Most of the prospective lessees, being poor farmers, could not provide the necessary security bonds. In addition, the region was in the midst of a drought that ruined the wheat and oat crops. Although Woodson was hopeful that the better Indian land would be taken up when other desirable land in the territory was occupied, the leases failed to materialize. Woodson's terms for leases were still too expensive for the small farmers and ranchers. A former leasing agent at the agency estimated that it would cost a farmer more than seven hundred dollars in cash over a five-year period, not counting the cost of the buildings, fences, wells, and orchards that the lease forms required. He contended that a five-year lease would cost only one-half as much as the outright purchase of comparable land in 1896. As a consequence of the criticisms of Woodson's leasing policy, the terms of the leasing contracts were liberalized for the benefit of the lessees, but still many Indian allotments remained unused by white farmers.[44]

After several years of failure to attract lessees, Woodson sought information from farmers to find out what they considered a fair price for renting Indian allotments. The farmers and ranchers, impoverished by two years of drought, were in no mood to be generous to the Indians. Most of them thought that the rental price for the allotments was more than three times too much, and some preferred to make no cash payment at all but give the Indians one-third of the crops grown or 20 per cent of the harvest if cotton or broom corn was cultivated. Ranchers were willing to pay only five to twenty-five dollars a year for a quarter section of grazing land for which Woodson was asking forty dollars. In the sections around El Reno and Kingfisher, where the land was more fertile and rainfall more abundant than in the western district, farmers were willing to pay more for the lease and would add substantial improvements if they were credited with the appraised value of the improvements at the end of the lease.[45]

Bureau of Indian Affairs officials agreed with the potential lessees that Agent Woodson was overpricing the Indians' lands. Woodson would not agree to allow payment of a share of the lessees' crops in lieu of cash, but he did slash the payments and the amount of improvements to be placed on the allotments. Even so, few farmers and ranchers appeared to sign leasing agreements. Woodson rationalized that the extended drought and low prices resulting from the panic of 1893 explained the slow leasing business. Then, inexplicably, Congress reinstated the three-year limit for agricultural leases, which further handicapped Woodson's efforts to lease Indian land.[46]

The number of leases taken up became greater in 1898 and 1899. By the latter year 850 leases had been approved or were in the process of receiving approval. Woodson estimated that more than two thousand allotments were available for leasing. They were the allotments of Cheyennes and Arapahoes who could not cultivate the land because of age or infirmities. Woodson adhered to his policy of not allowing Indians to lease their land if they were able-bodied and capable of working their own land.[47]

Even when the leases were properly completed, there was no assurance that the Indians' incomes would increase. When renters failed to make a crop either on their own or on leased land, the whites refused to honor their contractual obligations. Woodson's frequent appeals to the United States attorney for prosecution of the delinquent renters were usually ignored. The best that Woodson could do for George Bent, who had leased two sections of his family's land for $110 in cash, was to threaten the lessee with eviction as a trespasser when the payments were in arrears. Others would sign leases with no intention of farming the land, but only of stripping the allotment of timber, which was scarce and expensive in Oklahoma Territory. Judgments, however, were hard to obtain when a white violated an Indian's property rights, and the Cheyennes and Arapahoes were exploited by their white neighbors well into the twentieth century.[48]

The Indians also found it difficult to defend their property rights through the ballot box. Normally they were disinterested in the franchise, but when their property rights were involved in elections, they found it difficult and in some instances impossible to cast their votes. In the fall of 1893 cattlemen in the western portion of the agency were able to expand the area subject to range law, which meant that livestock was free to roam and that the farmer was responsible for protecting his crops with substantial fences. When the issue first came before the voters in 1893, the Indians found that every obstacle was placed in their way. Election officials demanded that the Cheyennes and Arapahoes swear in their votes individually, which intimidated most of the Indians. Faced with an unfavorable territorial law, Woodson tried to arrange for another vote in 1894, which would be easier than upsetting legislation in effect, by proving that fraudulent voting practices had resulted in the suspension of the herd law in western Oklahoma Territory. Agent Woodson, however, realized that the open-range advocates would again "intimidate and mislead the Indian voters" and that the Cheyennes and Arapahoes "must learn to take their place in the communities in which they reside and endeavor to acquaint themselves with matters" influencing their welfare.[49]

In 1894 in the western portion of the agency cattlemen and stock raisers, Woodson reported, continued to "over-run the Indian allotments with their cattle herds seemingly without restraint. They vote for free range and carry the elections without allowing the Indians to vote." Under the circumstances the Indian agent requested that the army keep cavalry units in the region to protect the Indians' land; otherwise, the bands of Red Moon, White Shield, and Spotted Horse would continue to "congregate in large camps for mutual protection." The large camps meant, of course, that the Indians could not work their individual allotments.[50]

Woodson fought tenaciously for the economic and political rights of the Cheyennes and Arapahoes and was successful in having a detachment of cavalry stationed in Roger Mills County, where tension between the cattlemen and the Indians was the greatest. Using information obtained from the troopers, Woodson managed to obtain some compensation for White Shield's and Red Moon's people for damages done by cattle to their crops and garden patches. But he was less successful in his opposition to laws that expanded the amount of land covered by open-range legislation.[51]

In early 1896 cattlemen continued to expand the open-range area despite Woodson's opposition. The Indian agent ordered district farmer N. W. Butler to "get all your Indians to the place of voting on the day fixed, and have them vote it down. . . . The Indians have a right to vote without question; and if they are prohibited, the election will be declared void. Have them all at home on that date to vote, and go the polls with them." As expected, the open-range advocates carried the election easily because the Indians were not permitted to vote. Also the cattlemen had the lines demarking the open-range and herd-law boundaries very carefully defined so that the former rule would apply only to the areas containing substantial numbers of Indian allotments and unclaimed land. The lands held by white farmers remained subject to herd law, and they therefore did not oppose the extension of the open range.[52]

Unable to stop the election or to influence its outcome, Woodson protested the legality of the balloting. He asked Caleb R. Brooks, United States attorney for Oklahoma Territory, "to enjoin the enforcement of the object of the so-called election," since the Indians had been denied the right to vote. As he was trying to invalidate the recent vote in Roger Mills County and County G, where the cattlemen's imposition on the economic interests of the Cheyennes and Arapahoes was becoming intolerable, the Indian agent very carefully called the commissioner of Indian affairs' attention to the implications of the new law. It was becoming increasingly difficult to "induce the Indians to go to voting precincts to register their votes" because of previous discrimination and intimidation. Woodson also warned the commissioner that after the passage of the open-range law the cattlemen would try to avoid payment when their cattle grazed on Indian allotments.[53]

Judson Harmon, attorney general of the United States, finally offered an opinion that upheld the Indians' right to vote and to occupy and profit from their allotments. He ruled that the legislative acts of the Territory of Oklahoma that discriminated against Indian citizens by disregarding their property rights under the open-range laws were repugnant to the act of Congress establishing the territory's government and to the Constitution of the United States. The attorney general suggested that Agent Woodson present some specific cases to the United States attorney for Oklahoma Territory, and the latter would be instructed by the Justice Department to secure to Indians those rights and privileges guaranteed under the Dawes Act.[54]

Woodson sought information from the district farmer in Custer County and from the county attorney of Roger Mills County. The district farmer failed to forward the names of cattlemen even when requested to do so by some of the Cheyennes and Arapahoes with allotments in his district. The county attorney of Roger Mills County merely avoided the issue in his response to an inquiry from the assistant United States attorney by saying that herd law was still in effect in his county and that crops were protected. One cattleman did pay damages to two Indians, Bobtail Coyote and Warpath Bear for hay destroyed on their allotments by his herd, although it was known that "stock of all kinds run at large through" the county.[55]

During the 1897 session of the Oklahoma territorial legislature a law was enacted that eliminated the need for the smaller open-range districts in the western part of the territory. The law affected about four hundred Indian allotments, over which the cattlemen immediately began to run their herds. The Indian Bureau did not respond to Woodson's request for a decision on the constitutionality of the new law and forced him to work out the problem directly with the cattlemen. As ranchers with larger herds began moving into western Oklahoma Territory, Woodson began renting blocks of Indian allotments in excess of eight sections for a maximum of thirty-two dollars annually for each allotment.[56]

White-Indian relations after the opening of the Cheyenne-Arapaho Reservation were tragic. Deep prejudice often bordering on racism marked whites' attitudes toward their Indian neighbors. With limited resources the Cheyennes and Arapahoes could ill afford to have any portion of their money or property diverted to the whites. If the Indians had possessed more economic potential, skills, and incentives to acquire additional or replacement property, the losses they suffered through fraud and theft would not have been so severe or irremediable. As it was, the discrimination, the loss of property, and the contempt in which the Indian was held by farmers and ranchers made it impossible for many of the Cheyennes and Arapahoes to follow the "white man's road." The first full mixing of the tribesmen with whites delayed and perhaps even prevented them from attaining the goal of self-support demanded by Congress and the Bureau of Indian Affairs. The native American was suffering because of discrimination, maladministration of policy, lack of adequate financial resources, and antagonism of his white neighbors.

CHAPTER VIII

An Indian Policy for New Citizens

WHEN THE CHEYENNES and Arapahoes were allotted their lands, only a handful were prepared to assume the responsibilities of citizenship and ownership of private property. Only one out of five could speak English; many of the younger, better-educated men and women were dying of tuberculosis; an Indian farm averaged about eight acres of cultivated land; few had accumulated any economic assets; the old way of life was crumbling but still had powerful adherents; the old chiefs still dominated the decisions of the tribes; and the likelihood of government assistance continuing as in the past was problematical. Extinction of the tribes was not likely, but neither was a full, worthwhile life for the Cheyennes and Arapahoes.

Governmental obligations to the Indians had not ended. As trustee for the Indian people, the United States government was required by law to protect the Cheyennes' land and property. Since citizenship had been forced upon them long before they could care for themselves, a moral obligation existed to support them with educational, vocational, and health programs that would eventually lead them toward individual self-sufficiency. How that could be done was the challenge faced by those who administered the affairs of the Cheyennes. But before improvement in the life of the Indians occurred, decades of failure would have to be endured.

For the first year after allotment Agent Ashley brought few innovations to agency policy. When Major A. E. Woodson became acting agent, however, he began to press the Indians more vigorously to change their way of life. He found most of the tribesmen living in camps away from the allotments on which they were supposed to be raising food and crops. In 1893 the traditional chiefs and leaders controlled their camps with "undisputed authority" so that they exercised their judgments over the "younger and more enlightened element." Woodson reported that in the camps the old customs and "superstitions" prevailed, and the people placed their trust in medicine men, continued plural marriages, and were inclined to "idleness, with lack of thrift and industry." Woodson fully expected any change in the Cheyennes' way of life to be opposed by the "older ones," who refused to contribute toward their own self-support.[1]

Woodson singled out for criticism certain chiefs of the Cheyennes. Cloud Chief, for example, one of the leaders who had willingly signed the 1891 agreement, was among the "coffee coolers" who lounged around the traders' stores and set a bad example for his people. Although the government had constructed a house for Cloud Chief on his allotment, the chief's land remained uncultivated, producing no food or income for him and his family. "He hangs about the Agency," complained Woodson, "a disgruntled and dissatisfied member of his tribe, and serves to create dissension and discord, by opposing the efforts of the Agent to get his people to locate on their allotments." It was the habit of Cloud Chief and others like him to camp on the agency reserve and plant only a small patch of ground for vegetables. The agent informed the Indians that he would not permit them to live in large camps near the agency for more than three days at a time. Because only idleness and dissipation occurred in the camps, he ordered the Indians to their allotments. Still, Young Whirlwind, who had been a bitter opponent of the 1891 cession agreement, until his death in May, 1895, was urging his band to settle on their allotments.[2]

In the spring of 1895, unwilling to rely upon persuasion, Woodson issued a series of orders. In the future no more than four families could congregate and settle near each other on one allotment. All able-bodied men over the age of eighteen were to live on their own land and by their labor provide for themselves and their families. If Indians refused to labor or to farm, the district farmers were ordered to discontinue issuing rations to them. If Indians were found outside the farming districts where their allotments were situated or if they were visiting for an extended period away from their home districts, the farmers were also ordered to discontinue rations. Unless the agency farmers and the Indian police strictly enforced these orders, they were threatened with "summary dismissal."[3]

Woodson had control over the Indian police and employees, but not the weather. A summer drought in 1895 made it impossible for many of the Indians to live on their allotments because they were without water and wood. The best that the Indian agent could hope for was to break the large camps into smaller ones located as near allotments as possible. It was not Woodson's intention to "inflict any undue hardship" on the Cheyennes and Arapahoes; therefore, he also permitted those tribal members disabled by disease or old age or young unmarried males to live with members of their families. The young men, however, were expected to aid and assist their relatives or friends in working the land. Woodson's campaign had some effect: in the Cantonment District, where many of the traditionalists lived, the largest camp in the area consisted of only nineteen lodges. White Horse, a Cheyenne chief, balked and maintained that he had been given permission to live in a large camp. Water was a problem; few of the allotments had wells, and it was impossible for many of the Indians to live where their allotments were located. Nevertheless, Woodson continued his systematic campaign to break up the large camps and reduce the power of the chiefs over their bands.[4]

Woodson expected that the older Indians and the chiefs would resent his program, and they did. "My regime," he reported to the commissioner of Indian affairs, "is distasteful with the older Indians. They only wish to be let alone and to drag along in the old way, confirmed in the belief that they will always be fed and clothed by a generous government, and nothing can be said that will convince them that the day will soon come when they will no longer be fed at its expense." He viewed the Cheyennes and Arapahoes as children who, when faced with a person of greater willpower, would eventually accept the new regulations. Breaking the power of the chiefs was the key to the "progress" of the tribes. The chiefs monopolized the councils and supervised the issuance of rations, clothing, and farming tools—always wanting more than their share of the issues and, when not consulted, refusing to co-operate with their agent. In Woodson's view "the sooner they are ignored and relegated to their proper sphere" the sooner the Cheyennes and Arapahoes would become self-sufficient.[5]

The Cheyenne chiefs fought back. White Shield talked to Quanah Parker, the Comanche chief whose lands had not yet been divided, about moving with his band to Parker's reservation. When Woodson blocked Old Crow; White Horse; White Bird, the son of Little Robe; and Bull Bear, the son of Heap-of-Birds, from visiting Washington, they found other means to make their complaints known to the government. They hired E. J. Simpson, a former superintendent of the Arapaho Boarding School, to effect the removal of Woodson as Indian agent. The chiefs did not want to be forced from their camps, to give up their religious ceremonies (which now included the use of peyote), to cease their visits among their neighbors and friends, to abandon all but one of their wives, or to discontinue taking the sick to the medicine men. Pressed to abandon their traditional ceremonies, the Arapahoes from Cantonment tried to placate the agent by telling him that if they were allowed to hold the "Crow Dance," which would last five days, they would pray to "the Father to bless the crops they were about to plant." One of Woodson's subordinates thought that, if permission would serve as an inducement for the Indians to go to work, "for goodness sake let them have it."

Woodson turned on the "coffee coolers" and "so-called chiefs" who lived in indolence and were dependent upon government support. He sought the aid of his military friends and the commissioner of Indian affairs. "I am too old a soldier," Woodson wrote the commissioner, "to cater to popularity or to curry favor with those under my command." With surprising speed Commissioner Browning approved of Woodson's actions, even the withholding of rations from the "non-progressive" Indians. Commissioner Browning may have been spurred on by persistent congressional criticism over continued support to Indians. Montana Congressman Charles S. Hartman rather crudely stated the issues when he argued: "We have given these big buck Indians, many of them physically equal to four white men, this subsistence year after year. . . . The result has been that fully 90 percent of them are loafers today. Not a single one of them desires to do any manual labor. . . . they remain wards, sponges, and leeches upon the United States Government." In Woodson's opinion the Cheyennes and Arapahoes had been made citizens too soon, and the Dawes Act should be amended to ensure that the Indians would remain totally under the control of the government as long as their lands were held in trust.[6]

With the permission of the commissioner of Indian affairs Woodson finally enforced the rule of withholding rations and annuities from those who opposed him. He decided to issue only butchered beef so that each family's ration was given out individually. The chiefs found themselves removed from the head of the ration lines, taking their places according to the ration list, "a most humiliating position for great men." Carl Sweezy, a noted Arapaho artist, late in life remembered, "Many a Cheyenne family went hungry until the proud chiefs of that tribe decided they must bow to authority and accept slaughtered beef." Cheyenne chiefs in the Cantonment District made such a fuss that the whites thought that an outbreak was imminent and requested that troops be sent to protect them from the Cheyennes. Woodson decided to withhold from the dissident Indians not only rations but also annuity goods due under the Treaty of Medicine Lodge; thus wagons, cooking and heating stoves, lumber, and canvas would be issued only to "deserving Indians who live upon and cultivate their allotments, and place their children in school."[7]

By 1897, Woodson's policies had begun to show results. Among the Arapahoes only one chief, Thunder Bull, continued to refuse to advise the tribesmen to send their children to school and to farm. Left Hand, Row-of-Lodges, Tall Bear, and White-Eyed Antelope were solidly behind Woodson and were trying to lead their people toward self-sufficiency. Among the Cheyenne chiefs Woodson was less successful. Twelve of the twenty-three chiefs led by Old Crow, White Shield, White Horse, Little Big Jake, Burnt-All-Over, Red Moon, and Pawnee Man still grimly resisted the new way of life. Even though most of the Cheyenne chiefs still opposed him, Agent Woodson believed that the struggle to break the power of the chiefs was almost over:

It has been a long and bitter struggle, but the end is near, and the opposition almost gone. One by one their followers have dropped off, and now those who once held undisputed sway over their people are deserted, their power gone, and nothing left to them but the inevitable. They must accept it or go down to their grave, maintaining to the last their efforts to retain their independence of the white man's control.[8]

Woodson seized every opportunity to reduce the strength of the dissident leaders. During the winter of 1897–98, when a delegation of Cheyennes and Arapahoes was being assembled to visit Washington, White Horse and Yellow Bear, two of the leaders who opposed Woodson, were elected, but the Indian agent refused to allow them to make the trip. The Cantonment Cheyennes would not elect others; therefore, Woodson filled out the list with more amenable leaders from other farming districts. After Woodson was promoted to major during his tenure as acting Indian agent, he offered to resign from the Indian Service. Commissioner of Indian Affairs W. A. Jones, however, wanted to retain his services because "his record in office is of the very best, *none better*."[9]

Woodson controlled even those who were not on the government payroll with an iron hand. The Reverend Rudolf Petter, the distinguished Mennonite missionary who compiled the first Cheyenne-English dictionary and grammar, wrote a letter supporting Little Man, a Cheyenne who opposed Woodson's programs. The Indian agent immediately rebuked Petter, calling Little Man a medicine man, a hypocrite, and a treacherous enemy of all those trying to civilize the Indians. If Petter was siding with the Indians, Woodson warned him, "I shall know where to place you in the future."[10]

Woodson's program to change the Cheyennes and Arapahoes was aimed at all parts of the tribes' lives. He required them to

live in permanent homes, on their allotments and to perform daily labor for their own support, to educate their children, to refrain from old time habits that continue them in idleness—such as tribal visiting, eating the mescal bean [peyote], gambling, drinking intoxicants, dancing, marriage, and divorce according to Indian customs, destruction of property on death of relatives, wife beating and desertion, living in adultery, selling timber from their allotments, using the property of relatives without their consent, and the habits of burial of the dead.

He could have added nonrecognition of traditional chiefs to the list of regulations that made him unpopular with the tribes. Toward the end of his tenure as agent Woodson could understand the opposition of the "older, ignorant, and superstitious Indians," but he could not ignore that of Cleaver Warden, Philip Cook, Grant Left Hand, Leonard Tyler, and Henry Roman Nose, all of whom had had the benefit of education at Darlington, Haskell, or Carlisle.[11]

Woodson also found the Cheyennes' and Arapahoes' ceremonies repugnant. Although he tried to crush all the traditional forms of worship among the Indians, many of his predecessors, such as Ashley, had not tried too hard to change the Indians' beliefs. Ashley's only prohibition against ceremonies and dances had been that they should not be held within five miles of the agency schools. Otherwise, the Indians could gather as they pleased, and they did so every six weeks after 1890 to participate in Ghost Dances. Not until the new belief had reached its peak among the Sioux did the Cheyennes and Arapahoes really become interested in Wovoka, the new Messiah, and his teachings.[12]

During the summer of 1890 a number of Cheyennes and Arapahoes had gone north in search of Wovoka. Four Cheyennes were perhaps in the party—Tall Bull, Heap-of-Crows (Red Moon's son), Little Chief, and Thunder—who may have seen the Indian Messiah in the northern Rockies. While the Cheyennes were apparently unimpressed, the Arapahoes became devotees of Wovoka. The teachings of the Indian redeemer were spread on the Southern Plains by Sitting Bull (Scabby Bull), a Northern Arapaho who had established his camp in the Red Hills east of Cantonment. Among the adherents of the new religion were Left Hand and Row-of-Lodges, important chiefs of the Southern Arapaho bands, who regularly gathered in large camps to pray to the Great Spirit. Row-of-Lodges assured Agent Ashley that during the Ghost Dances his people prayed to the Great Spirit to make them a better, more prosperous and happy people and to enlighten them in the ways of the white man. The Ghost Dance songs were little different from those sung by the Indian school children, and, because the Ghost Dance did not hamper the Indians' industrial pursuits, Ashley did not interfere but accepted the Ghost Dance as a "long step in the direction of true religion, as compared with their former customs of worship."

The impact of the Ghost Dance on the Cheyennes is difficult to assess. The Mennonites reported that during the latter months of 1890 both the Cheyennes and the Arapahoes were spending a great deal of their time in camps away from their homes, neglecting their farms and the education of their children. Fenton Antelope, who had completed three years of study at Haskell and was the son of White Antelope, scoffed when asked about Wovoka: "The boys who have been away to school . . . know better than to believe in a Messiah." For the most part Cheyennes participated only as individuals in the Arapaho Ghost Dances, which were held less frequently by the spring of 1892. They continued as smaller dances possibly as late as 1902, but no longer with the fervor of earlier ceremonies. When Woodson became agent, he looked on the Ghost Dances as only another ceremony to be stamped out, and he refused permission for the Indians to assemble for any ceremony that lasted for more than twelve hours.[13]

In the spring of 1894, Woodson learned of a new ritual among the Cheyennes and Arapahoes. At the outset of his investigations he erroneously believed that the new ceremony was linked to the use of mescal beans. Actually the new rituals utilized peyote, and Woodson's failure to distinguish mescal from peyote caused his successors difficulties when, at a later date, efforts were made to eradicate the peyote ceremony among the Cheyennes and Arapahoes. Peyote is the buttonlike top of the cactus *Lophophora williamsii*, while mescal beans are the seeds of the shrubby legume *Sophora secundiflora*. Both peyote and mescal beans have hallucinogenic effects. In 1895, Woodson issued, among other orders to the tribes, the following regulation: "The habit of gambling and the use of the mescal bean which have heretofore been so prevalent, are strictly prohibited in future; and all old-time customs that existed during the reservation system which served to keep alive superstitions and barbarous practices must be abandoned." The tribesmen often ignored the agent's regulations, however, as did the Cheyennes in September, 1894, when five hundred people, led by the old warriors Yellow Dog, White Bear, and Red Moon, visited the Oto Agency. It was through these intertribal visits that the peyote ceremony diffused through the Indian tribes of the Oklahoma and Indian territories.[14]

In the agent's opinion traditional ceremonies and tribal visits prevented the Indians from contributing to their self-support. When the Indians gathered together, they gambled and feasted long into the night, which meant that their farm work was neglected. Then, he said, the Indians complained that they had nothing to eat. The agency farmers were instructed by Woodson to break up the gatherings, "by force if necessary," using the agency Indian police. Woodson told his subordinates that if the tribesmen complained to him they would receive no sympathy.[15]

Woodson believed that change within the tribes was most seriously retarded by the "councils, dances and the intermingling of the tribes. It enables the chiefs and 'medicine men' to wield their vicious influence over the rising generation of young men and women who have been educated and who otherwise willingly throw off the yoke of tribal bondage." In 1896, he denied the Cheyennes permission to hold their annual Sun Dance and urged them to continue their farming operations. The Arapahoes, also forbidden to hold their Sun Dance, petitioned the agent for permission to hold a Willow Dance, a request that Woodson granted. In retrospect however, Woodson thought his decision to allow the dance was a mistake because it afforded the Cheyennes and Arapahoes in the Cantonment District the chance "to council and talk about the policy of the Government, and no doubt result in bad influence being exercised over those who would otherwise be disposed to follow the advice of their Agent." When Little Raven and Heap-of-Crows from Cantonment requested permission to hold another ceremony in the fall of 1896, Woodson denied their request. Despite all of Woodson's pressure, however, the Cheyennes and Arapahoes continued to hold their ceremonies. In the spring of 1898 more than one thousand members of the tribes gathered near Cantonment for traditional rites.[16]

In 1899, Woodson launched a vigorous attack against both medicine men and peyote, which he continued to confuse with the mescal bean. As yet agency officials had not mentioned peyote in their recommendations and correspondence. According to the agent, among the "immoral and debasing customs" practiced by the Cheyennes and Arapahoes was the use of the "mescal bean," which when used to excess injured the nervous system and resulted in "mental debility and total loss of energy." Woodson wanted the Oklahoma territorial legislature not only to suppress the use of "mescal" but also to suppress the activities of tribal medicine men. He charged that small children and older tribal members frequently became victims of the practice, and he especially deplored the medicine men's treatment of women, who were "frequently subjected to the most horrible and demoralizing abuse at their hands, involving inhumane treatment and loss of virtue." One medicine man, Woodson alleged, debauched a woman and required the husband to pay a large sum of money on the pretext of ridding her of an evil spirit. In his recommendation for legislation Woodson carefully noted that it should apply only to those Indians who had become citizens under the terms of the Dawes Act.[17]

Dr. George R. Westfall, the agency physician, supported Woodson's plea for legislation. Also mistaking peyote for the "mescal button or bean," Dr. Westfall claimed that it was as dangerous as opium, cocaine, or Indian hemp. Informants had told him that when an individual was

fully under the influence of mescal . . . the most pleasurable mental state imaginable exists. The knowledge of time is lost; owing to the number and variety of images which occupy the mind, a few minutes appears to be hours, days, or months. When the effect of the drug passes off, they are left in an exhausted, debilitated condition, similar to that of a person who has been on a prolonged spree. Furthermore, it incapacitates them for all mental and bodily exercise.

Utterly without sympathy for Indian medicine, Dr. Westfall denounced Indian medicine men for using only "incantations, exposure in the sweat house, and mutilations of the body." Both newborn infants and the old were subjected to the same treatments, which Westfall asserted usually resulted in the patients' deaths.[18]

By the time Woodson began his assault on the use of peyote, the ceremony had been practiced by the Cheyennes and Arapahoes for at least a decade. Jess Rowlodge, a present-day Arapaho chief and peyotist, believes that in 1888 Medicine Bird, an Arapaho, brought in peyote rituals from the Kiowas and Apaches. The Cheyennes, according to Rowlodge, did not practice the peyote ceremonies until 1901, when members of the tribe were living around Watonga. At that time they adopted the ceremonies of the Kiowas, which were based on the teachings of Quanah Parker, a distinguished Comanche chief and peyote-cult leader. Woodson urged Senator George W. Ballamy, a member of the Oklahoma Territorial Council, to do everything in his power to have mescal outlawed. "The use of the mescal bean," Woodson wrote, "has become so prevalent now that we have hundreds of Indians so confirmed in the habit that they have lost all energy and all desire to support themselves, and are simply worthless vagabonds, better dead than alive." Woodson forwarded to Senator Ballamy a draft of a bill that he wanted revised into proper legal terminology so that mescal would be prohibited and medicine men prevented from practicing their arts.[19]

The "mescal and medicine man" bill passed both houses of the Oklahoma territorial legislature. Woodson then turned to Territorial Governor C. M. Barnes, who was receiving requests from "nonprogressive" Indians to refuse to sign the bill. Woodson assured Barnes that the bill had the approval of the Indian Rights Association, the missionaries working with the Indians, the commissioner of Indian affairs, and the secretary of the interior. There would be no trouble in Washington because the commissioner and the secretary had long worked to curtail the "baneful and immoral practices of the medicine men and suppress the use of the mescal bean." After considerable thought, Governor Barnes signed the bill. With the activities of medicine men and the use of peyote under control—or at least prohibited by territorial law—Agent Woodson believed that the Cheyennes and Arapahoes were ready to take "an advanced step in their civilization." But the peyote cult continued to expand, and the law proved defective when its enforcement was attempted eight years later.[20]

Cheyenne and Arapaho Indian agents were also deeply concerned about the continuation of traditional Indian marriage customs. Soon after the Indians became citizens, Agent Ashley considered initiating court actions against men who took second and third wives according to tribal customs. When three Arapaho schoolgirls at Cantonment became wives of men who had not abandoned their other wives, Ashley suggested that the men be taken into court. One of the men was Little Raven, who took Susie Mixed Hair into his lodge. The chief and the other men acknowledged their "guilt, but sought to excuse themselves by stating that they would immediately put the girls away." William M. Pulling, the issue clerk at Cantonment, persuaded Ashley not to call the girls as witnesses in court. Pulling explained that the girls knew of the other wives, "but on account of the status of a woman among the Indians, and the influences often brought to bear, are these girls not more sinned against than sinning? I think so."[21]

Woodson was less understanding than his predecessors. He immediately began to work for the eradication of plural marriages among the Cheyennes and Arapahoes. The Bureau of Indian Affairs, Woodson pointed out, had already established regulations by which a man would be allowed to receive annuities or other payments for only one wife and her minor children. Other wives and their children would receive their annuities, payments, and rations apart from their former husbands. At that time, however, plural marriages were still common among the Cheyennes and Arapahoes. Few of them, Woodson claimed, followed the example of Dan Tucker, a full-blood Arapaho and a graduate of Carlisle, in 1882, who married Maude McIntyre, a white schoolteacher at Darlington. After their marriage the Tuckers moved to his improved allotment near Cantonment, where Tucker had about one hundred head of cattle and a bank account of one thousand dollars. Woodson believed that it was much more common for an Indian man to "throw away" his wife or wives and their children to marry another woman. He reported that Little Hawk, a Cheyenne, did precisely that when he took as his wife in an Indian marriage ceremony Julia Bent, a daughter of George Bent who had returned from Carlisle after six or seven years of schooling. Julia was offered a position on the agency staff if she would not live with Little Hawk, but she preferred her husband to the appointment. Woodson hoped to use territorial courts to terminate marriages that were based on Indian customs.[22]

Woodson reported that Cheyenne and Arapaho men could not understand why they had to live with only one wife. Nor could they understand why the relatives of a wife could not take her back if the husband did not respond to their demands for food or property. The tribesmen preferred their old marriage customs, just as they did the custom of sharing their food and homes with their relatives. If the government, they reasoned, had provided for them in the past, they saw no reason why clothing and food given to them should not be used for the benefit of their families and friends. Woodson also found the territorial legal code ambiguous. It merely stated, "Indians contracting marriage according to Indian custom, and cohabiting as husband and wife, are lawfully married," ignoring the possible interpretation that a man could have more than one wife if he married another woman according to Indian customs. In 1895, Woodson issued an order prohibiting plural marriages as contrary to territorial law, and he instructed district farmers and Indian police to report all violations of his regulation so that he could punish the "bigamists" in courts of law.[23]

Woodson was angry when newspapers reported that the Cheyennes and Arapahoes were still contracting plural marriages. A story had appeared that an Arapaho school girl had been sold to a man who was already married. The newspapers had reported the wrong name of the girl involved, but such a marriage had occurred. Lula Blind had married White Shirt, her brother-in-law, according to Arapaho customs, after White Shirt paid Lula's father a considerable number of horses for her. When Lula returned to the Arapaho Boarding School at Darlington in the fall of 1894, however, the older girls teased her about being married. Lula broke down under the ridicule and finally told the school superintendent that she had married White Shirt but that she did not want to live with him and would rather remain in school. Lula remained in school, and White Shirt did not press the matter.[24]

When Indian employees were involved in plural marriages or married according to tribal custom, Woodson punished them. Paul Good Bear, a Cheyenne who was highly recommended by Captain Pratt, was employed at the Cheyenne Boarding School as a shoemaker and disciplinarian. He married a girl but did not conform to the law of the territory by seeking out a minister or a justice of the peace. Good Bear had acquired the right to marry the girl by presenting ponies to her family. For violating the regulations of the agent and the Bureau of Indian Affairs, he was summarily dismissed from his position at the school.[25]

Left Hand, the distinguished Arapaho chief, arranged for his daughter to be married by a minister, but many tribal members were willing to suffer the displeasure of their agent and his interpretation of the territorial laws. Almost daily Woodson was told about someone who had left his family to marry another woman or who, after taking a second wife, was living "in bigamy with them both." Woodson's objections to Indian marriages not in agreement with his interpretation of the territorial laws were also based upon economic considerations. He held that offspring of marriages based on Indian custom were not legal heirs of their natural father. He suggested that Indian marriages according to Indian customs be tested in the courts, but nothing came of the suggestion.[26]

On occasion a woman would also shown her disdain for white man's law. The wife of Big Belly, a Cheyenne, voluntarily left her husband and began living with Black Bull. The woman was, according to Woodson, "outspoken in her determination not to live with her husband and insists on living apart from him in adultery with Black Bull." Big Belly, through Woodson, asked the Canadian County attorney to prosecute his wife, but all Woodson could do was fume that it was necessary to make some of the alleged violators of the law "forcible examples in order to deter others from committing like offenses."[27]

Until the territorial laws were changed, there was little that Woodson could do but complain. In 1896 he wrote that, despite his regulations and those of the Bureau of Indian Affairs,

plural marriages and the barter and sale of women as wives, the abandonment of wives at the will of the husband, the taking away of wives from husbands by parents and relatives for trivial causes or on failure of the husband to share his goods and chattels with the wife's relatives, total disregard to the laws governing marital relations, marriages according to Indian custom (which are frequently incestuous as well as bigamous), consummated between those of unlawful age, and the frequent crimes of seduction, abduction, rape, etc., constitute a list of offences against law and civil government.

In 1897 he presented the problems to the Oklahoma territorial legislature and suggested a change in the statutes governing marriages.[28]

Woodson presented his point of view to the legislature at Guthrie in February, 1897. Before legislative committees he testified that it was proper for marriages consummated by Indian customs before allotment to be viewed as legal but that all subsequent marriages should be solemnized in the same manner as that prescribed for white citizens. While before the committees Woodson also sought means to restrict marriages between whites and Indians, because, he said, many worthless non-Indian men married Indian women for the sole purpose of receiving rations and a share in the women's lands and annuities. With legal advice Woodson presented a draft of a bill for the legislature's consideration that declared plural marriages illegal. The "rejected wife" was protected in her economic rights when her husband chose one of his other wives for his marital companion, and the rejected wife would also be given custody of her children unless cogent reasons could be presented to provide for them otherwise. Woodson also suggested that Oklahoma Territory should legalize divorces for those Indian men with more than one wife so that the rejected women could have the right of remarriage.[29]

The statute passed by the territorial legislature and approved on March 12, 1897, contained much that Woodson advocated. All marriages and divorces among Indian citizens before passage of the act were validated, but thereafter marriages or divorces according to Indian customs were punishable under the territory's criminal code.

After July 1, 1897, all men with more than one wife were required to select one as their lawful wife, and to cohabit with any other woman was bigamy. Each county was required to compile a list of men allotted under the Dawes Act, the list to include the names of the wives selected from each group of multiple wives and the names of the "Indian wives rejected."[30]

Enforcement under the law was not strict. The fifty Cheyenne and Arapaho men who still had multiple wives in 1897 were allowed to live with them, especially if the women had children. Agent Woodson informed the commissioner of Indian affairs that, by agreement with the attorney general of Oklahoma Territory, "none of the old Indians [will be] prosecuted who have more than one wife, taken prior to the enactment of the Indian Marriage Law. . . . It is deemed best to allow old Indians to keep their wives, by whom they had children, rather than to impose the penalties prescribed." But when younger people persisted in marrying according to tribal customs, Woodson took them to court. Two educated Cheyennes from the Watonga District, Hugh Antelope and Veseva Star, who were married by tribal custom, were arrested, convicted, and confined in the Blaine County jail for thirty days.[31]

The older Indians probably would have ignored the marriage law of the territory if it had been enforced. Left Hand told Woodson: "The good God above gave me children and by His help, I will stand and protect them while there is a breath of life in my body. I will not part with any of my wives, but will obey the law and not marry any more. Those whom I have got I will protect for my children's sake." A Cheyenne spokesman expressed his views even more vividly: "If the white man wants to take our children away from us it would be far better they should take us out on the broad prairie and let the soldiers from the fort shoot us down like dogs. . . . A Cheyenne will never give up his wife and children."[32]

Tribal marriage customs persisted for some years beyond 1897. The Indian agent encountered iron-willed mothers who intervened in their daughters' marriages when their wishes were not followed. Often a mother sided with her daughter when marital conflict occurred, and the agent often found it impossible to change the decision that the daughter leave her husband. Despite the difficulties, Woodson thought that the new marriage law would improve the status of women in the tribes since they would no longer be "bartered and sold for ponies and chattels, and divorced at will, for trivial causes." But in February, 1900, within a few months after assuming his administrative duties, George W. H. Stouch, Woodson's successor, noted that violations of the territorial marriage law were sharply increasing within the tribes, and greater pressure would have to be applied if the customs of Indian marriage were to be eradicated.[33]

Marriage customs were not the only problems encountered by the agents. Liquor was easily obtained by the Cheyennes and Arapahoes during the 1890's, and it was used to excess by many of the Indians. The source of the whisky was, of course, the saloons, which proliferated in the small towns that sprang up throughout the Cheyenne-Arapaho country. Near Darlington the agents used Indian police to restrict the sale of liquor to Indians, but even when a liquor peddler was arrested for selling liquor to them, the fines levied by the local courts, sometimes as little as one dollar, did not diminish the profitable sales. Only sporadically did Agent Woodson move against the liquor dealers. Sometimes he worked with local ministerial associations or the officials of county fairs, but most of the time he was too preoccupied with other matters to enforce the liquor laws.[34]

Until 1898, Woodson denied that liquor caused many problems among the tribesmen. Then either he became aware of the problem for the first time (which was unlikely) or the quantity of liquor being sold to the Indians increased sharply. George Bent was accused of being a middle man in some of the liquor sales, and Indians were sought to testify against Bent in court. The sale of whisky to Indians in El Reno was particularly annoying to Woodson. He complained to a law officer in that town not only that older Indians were drinking too much but that younger men just returned from off-reservation schools were going on long sprees. Any effective curtailment of the usage of alcohol by the tribes, however, had to wait for a new agent and more effective enforcement procedures a decade later.[35]

Education, a key to the governmental policy of assimilation, was not flourishing among the Cheyennes and Arapahoes when the reservation was opened to white settlement. There were reservation schools available at Darlington and Colony, and the Mennonites operated mission schools at Darlington and Cantonment. Every year when the fall term began, the agents and their subordinates struggled to fill the schools. Few students attended the schools on the first day of classes, and various means of persuasion were used to gain more pupils. Threats of withholding food raised enrollments slightly, but promises of a bonus of meat during rationing was more effective. In the fall of 1892, William Pulling, the issue clerk at Cantonment, used that scheme successfully among the more traditionalist bands. The day after Pulling's announcement five "companies of Dog Soldiers" turned up at the school, mounted and armed with their Winchesters. Drawing themselves into orderly line, they fired their rifles in the air and asked Pulling whether he was afraid. Then they made a few speeches and produced enough Cheyenne boys and girls to fill the Cantonment Mission School to its capacity. After the Cheyennes received their meat and a "small feast," they went away happy.[36]

A Mennonite missionary complained that Agent Ashley was too lenient toward the Indians. Ashley refused to break up the Indians' dances and ceremonies during the fall of 1892, causing the Reverend J. S. Krehbiel to remark, "Our Agent is too easy with them or things would be in better shape." The agent, however, had his problems, too. Older, traditionalist chiefs used any excuse to delay the children's enrollment or withdraw them from the schools. When the beef ration was cut by 50 per cent in 1892, even the more progressive faction, headed by Little Big Jake and Little Medicine, from the Seger District, told the agent that they had little interest in sending their youngsters to school. Red Moon and White Shield, from the western portion of the agency, said that they would send their children to school only when buildings were constructed for them near their camps. Since some of the Indians still had money from the payments for the reservation, the usual threat of withholding rations when they kept their children out of school had little impact on the traditionalist bands.[37]

When Woodson became agent in 1893, five schools were operating for the Cheyennes and Arapahoes. About half of the tribes' children of school age attended the schools, the largest number being educated at the two Darlington government boarding schools. The number of pupils at the mission schools dropped from year to year as the capacity of the school maintained by federal funds increased. In an effort to overcome the Indians' reluctance to send their children away to a boarding school some distance from their homes, Woodson suggested constructing additional educational facilities. A new school operated by John Seger at Colony opened in January, 1893, but others were needed at Watonga and in the far-western part of the agency.[38]

As citizens the Cheyennes and Arapahoes could send their children to the public schools of the territory. They were reluctant to do so, although local school administrators were at first eager for Indian pupils to attend with white students. Woodson denied that he had threatened to cut off rations from the Indians if they sent their children to public rather than the agency boarding or mission schools. He explained, "I have labored assiduously to induce the Indians of this Agency to place their children in school; but I have in no instance hindered or prevented or attempted to prevent their attendance at neighborhood schools."[39]

Although by 1895 Woodson had broken down the opposition to reservation boarding schools through threats of curtailment of rations, the function of education among the Cheyennes and Arapahoes remained uncertain. Few questioned that it would eventually lead to a different way of life for the Indians. Some of the pupils from Haskell and Carlisle were employed at the schools as disciplinarians or in the school shops, where crafts were taught to the boys. A few others were provided with jobs at the agency office or issue stations. In 1895 seven young men from Haskell and Carlisle worked with fair success as government employees, but others less fortunate drifted back into camp life. Deforest Antelope, the son of White Antelope of the Cheyennes, worked at the Cheyenne Boarding School at Darlington. Another Cheyenne chief's son, Meat, whose father was Old Crow, returned to the agency from Carlisle but found no opportunity to work at his craft as a typesetter. A newspaper editor commented: "Of course since he had gotten back in his tribe, they will compel him to be an Indian again, or make his life wretched. A few months from now he will probably refuse to speak English."[40]

In the mid-1890's approximately one-half of the agency's school-age children were not attending schools. Among the Cheyennes there were 589 children of school age, of whom 283 attended school, while 310 out of 314 Arapaho school-age youths were apparently being educated. The Arapaho statistics are doubtful because an inspection of the reservation schools in late 1894 showed that only 134 Arapaho pupils were actually attending classes. Many of the students in school attended only irregularly. They ran away from the dormitories when they became unhappy or when discipline became too severe; parents withdrew their sons and daughters when they became ill, even though the illnesses were minor; many were forced to attend religious ceremonies and dances through the regular school year; and some were withheld from school when the tribal leaders became displeased with government or agency policies. Many of the students could not benefit from educational instruction because of debilitating diseases: tuberculosis was prevalent among them, trachoma was endemic in the schools (and was not to be curbed until the twentieth century), and many came to the schools suffering severely from malnutrition. Yet Woodson believed that the government schools were particularly important for children because "the longer children are kept away from the uncivilizing influences of camp life the better it will be for them."[41]

Enrollment of Indian students in the public schools did not appear to be the answer to Indian education. Public schools received ten dollars a quarter for each Indian child enrolled in school districts under the control of county governments. Teachers and local officials, however, had no means of enforcing the attendance of enrolled Indian pupils. Too frequently the parents of children attending the public schools allowed them to stay at home whenever they wanted to. Woodson objected to sending the Indian pupils to public schools because no industrial education was provided for them as it was in the government boarding schools. Although one county received tuition for twenty-five students during the 1895–96 school year, fraud was apparent. When he investigated, Woodson discovered that none of the alleged pupils attended school in the county and that in fact the school "did not exist except on paper."[42]

A few Indian primary pupils attended the public schools in Watonga, Blaine County, during the fall of 1896. While Woodson approved the idea of Indian children attending school with non-Indian children, because it aided "the speed in which Indian children acquire the white way of life," problems arose. Indian children, especially the girls, lacked proper clothing to attend school with non-Indian children. Even when the Indian pupils did attend the schools, there was little social contact with non-Indian students. School officials provided the same curriculum and classroom facilities for both Indians and whites, but when the Indians were outside the classroom and at play they were "shunned by white pupils on account of their lack of cleanliness in person and clothing." Woodson further suspected that the Watonga Board of Education had little interest in the Indian pupils except to collect the tuition paid by the Bureau of Indian Affairs.[43]

The experiment of enrolling Indian pupils in the public primary schools in Watonga lasted only one year. The school board decided not to accept Indian pupils for the fall term of 1897 because the patrons of the school were considering challenging the legality of Indians and whites attending the same school. A local law prohibited "COLORED children in WHITE schools." Mrs. Mary L. Woodworth, a former secretary of the Watonga School Board, sought a contract to teach forty Indian pupils whose homes were in or near Watonga. Woodson did not recommend offering a contract to Mrs. Woodworth for several reasons: If pupils came from any distance, their parents were likely to leave their allotments and camp near the school. Any large concentration of Indian children in a school would result in their association with each other and avoidance by non-Indian pupils which would emphasize the "race prejudice" that already existed in Blaine County. The discipline in public schools was too lax in his opinion, and such permissiveness would create opposition to the government boarding schools.[44]

Rather than sending Indian children to white primary schools, government officials authorized another boarding school at Hammon. Until 1898, Red Moon and White Shield and their bands did not send their children to the boarding schools in the eastern and central portions of the agency, some distance from their camps. Even when the bands' rations were withheld because their children were not attending schools, the Indians obtained credit from a trader in Cantonment so that they could have food for their families. The new school was small and added only twenty more places for Cheyenne and Arapaho students because the population of Red Moon's and White Shield's bands was less than two hundred people.[45]

At the end of the nineteenth century the agency schools had a capacity of 660, although there were 833 children between the ages of six and eighteen who were expected to attend school. About 10 per cent of the school population attended nonagency schools, such as Carlisle, Haskell, or Chilocco, while another 2 per cent were enrolled in schools supported by the county governments of Oklahoma Territory. Rarely were the agency schools filled to capacity, which meant that probably 250 Cheyenne and Arapaho youngsters still were not receiving an education that would enable them to fulfill the government's expectation of merging them with the non-Indian population of the United States. Less than 15 per cent of the children received more than a few years of primary schooling, which at best ill-prepared them to exercise their rights and privileges as United States citizens and to be trained for a life of independence and self-sufficiency.[46]

CHAPTER IX

Allotments and Farming

ALLOTMENT OF LAND was the key to the success or failure of the Dawes Act. From the 1850's on, all those concerned with Indian affairs assumed that if the Indians were to be assimilated into white culture agriculture would be the vehicle for change. Indian agents such as Woodson had a twofold program: to destroy the old Indian society as completely as possible, and to introduce changes that would make the Indians self-sufficient. Schools maintained by the Bureau of Indian Affairs would teach the young Indians reading, writing, arithmetic, and perhaps the few simple trades required in an agrarian society; the older Indians would be taught agriculture by example. On the Plains the efforts to transform the Cheyennes and Arapahoes into farmers encountered formidable obstacles.

In the culture of the Plains Indians adult males did no domestic manual labor; work in the fields and gardens was for women. Even if the Cheyenne and Arapaho men had been convinced that regular labor was necessary and good, they needed more than their allotments of land to become self-sufficient. The Indians had few machines or implements; had only a limited desire to farm; owned little stock other than their ponies; had few houses, barns, or storage sheds; and had accumulated little capital with which to buy seeds or other farming needs. As the allotment period began, the Cheyennes and Arapahoes were still receiving some assistance from the government. Annuities from the 1867 Medicine Lodge Treaty would not end until 1898, cash payments were being made in the early 1890's for the sale of the reservation's surplus lands, interest from the one million dollars on deposit in the United States Treasury continued, and a few of the tribesmen were employed at the agency, in the schools, or by the traders. For the vast majority, however, utilization of the allotments was the only means of assuring a stable and permanent income.

By 1893 the tribal reserve fund in the United States Treasury had become important to the Indians and their agent. The $432,500 paid directly to the Cheyennes and Arapahoes for the reservation's surplus lands was gone, and the tribes failed to recover the $67,500 payment to Crawford and his co-conspirators. Needing more money and urged on by merchants, Young Whirlwind and the Cantonment chiefs petitioned for a distribution of $75 for each tribal member from the $1 million reserve. The commissioner of Indian affairs rejected the petition because he felt that unsupervised expenditures of funds would do the people little more permanent good than the cash payments from the 1891 agreement.[1]

As long as the reserve funds were in the Treasury, there was little chance that Congress would provide the additional money required to establish the Cheyennes and Arapahoes on their allotments as farmers. Woodson's preliminary suggestions had two objectives: If the allotments were made livable and productive for the Indians, they would remain on them, either willingly or by force, and leave the large camps. He therefore advocated that funds be made available to the Cheyennes and Arapahoes so that they could break the sod, buy seeds, dig wells, build homes, and purchase agricultural implements. Competent farmers should be distributed throughout the agency to furnish agricultural instruction, and shops for the repair of farm machines and tools should be constructed near the Indian population centers. In the shops young Indians educated as artisans at Carlisle and Haskell could be employed. Woodson wrote to the commissioner of Indian affairs that if the Cheyennes and Arapahoes were "placed on their allotments and required to maintain a residence thereon, they would no longer assemble in camps and villages. Their congregation in large numbers promoted dissipation and keeps alive barbarous customs and the habit of dancing and indolence. Tribal relations will never be broken up if they continue to live as now."[2]

Early in 1894, Woodson began holding meetings to explain his plans for improving the allotments, but the traditionalist chiefs managed to defeat his proposals. Even among the Cheyennes and Arapahoes in John H. Seger's district on the Washita River, Little Big Jake and his fellow chiefs managed to hold onto their position of authority in tribal councils. Seger proposed to have the tribes vote through the heads of the "beef bands," who were somewhat younger and better educated than the chiefs. When Seger called upon the younger leaders for their votes, Little Big Jake interrupted; "Hold on, we don't want to vote that way." The Cheyenne chief then asked the older chiefs to vote first, and only three of the younger men were willing to oppose their elders when the vote tally was counted. Although, in Seger's opinion, most of the Cheyennes were willing to follow the suggestions of their agent, the chiefs not only on the Washita but also at Cantonment and along the South Canadian River wanted the money in cash, to be spent without the agent's supervision.[3]

The chiefs' victory did not discourage Woodson. He told his subordinates in the field to keep the proposal before the Indians whenever rations were issued. Use of the reserve funds was the only means of bringing the Indians' allotments into production. Many of the older people, Woodson believed, would realize no benefit from the tribal funds unless they were spent in part for homes, machines, and farm animals. Seger's second meeting with the Indians living on the Washita River was more successful. "The old men," Seger reported, "came in late and did some grumbling and objecting on general principles, but it was evident all through the meeting that they had lost their grip and that the young men were throwing off the yoke." Even in his district, however, Seger did not think that the Indians would approve the use of their money unless a majority of both tribes agreed with their agent.[4]

During April, 1894, Woodson traveled over the agency explaining his plans to Indians and whites. He explained that $500,000 should be diverted from the reserve funds. Each individual would receive $166.66; a family of four would receive $665 with which to improve its allotment. A family of four with a section of land would be able to build a fence for 160 acres of its land, construct a house, dig a well, and have some money for the purchase of farm machines. The remaining allotments of the family, the agent suggested, could then be leased to white farmers and ranchers for income needed for food and clothing. Newspaper editors reacted favorably to Woodson's proposals because the Indians' lands would thus become productive, enabling them to "bear a fair share of the common burdens of the community." Woodson's swing through the agency did little to change the Indians' minds. The older people and chiefs still wanted the money distributed for expenditure as they saw fit, while the younger people were willing to take a chance on Woodson's plan.[5]

In mid-summer, 1894, Woodson identified the source of the Cheyennes' objections to his program. E. F. Mitchell, the former trader at Darlington who had profited so handsomely when the cash payments had been made in 1892, had persuaded the chiefs to demand their money without the agent's supervision so that they could again buy horses, wagons, and other goods from him. Woodson, believing that he had three-quarters of the adult males on his side, called for a council of the tribes to be held at Darlington toward the end of June. The council was not as pliable as Woodson had hoped, and the Indians subjected him to vigorous criticism. They even questioned his personal motives and suggested that he would make a substantial sum from the payment, since one-half million dollars could pass through his hands. One observer commented, "I could not help thinking that if I were in their places, after having been deceived so many times, I would be very slow to accept any propositions from the white men."[6]

It was Woodson's belief that without adequate supervision the Cheyennes and Arapahoes would squander their money as they had before. Discussing the cash payments of 1892, he maintained that the Indians "had no appreciation of the value of money, and it was foolishly spent for all sorts of articles and trifles that they did not require. They easily became the prey of designing men, who managed to fleece them of the money that should have been to supply them with useful articles." Woodson proposed to use a portion of the reserve fund to purchase for the Indians the things necessary "in their farming operations, and to build suitable houses and provide them with a few cows, chickens and pigs." If his plan was implemented, Woodson was sure, white profiteers could not take the Indians' money, and the Indians would become "industrious and worthy citizens." Nevertheless, as a tribe the Cheyennes were unwilling to accept Woodson's plan despite the poverty and privation that many of their people were experiencing.[7]

Unquestionably the Cheyennes and Arapahoes needed assistance in the use of their allotments. From annuity payments and interest on the reserve fund each person in both tribes received twenty-five dollars a year. Adult Indians received rations that were the equivalent of 43 per cent of an army ration and schoolchildren, 70 per cent. Captain Jesse M. Lee, a former Indian agent at Darlington, in supporting Woodson's program, reported that, since the Cheyennes and Arapahoes had citizenship and allotments suddenly thrust upon them, they required "greater care, instructions and protection than ever before.... If left to themselves—in competition with the whites around them— they will 'go to the wall.' "[8]

The deadlock between the Indian agent and the Cheyennes continued over the proper manner by which to utilize a part of the reserve fund. Behind the Cheyennes, of course, were such men as E. F. Mitchell and former agent Ashley, who were ready to assist the Indians in spending their money as before. If Mitchell and Ashley had their way, any distribution of the reserve fund would do little good because conditions similar to the per capita payment of interest money would occur "when merchants and traders sell them goods on credit and take chattel mortgages on their stock, wagons, and harness, which, when lifted at the time of the payment, in most instances leaves absolutely nothing for the Indians." Mitchell persisted in his battle with Woodson. He collected money from many Cheyennes when they received their annuity in November, 1894, so that he could lead a delegation of Cheyennes to Washington. Later he sought to become the attorney for the Cheyennes to represent the tribe in court actions and in all matters before the Bureau of Indian Affairs. Mitchell's interest was clear to Woodson. The former trader hoped to sell the Indians "extravagent shawls and vehicles and broken down horses," as he had in 1892.[9]

Greed drove Mitchell to launch an attack on Agent Woodson's whole administration. In payment for his services as tribal attorney for the Cheyennes, Mitchell expected an annual fee of twenty-five cents from each person on the tribe's roll, with other expenses to be paid from funds under the control of the Bureau of Indian Affairs. He charged that the use of the reserve fund was not the real issue but rather that Woodson had lost the confidence of the tribes. The Indian agent, Mitchell charged, refused to seek means to lease unutilized allotments to whites, would not allow the Indians to send a delegation to Washington, where they could make their needs known, and threatened to discharge an agency Indian employee if he co-operated with Mitchell. Mitchell claimed to have a petition in his possession with 1,364 signatures, which granted him the power of attorney for the Cheyenne tribe. He would voluntarily relinquish the contract as tribal attorney if the Indian commissioner would appoint him leasing agent for the Cheyenne and Arapaho allotments.[10]

An unwary person unfamiliar with Mitchell's character might accept the merchant's schemes as plausible. He argued that most of the 528,000 acres of land alloted to the Cheyennes and Arapahoes was not being used in 1894. Less than 25 per cent of the allotments could be cultivated profitably by the Cheyennes and Arapahoes, and the remainder could be leased to white farmers and ranchers for an estimated $137,000 annually. He claimed that an inspection of the agency in the winter of 1894–95 revealed that the Indians cultivated 5,552 acres, while 4,000 acres were leased for use by whites. Indians, despite assistance from agency farmers, gave little care to their crops. They did not realize "how disastrous it is to leave a half-grown crop and go to visit their relatives. They think that a crop, once planted, should grow—and this only among the younger ones; the older ones do not take to any kind of work that will interfere with their social relations." If the allotments were leased to white farmers, more taxable property would be brought into the counties of Indian Territory to assist in the support of schools, roads, and public expenditures. Mitchell let it be known that he advocated giving Indian families about $220 each to make their existence more comfortable and that he felt that eventually the Indians would benefit from the improvements made upon the allotments by the lessees.[11]

Both Agent Woodson's and Mitchell's programs were disapproved. An intertribal delegation of chiefs visited Washington in March, 1895, to settle the status of the reserve fund. From the outset of conversations with Commissioner of Indian Affairs D. M. Browning it was apparent that the two tribes disagreed—the Cheyennes did not want the money in the Treasury used to fulfill Woodson's program, while the Arapahoes were willing to spend some of it under the supervision of their agent. The chiefs of both tribes expressed similar desires, except in regard to the utilization of the reserve fund. The Indians, Young Whirlwind maintained, were willing to work, but they had no machines or implements to till the soil or harvest their crops. The Cheyenne leader from Cantonment told the commissioner:

We have not enough mowing machines. They are so limited that they cannot get around, by the time they reach one . . . it is too late to cut hay. We do not want to put in small grain because we cannot get binding and threshing machines and we are not able to hire white men for this work. With old men like me the only way we can do to get Indians to work is to talk with the youth. We cannot catch hold the plow and show how. These young men can not only talk, but they can catch hold of the plow and talk that way also.

Left Hand and Row-of-Lodges of the Arapahoes were willing to use the reserve fund to improve allotments and purchase farming equipment. They considered helping the younger men a commendable use of the money because the Indians were in a "very bad fix" for cash. Row-of-Lodges in particular stressed the poverty of his people, calling the commissioner's attention to the needs of those who were trying to farm:

We must have wagons, harness, teams and other things; but without money we cannot purchase them. These Indians are poor and at the point of starvation, and are told that we must work for their bread as white people do. . . . While I am here I have better food than the folks at home; a good many of them have nothing to eat this morning.

Since the tribes could not agree, the funds remained in the Treasury, drawing 5 per cent annual interest, which was distributed in per capita payments among the tribesmen.[12]

Despite the rebuff Woodson pushed other portions of his program. Essentially he hoped to break up the Indians' camp life and force them to live on their allotments, and begin farming. He was disappointed when the commissioner's office cautioned him about withholding rations from Indians who refused to obey his regulations. Thomas Smith, acting commissioner of Indian affairs, pointed out that the Indians were guaranteed their annuity goods, which included food, by treaties and agreements with the government. Woodson maintained that the Treaty of Medicine Lodge required only the issuance of clothing and not food, and he reminded Acting Commissioner Smith, "you know quite well how little respect Indians generally have for an agent who is not backed up by the Dept." Although a few Indians opposed him and tried to convince others that he was acting without the approval of Washington, Woodson claimed that there was little hostility to him within the tribes. Unless full support was forthcoming from Washington, he declared, however, "my influence over these Indians to accomplish good results is ended."[13]

Only Rule Five of Woodson's orders was not approved by the commissioner of Indian affairs. By threatening to withhold food rations, Woodson had hoped to prevent Indians from visiting or living outside their ration or farming districts for extended periods of time without his permission. The commissioner noted that as citizens the Indians could not be denied their freedom to visit outside their districts or be deprived of their rations, especially since an extended drought in Oklahoma Territory had destroyed the Indians' crops, leaving them little to live on. Otherwise, the commissioner said, Woodson could expect support "by all proper and lawful means," and he was urged to "exercise lenience, patience, and forbearance to the end that hardship may be avoided."[14]

Only the older Indians found Woodson's rules distasteful. All others complied willingly to the new regulations, especially when he treated them firmly and kindly. He predicted that as the Cheyennes and Arapahoes found that evasion of the edicts to go to work on their allotments would not be tolerated, they would "become sub-servient to the control of the agent in carrying out the instructions of the Department with surprising acquiescence." Woodson continued to insist that issuing rations to every Indian regardless of his efforts to self-support hindered "any rapid advancement of the Indians." He preferred to discontinue issuing food from annuity funds and to allocate money from congressional appropriations for that purpose. Rations, he maintained, should be given only to the "deserving Indians" as a "reward for industry" and to others "incapacitated by disease, age, or physical infirmity."[15]

Blocked in an effort to have the tribal reserve funds distributed to all Cheyennes and Arapahoes, Woodson devised a plan so that funds could be obtained by individuals. He drafted legislation to be introduced into Congress that would permit tribal members to apply through their agent to the secretary of the interior for their share of the permanent funds. If the bill passed Congress and if the secretary of the interior approved the application, the "segregated" money would be spent for the purpose of "having improvements made on his or her allotment, or for the purchase of stock, wagons, harness, farming utensils and such other articles as may be deemed necessary by the Secretary of the Interior for their progress and civilization." When the funds were withdrawn from the reserve, the individual would no longer share in the tribes' interest payments. No legislation was required because Woodson's modified plan received the approval of the secretary of the interior.[16]

Unless money became available to the Cheyennes and Arapahoes, Woodson contended, they would become "vagrants and paupers." With assistance the younger people especially had the chance of becoming "good citizens contributing their share of the revenues for local government." As in the previous years the Indian agent insisted that the expenditure of the funds should be controlled by his office since the Cheyennes and Arapahoes were not "intelligent" enough to make "proper and judicious" use of their money. Since 1892 the tribes had received more than $700,000 in cash payments. "This large sum," Woodson told Dennis T. Flynn, an Oklahoma territorial delegate, "was wasted and but little of it used for improvement of their allotments—so that to-day they are even worse off than when they held their reservation in common." The Indians' white neighbors would also benefit from the supervised distribution of the money because they could be employed to build houses and make improvements on the allotments which the Indians could not do because of their lack of skills. Although some Indians could withdraw funds from the Treasury, Woodson was still forced to rely on annual appropriations to bring changes in the Indians' economic activities.[17]

As pressure from Woodson increased for the Cheyennes and Arapahoes to live on and work their allotments, the Cheyennes particularly came to resent their agent. Old Crow was especially bitter and demanded that the Indian agent be dismissed from his post within thirty days. He and his fellow chiefs decried Woodson's withholding of rations from able-bodied Indians who refused to work, the curtailment of their traditional ceremonies which included the use of the "mescal bean" (peyote), and the prohibition of plural marriages. Consequently, the Cheyenne chiefs retained an attorney to negotiate with the government for more money for the sale of their reservation and to press charges against Woodson.[18]

Woodson received official support in his struggle with the older Cheyenne chiefs. The commissioner of Indian affairs conceded that the food issued to the Indians from congressional appropriations was not a right as defined by treaties with the Cheyennes. He ruled that beef, flour, and other foods purchased from funds provided by Congress to the Bureau of Indian Affairs were a gratuity from the government which could be terminated at any time by Congress. The commissioner instructed Woodson to inform the Indians that the full power of the government stood behind him and that annual appropriations of Congress would not be used to support them in idleness. The stand of the commissioner and endorsements from high ranking army officers and the chairman of the Board of Indian Commissioners quieted the Cheyennes' dissension for a time.[19]

By 1897, Woodson thought that he observed some progress toward self-support among the tribes. John H. Seger was the most successful of the agency employees in persuading the Indians to grow crops. Thirty-three Cheyenne and Arapaho men from Seger's district brought into El Reno wagonloads of wheat, cotton, and wool, which they exchanged for lumber and food. Several other men whom Seger was instructing had hired themselves out to white farmers to pick cotton. Woodson accounted for this improvement by the firm and decisive decisions of his superiors and the shrewdness of the chiefs, who finally realized that opposition to the agent would not succeed. After a long and tedious struggle Woodson thought that the resistance of the chiefs was beginning to crack and that the younger, educated men would be able to play a more active role in planning tribal affairs.[20]

The chiefs' power, however, was never entirely crushed. As a group they blocked the sending of an intertribal delegation to Washington in 1898, when Woodson wanted to reopen discussions about the tribal reserve funds. Although the Arapaho chiefs were willing to talk, the Cheyennes took no part in the preliminary councils at Darlington. Until 1898 the interest payments were made semiannually. Usually the amount was so little—$7.50 for each person—that the Indians squandered or gambled away the money before they left the places where the money was distributed. To make more effective use of the money, Woodson changed the interest payment to once a year, in early winter, so that the Indians would have some cash to buy food and clothing when their resources were generally the lowest. The Indian agent was disturbed by the previous spring payments, which had caused the Indians to gather away from their allotments for several weeks. Merchants in the towns were willing to extend credit to the Cheyennes and Arapahoes up to the amount of the interest payment so that they could live in camps and feast and gamble. Cultivation and planting of crops ceased as long as the credit lasted.[21]

Regardless of the policies initiated in Washington or Darlington, the Indians needed food, clothing, and homes. The objective of the Dawes Act was to sever the Indians from dependence upon congressional appropriations and to force them as a people to assume responsibility for their own livelihood. Since the Cheyennes and Arapahoes were virtually unprepared to do so in 1892, the amount of money made available by Congress to the Indian agents was of vital concern. Within a few months the Cheyennes and Arapahoes had used up the payments made for the sale of the reservation. As long as the money lasted, they ate well. One reporter described an Indian family's purchase of a cow in Arapaho and their butchering of it at the nearest convenient place. He wrote that, after the animal had been killed by the men,

the squaws of the family took charge of the entrails, cleaning them carefully and now and then cutting off generous hunks of the choicest portions which were distributed among their numerous progeny. The kids sat crosslegged on the ground and contentedly munching away on these dainty morsels, chatting gaily all the while, much the same as a parcel of white children would with a snack of chocolate creams. They carted off everything pertaining to the animal except what blood soaked into the ground.[22]

In 1892 money was soon scarce among the tribes and they began grumbling about the shortages of beef resulting from smaller congressional appropriations. They began to sell ponies for meat; others with cattle killed them for food, which quickly depleted the small herds and lessened the Indians' ability to live off their herds' natural growth. When Agent Ashley heard that the Cheyennes and Arapahoes were becoming "restless, cross and liable to make trouble by reason of insufficient subsistence," he made a brief tour through the agency and found none of the people "in a starving condition or suffering from hunger." The forthcoming interest payment, nineteen dollars for each person, the sale of ponies, and a temporary 25 per cent increase in beef rations, he thought, would see the Cheyennes and Arapahoes through even a severe winter.[23]

In 1892 the Cheyennes and Arapahoes cultivated less than one acre of land for each person. Even that small acreage decreased if there was any reason not to cultivate the fields and gardens, such as the cash payments resulting from the 1891 agreement. John Seger observed that the Seger colonists fared "sumptiously" while the payment money lasted and that "ghost dancing was freely indulged in to the exclusion of farm work." For the sponsors the Ghost Dances were an intense religious experience, but for most of the six hundred Cheyennes and Arapahoes over whom Seger had supervision the dances were merely an opportunity to visit and feast with their friends and neighbors. The exceptional Indian family, such as that of Prairie Chief, invested their money in cattle. Prairie Chief's people had accumulated a herd of 162 cattle, but during the feasts that followed the sale of the reservation, the Seger colonists had "killed or eaten more of their own cattle than in the five years previous, and this at a time when they have had more money to help themselves with than at any previous time."[24]

After the allotment of Cheyenne and Arapaho land Congress slashed the funds available to purchase food for the tribes. Actually more food was needed immediately after 1891 than before. During the reservation period cattlemen had made presents of beef to the Indians so that herds of cattle could be run on the rangeland, and money previously earned by the Indians transporting agency supplies from Kansas lessened because railroads had been constructed to towns near Darlington. Reported Agent Woodson, the Cheyennes living in the western portion of the agency were "in the wildest condition of blanket Indians. . . . The issue of beef once a month and other stores twice a month, does not keep them from suffering from a lack of food." In 1894, Congress reduced the beef ration by three pounds, the amount of flour by one and one-fourth pounds, and other essential items of food proportionally. Indian crops were small because of a severe drought and lack of sufficient implements to cultivate allotments. Wealthier Indians survived by selling off their ponies to buy food, others in a less fortunate position, said Agent Woodson, were in a "pitiable" condition.[25]

With less money to buy beef, Woodson also found that the meat for rations had become more expensive. White farmers and ranchers whose improved stock was imperiled by Texas fever demanded effective quarantines against herds taken to Darlington from Texas ranges or from the Indian agencies southwest of Darlington. By 1892 the governor of Oklahoma Territory was enforcing the quarantine laws passed by the territorial legislature. Woodson could receive the herds delivered by the beef contractor at Darlington, since Canadian County was not within the quarantine boundary lines, but he could not easily distribute the cattle to outlying issue stations. The only alternative available to the Indian agent was to slaughter the beef at

Darlington and transport the butchered meat to the issue stations. Transportation and butchering cost money, and the amount of spoilage rose sharply. If Woodson ignored the quarantine laws and boundaries, the cattle intended for issue to the Indians could be seized by county officials, and the Indian agent was subject to fines for the violations of the statutes.[26]

To avoid the quarantines, Woodson tried to purchase the 2.5 million pounds of live cattle within the quarantine-free area of Oklahoma Territory. The beef contractors, however, complained that they could purchase cattle more cheaply in Texas, and they were unwilling to absorb the losses if they were required to buy more expensive cattle. After months of delay Woodson managed to find an inspector from the Bureau of Animal Husbandry who would certify that the beef contractors' cattle were free from infectious diseases. Nevertheless, when the inspector issued the permits to move cattle from Darlington to Cantonment and other agency issue stations, farmers and county officials stopped the herds. Woodson was charged with neglecting the interests of the farmers and small ranchers scattered throughout the agency.[27]

While the farmers and the agent bickered, the Indians suffered. Often the beef rations, upon which they depended as the main staple of their diet, were delayed for weeks. The farmers would not accept Woodson's assurances that only cattle free from Texas fever were being moved through the agency to the issue stations. And, Woodson admitted, the farmers had legitimate grievances since the school herds and those owned by agency employees had suffered from Texas fever. Finally, after a year of effort, Woodson solved the problem with the farmers by having the beef contractors purchase their cattle either in Oklahoma Territory or in areas not infected with Texas fever. The Indian agent also instructed the beef contractors to keep their cattle on carefully marked routes to avoid as much as possible the improved stock of the residents.[28]

Once Woodson had satisfied the farmers and ranchers, the Indians began to complain. As the distribution of butchered meat began, the old chiefs who controlled the issuance of rations demanded permission to place their complaints before the commissioner of Indian affairs in Washington. Every two weeks each family or beef band received its ration of meat, but the old chiefs no longer could claim a larger portion as they had previously, and, of course, they could not dole out the meat to their favorites. The new system begun by Woodson was more equitable but was politically unpopular with the chiefs. Woodson required his subordinates to tell the Indians bluntly that "it is useless for them to send anyone to Washington relative to the issue of beef, and you are hereby directed to carry out your instructions to the letter relative to the issue of beef from the block, and you will be sustained by this office." A few of the chiefs, such as White Shield, were still popular enough with their bands to be able to refuse altering the manner in which meat was issued. Many of the 175 Cheyennes led by White Shield would not accept butchered meat. They boycotted the issue stations for three years before accepting beef from the cutting blocks.[29]

Toward the end of his administration Woodson thought it wise to reduce the amount of beef furnished to the Cheyennes and Arapahoes. In 1899 he suggested that the one million pounds of cattle, liveweight, be cut by 25 per cent. Woodson did not advocate a sudden withdrawal of rations, especially for old and infirm Indians, but for others the quantity of meat provided to the Cheyennes and Arapahoes retarded "their ultimate independence of Government support." Rather than continue to spend such large sums for beef, Woodson suggested that more congressional funds be used to purchase foundation stock for Indian herds or for improvements upon allotments.[30]

For a few years following allotment, Agents Ashley and Woodson paid little attention to the Indians' homes. Both were more concerned with providing food and clothing for the Indians and protecting the new citizens' property from being seized by the incoming white population. In 1893, Woodson became disturbed about the condition of the Indian camps where most of the tribes lived. "Long residence," he wrote, "in one locality without efforts to maintain proper police regulations renders it unhealthful. Only when the place becomes foul will they voluntarily change their location." In the camps there was a high incidence of disease caused by contaminated water supplies and large accumulations of camp and human refuse. A few of the tribesmen requested that homes be built for them, but Woodson thought that the money could be better spent for other purposes.[31]

Until 1896 the Cheyennes and Arapahoes seeking permanent houses for their families were usually not given much support from Agent Woodson. When, in 1894, Richard Davis, an educated Cheyenne who was working as an "additional agency farmer," inquired about constructing houses for his people, Woodson replied that it was not contemplated furnishing the Indians with them until they could be used. Rather than "waste" money on houses, Woodson preferred to spend money obtained from Congress on the purchase of horses, plows, and other agricultural implements so that the Indian allotments could be made more productive. Woodson could also have pointed out that of the 125 homes built for the Cheyennes and Arapahoes, only 31 were continuously occupied.[32]

Perhaps Woodson delayed a housing-construction program because the Cheyennes and Arapahoes were unwilling to commit a portion of their reserve fund for improvements on their allotments. Finally, in 1896, Woodson was willing to support with congressional funds the building of fifty houses for the more progressive members of the tribes. Woodson believed that it would not be productive to build houses similar to those undertaken during the administration of Agent Ashley; they were "simply shells, without plastering or ceiling, and afforded insufficient shelter in cold weather, making it more comfortable for the inmates to live in teepees during the winter months." In providing houses that would be comfortable during the winter, Woodson estimated that he would have to spend at least $250 for each dwelling, twice the amount spent by Ashley. To launch the building program, Woodson requested authority to hire carpenters to assist the Indians in constructing their houses and money to buy flooring, shingles, doors, windows, and other hardware. Each two-room house contained 384 square feet of floor space, a size that the Indian agent hoped would "induce these Indians to establish permanent homes on their allotments. . . . Their inability to procure proper shelter and water, hinders many of them from having permanent abodes."[33]

From the outset Woodson restricted construction of homes to those

Indians who were "actively engaged in the work of establishing homes and making other necessary, permanent improvements on their allotments." He justified the limited size of the program because he had found that the dwellings constructed entirely with government funds were soon abandoned by their owners. Most assistance was directed toward those tribesmen who had accumulated funds from freighting, hauling and cutting wood, and other labor. In 1898, Woodson found that more of the Cheyennes and Arapahoes wanted houses. They had discovered that they could not adopt the habits of their white neighbors while they lived in canvas-covered lodges. Such associations caused many of the Indians to want the small two-room houses usually constructed for them, while a few of the more "progressive" families owned larger homes containing three or four rooms.[34]

It was difficult for Woodson to assist even the "deserving" Indians in building houses on their allotments. He saved the money obtained from the sale of cattle hides from the beef issues to help in the program, but that amounted to only about fifteen hundred dollars a year. Other funds would have to come from annual congressional appropriations, which were cut by thirty-eight thousand dollars for the 1898–99 fiscal year after annuities guaranteed by the Treaty of Medicine Lodge had expired. All expenses other than that for education at the agency would have to come from the ninety thousand dollars provided by Congress. After food, clothing, and the needs of the older Cheyennes and Arapahoes were provided for and the salaries of the agency employees were paid, little money remained to assist the Indians in any way to establish themselves on their allotments.[35]

At the turn of the century seven out of eight Cheyenne and Arapaho families still lived in tipis or lodges, and in the immediate future Woodson could not anticipate additional funding from Congress. With the expiration of annuities provided for during the preceding thirty years, Woodson commented that the government would no longer "feed" the Indians. The Cheyennes and Arapahoes did not have a treaty "with the Government and it is not bound to give them anything." Within several years the "indiscriminate gratuitous" issues of rations were viewed by Acting Commissioner A. C. Tonner as a "hindrance rather than a help" to Indians. The old and helpless would continue to receive assistance, but the able-bodied and those educated in Indian schools would receive food only if they labored. Commissioner Tonner warned that the time was soon approaching when "all Government support will be withdrawn, and . . . [the Indians] will have to depend entirely upon their own resources for a livelihood."[36]

After 1891 it was crucial that the Indian allotments become productive. When the Cheyennes and Arapahoes came into possession of their individual tracts of land, only 2,966 acres of land, or less than 1 acre for each person, were planted in crops. The 1892 crop was nearly a failure because of the customary dry summer season. Corn, for example, produced only 15 per cent of the expected yield because the agency farmers were still instructing the Indians in the planting, cultivating, and harvesting cycle used in the more arable and cooler regions of the United States. Other factors also contributed to the low agricultural productivity. Cash payments from the 1891 Agreement were used by the Indians to buy their necessities, and the "utmost efforts failed to induce them to engage in their farm work." Some Indians bought cattle with their portion of the funds distributed throughout the tribes. Many of the cattle, however, died from the lack of forage, and the remainder were sold to whites for nominal sums. Seger did not believe that insufficient rainfall caused the failure of field crops. Rather, the Indians neglected corn at particularly critical times, a pattern that would continue, in Seger's view, until "necessity compels them to work for their necessaries." When the Indians grew wheat, the crop was not profitable to them. Because it cost the Indian farmers fifty-five cents a hundredweight to transport grain from the Seger District to the nearest railroad, an adequate margin of profit was destroyed.[37]

The distribution of slightly less than five hundred thousand dollars to the Cheyennes and Arapahoes during 1892 made little impact on their ability to live on their allotments. Actually the funds probably caused most of the tribesmen to labor less for a period of time. When the second installment of the payment was to be made, all the tribesmen, except for some of the Cantonment Cheyennes, gathered at

Darlington on May 20 and remained there until June 30. During that period all crops and livestock were neglected. The Indians spent their money for food and luxuries; they gambled and were preyed upon by the white merchants of El Reno and other nearby towns. Only thirty-five families of the two tribes were engaged in farming, and all of them had begun their efforts before the allotment process had begun. Too few of the Indians used the money to build homes or fences or to dig wells so that they could live on the lands that they had chosen or that had been assigned to them. As a group the Cheyennes and Arapahoes were not prepared to benefit from citizenship or from the lands held in trust for them under the Dawes Act.[38]

In the day-to-day administration of agency affairs the Indian agents faced perplexing problems. Red Moon's, Spotted Horse's, and White Shield's bands were completely unwilling to undertake any kind of work and would not labor on their allotments. Some of the agency additional farmers employed to assist the Indians in farming were too old or incompetent to be of any assistance. Whenever annuities or interest payments were to be made, the Indians moved to Darlington for weeks of visiting and dancing. Once at Darlington, the money disappeared almost as quickly as the agent distributed it. Although Ashley insisted that the prices for the goods and food were as low near Darlington as in the towns in other counties, El Reno merchants and liquor dealers periodically enjoyed windfalls of large profits. The Indian agent denied that the young men were "unduly influenced . . . to spend their money in gambling, horse racing, and many other ways detrimental to them" while they were at Darlington, but he did not mention what happened when the young citizens wandered into nearby El Reno with money in their pockets. An attempt to purchase a self-binder for the agency schools to be used for the instruction of Indian boys in harvesting grain was blocked by the commissioner of Indian affairs because the young men would not be able to buy such expensive machinery for their farms. The commissioner was not moved by the explanation that the Indians needed a self-binder for grains, particularly oats, since the dry harvest season dried out the mature crop too rapidly to permit efficient gathering by hand labor.[39]

When Woodson became Indian agent at Darlington in July, 1893, he immediately set out to increase the agricultural productivity of the Cheyennes and Arapahoes. For the few Indians who had surplus grain to sell he found a market at Fort Reno and Fort Supply; he believed it important that they be encouraged with all possible income for their labor. To improve the Indians' workstock, he suggested the use of stallions of greater size than the Indian ponies so that the Cheyennes and Arapahoes would not have to spend their limited funds in purchasing draft animals. Educated Indian youths were advocated as agency assistant farmers so that instruction could be begun with most of the tribesmen who could not understand even a limited amount of English. Agent Woodson also found that the Indians were spending too much time traveling to Darlington semi-monthly to pick up their rations. Many of the Indians spent at least seven days out of every two weeks traveling to and from the town. During their absence from their allotments white neighbors carried off "farming implements, tools, fence wire, or anything they find lying about, and as yet no convictions for larceny or theft by such people have been obtained." To prevent such losses of property, Woodson suggested that issue stations be established at Hammon, Cantonment, and Watonga.[40]

After six months at Darlington, Woodson knew that some changes were necessary in the Indians' way of life. If the Cheyennes and Arapahoes continued to live in camps away from their allotments, to visit their friends for weeks at a time, and generally to ignore their land and crops, there was little hope of their becoming self-sufficient. First the Indians would have to be compelled to live on their lands, and to do so additional agency Indian police would be needed. Then more money would be required from Congress so that a part of each allotment could be plowed, fences built, wells dug, houses constructed, and farming tools purchased. Additional issue stations would have to be scattered over the agency so that the Indians who lived away from Darlington would not have to spend up to seven days traveling to and from the agency headquarters. Young, educated Indians could be employed at the new issue stations to assist other tribesmen in the repair and use of farm machines and implements. Many of the Indians, Woodson informed the commissioner of Indian affairs, "have never lived on their allotments, and some . . . even do not know where their lands are situated; while others still maintain that they have never parted with their right to their reservation lands." For any measure of success Woodson needed more funds from Congress and the support of the Bureau of Indian Affairs.[41]

D. M. Browning, the commissioner of Indian affairs, agreed with Woodson in principle. It was the determination of the Bureau of Indian Affairs to make all Indians "self-supporting and respectable members of the community." But there the commissioner stopped. It was unlikely that Congress would provide larger appropriations for them, especially since they had a reserve fund of one million dollars in the United States Treasury. Browning suggested that Woodson approach the chiefs of the tribes and other leaders and seek approval to expend some of the reserve funds on the allotments.[42]

Teaching the Cheyennes and Arapahoes to become farmers was difficult. They were averse to agricultural labor, and the agency employees hired to assist them were ineffective or incompetent or both. Agent Woodson maintained that the "progress of the Indian depends largely on the competency and fitness of men appointed farmers." Unfortunately, most whites employed as additional or assistant farmers could not speak Cheyenne or Arapaho and therefore could not communicate with the people they were trying to instruct, while young, educated Indians who could talk to their fellow tribesmen were insufficiently trained in business matters or farming supervision to be effective as employees. Woodson wanted better employees to work with the Indians, but finding them was difficult.[43]

Richard Davis, a full-blood Cheyenne, became an agency additional farmer. Recently returned from Carlisle Institute, Davis was well recommended, and it was believed that his appointment would be fully accepted by the Indians. After Davis assumed his post in mid-July, 1894, Woodson worked closely with him with success. Woodson hoped to appoint other Indians to similar positions, but he recommended that since they would be less efficient than white employees their salaries should be less than those of whites with similar appointments. Within a few months four other young men were working throughout the agency. Andrew Tasso and Stacy Riggs, Cheyennes, and Henry D. North and Lewis H. Miller, Arapahoes, joined Richard Davis as additional farmers at salaries of $720 a year.[44]

Within a year Woodson's experiment with the Indian additional farmers was in difficulty. Davis tried to work too independently, and he lacked experience to make his ideas successful. Intertribal jealousy also presented some problems because people from both tribes lived in the various farming districts. It was alleged that Davis was favoring Cheyennes in the distribution of agricultural implements. The report brought a sharp reprimand to Davis from Woodson:

How can you expect the Indians to become progressive and industrious unless you will set them a practical lesson and show by your actions that you are governed by a proper sense of justice in the distribution of the articles placed in your charge? These Indians must learn to work, and you are placed over them to instruct them and encourage them in doing so. You should have no favorites, and be fully alive to the responsibility resting in you; and the Arapahoes should receive from you as much consideration as the Cheyennes.[45]

Less than a year after the appointments Woodson decided that the five Cheyennes and Arapahoes were not competent to be additional farmers. He claimed that they were not intelligent enough to resolve frictions that arose between the allottees and their white neighbors. The young men did not possess sufficient knowledge of local laws to prevent whites from infringing on the rights of Indian citizens, and they were not prepared to teach other Indians proper farming techniques. As a group the Indian additional farmers did not possess the "power and force of character" to force other Indians to observe agency regulations. Woodson also charged that the young men would not distribute farming equipment equitably; that they lacked "energy, industry and close attention" to their duties; that they would not report violations of orders dealing with plural marriages, peyote, gambling, and other "vices"; that trespassers on Indian allotments remained unreported by the Indian additional farmers; and that they would not assist in the apprehension of whites who stole Indian property. Since the young Indians could not discharge the duties assigned to additional farmers, Woodson recommended that they be dismissed from their appointments and reassigned as assistant farmers with reductions in salary up to 100 per cent.[46]

Davis "indignantly" declined to accept his demotion. He charged that Woodson was motivated by political considerations and gave preference to Republicans. Thomas A. Butler, who replaced Davis in Farming District 8, had been recommended to Woodson by Dennis T. Flynn, a Republican congressional delegate of the Territory of Oklahoma. The Indian agent, of course, denied Davis' charge and simply responded that he would have appointed a Democrat if he could have found one who was qualified for the position.[47]

White additional farmers also neglected their duties, but the Indian agent did not summarily dismiss them. An additional farmer whose district was adjacent to Darlington was warned: "Your visits through your district have been few and far between; not more than three times during the whole farming season. You have left the entire management of this district to your Indian Assistants."[48]

During his years as Indian agent, Woodson never was satisfied with the men who were teaching the Indians to farm. Further problems arose in 1899, when Congress decided to limit the amount for all wages for whites on Indian agencies to ten thousand dollars. When the new regulation became effective, the Indian agent would have no choice but to employ Cheyennes and Arapahoes who could be hired for smaller salaries than those of whites.[49]

At first glance the Cheyennes and Arapahoes appeared to have enough instructors to help them in their farming endeavors. In 1897 the agency was assigned one superintendent of farming, nine additional farmers, and nine assistant farmers, the latter group being members of the tribes. Seven Indian blacksmiths worked in seven of the nine farming districts repairing agricultural machines, and there were twenty-nine Indian police to maintain discipline and the regulations of the agency. The farmers had more contact with the Indians than did the Indian agent, who spent most of his time in Darlington. Each farming district was virtually a subagency in which most of the needs of the Indians could be met except for schooling and medical care. Through the additional farmers the Indian agent learned of those able-bodied men who refused to work, of the mar-

riages that occurred, of the legal problems that the Indians encountered, and of the successes and failures as the Indians tried to work
at growing crops.[50]

Nearly every part of Woodson's program was resisted by the
Cheyennes and Arapahoes. An illustration of the conflict between
the Indians and their agent occurred when the latter tried to improve
the quality of workstock throughout the agency. Indian ponies were
too small and weak to serve as draft animals to work the allotments,
and Agent Woodson wanted to breed the Indians' mares to French
Coach stallions, and he purchased a number of them to stand at the
issue stations. Even the more co-operative Indian leaders refused to
bring in their mares to be serviced by the stallions because they
wanted to keep their prized ponies. As a result the Indian pony
stallions continued to run freely with the mares. After four years of
effort the Indians won the struggle. Woodson admitted that the
French Coach stallions "have been patronized to a limited extent
only, the Indian being very much wedded to his pony and indifferent
to the importance of breeding better and more useful animals." Upon
advice from agricultural specialists from Oklahoma Agricultural and
Mechanical College, Woodson finally purchased four jacks so that
the Indians could choose between having their mares serviced by
stallions or jacks. The Indians, however, did not respond to Woodson's new venture because they undoubtedly understood that better
work animals would bring increased demands for their use in the
fields.[51]

Despite the slowness with which the Indians responded to efforts
to assist them in becoming farmers, Woodson paid close attention to
what he believed were their best interests. By careful economy the
Indian agent was able to assemble at each issue station sets of agricultural machines other than the more expensive items, such as self-
binders and threshing equipment. Additional farmers were warned
to issue the implements to "deserving Indians only," but large numbers of farming tools continued to be stolen by or sold to white
farmers. Indian farmers owning twenty-five or more acres of broken
land were advised to plant more of it in corn, kaffir corn, and other
productive grains. To ensure that the Indians would be on their

allotments during the planting season, Woodson wanted credit to the Cheyennes and Arapahoes limited until mid-May, when most of the crops would have been planted. "Experience has shown," he wrote, "that as soon as goods are offered by the traders on credit—secured by chattel mortgages on the teams and wagons—that they flock to the Agency, abandoning their allotments and crops for the time being, where they remain until their credit is exhausted."[52]

Recommendations were made to use better varieties of seed and to shift to different crops more adaptable to the climate of Oklahoma Territory. Additional farmers were informed about the availability of improved seeds and were given instructions on the proper planting and cultivation of crops. Particular attention was given to cotton, and some Indian farmers, because of the success they had with it in 1897, expanded their acreage the following year. In some of the farming districts, especially around Watonga, Indians were employed by white farmers to pick cotton, employment that produced some income for them.[53]

A few members of the tribes tried the "white man's road" and raised crops. With pride Agent Woodson could point to Standing Bird, a Cheyenne, who, Woodson said, was a "blanket Indian" in 1892 but five years later "raised and dug 30 bushels of Irish potatoes, has a good field of corn and kaffir corn, and has 4 acres of the finest cotton in Custer County." Most Cheyennes and Arapahoes, however, had to be coerced into farming by the threat of cancellation of rations. For some, no amount of pressure from the agent would make them change their way of life or contribute to their self-sufficiency. Unfortunately, allotting agents in 1891 had placed some Cheyennes and Arapahoes on land that was not fertile and could only be used for grazing. Those Indians, Woodson concluded, would always be "heavily handicapped in the effort to derive self-support by the cultivation" of their allotments.[54]

By the end of the nineteenth century the Cheyennes and Arapahoes had made some progress in agriculture. Indian farmers grew corn, kaffir corn, wheat, oats, millet, sorghum, cotton, and vegetables. When the elements favored the farmer, as they did in 1899, fields cultivated by Indians produced as much as forty bushels of corn an acre. 1899, however, was an exceptional year, when the Indians' grain was not destroyed by drought or severe storms. Rather than face the disappointments of crop failures, many of the tribes began to lease their allotments to white farmers and ranchers, who eagerly sought to make the necessary arrangements through the Indian agent. Depending on the quality of the soil and whether crops could be raised or cattle grazed, Indian allotments were rented to whites for sums ranging from twenty cents to one dollar an acre. In 1899 out of the 3,295 allotments in the agency 1,072 were leased by the Indians. Ostensibly those leases covered the lands of Indians who were old or physically infirm, or children who could not yet work productively on their allotments. Such was not always the case.[55]

At least one-third of the allotments contained insufficient fertile land on which crops and vegetables could be raised to add appreciably to an Indian family's income. It is difficult to estimate family incomes for the Cheyennes and Arapahoes during this period. Fewer than ten members of the two tribes had cash incomes of five hundred dollars or more a year each. All members of the tribes received a minimum of sixteen dollars a year when the interest on the reserve fund was distributed on a per capita basis. How many of the Cheyennes and Arapahoes worked as agricultural laborers or freighters in 1899 is not known, but certainly no more than a few thousand dollars were earned in aggregate from those sources.

In his 1899 reports to the commissioner of Indian affairs, Agent Woodson claimed that 95 per cent of the able-bodied males of the tribes were living on their allotments. If the Indian agent's statements were true, the struggle to break up camp life had been won, and in the future the quality of life for the Cheyennes and Arapahoes would depend upon the retention of the allotments and the degree to which those lands became agriculturally productive.[56]

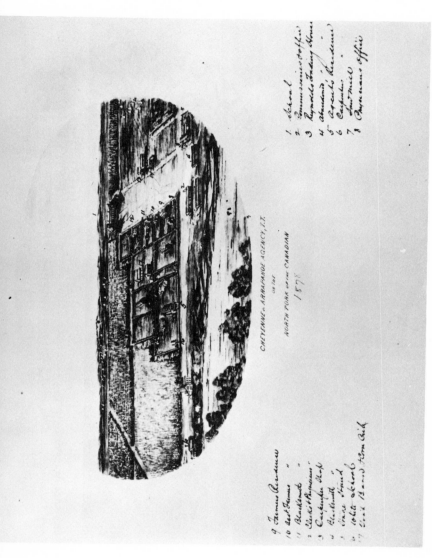

Cheyenne-Arapaho Agency at Darlington in 1878. *Courtesy Western History Collections, University of Oklahoma Library.*

Cheyenne-Arapaho Agency at Darlington during the late nineteenth century. *Courtesy Western History Collections, University of Oklahoma Library.*

Baker's Store and Murray Hotel, Darlington, Indian Territory. *Courtesy Oklahoma Historical Society.*

A mission building, Darlington, Indian Territory. *Courtesy Western History Collections, University of Oklahoma Library.*

Seger Indian School, Colony, Oklahoma Territory. *Courtesy Western History Collections, University of Oklahoma Library.*

Indian girls entering Seger Indian School, Colony, Oklahoma Territory. *Courtesy Western History Collections, University of Oklahoma Library.*

Indian boys cleaning the grounds of the Seger Indian School, Colony, Oklahoma Territory. *Courtesy Western History Collections, University of Oklahoma Library.*

John H. Seger, seated on bank, supervising a work crew of Indians at Colony, Oklahoma Territory. *Courtesy Western History Collections, University of Oklahoma Library.*

CHAPTER X

The Law of the White Man—
The Pressure for Conformity

WHEN INDIAN AGENT Woodson claimed that 95 per cent of the able-bodied Cheyennes and Arapahoes were living on their allotments, he made a misleading statement. If he had included other information, such as the fact that 2,500 Cheyennes and Arapahoes out of a total population of 3,018 were still dependent on rations issued through the Indian agent's office in 1900, a more realistic description of the tribes' condition would have been presented. The ration system, in the view of the commissioner of Indian affairs, had to be eliminated because it encouraged idleness, promoted beggary, suppressed independence, perpetuated pauperism, and stifled industry. Congress in 1875 enacted a statute requiring Indians to contribute to their own support by labor in return for food, clothing, and other goods supplied to them by Congress through either supplemental congressional appropriations or annuities due from treaties and agreements. But the ration system was little better than the reservation system, which the Dawes Act was intended to destroy.[1]

On January 1, 1900, a new Indian agent, Major George W. H. Stouch, took charge of the offices at Darlington. As he became familiar with the condition of Indian life throughout the agency, he reacted vigorously against the apparent stagnation and lack of progress toward self-sufficiency. Agent Stouch learned that only 15 to 18 per cent of the Cheyennes and Arapahoes were actually growing crops or gardens on their allotments. Seeds issued to the Indians were fed to ponies or destroyed. For the most part the Cheyennes and

Arapahoes "had citizenship thrust upon them when they were so fearfully unprepared for it." Few of the people could protect themselves from unscrupulous whites, even though as citizens they were supposed to receive the same treatment as whites in the territorial courts. With no money to hire lawyers to represent their interests, the Indians relied upon the agent, who was too busy with other matters to see that they were given a fair hearing in court cases. Even the money received from land rentals was, in Stouch's opinion, too little. During the 1899–1900 fiscal year the Cheyennes and Arapahoes received $42,120.83 from rents or leases of their allotments. As the leases came to the agency headquarters for renewal, Stouch expected to double the rentals for productive cropland and thereby measurably to increase the Indians' income.[2]

Indian life in the homes and camps was depressing. Cheyenne and Arapaho women clung to their old customs even more tenaciously than did the men of the tribes. Young women who returned from the schools with homemaking skills soon lapsed back into the traditional camp life, especially when they were ridiculed by the old women. Few of the Indian families supplemented their rations by growing vegetables. Every two weeks the Indian families went to the issue stations for rations, even in inclement weather, which caused suffering among the children because of improper care and clothing. Since the Indians did not grow foods or raise chickens and swine, after the inadequate rations were exhausted, "gaunt hunger stalks them until the next issue." One field matron complained that her efforts to assist the Indian families had only limited success because, while a few Indians had gardens, "the majority have none and don't seem to want any. I do not know what more to do than I am doing, it seems impossible to get some of them to see what is for there [sic] own good. It is just like washing clothes. The same thing over and over, year in and year out."

As lease money from allotments increased, more of the tribesmen abandoned their fields and gardens. It was believed by them that rations and lease money would support them in the future; yet there were exceptions. Some Indian women were willing to sew clothing for their families if the field matrons would first cut the cloth. When

White Antelope, the old Cheyenne chief, died, Mary E. Lyons claimed that a "better hearted Indian" never lived. Despite his age and crippling infirmities, he farmed as much as any younger, educated man, and his wife learned to bake bread and performed many of the customary household chores. As Mrs. Lyons visited White Antelope and his wife, the chief always "met me kindly saying, 'Good Squaw, come back.'"[3]

The Cheyennes living in the westernmost portion of the agency refused to co-operate with their agent's programs. Led by White Shield and numbering 186 people, 49 of the families still lived in tipis, and only 7 families occupied houses for a part of the year. In some instances families of 3 to 10 people occupied tipis or tents that measured sixteen by fourteen feet. It is not surprising then that among this band tuberculosis was extremely prevalent. When the Red Moon Day School was constructed for their children, the leaders refused to enroll their youngsters. They preferred to send them to Cantonment, where they also favored planting their crops. Agent Stouch encouraged the superintendent of the Red Moon School to enforce the governmental policies and to see that White Shield and his followers realized that the "day when the Government will withdraw its support is near at hand, and when it comes the Indians, by their habitual diligence, application and perserverance, from now on, will determine whether it is a question of independence or pauperism with them."[4]

White Shield preferred not to build a "comfortable home" and become a farmer. Instead he chose traveling and visiting his friends. White Shield prevailed upon Temple Houston to see whether Oklahoma Territorial Delegate Dennis T. Flynn could obtain permission for him and his band to take an extended trip to Colorado to visit the Utes. Agent Stouch recommended denying permission to the band, although he acknowledged that as citizens the Indians could move about as they pleased. He reminded the commissioner of Indian affairs that White Shield's band had been "the direct cause of more trouble and annoyance to your office and this, than had all the other bands put together. It has been a retarding element and despite the many efforts made to eliminate its influence it seems to go from bad to worse." Since the Cheyennes and Arapahoes could not compete with whites as skilled or semiskilled artisans, he said, the only occupation available to them was farming. Admitting that the Indians were limited in sources of income, the agent still deplored "their total disregard of economy and their inability to foster their substance places them at a disadvantage; and where the white man would thrive, they would go poorly clad and fed." What Stouch did not mention was that few if any white men could thrive where White Shield and his people had been assigned allotments.[5]

White Shield made his trip to Colorado, but most of his band stayed home. A few years later, after his wife died, the chief, complaining that he was lonely, decided to visit the Northern Cheyennes in Montana. Seger, who knew White Shield very well, thought the chief just wanted to go on a "tramp" through the countryside and spend the several hundred dollars in his account at Darlington that had been acquired from the sale of inherited land. Since White Shield had not as yet placed any improvements on his allotment, upon Seger's recommendation White Shield was denied permission to travel. Even without permission, however, White Shield made his journey to the Tongue River Agency in Montana and obtained a new wife. It was reported that Rosa Medicine Rock, a young Northern Cheyenne woman, set out from her agency with White Shield and they headed for the chief's home near Hammon.[6]

While White Shield simply ignored regulations and policies, other traditionalist Cheyenne leaders organized their followers against the agency force. Little Man, who lived near Cantonment and was the keeper of the sacred Medicine Arrows, a key to many of the programs initiated by the Indian agents. When Paul Good Bear's eighteen-year-old brother ran away from school, Horace E. Wilson, the superintendent of the Cantonment School, decided to use the Indian police to apprehend the youth at an issue dance. Little Man intervened and pushed Wilson away from the boy, forcing the superintendent toward a door in the building in which the dance was being held. Through an interpreter Wilson told Little Man that he would "knock him down if he put his hand on me," which so angered Little Man's wife that she attacked Wilson and tore off his coat. Throwing blankets over their heads to prevent recognition, Little Man's followers forced Wilson and the police out of the building. Wilson wanted to punish Little Man to destroy his influence and force the priest to observe the regulations of the agency, but no action was taken by the superintendent because leaders who were co-operating with him at Cantonment, such as Mower, Flying Bird, Sage, Sweet Water, and Wolf Chief, advised him that the arrest of Little Man would "make me some bad enemies."[7]

When Little Man lost favor with Superintendent Wilson, all but seven or eight Cheyenne men abandoned the priest. Then Wilson forced the issue as the time approached to send the children from Cantonment to Darlington for the regular school term during the fall of 1901. The threat to cut off "all courtesies and rations" forced Little Man to capitulate, and the priest sent one of his three children to the Darlington Boarding School. Rather than recognize that the priest had acceded to his demands, Superintendent Wilson explained, "it is better that he oppose than favor us, we cannot afford to restore him to his lost throne."[8]

As the Indian agents worried about the traditionalist chiefs, other problems gradually assumed greater significance. Because of congressional legislation, Indian allotments beginning in 1891 could be leased to non-Indians for specified periods of time. The land allotted to the Cheyennes and Arapahoes in 1891 constituted their greatest economic resource. From it they were expected to derive their livelihood either by using the land for farms or by renting the allotments to their white neighbors. Great care had to be taken by the Indian agents when leases were signed, because as legal documents the leases conveyed certain rights to the lessees. And Congress and the Bureau of Indian Affairs were concerned that capable Indians use their lands to produce crops that would enable them to become self-supporting. As far as possible it was governmental policy to persuade the Indians to farm their own lands rather than to depend on lease or rental money. Congress, however, had difficulty defining consistently which groups of Indians should be required to farm their lands and which groups should be free to lease the allotments.

The first general leasing statute of 1891 provided that an Indian allottee could lease an allotment if he could not use it because of age or other inability. Three years later Congress added "disability" as a criterion for permitting an allotment to be leased and increased the period of the leases for farming and grazing purposes from three to five years. Then, in 1897, Congress dropped to word "inability" from the criteria and changed the leasing period from five to three years. Finally, in 1900, the national legislators restored the "inability" criterion and limited leases to those for farming purposes and restored the five-year term to new leases. As interpreted by Indian agents and Bureau of Indian Affairs personnel, inability meant that an Indian allotment could be leased if the land could not be used for any reason. The commissioner of Indian affairs did not fully agree either with the interpretations used by his subordinates or with the latitude of discretion given to them by congressional action. In his view, lease money, like gratuitous issues or rations, fostered indolence and suppressed the incentive of labor, thus defeating the intent of the Dawes Act.[9]

In the first years of the leasing program the Indian agents were lax in protecting the Indians' interests. Regulations prohibited lessees from subleasing the allotments. Yet some people systematically obtained leases for speculative purposes, and as prime agricultural land became less plentiful, substantial profits were made. Those profits rightfully belonged to the Indians. Individuals with subleases often could not be held responsible for the terms of the lease and would either default on payments or strip the allotment of valuable improvements. Normally the original leases required bonds for performance of the lease's stipulations, and the sublessee often escaped from his obligations even when hailed into court.[10]

To illustrate the problems involved in leasing, there is the example of the difficulties of Bear Robe, an Arapaho who leased his land to John C. Dyer. On July 27, 1899, Dyer's lease was canceled by Acting Commissioner of Indian Affairs A. C. Tonner, because Dyer had subleased to "very undesirable persons." Before the cancellation became effective, the sublessees carried away all the improvements on the allotment, even the fence wire that had been issued to Bear Robe by the Indian agent. Following the eviction of Dyer, another lease, properly approved by the Indian agent and the secretary of the interior, was granted to John Wakefield, who occupied the allotment and planted crops. Well after Wakefield planted his crops, Dyer went into the Canadian County Probate Court and obtained a ruling that he could resume occupation of the allotment and harvest Wakefield's crops. In all this legal maneuvering the interests of Bear Robe were forgotten.

Wakefield was a poor man without means of retaining a lawyer. When he heard of the judge's decision, Wakefield presented his receipts for the lease payment to the judge, who said that "the case was closed and that the papers had nothing to do with his Court and would not be reconsidered; that the Acting Indian Agent [A. E. Woodson] was not running his Court." Since the case involved Indian property, Agent Woodson took the matter to the United States attorney, who was bound by federal statute to represent all Indians who sued and were sued in the courts of Oklahoma Territory. Much to the consternation of Woodson, the United States attorney offered the opinion that the secretary of the interior had no right to cancel a lease; the legal issue had to be decided in the U.S. District Court, where proof must be presented that the lessee had violated his contract. Appeals either to the United States District Court or the Supreme Court of Oklahoma Territory could take years before the issue would be settled.

To shorten the process, Agent Stouch, who had inherited the case when he came to Darlington, worked through the United States Department of Justice. The Justice Department ruled that the secretary of the interior was vested by Congress with the authority to cancel leases since he was charged by law to determine whether or not the conditions of the lease had been fulfilled. In essence it was held that the jurisdiction of the secretary of the interior did not cease when the lease was granted because the United States was still the trustee of allotments under the terms of the Dawes Act. With this ruling Agent Stouch negotiated a new lease with John Wakefield for Bear Robe's allotment, which called for a payment of $130 a year and allowed Wakefield to cultivate 120 acres of land and to use the remaining land as a pasture. Both Bear Robe and Wakefield suffered.

The Indian lost rentals due him under the original lease and the improvements and fences on the allotment, while Wakefield lost one year's crops and a mule, which was sold to cover the court costs when Dyer won his case in the Canadian County Probate Court.[11]

During the late summer of 1900, Agent Stouch began to tighten up the leasing procedures of the agency. He knew that the Indians desperately needed the income from their lands to live on and had earlier written to the commissioner of Indian affairs that the "leasing of allotted lands is firmly established at this Agency; it is deeply rooted in the necessities of hundreds of allottees; for better or worse, it is here to stay." On July 16, 1900, the specifications for lease payments were changed by the acting secretary of the interior. After that date leases could not be made for a cash payment only. The secretary thought a money consideration only was "injurious to the best interests of the Indian owners," and suggested that "in the future allotted land shall be leased with a view of their permanent improvement, so that the allottee, when capable of taking charge of and working his land shall have something more than bare land, which he would only have under the present system of leasing."[12]

The realities of leasing problems forced Stouch to change his initial ideas. Although he found many whites using Indian allotments without either the approval of his or the Washington offices, Stouch admitted that some of the farmers through no fault of their own could not plow and plant crops on the leased allotment. Often the white farmers had insufficient work animals to till the leased land, and thus the acreage would be broken and seeded by a neighbor for one-third of the grain harvested. Cattlemen who were renting thousands of acres wanted more than a one-year agreement because to use the land the ranchers had to build fences, dig wells, build water tanks, and install windmills. If the cattlemen were forced to abandon their use of allotments, thousands of acres of land on the agency would lie idle because the grazing lands were unsuited for crops. It was also pointed out to the Indian agent that if improvements were placed on the allotments of minors, the buildings would be of little use to the children by the time they began to live off their lands. Also, improvements, the breaking of land, and a cash consideration of thirty-five dollars a year for agricultural land made the leases too expensive because an individual could expect no income until the second year of the lease. Because the allotments were still sixty miles or more away from the nearest railroad, lack of transportation made it difficult for farmers to dispose of the surplus crops profitably and also made building materials expensive.[13]

The Bureau of Indian Affairs finally gave the Indian agent more flexibility in arranging the terms for land leases. If improvements were part of the leasing stipulations, the agent could provide for as many as five years of land use by the lessee, and if cash alone was the consideration, leases for one year for pasture land and two years for cropland could be arranged. With this latitude and with increased attention to the supervision of leases, Stouch during his first year as Indian agent was able to add $12,000 of new lease money to the Indians' income. As old leases came into Darlington for renewal, Stouch increased the payments, especially for good land near railroads. Allotments containing prime cropland within two years were bringing as much as $200, ten times as much as grazing land in the western portion of the agency.

During the 1901–1902 fiscal year the Cheyennes and Arapahoes received $71,298.66 from leases; in 1902–1903, $76,916.48. Thereafter the Cheyenne and Arapaho Agency was divided into three autonomous districts, which included Darlington, Seger, and Cantonment, each with a superintendent who was responsible for his own annual reports. Depending upon the superintendents' thoroughness, financial statements varied considerably in accuracy and completeness.[14]

Not all the Indians on the agency rolls were without guile in their relations with white men. Such a man was Benjamin, or Bennie, Keith, who had leased a part of his allotment since 1892. Of one-quarter Arapaho blood, Keith had received an adequate education. He hired lawyers in El Reno to handle the arrangements for leases when they were renewed and conducted his own business affairs. One of the leases provided that certain improvements on the allotment, such as fencing and buildings, would remain the property of the lessee upon payment of stated sums of money which the lessee, George O. Convill, owed to Keith. Early in 1902, Keith decided that

Convill's lease was not in his best interest and claimed that he was being defrauded when Convill decided to remove the improvements from the allotment. He further maintained that he had never understood the terms of the leases when they were signed. If the buildings and fence were to remain, Convill asked for four hundred dollars from Keith as compensation for giving title to the improvements.

Agent Stouch's view of the problem differed entirely from Keith's. After investigating the matter, Stouch learned that Keith was capable of understanding the terms of the contracts and that he was trying to squeeze more money from Convill, which he had done on several previous occasions. Nor did the Indian agent believe that Keith had any intention of working the forty acres of the allotment as required by departmental regulations. All of Keith's complaints were designed, Stouch maintained, "to get control of his land and place it in the hands of some other white man. I find, I am sorry to say that Benny Keith is not to be trusted. In another communication I have recommended him for citizenship. He is as fit now for such a change as he will ever be and the rest of the Indians will be better off when he and his kind are erased from the rolls." Of course, Keith was already a citizen, and the Indian agent only meant that he should be severed from the tribal rolls so that he could assume full responsibility for his economic activities.[15]

While Bennie Keith was perfectly capable of looking after his own financial affairs, other Indian people were not, especially minors and orphans. The regulations of the Bureau of Indian Affairs did not sufficiently protect the estates of minors, which were systematically looted by court-appointed administrators regardless of whether they were Indians or whites. A. C. Tonner, acting commissioner of Indian affairs, thought that it might be worthwhile for Indians to act as administrators of the estates of minors and orphans as another way for the Indian to come in "touch with local laws and the ways of his white neighbors." With the permission of the proper judge, the Indian agent could examine the estate's records to determine whether the moneys had been used wisely. If maladministration was evident, the agent could withhold money derived from federal sources.[16]

Indians in some instances would have nothing to do with legal papers because they did not understand and therefore feared them. In addition, some missionaries refused to accept the responsibilities of guardianship, claiming that they had no training and could not carry out their obligations. As a result, Agents Woodson and Stouch were forced to depend on dishonest whites, who charged the estates exorbitant fees for their activities. Knowing that neither the Indians nor many of the white administrators or guardians would fulfill their obligations to their wards, Agent Stouch, shortly after his arrival at Darlington, tried to remedy the situation. He recommended that he be appointed as guardian and administrator for many of the Indian children until they reached majority. Stouch suggested that he be given control over the lease money from the children's allotments in addition to the funds derived from federal sources. He wrote to the commissioner of Indian affairs:

To pay rental over to relatives of minors is just like throwing it away; the rightful owner derives no benefit from the money, and when he marries and settles down on his allotment, he finds it requires fencing, that he needs a dwelling, and stock and farming implements, he then will have to begin to save and work out half his life before he will be able to say he is owner of his own house. . . . The condition of these Indians today is little better than it ever was; they have no conception of economy, they make no provisions for the morrow, when their substance is gone they help their neighbors dispose of theirs, and no matter how much money they get, it all goes. They are in no way provident and will never learn to be, while they have the strong arm of the generous government to lean on.[17]

Some minor Indian children's funds did come under Stouch's supervision. An Indian girl named Jennie Short Teeth married at the age of fifteen and demanded through lawyers that the money that had accumulated in her United States Treasury account be paid to her. Stouch objected, believing that, if the accounts were paid out, "every orphan girl, minor, to whose credit you have money, will be persuaded to marry while she is at home during the summer vacation, frequently to be deserted as soon as . . . the unworthy husband has had time to 'blow it in.'" Jennie was denied her funds until she came of age.[18]

After a delay of six years Indian agents and superintendents finally were instructed to have themselves appointed guardians of orphans. In the interim much of the income and financial resources of the children were wasted away despite the efforts of Agent Stouch. It was found, for example, that one banker who acted as his own attorney in collusion with a probate judge had systematically despoiled the accounts of eighteen minor heirs for whom he had been appointed guardian. Penniless at adulthood, the young men and women were nonetheless expected to provide for themselves from that time onward.[19]

As fertile land became less plentiful in Oklahoma Territory, whites found still another means to harass the Indians. When the allotments were assigned the Cheyennes and Arapahoes in 1891, a person might be given two allotments of land because Indians often had more than one name. Upon the discovery of the double allotment, the Indian was usually given the choice of which allotment he wanted to retain, and the other would be canceled. If the Indian died shortly before the alloting process was completed, the heirs were required to divest themselves of the land. The few cases of double or improper assignment of allotments, however, caused whites to try to prove that the practice was common, and court proceedings resulted in which it was contended that the Indians' land should be subject to a homestead entry.

Typical of these contests was the struggle over the allotments of Rosa and Ella Romero.[20] Rosa, or Rosey, Romero was the daughter of Rafael Romero and a Cheyenne woman, Woman-Stands-in-the-Sand-Hill. Rafael, of Spanish-American extraction, had worked as a teamster and employee of agency or post traders since the 1870's. It was alleged that the mother selected one allotment for Rosey, and Rafael selected the other. It was maintained that, as a result, Rosey Romero received two tracts of land as Cheyenne and Arapaho Allottees Nos. 518 and 3067, the latter allotment being listed under the name of Corn, a shortened version of Corn-e-o-tah, by which Rosey was known among the Cheyennes. One allotment, near El Reno, was valuable and coveted by whites, who influenced Rafael to submit an affidavit that his daughter had received two allotments. Agent

Stouch was ordered to investigate the allegations and report to the Department of Indian Affairs.[21]

As Stouch conducted a review of the matter, he found a rather sordid record. Rafael Romero was described by the Indian agent as an "irresponsible, unscrupulous and ignorant Mexican, who drinks to excess . . ., married to a Cheyenne woman but never adopted by the tribe," who cared only about the money he could obtain if the El Reno allotment of his daughter could be claimed by John W. Laird. Laird, unlike others claiming double allotments, would not accept the agency records as valid and persisted in pressing his claim. Three hundred dollars was on deposit in an Oklahoma City bank to be paid to Rafael if Laird came into possession of the allotment. Romero's affidavit was supported by James Frost, who claimed to be a Northern Cheyenne, but whose base of operations was usually the Ute Reservation in Colorado. Frost was said to be a troublesome man who could not be trusted since he was a "rascal, renegade, vagabond and refuge from justice." During one of his periodic stays in Indian Territory, Frost had married a Cheyenne woman, whom he later deserted. He was charged with larceny and illegal sale of liquor to Cheyennes and Arapahoes. To acquire a few easy dollars, Frost let it be known that he had information about several double allotments, including those of the Romero sisters, and would furnish information to those willing to pay him. Believing Romero and Frost, Laird had moved onto Rosey Romero's allotment near El Reno and refused to vacate it. Just as dangerous to the Indian family was the fact that under the laws of Oklahoma Territory Rafael had become the sole heir of Rosey, who had died unmarried without issue. Money derived from the allotment, therefore, went to Rafael and did not benefit Rosey's Indian relatives. Stouch wanted to make an example of Laird, an "allotment jumper," so that others would not follow his example, but when the local courts would not co-operate with him, he sought from Washington information about how he could proceed legally against Laird.[22]

While Rosey Romero's allotment was under contest, James Ford initiated a claim for the allotment of Ella Romero. Ford maintained that Ella Romero and Pipe Woman were one and the same person and

277

that Ella's allotment, also near El Reno, should be canceled. After the acting commissioner of Indian affairs received information from Ford and two affidavits from members of the Cheyenne tribes that Ella and Pipe Woman were two names for the same person, Stouch was again ordered to investigate. Agency records revealed that Ella was the daughter of Rafael Romero and Coming-in-Sight, or Mrs. Rufus Gilbert, while Pipe Woman was the daughter of Twins, or Two Sons, and Medicine Woman.[23]

The contest over Ella's allotment continued despite Stouch's report. Ford's attorney, J. H. Everest of Oklahoma City, transmitted a notarized statement from Washee, who claimed to be a chief of the Cheyennes. Since the Washington office always considered Washee "a reliable Indian, worthy of credence," Stouch was asked to re-investigate the controversy over Ella Romero's allotment. The Indian agent was amazed that Washee's reputation for credibility "ever reached Washington ... [because] it is at variance with his reputation here, for he has none—save that of a common drunkard. He is a worthless character and is not entitled to the credit you give him; why his own people refuse to have any dealing with him when they can avoid it." After Stouch called Washee to his office and confronted him with the office records and the affidavit sent to Washington, Washee recounted for Stouch how he had signed the document. A man from El Reno, whose name Washee did not remember, kept pressing him to sign a paper about Ella Romero's double allotment. The Cheyenne told the man that he was no chief and that he knew nothing about the double allotment. Finally Washee met the man in an El Reno saloon, and after a couple of glasses of beer, they went to the office of a notary public, where Washee signed the paper, although the contents of the document were unknown to him. Washee admitted that he did not know either Ella Romero or Pipe Woman. For the moment at least the allotments were safe, and Stouch did not change his determinations.[24]

Other white neighbors of the Indians found additional means to question the validity of the allotting process. It was contended that some children had not been born or that old Indians had died before the allotting of the reservation had been concluded and were, therefore, not eligible for land. Mrs. Anna Sechtem, claiming that Ha-o-ma-ista, or Red Woman, died before the allotments were assigned, occupied the allotment without permission from the Indian agent and paid no lease money during the interim. After talking to older Indians acquainted with Red Woman's family, Stouch found that Mrs. Sechtem's statements were false, and he succeeded in having her evicted from the allotment by court action. John M. Sweeny, of Kingfisher, insisted that Curley Hair died before allotment and that the allotment should be canceled so that he could file a claim for it. Curley Hair, Stouch learned, had indeed died, but Deaf Woman, Curley Hair's mother, had taken his name upon her son's death, a common custom among the older Cheyenne women. Again Agent Stouch maintained that the allotment was properly made and that the land was not subject to a claim under the homestead law.[25]

As challenges to Indian allotments continued, Stouch carefully examined the records of the agency. Most of the contests were resolved in favor of the Indians. Unless the agent protected the Indians, however, allotments would be taken from them. Commenting upon the contest over Beaver Woman's land, Stouch wrote:

This contest, I am sure like a great many more that have been filed, was prompted by inquiry among the Indians, many of whom upon the solicitation of unscrupulous white men, backed up by the tender of a small sum of money, will testify to matters upon which they are not well posted and about which hearsay is taken, many times signing documents the purport of which is not known to them.[26]

When it was found that Nat Murphy, a thirty-two-year-old Cheyenne, had also been allotted under the name Night, Stouch worked with the young man so that he could retain the more valuable of the two allotments. A white family named Payne, occupying Murphy's allotment near El Reno, was trying to influence him to cancel it and retain his land much farther west on the Washita River. The Cheyenne denied that he ever signed a relinquishment to the El Reno land but stated that he had done so seven years earlier to the tract on the Washita. When faced with the choice, Murphy stated, "I want to retain this one near here, not far from Fort Reno, because it is good level land, well located, believing it to be in my best interest to keep it, it being worth more money than the other." Stouch added that Murphy was "an Indian of sufficient intelligence to know what he wants. . . . I am sure if I had a choice between the two pieces of land, I would select the same allotment the Indian has."[27]

On May 27, 1902, Congress passed legislation that significantly altered the intent of the Dawes Act. Under Section Seven of the 1902 Indian Appropriation Act it became possible for "adult heirs of any deceased Indian to whom a trust or other patent containing restriction upon alienation has been or shall be issued for lands allotted to him may sell and convey the lands inherited." The allotments of minor heirs could be sold by their guardians, and all conveyances were made subject to the approval of the secretary of the interior. Money derived from the sale of the lands would be paid directly to the heirs or if the heirs were not of age, the funds would be administered by the guardian. Exceptions to the legislation did not apply to the Cheyennes and Arapahoes, whose lands were becoming desirable to farmers and ranchers in Oklahoma Territory. The commissioner of Indian affairs noted that the heirs would not be compelled to sell their land and that as Indians continued to die their allotments would fall under the provisions of the act. Even before the legislation was passed, one territorial newspaper noted that 69 per cent of the land allotted to the Cheyennes and Arapahoes belonged to "dead Indians." In the view of the newspaper's editor, nothing could benefit Blaine County more than to have the allotments cultivated and worked by white farmers. A ready market existed for the allotments of "dead Indians," and from that fact the legislation came to be known as the Dead Indian Land Act.[28]

By August, 1902, many inquiries had been received at Darlington about allotments available for sale. Almost daily Agent Stouch was asked by lessees whether they would be protected in their rights since most of them were too poor to purchase allotments. Cheyennes and Arapahoes also inquired about the sale of their inherited lands, because if the leases were not to be renewed and renegotiated, they did not want to complete new leases. Many Indians indicated that, if they had a choice, they preferred to lease the inherited lands and not sell, but Stouch felt that they could change their minds at any time. He believed that "there would be a great demand for Indian Land. It will be the object of real estate firms in the Territory to get hold of as much of the land at as low a price as is possible."[29]

Although the Indians needed protection from real-estate firms and others, instances occurred where they were dealt with and prices for allotments were negotiated without the knowledge or advice of the Indian agent. To prevent whites from taking unfair advantage of Indians, Stouch instructed the agency farmers to make honest appraisals of the lands in question so that the Indians would receive all that the lands were worth. Stouch also denied individuals seeking out inherited allotments access to the agency records and forced them to initiate a discussion in the first instance with the agency staff.[30]

Stouch consistently refused to approve bids for inherited allotments because he believed that the offers were insufficient. In addition, the Bureau of Indian Affairs suspended the sale of inherited land for a few months until regulations could be developed to ensure a system of competitive bidding. Even Ben Clark, the old army scout and confidant of General Phil Sheridan, was denied permission to sell the allotments of three of his children who had died because his sales did not conform to the bureau's regulations. But the pressure for the sale of the inherited allotments continued as bankers and real-estate firms sought to identify the allotments available for purchase by their clients. One banker organized excursions on railroads to interest prospective buyers in the Indians' allotments.[31]

After five months of consideration the Bureau of Indian Affairs announced rules for the sale of inherited land. The commissioner of Indian affairs decreed that after an heir or heirs had petitioned to sell the inherited land, notices about the anticipated sale of the land had to be posted in the office of the Indian agent for a period of not less than ninety days. Also, the sale of the land had to be advertised in the newspaper of widest circulation of the county in which the allotment lay, and the buyer had to assume the cost of the conveyance of the title.

Difficulties arose under the act of May 27, 1902. Heirship was determined by the states or territories in which the Indians resided.

Many of the states and territories, including Oklahoma Territory, provided by statute that the father inherited all of the land of his deceased offspring to the exclusion of the mother, brothers, and sisters. If the husband deserted his Indian family, he alone stood to profit if his child or children died without issue. Nevertheless, inherited land began to be sold on March 4, 1903. Sale began slowly among the Cheyennes and Arapahoes, and by the late summer of 1903, only sixteen allotments had been sold, for slightly more than thirty-eight thousand dollars.[32]

Agent Stouch was questioned by his superiors in Washington about the lack of competitive bidding for the allotments. The commissioner of Indian affairs seemed to imply that those bidding on the allotments were acting in combination and were receiving advance information about the appraised value of the tracts offered for sale. Stouch informed the commissioner that when the agency farmers sent their appraisals to him they were placed in sealed envelopes and stored in a strongbox until the bids for the land were opened. As more desirable land was advertised, the bids increased. Some allotments sold for as much as $5,000, but the average was much lower. During the 1903–1904 fiscal year the Cheyennes and Arapahoes sold more than eighteen thousand acres of their land for more than $212,600. The average price an acre received by the Indians was $11.78.[33]

With several hundred thousand dollars of additional income coming into the hands of the Cheyennes and Arapahoes, white merchants and bankers were ready to take unfair advantage of them. "Some Indians," Stouch wrote to the governor of Oklahoma Territory, "used the money judiciously, paying their debts and buying horses and wagons, while others spent their money foolishly. . . . Their worst evils are whisky, mescal [peyote] and borrowing money at high interest, frequently paying from 24 to 200 percent interest, and sometimes a higher rate." Even if Indians tried to use their money wisely, merchants would try to defraud them. Big Knee, a Cheyenne who lived near Watonga, purchased from Roy Caton six cows, eight yearlings, and twelve heifers for $580 and a horse. The horse was given to Caton, and it was agreed that the money would be paid when Cedar Woman, Big Knee's wife, received her funds from the sale of inherited lands. Three witnesses, two educated Indians and an Indian trader, saw Big Knee pay Caton the money. But Caton refused to deliver the cattle to Big Knee because he alleged that the debt was not fully settled.[34]

Again precious money was slipping away from the Cheyennes and Arapahoes. To protect the Indians' funds and to tighten up administrative procedures, it was decided by the Washington office and Superintendent Stouch[35] that between August 22, 1904, and January 1, 1905, no additional inherited land would be posted for sale. The commissioner of Indian affairs noted that

to the average land speculator the Indian seems to be considered common prey, and there had been disclosed . . . cliques and combinations of schemers in the vicinity of nearly every agency where large quantities of land are being sold, who, by various means fleece the Indian to the last penny within a few hours after the agent had turned over to him the proceeds of a sale.

After September 16, 1904, agents or superintendents were authorized to assume control over the money received from the sale of inherited lands. It was expected that just debts would be settled and that Stouch would limit expenditures of Indians who had sold inherited lands to ten dollars a month. Sums in excess of that amount would have to be approved by Stouch and the Washington office.[36] Many of the Cheyennes wanted to settle their debts quickly so that the merchants would continue to give them credit. At first Commissioner Jones refused to allow Stouch to settle even those bills which had been contracted before the September, 1904 regulation went into effect. A new commissioner of Indian affairs, Francis E. Leupp, reversed his predecessor and permitted settlement of debts contracted before September 30, 1904. Thereafter, however, those who extended credit to Indians without authorization did so at their own risk. Some of the better-educated and mixed blood tribesmen resented being limited to ten dollars a month from their accounts. Led by Charles Keith and Jock Bull Bear, the "progressive" Indians met with Superintendent Stouch and threatened to sell no more land if they could not obtain a more liberal policy. Stouch refused to modify

283

the ten-dollar limit. He met with the tribesmen at Darlington, explaining the new rules in detail and warning them against "bad white men, bankers, money loaners, and others who are seeking to rob them."[37]

Money derived from the sale of inherited land was deposited in local banks at 3 per cent annual interest. Withdrawals of amounts larger than $10 required the approval of the superintendent and the Washington office. If the depositor could not sign his or her name, the X mark had to be witnessed by two other persons and approved by the superintendent. When Superintendent Stouch was convinced that a person would benefit by the use of a substantial portion of the funds, he approved. Casper Edson, for example, an Indian who had been employed at the agency for many years, requested that he be allowed to spend $625 from his $1,404 account for a team of horses, harness, a registered bull, six heifers, two brood sows, a farm wagon, and enough money to repair his house. Stouch approved Edson's request.[38]

At the Cantonment Subagency, the problems arising from the sale of inherited land were similar to those at Darlington. Some permanent impact was made by the wise use of funds. More often, however, Indians were left stranded without either their land or their newly purchased teams or farming equipment. The system used by white creditors was simple but ingenious. A group of creditors would allow an Indian who was selling inherited land to purchase more than the price the allotment would bring. The principal creditor would be satisfied when the money was paid to the Indian, but the minor creditors would place a levy on all of the property through a court judgment. Since the principal items of the Indians' purchases were used, their worth rapidly depreciated, and the courts would require the forced sale or seizure of the newly acquired teams, buggies, wagons, and other articles. Byron E. White, the superintendent at Cantonment, called the bureau's attention to a typical case, that of White Fool. The old Cheyenne owed $1,800. His inherited land had sold for $1,400. The principal creditor had sold him a team of horses, a wagon, and a buggy for $1,275, while a number of others who had sold White Fool other goods were in the process of taking, through legal action, the horses, wagon, and buggy. White Fool had a little income from rental of his allotment, but he would not be any better off than he was before the sale of the inherited land. Eventually a ruling came from Washington that property purchased by money derived from the sale of inherited land was trust property and therefore could not be alienated.[39] But the rule came too late to help White Fool or other Indians similarly imposed upon.

Imbued with the work ethic, Theodore Roosevelt's commissioner of Indian affairs, William A. Jones, had decided to force the Indians to take another step toward self-support. Since 1875, Indian agents, commissioners of Indian affairs, and the Congress had been seeking implementation of a policy to make the Indians self-sufficient, thereby reducing their dependence upon rations or gratuities, and then severing them from the tribal rolls. It was a logical, if rather callous, progression to and from the Dawes Act. Commissioner Jones suggested two plans whereby Agent Stouch would withhold "a large per cent of the subsistence and all clothing" from the Cheyennes and Arapahoes. All able-bodied male Indians would be expected to work eight hour days on the reservation for $1.25 a day. The funds would come from the money usually spent for rations and clothing. Dams, reservoirs, irrigation ditches, fences, and roads could be constructed throughout the agency, or the Indians could be employed at other productive labor that would produce lasting benefit to them and would lead to their self-support. It was also suggested that the Cheyennes and Arapahoes find work with the assistance of their agent on ranches or farms or on the railroads. Rations would continue for those Indians who, by reason of age or infirmity, could not work. Stouch was instructed to tell the Cheyennes and Arapahoes that the "Government is very much in earnest to carry out this new policy in helping them to become self-supporting and that no good will be accomplished by protesting." In the future the Indian agency would not be a "center for the gratuitous distribution of supplies," but rather an "employment agency." The commissioner estimated that if Agent Stouch would inform farmers, employment agencies, railroads, and other likely employers that he could furnish skilled Indian mechanics, carpenters, and artisans from among the returned Carlisle and Haskell students and if girls could be placed in "good respectable white families," 25 per cent could be saved in rations and clothing.[40]

The Indians did not appreciate the policy of curtailed rations and clothing. Groups of tribesmen were meeting and were "chewing over their rations being taken away. The old Indians don't make as much of a do about it as those that are educated," reported a field matron. Mrs. Lyons, with ten years' experience in the Indian Service, maintained that the younger Indians who were capable of working would not support their elders. "Some will contend," Mrs. Lyons wrote, "the young ones will care for the old, I say *they will not*." When Commissioner Jones heard that the Cheyennes and Arapahoes wanted to send a delegation to Washington to protest the changed criteria for issuing rations, he directed Agent Stouch to "inform the Cheyennes and Arapahoes that the instructions given you about striking the names of able-bodied and self-supporting Indians from the ration roll will be strictly followed, and no change will be made." Two months later Commissioner Jones softened his attitude and indicated that he was willing to see Three Fingers of the Cheyennes and Black Coyote of the Arapahoes with an interpreter if they paid their own expenses to Washington. If the delegation became stranded during their journey, they would receive no funds from government sources.[41]

Not all able-bodied Indians, however, were expunged from the ration and clothing lists. Agent Stouch rationalized his action by writing to his subordinates that some of the younger people did not "have the means of support that warrants them being cut off" during the winter season. Stouch decided to modify the commissioner's instructions until July 1, 1902, but the Cheyennes and Arapahoes were to be told "emphatically that the time has arrived when they must do something for themselves and they had just as well begin." Stouch's judgment had merit. Later, in the Cantonment District for example, it was determined that among slightly less than eight hundred Cheyennes and Arapahoes only forty Cheyenne and twenty-nine Arapaho men were capable of working so that their families could be fed, clothed, and housed.[42]

Some of the Indians, particularly the traditionalist chiefs, were dissatisfied with the limitations placed upon the gratuitous issues.

Crow Chief, a spokesman for the Cheyennes living around Cantonment, heard two different versions of the new regulation. Rudolf Petter, the Mennonite missionary, expressed Crow Chief's concern to Agent Stouch: "You wrote to me that after the 4th of July [1902] all the old people shall get rations and the other day we were told here that rations would be cut off for all the Indians! But I believe your word to be true and I keep your letter." Despite Stouch's effort to minimize the impact of the regulation on the Cheyennes and Arapahoes, they demanded that a delegation visit Washington to "get the words right from your mouth, and not get it second handed, like in a letter," Stouch wrote to the commissioner of Indian affairs. The Indian agent admitted that the list of people of the two tribes qualified for rations still included some able-bodied Indians because he took into account rentals received by a family, education, and the total resources of the family to exist without free food and clothing. As of January 2, 1903, Stouch had removed 946 from the ration list out of a total population of the agency of 2,259. It was his intention to shorten the list of those to be rationed after July 1, 1903, so that only "old and indigent" Indians would receive the customary issues from the government.[43]

Reduction in rations was only one part of a broader plan to eliminate Indian dependence on the federal government. Commissioner Jones thought that it was time to trim the tribal rolls of those individuals who through education or training could fend for themselves. He argued that, through controlled payments from the United States Treasury, Indians tended to "huddle" on reservations rather than striking out for themselves. He further maintained that, when an Indian demonstrated competence to assume the responsibilities of citizenship, "start a business himself, to manage his own affairs, to work his own allotment and to earn his support," he should be given his pro rata share of the tribal fund and "cease to be a ward of the Government." Agent Stouch cautioned the commissioner not to proceed too rapidly with his ideas. Among the Cheyennes and Arapahoes, Stouch countered, those who were seeking their pro rata share of the tribal funds and patents to their land in fee simple were the "very ones who are least fitted for such a change. They are weak characters who

are easily influenced by the worst elements of white men who sur-
round them and set like hawks watching for their prey." Funds given
to those people would only be squandered, and "the Government
would have to assume guardianship of them again, or they would
become charges of the county and State in which they reside."

Although Stouch contended that most of the whites would not
take unfair advantage of the Indians, others less interested in the
welfare of Indians were waiting for the day when the Indians had
cash to spend or squander. Well-informed Indians, such as Robert
Burns and Robert Black, who worked in the agency office as clerks,
did not want either their share of the tribal funds or their lands
patented to them in fee simple. Nor did they want gratuitous issues
from the government. One group of Indians, Stouch did believe,
could be stricken from the tribal rolls—the mixed bloods of the two
tribes who with their families numbered 101 people. Most of them
had controlled their own financial affairs for some time, and Stouch
could see no reason why the government should maintain guardianship over them. Educated full bloods such as William Fletcher were
given the opportunity of leasing allotments by themselves. Stouch
agreed to Fletcher's request to lease his own land because "it would
be good experience for him and a lesson to his neighbors." Stouch
estimated that, after the ration rolls were purged of those who could
support themselves, 750 old and indigent Indians would continue to
need rations.[44]

Commissioner Jones hammered away at his program of reducing
subsistence provided to able-bodied Indians. To the agents and superintendents supervising the distribution of food and clothing, Jones
wrote: "The Department is very earnest in its desire to withdraw
Government support from the Indians to make all those who are able-
bodied self supporting. This matter is no passing fad." He insisted
that the agents see that the Indians took care of their cattle and crops,
that the able-bodied were given employment either on or off the reservations, and that the money saved by fewer rations be spent constructing water-storage reservoirs, fences, roads, and bridges. What
Jones did not apparently realize was that in Oklahoma Territory few
jobs were available for Indians other than as part-time agricultural

laborers. The economy of the territory was not sufficiently diversified to absorb more than a few Indians who had been trained in the Indian schools as artisans. Henceforth, Jones warned, agents and superintendents would be judged upon the progress of Indians within their jurisdictions toward self-support, and concluded his warning by saying that the Indian Office intended to reduce the "amount of subsistence furnished to all Indians through the U. S. to the lowest possible limit."[45]

At the Cheyenne and Arapaho Agency some money was saved by cutting food and clothing issues, but not enough to make any measurable change in the incomes of Indians who could work. Stouch was able to divert only eight thousand dollars from food and clothing to Indian labor throughout the agency. Some of the Indians with good education were employed as clerks in governmental and agency offices and in the schools, while others managed to find a little employment during the harvest season working for white farmers and ranchers. Very few of the Cheyennes and Arapahoes were willing to seek employment outside the agency. What money most Indians had available came from leasing allotments and the interest on tribal funds. Cash derived from those sources was often wasted. According to an El Reno newspaper account, pay days were a "jolly" time at Darlington and El Reno, a time when "money is plenty thereabouts, and one would imagine that it grew on bushes along the Canadian. . . . The Indian always lives high while the money lasts . . . and it is amusing to see the stolid buck maneuver with a slick white man to get a bottle of firewater which they succeed in doing despite the rigid law against it."

At least the Cheyennes and Arapahoes were free from large debts, Agent Stouch claimed, and were not retrogressing in their agricultural endeavors. Indian farmers were encouraged to plant more wheat, and seeds were furnished by the agency if the Indian had broken new land. Despite decades of persuasion, however, the Cheyennes and Arapahoes still refused to become farmers; unless the Indian "felt that success as a farmer is assured, he prefers his old irresponsible life." After July 1, 1903, only old and physically handicapped Indians received rations from government funds.[46]

How the Indians obtained their livelihood was important, as were their customs and manner of living. Whether Indian men and youths wore their hair long or short worried Indian agents and commissioners of Indian affairs. Stouch ordered all educated men to cut their hair, but he delayed enforcing the regulation until April 1, 1900, thereby removing "the liability to catching cold as a result of cutting hair during the unsettled weather." Then Stouch changed his mind when spring came. He informed those in charge of distributing food and clothing that, while he would be gratified if Indian men would cut their hair as an evidence of civilization, he did not think that withholding rations was the way to lead the Indians toward farming and the white man's way of life. Commissioner Jones, however, was of a different opinion. He wanted all Indian males to wear "short hair" and suggested that noncompliance should be sufficient cause to terminate the issuance of free food and clothing.[47]

If Indian men would not cut their hair, Agent Stouch believed he could at least make them live with the women to whom they were legally married. The immediate focus was a returned student from Carlisle, William Goodsell. A young Cheyenne, Goodsell had married Day Woman, a woman nine years his elder, with whom he had lived for several years before the Territorial Marriage Law of 1897 legalized their marriage. Goodsell, who understood English well, ignored the marriage law, abandoned Day Woman, and married Curved Nose Woman, the widow of Yellow Shirt. For his second marriage Goodsell had to obtain a license from a probate judge in Watonga, and the marriage ceremony was performed by the Reverend Robert Hamilton. Since Goodsell had not been divorced from Day Woman, by law he became a bigamist. Readily admitting to Agent Stouch that he had abandoned Day Woman, Goodsell commented that he thought, as did other Indians, that the 1897 Marriage Law was a "dead number" and that it did not apply to him. After talking to Goodsell in Darlington, Stouch instructed the agency farmer at Watonga, George E. Coleman, to co-operate with the Office of the United States Attorney so that Goodsell could be properly indicted and punished.

"This is a case," Stouch wrote to Coleman, "that the Indians are watching and it must be won if possible for if it is won and William is properly punished, it will make the work of breaking up dual marriages among our Indians a much easier task." When the Indian agent received an order that Goodsell be issued an ax, a hoe, and a rake, Stouch reminded Coleman that Goodsell was on trial for bigamy and that if the charge was proved the Cheyenne would not "likely need these articles" in prison.[48]

Little was left to chance in the effort to convict William Goodsell. Agent Stouch wrote directly to the trial judge to make certain that it was understood that Goodsell was guilty of bigamy. If the Cheyenne was found guilty of the crime as charged, Stouch asked that when he came before the court for sentencing, "you will give him the extent of the law." The Indian agent stressed that if Goodsell was turned loose, it would be a "signal for numerous offenses, if he is punished as he should be it will be a warning to the other Indians and will go far toward helping me in my efforts to break up the nefarious practice of a total disregard of marital laws among these Indians." It was also necessary that the Cheyennes and Arapahoes be taught that they were citizens of the United States and the Territory of Oklahoma and were governed by the laws of the nation and territory. Goodsell's case, Stouch concluded, must be won "if dual marriages with the Cheyennes and Arapahoes are to be suppressed to any great extent." To his subordinate, Agency Farmer Coleman, Stouch made it clear that he wanted Goodsell to receive the full penalty of the law in order to force the Indians to abandon multiple marriages.[49]

William Goodsell was not convicted of bigamy. The trial was delayed until November 28, 1902, and when it was held, the judge refused to convict the Cheyenne because of technicalities and ruled that the verbal testimony against Goodsell was insufficient. Stouch wanted to reopen the case but was not successful; Goodsell remained free to live with his second wife.[50]

The lack of stability among Indian marriages on occasion raised problems over heirship. When a young Arapaho boy, Yellow Bird, died, his mother, Shaking Timber, advertized for sale one-half of her deceased son's allotment. The boy's father, John Poisal, an Arapaho mixed blood, retained a law firm to put forward his claim for one-half interest in the allotment, an action that angered Stouch. Poisal was by tribal standards a wealthy young man who had little trouble changing wives with considerable frequency. Shaking Timber and Poisal had lived together for only a short period, during which time the young woman became pregnant; soon thereafter Poisal deserted her and never contributed to the support of either Shaking Timber or Yellow Bird. In this case, however, the 1897 Marriage Law recognized the separation that had occurred before the statute's enactment as a divorce according to Indian custom, and Shaking Timber rather than Poisal became the sole heir of their son's property. If such a ruling was not possible, Stouch warned, cases would arise at the agency when men could abandon wives and children, to return only when allotments were to be sold and claim portions of the settlements as their legal right. Poisal and other men were thus denied the right to share in the division of their children's property when they had deserted their families before the enactment of the 1897 statute.[51]

Social customs among the Cheyennes and Arapahoes changed slowly. Despite the pressure of the agency officials, many Indians refused to obtain marriage licenses and declined to have their ceremonies performed before a minister or a civil officer. John Seger reported that during the 1902–1903 fiscal year among the Indians of his jurisdiction only two Indian marriages conformed to territorial statutes. During the annual Sun Dance, Indian youths often began living together, and Seger complained that in some instances one or both of the young people had attended school and knew of the marriage laws. The agency farmers, who were charged with keeping social and economic statistics, noted that only on rare occasions was an Indian couple married by either a minister or a justice of the peace.[52]

The Cheyennes and Arapahoes, especially the older ones, grieved when their traditional ceremonies were curtailed. During the spring of 1901, older Cheyennes pleaded with Agent Stouch for permission to hold the Sun Dance; permission was granted. Held later that year with more than three thousand Indians in attendance, the Sun Dance was witnessed by George A. Dorsey, of the Field Columbian Museum, Chicago, Illinois. Dorsey advised that the tribes be permitted to continue holding the Sun Dance for a period of five to ten years.

The ceremony as practiced in 1901 was, in Dorsey's opinion, "absolutely devoid of disgusting, shocking or harmful features." The dance was well ordered, and Stouch thought that no harm could come from it. He recommended that the two tribes be permitted to hold their annual Sun Dance.

Left Hand, the sixty-three-year-old Arapaho chief, made a touching appeal to the Indian agent:

We old Indians have our God, and while you may not know it, it is the same God as yours. . . . Why should we not be allowed to worship God in our own way. We give up our children to the schools you have built for them, and we allow you to teach them to worship God in the manner you think best. You instruct them in your way of thinking and believing, and in a little while some one will come and take your place, and teach them another way altogether—not only another way to believe but another way to worship. It has been going on this way ever since I can remember anything about it. Many of us are getting old, very old. . . . When we die our mode of worship will die with us. Our children will have the same God, but will worship him in the way they are taught. We are so sure that our God and your God are one that we do not wish to take our children from you; go and teach them your way to worship—it is good, but we do not understand it. . . . You will be welcome to visit with us through the ceremonies, and you will go away satisfied that they rest upon a foundation as ancient as our race, and that they contain nothing harmful, but show our homage paid to God in our own way.

Stouch could not disagree with the words of Left Hand.[53]

While Stouch thought it was wise to allow the Indians to continue the Sun Dance and other ceremonies, Seger did not. The Sun Dance, Seger claimed, had largely been discarded by the Cheyennes and Arapahoes during the period when the Ghost Dance was important among the tribes. Recently demands for the Sun Dance had revived, and three were held from 1901 through 1903. The Sun Dance was once a worthwhile religious ceremony which also aided in solidifying the organization of the tribes. Seger claimed, however, that the Sun Dances held in 1903 were simply fakes and sponsored by white men.[54]

Seger was incensed because the Indians stayed away from their homes for as long as three weeks during July, a time when they should have been putting up hay and harvesting their crops. The Indians' stock was uncared for during the Sun Dance and wandered away, only to be taken by whites and held until the Indians redeemed their stock and compensated their white neighbors for the damages the ponies and cattle had caused. Although physical torture at the Sun Dance had been forbidden by the Indian Office, it occurred at the 1903 dance. "To me," Seger wrote, "the most disgusting thing about it was to see two scientists eagerly point their cameras at the tortured man to get his picture, and to see them pose the victim so as to give the best effect."[55]

Even the torture at the 1903 Sun Dance was faked, according to Seger. He insisted that it was staged and paid for by James L. Mooney, of the American Bureau of Ethnology, and Dorsey. It was alleged that Red Leggings, a Cheyenne, was paid fifteen dollars to undergo his painful experience. Seger, in company with three missionaries, witnessed Red Leggings circle around the dance site with a portion of a buffalo head attached to a lariat and then to a wooden pin, which was inserted under the skin of the Cheyenne's back. When Red Leggings reached the point where Mooney, Dorsey, and other men with cameras were standing, he

stopped and let them take snapshots of him in different positions. As it is reported that sometimes the victim of torture sinks down with exhaustion and as Red Leggings had only been encumbered with a small portion of the buffalo head, it took a special effort for him to sink down exhausted. Some twenty five years ago I saw these Indians voluntarily undergo this torture, and there was as much difference then and now as there is between night and day. The old way of torturing was the real thing.[56]

Seger's complaints caused some concern in Washington. A. C. Tonner, the acting commissioner of Indian affairs, requested an investigation that proved little. Mooney and Dorsey, of course, denied that they had arranged the dance and the torture exhibitions by the Cheyennes. Yet Seger and Byron White went through the motions and talked to the dance's sponsors, Bull Tongue and Hawk, and tried unsuccessfully to find the men who had been photographed by Mooney and Dorsey. Most of the Indians simply claimed they knew nothing about the Sun Dance and did not see Red Leggings, Bull Tongue, or Short Nose undergo their ordeal.[57]

Every aspect of Cheyenne culture was under stress, and the old ways of life were changing: the Indian could no longer dress as he wanted or wear his hair as had the old warriors; Indian marriages were illegal (though still practiced); wood-frame houses replaced the tipi; the children were in the missionary, government, and public schools; Indians had to live among increasing numbers of white men and women; and all had to conform to the law of the white man. Basically the Indian policy of the federal government did not change. Indians were only under greater pressure to assimilate after 1900 than before. Most importantly, however, the final erosion of the Indians' land base had begun with the enactment of the 1902 Dead Indian Land Act, which in time would cause most of the Cheyennes and Arapahoes to become utterly landless. Perhaps those who enacted or suggested the statute did not understand the significance of the law, but its effects were devastating. As long as an Indian possessed an allotment, he was assured an income. But without land, the Indian had no choice but to labor for his food in the white man's ways.

CHAPTER XI

Stagnation and Decay

Francis E. Leupp became the new commissioner of Indian affairs during the middle of the 1904–1905 fiscal year. In his policy he seemed more sensitive to the needs of the Indian people because he realized that an Indian was not "a white man with a red skin" but rather that an Indian should be measured by "his own standards." Leupp recognized that the reservation and ration system had failed and that little could be done for the Indian who "has already passed middle life." The hope for the future was among the Indian youths, who would profit from a more practical, basic education that would enable them to manage their own financial affairs and yet preserve their native artistic ability and their appreciation of Indian music. No longer would Indian youths be encouraged to "despise the aged and non-progressive members of their families." The commissioner hoped to adopt a more humane plan that would nurture the youths' love of their mothers and fathers so that affection within families would not be destroyed.[1]

Commissioner Leupp proudly announced that he had "nipped in the bud many schemes for despoiling the Indians." Early in his administration he limited payments to Indians from the funds derived from the sale of inherited lands to $10 a month. Before the regulation became effective, claims against Indian accounts often exceeded the amount of money received from the sale of inherited land. Efforts were being made to separate legitimate from illegitimate claims, and after March 21, 1905, all Indian funds could be deposited only in banks or other financial institutions that would post sufficient bonds to guarantee the safety of the Indians' money. As of July 1, 1905, Cheyennes and Arapahoes possessed bank accounts totaling $62,314.60, largely obtained from the sale of 11,830.39 acres of inherited land for which they had received $132,639.75.[2]

Commissioner Leupp's statement was misleading. By implication he gave the impression that the funds on deposit were free of claims and could be used for living expenses of the Indians at the rate of $10 a month. Superintendent Stouch, however, claimed that, although the Indians in the Darlington Agency had $25,364.08 on deposit in banks as of July 1, 1905, much of the money was encumbered by debts already contracted by the Indians. He did not mention what portion of the $65,709.75 resulting from the sale of inherited lands during the year 1904–1905 remained for the future use of the Cheyennes and Arapahoes. Land sales constituted 36.72 per cent; rental of allotments, 33.99 per cent; farming and labor proceeds, 16.34 per cent; and interest from the permanent fund in the United States Treasury, 12.98 per cent of the cash income of the Cheyennes and Arapahoes administered by the Darlington Agency. The total cash income for the 1,286 Cheyennes and Arapahoes controlled by Superintendent Stouch was $178,965.37, or a per capita income of $139.16 during 1904–1905. That income, however, was unevenly distributed through the population, since those who did not sell inherited land or rent allotments to white farmers shared slightly more than 30 per cent of the total cash income of the group. If an Indian did not sell or rent land, his income might be less than $100 and, if he was old and unable to work, less than $20 a year.[3]

Because the Indians' incomes were too low to support their families and money was needed to purchase the necessities of life, funds were often borrowed from bankers and money lenders, or credit was obtained from merchants. When the loans came due, Indians found that they were charged usurious interest rates. Arnold Woolworth, an Arapaho, borrowed $150 from a banker in Geary and repaid $115 on his note. Woolworth was warned by the banker, John D. Dillon, that, if the additional $61.50 due on the principal and interest was not paid soon after the anniversary date of the note, he would foreclose on Woolworth's team of horses. Because the Arapaho had no cash, the foreclosure sale was held. The horses brought $65 at the public auction. The banker then informed Woolworth that an additional $12 was still due for attorney fees and other unspecified charges. Compared with some of his fellow tribesmen, Woolworth was fortunate, since he was charged only 16.66 per cent interest on his loan. Clarence Powder Face borrowed $8 from Dillon's bank in Geary for a period of two months and repaid $10. He had been charged 150 per cent interest for his loan. Again needing money, Powder Face returned to Dillon's bank and borrowed another $8. When the small note came due, the Arapaho could not redeem it, and the note was signed over to T. J. Ballew by Dillon. The former told Powder Face that he owed $45, and a new note was written a year later when the Indian paid $25 in cash and secured the balance of $20 with his team of horses. After Powder Face borrowed another $4 from Ballew and could not repay the debt, Powder Face lost his team, valued at $60. In two years Powder Face had borrowed $12, for which he was charged more than 350 per cent interest a year. In a report to the United States attorney, Superintendent Stouch cited other cases of usury and asked that court cases be initiated against Dillon and Ballew.[4]

Merchants were as unmerciful to the Indians as were the bankers. Henry Roman Nose, a Cheyenne chief who had been educated at Carlisle, purchased a team, harness, and halter from merchants in Watonga. The bill came to $305, but the team of horses were valued at $300. Roman Nose paid the merchants $150 in cash and signed a promissory note for the remainder. When no other payments were made, the merchants seized the team at Roman Nose's home and held the horses until the chief could redeem them. That was impossible, because Roman Nose had spent all of his available money. The merchants kept the horses. Superintendent White at Cantonment stated that Roman Nose's case was only one among many in his agency.[5]

The superintendents received little encouragement in their search for justice from the Office of the United States Attorney. It was clear to J. W. Scothorn, assistant United States attorney, that unscrupulous persons were robbing the Indians. But Scothorn reminded Superintendent Stouch that when the Cheyennes and Arapahoes took their allotments in severalty they had become citizens who then had the right to make contracts and sue or be sued in courts of law. Commenting on the group of Cheyennes and Arapahoes discussed in Stouch's letters, Scothorn wrote that they were "fairly intelligent and know what it means to mortgage their property; they make contracts and agree to give any rate of interest demanded; the contracts are made without any witness except to the signing of the mortgage." It was conceded that court cases could be initiated in the territorial courts—not, however, in federal courts—to recover usurious interest, but the Indians would be required to give security for court costs in case the suits were rejected. Such a case would involve a jury, and recovery would depend on "the amount of credence that would be given to the Indians over the white man, and our observation has been that as a general rule juries do not take kindly to the testimony of the Indians, but regard them as unreliable." Scothorn's only suggestion for protecting the Indians was to have them offer before witnesses to pay 12 per cent above the capital or principal involved and then refuse to deliver the property claimed by the creditor. The creditor would then become the plaintiff in a court case and would become liable for the court costs if the recovery did not exceed the amount offered by the Indian debtor.[6]

County officials were indifferent toward crimes committed by Indians against their own people. Wolf Ahead, a Cheyenne man, was accused of raping a school girl. The youngster was sent to the Office of the County Attorney, and the girl's account of the crime led to Wolf Ahead's arrest and imprisonment. Wolf Ahead's wife intervened and offered the acting county attorney for Canadian County $45 in cash and $205 more at a later time for his legal services. E. T. Marsh, the acting county attorney, took the money, investigated the crime, and reported to the sheriff that there was no truth in the girl's allegations and that he should release Wolf Ahead. Superintendent Stouch complained to County Attorney James Frame that a full investigation should be conducted and that Marsh should be disbarred. Nothing, however, was done in the matter.[7]

Economic conditions among the Cheyennes and Arapahoes were stagnant. Practically none of them farmed more than forty acres of their allotments, and the crop yield was mediocre. Corn produced an average of fifteen bushels to the acre, hay cuttings were limited by the lack of mowers, wheat was planted in minimal amounts because the Indians lacked the required farming implements and depended upon their white neighbors to cultivate and harvest the grain, kaffir corn was neglected and usually used as fodder for their few animals, and even gardens were unattended. Too many of the Cheyennes and Arapahoes still lived in "camps or on the road" to use the land effectively for agricultural purposes. Regulations stipulated that Indian males reserve at least forty acres of their allotments for farming purposes, but few of the Cheyennes and Arapahoes lived on their allotments. Instead they usually rented informally their reserved forty acres to white farmers, who worked the other 120 acres. That arrangement freed the Indians to live where they chose.

Indians employed as additional farmers were a little more optimistic in reports about the economic condition of their people than were their white counterparts. More sensitive and aware of the changes within the Indian society and culture, however small they might be, the Indian farmers were of the opinion that their tribesmen learned farming techniques when the men were employed as agricultural laborers. Two of the three Indian farmers thought that the Cheyennes and Arapahoes were making "satisfactory progress," but the third stated, "These Indians are in a bad condition and doing very poor progress towards self-support."[8]

Preparations were under way in Washington for a major revision of Indian policy. There was little doubt that the objectives of the Dawes Act had not yet been attained and that the basic statute for Indian policy needed revision. If conditions at the Cheyenne and Arapaho agencies were typical of other Indian jurisdictions, additional money was needed to assist the Indians while they made adjustments to citizenship and self-support.

Superintendent Stouch's evaluation of the conditions at his agency revealed the failure of the policies initiated under the Dawes Act. After the division of the agency into three jurisdictions, 1,549 allotments remained under the supervision of the superintendent at Darlington. Late in 1905, however, only 1,289 Indians were assisted from the Darlington office, an indication that the population had declined by 260 persons. Since 1892 in all three jurisdictions 639 Cheyennes and Arapahoes had died, which meant that their allotments were available for sale under the 1902 Dead Indian Land Act. At Darlington, 745 allotments were rented to whites, and only 143 Indians were actually living on their land. Among all the 1,289 Cheyennes and Arapahoes under his charge, Stouch believed that only 12 or 13 adult Indians were "intelligent, sober and industrious enough to handle their own shares of tribal funds wisely and properly." When sale of allotments was being discussed in the United States Senate, John C. Spooner of Wisconsin warned that Indians needed protection. Otherwise, "the white man will have the land and the white man will have the money, and the Indian will have the experience."[9]

The Burke Act of May 8, 1906, modified the 1887 Dawes Act in several important ways. The statute provided that in the future the act of allotment alone was an insufficient basis for the granting of citizenship to the Indians. Congress agreed with South Dakota Republican Representative Charles H. Burke, one of the act's sponsors, that "blanket Indians" were unfit to exercise the privilege of suffrage. Henceforth citizenship would be granted only when an Indian received his allotment in fee simple and not during the trust period, when the government of the United States acted as a guardian to the Indian. Congress bestowed on the president the authority to extend the trust period at his discretion. The portion of the act that was particularly pertinent to the Cheyennes and Arapahoes defined the manner by which they could receive title to their allotments in fee simple.[10]

Indians varied, congressmen commented, in their ability to control their lives because of differences in intelligence and industry. In the future Cheyennes and Arapahoes could receive a patent to their allotment in fee simple whenever the secretary of the interior was satisfied that a person could take care of his or her own financial affairs. Commissioner of Indian Affairs Leupp indicated that the Indian's occupation and industry would be the primary test in determining competency. Before the passage of the Burke Act, the wardship status of an Indian could only be terminated by a special act of Congress, too cumbersome a process. Also, the statute outlined the proper manner by which heirs of deceased Indian allottees were to be determined. As with other policies, whether or not the law would be beneficial to the Cheyennes and Arapahoes would be settled only if the superintendents were able to guard Indians who were unable to protect their allotments and other financial resources from unethical and money-hungry residents of Oklahoma Territory.[11]

No immediate change occurred at the Cheyenne and Arapaho agencies as a result of the Burke Act. The sale of inherited lands continued to be a significant source of additional income to the tribesmen. During the 1905–1906 fiscal year, 77 tracts of land containing 11,340.06 acres were sold for $123,177.33 at the three agencies. There were 1,024 leases in effect throughout the Cheyenne and Arapaho country, furnishing rents to the Indians; varying from $.10 to $.87 for grazing land to $.31 to $10 an acre a year for agricultural land. Well over one-half of the leased land lay within the Darlington area, which brought to the Cheyennes and Arapahoes $60,021.95. Superintendent Stouch noted that the cash income of the Indians in his agency for the year 1905–1906 amounted to $110,721.49, a decline of more than 38 per cent from the previous year's cash income. The loss of income resulted from fewer sales of inherited land and less income from labor and crops.[12]

At Darlington during the summer of 1906, Charles E. Shell succeeded Stouch as superintendent and special disbursing agent. Soon the new superintendent began inquiries into the lives and habits of the Cheyennes and Arapahoes so that greater conformity to statutes and regulations of the Bureau of Indian Affairs would result. Superintendent Shell began to concern himself with the availability of liquor to the Indians, their traditional ceremonies, Indian education, the leasing of land and the use of the funds derived from the sale of allotments, the competency of the Cheyennes and Arapahoes to manage their own financial affairs, and the use of peyote. Despite denials by the agents and superintendents assigned to the Cheyennes and Arapahoes, the volume of liquor used by the Indians was considerable not only in western Oklahoma Territory but also in Indian Territory. To investigate conditions and reduce the flow of whisky, the Bureau of Indian Affairs appointed William E. Johnson as a special officer to work with the Indian superintendents in the two territories.

Superintendent Shell did not share the view that the sale of liquor to Indians was being "very successfully regulated" by local authorities. When he began preparing to distribute the per capita payments and lease money to the Cheyennes and Arapahoes at Darlington, he expected whisky peddlers to ply their trade and requested funds to hire detectives to obtain evidence so that those violating the prohibition laws could be prosecuted in courts of law. One of Special Officer Johnson's men attended the distribution of money on October 12, 1906, when almost $43,000 was paid over to the Indians. A few arrests were made by the Indian police. Still, Indians with long experience at evading the laws found ways to obtain liquor. John Poisal, a mixed-blood Arapaho, brought his liquor with him to the pay table; he was arrested, and his bottle was taken from him by the captain of the Indian police. Other Indians were willing to name in court the whites who sold liquor to them, but no prosecutions resulted, despite Shell's vigilance.[13]

Encouraged by even the limited success of his first antiliquor effort, Shell began to watch the saloons in the small towns for illegal sale of intoxicating beverages to Indians. He asked Johnson to send one of his men to Calumet to watch a saloon at which Indians were buying a drink called "tin-top." Since Cheyennes and Arapahoes were obtaining liquor in Kingfisher, Shell reminded the Friends of Temperance in that city that it was a federal crime to sell, barter, give, exchange, or in any other way dispose of intoxicating liquors to either reservation Indians or Indians whose lands were held in trust by the United States government. If two or more witnesses could be provided who would testify in court to such a crime, Shell promised prosecution of the matter in federal courts.[14]

In nearby El Reno constant observation of saloons and whisky peddlers reduced the sale of liquor to Indians, but in the small towns scattered throughout the agency control of the liquor traffic was a much more difficult matter. Shell knew that in Fay, Calumet, Geary,

303

Kingfisher, and other towns the Indians could obtain liquor and beer without much difficulty. Because he and his staff were well known, the only way to apprehend those selling liquor to Indians was for "a stranger to come to these places and play detective." Reports continued to come into Shell's hands indicating that Johnson, the ministers, and the Anti-Saloon League had not dried up the liquor traffic completely. Man-Going-Up-Hill sold whisky and a gun in Geary; he was arrested and fined thirty-one dollars and was bailed out of jail when his lessee paid his fine. The additional farmer at Geary complained that if "one of Geary's favorites" had been arrested he "would have gotten off without a fine. I do not think this Indian has had fair treatment and have requested Geary people to do the fair thing." Dan Webster, an Arapaho, was accused of drinking and fighting in Kingfisher. In a drunken rage he had charged Mrs. John Poisal with killing her husband, and he had then struck the woman, grabbed her hair, and thrown her to the ground. When an Indian named Fire and his wife tried to intervene, Webster attacked them as well.[15]

Increased surveillance somewhat reduced the Indians' ready access to liquor. When money was available, however, they still managed to find sources of liquor. After the payment of interest and lease money in the summer of 1907, Shell learned that the "Indians congregated in a canyon near Bridgeport and had a glorious old drunk. It is said that the joints and bootleggers furnished the dope in exchange of the Indians' cash." With too few enforcement officers and the general prevalence of liquor, Shell and his staff could do little more than occasionally haul a few of the offenders into court and try to make examples of them.[16]

Indians were also jailed for violating laws other than public drunkenness. Substantial doubt always existed whether the Indians were treated fairly and in the same way as whites accused of the same misdemeanors. Ten Cheyenne youths were arrested for gambling in the Watonga city park by the town marshal on the morning of August 7, 1907. They were jailed and within a few days were tried by a jury. William Goodsell, who seemed to be sponsoring the gambling, was fined $31 and court costs. The other nine, who were each fined $5 and $10 court costs, did not have the money to pay the assessments and remained in jail until Charles W. Ruckman, the additional farmer at Watonga, arranged for an appeal bond. The boys maintained to Ruckman and "two colored and one white lawyer" that they were innocent and were only in the tent with Goodsell. Ruckman thought Goodsell guilty of gambling. Ruckman wrote to his superintendent, "It looks as if it were a 'graft' on the part of the city authorities and that, because they could do so, they took unfair advantage of the boys because they were Indians." Charlie Jackson, Watonga's town marshal, advised Shell that the boys should pay the fines because that would be less expensive than trying to appeal the cases to superior courts. Jackson explained: "We are trying to do the right thing here and enforce the laws. We have had very little trouble with the Indians. Out of about sixty cases in the last two months, excepting two cases of drunkenness, this is the first time we have had to arrest any of the Indian boys." Whether Shell's intercession on behalf of the youths was successful or not is not known.[17]

It was even more difficult to assist Indians in obtaining their allotment lease money from whites than it was to shield Indian citizens from discriminatory treatment by local law officers. The superintendent found that the territorial courts were often hostile to the Indians and the agency officials. Technically, the federal courts were the proper courts to assume jurisdiction of the cases, but actions before them were slow, and the Office of the United States Attorney rarely could assemble the facts with sufficient rapidity to prevent economic injustice from occurring.

To regularize the leasing procedures, Shell attempted to evict white farmers who had only informal leases for Indians' allotments. When he found lessees delinquent in payments, he tried to attach their unharvested crops. Soon he found that he was powerless to act in the name of the Indians because Judge C. F. Irwin, who presided over the district court, had held that the superintendent as a government officer had no authority to bring into United States courts suits on behalf of citizen Indians. Shell could obtain a writ through the Office of Indian Affairs and the Department of Justice, but by that time the lessees who were delinquent in their payments would have harvested their crops and moved beyond the reach of the court. Louis E.

McKnight, assistant United States attorney, advised Shell that if he wanted to file an attachment bond and personally deposit fifteen dollars for security against court costs, his office would initiate a case in a territorial court. Shell believed that he should not be obligated to stand the cost of prosecutions in the territorial courts. During the discussion Shell refused to renew leases to persons who had defaulted on lease payments, and he also rejected bondsmen who had failed to fulfill the conditions of the leases that had been guaranteed. Within a short time lessees learned of the impasse, and unprincipled men began taking advantage of the Indians.[18]

For a few months Shell tried to find other solutions to the leasing problem. He considered requesting federal troops to evict white farmers occupying allotments without formal leases on the grounds that they were squatters. The Indian police of the agency were, of course, available to Shell, but he doubted that they would remove by force whites who were evading leasing regulations. Similarly, the territorial courts did not offer much hope because "a jury of white farmers would be prejudiced against the Indians and in favor of the white man." The only alternative was to bluff the lessees into settling up their accounts. When one man removed his crop without paying lease money due an Indian, Shell wrote: "In so doing, it seems that you have sold mortgaged property and have thus thrown yourself liable to imprisonment. If you do not come to this office immediately or send sufficient money to settle your indebtedness of $183.33, action will be taken against you without delay." Neither the man nor the money appeared in the agency office, however.[19]

As he developed his leasing program, Shell assumed that all Indians within the agency would be subject to the same rules and regulations. The mixed bloods led by the Balenti family dissented vehemently. George Balenti visited Darlington with his parents to insist that while at Carlisle he had been told by the commissioner of Indian affairs "to go home and go to work and manage all of his own business." The young man interpreted the commissioner's remarks to mean that he did not have to consult the superintendent when he wanted to lease his allotment. Shell conceded that as a family the Balentis were "thoroughly capable to attending to their own affairs; it is also true

306

that they send their children to a public school, which action I most heartily commend." The superintendent continued with the comment that the Balentis were the "most prosperous people" around Calumet and that he had urged them to apply for patents for their land; the members of the family refused to do so because then their allotments would be liable for taxes. Shell asked the commissioner of Indian affairs if the rules and regulations should be suspended for George Balenti and others with similar abilities and resources. If the restrictions were lifted, Shell wanted to know what new guidelines should be followed.[20]

The Balentis continued to put pressure upon Superintendent Shell because they wanted to manage their own leases and obtain patents to their allotments. George and other members of the family were assured by Shell that he would do nothing "to prevent you from getting your patent in fee for your land, but will lend every assistance in my power to aid you in such matter." The superintendent, however, warned George that use of lawyers to obtain patents would do no good since he alone could make the necessary determinations. Information had reached the Darlington office that George's father "had been in consultation with certain lawyers and curbstone real estate men and that they pretend to assist him in getting a patent. Now if he, you or your mother are paying anything for such assistance, you may just as well burn so much money, as they can be of no assistance to you." The Balentis, nevertheless, worked out their leases without the assistance of the agency personnel and the superintendent. One Bernard Bloom obtained the right to plant crops on the allotments of George, John, and William Balenti. Shell did not object since two of the young men were in the process of petitioning for patents to their lands. Shell still thought that the leases for the allotments of other minor children of Michael and Belle Balenti should be processed in the normal manner and that the incomes should be placed in a trust account until the children reached majority. "It is no unusual thing," Shell wrote to Bloom's attorney, "to have young men come to me at the age of 21 saying that they cannot farm their places for lack of horses and implements." Had their lands been regularly leased, and their funds kept on deposit at interest, he said, such "excuses" would not have occurred. For the time, Shell insisted that the lease for John Balenti's land be handled through the agency office.[21]

Others accustomed to handling their own financial affairs also disagreed with Shell's interpretations of leasing regulations. Charles Keith, a mixed-blood Arapaho, and Frederick Haag, a white man married to a Cheyenne woman, retained an El Reno lawyer to represent them in their conflicts with Shell. When the superintendent was accused of ignoring the interests of the Indians, he replied angrily that he was acting in accordance with the regulations issued by the secretary of the interior and that he was not intimidated by the lawyer's "ravings." It appeared to Shell that Indians such as Keith

desire to have all the benefits of other citizens without bearing the burdens which such citizenship should carry. Then you talk to me about keeping the Indians in a state of pupilage. You appear to think that these persons should be white in benefits and Indians in the matter of payment for such payments. . . . I know of no reasons why lawyers and their clients should undertake to instruct me in my duties. My superiors at Washington are the only persons who have any right to give such instructions.[22]

Despite the objections raised by a few of the Indians, Shell continued his program of regularizing the leases held by white farmers throughout the Cheyenne and Arapaho Agency. No exceptions were made for individuals such as George Bent or John Otterby, who had leased their own lands and those of their dependents. It was Shell's intention that after July 1 or December 31, 1907, there would be no informal leases on the lands of the agency. If Indians refused to comply with the wishes of the superintendent, they were to be told by the additional farmers to apply for a patent to their allotments. To the white farmers using allotments without formally approved leases Shell usually wrote, "You are notified to at once vacate any and all Indian allotments used, occupied, or cultivated by you, and if you do not do so within 20 days from the date of this notice, I shall present the matter to the United States Attorney."[23]

Even intermarried white men who usually handled their family's business or who had used the lands of the family were required to file lease forms. Frederick Haag worked not only his wife's allot-ment but also those of two minor sons, one of whom was attending Hampton Institute. Through an El Reno lawyer Haag complained that the family did not want to lease the land through the agency office because it produced one-third less in income than when Haag worked it or negotiated for its use. Still Shell would not depart from the rules as he interpreted them. Without variance Shell informed the Indians and others that the lands were being used without authority, that the informal lessee would have to abandon the land in question, and that, if the Indian persisted in leasing the land himself, he could apply for a patent and assume the full responsibility of citizenship, which meant payment of taxes on the property. Because in most cases the Indians did not want a patent to their land because of the tax, Shell was able to use the tax threat to force the Indians to conform to his interpretation of leasing regulations.[24]

Revision of the leasing regulations by Washington officials on May 6, 1907, disturbed him. Under the new rule those Indians deemed capable of managing their own affairs after that date did not have to follow previous guidelines. Shell interpreted the new rule rather strictly. He immediately excluded income from the allotment of minors from the new regulation and viewed the new privilege as merely probationary: if an Indian "abandons his place and roams about the country making no attempt at self-support, the privilege will be taken from him." Each adult male was still expected to farm at least forty acres of his allotment or to engage in some permanent occupation to provide for his family. The form of the new lease between the Indian and his lessee would have to be approved by the superintendent, but the latter would not collect the lease money, and the Indian would be responsible for any suit involving the terms of the lease. The new plan, Shell commented, did not permit the Indian to "have nothing to do but enjoy himself. He must learn to be a self-respecting, self-supporting citizen."[25]

If white farmers did not adhere to either the new or the old regulations, Shell brought legal action against them. He sought in-junctions against some to prevent trespassing on Indian allotments;

against others he sought temporary restraining orders so that the debtors of the Indians could not remove their crops until the money due the Indians was paid. John Embry, the United States attorney for Oklahoma Territory, cautioned Shell to have the legal questions settled in the proper manner rather than speedily. Shell was advised to keep the cases out of the territorial courts because cases so begun could not be transferred to the federal courts once statehood was granted to the Twin Territories of Oklahoma. "In this Indian litigation," Embry told Shell, "we are encountering a great many new questions which will be of importance to the Indian for 15 or 20 years to come."[26]

Despite Embry's warnings Shell decided to press for actions in the territorial courts. He focused his attention around Watonga, where at least five persons were growing cotton and corn on Indian allotments with no more than a verbal agreement between the Indian and the farmer. With evident racism, Shell singled out one Will Wright, a Negro, for particular attention. He described Wright as a man "of ill reputation in his neighborhood and some of his white neighbors appear to be afraid to appear in any action against him." Shell was certain that Wright, if brought to court, would fight the case and plead that he had already paid money directly to the Indian lessor. Even if a temporary restraining order was issued by the court, Wright would still have time to remove his crops from the land he used and for which no lease had been recorded for more than a year. If it appeared to the superintendent that he would be unable to protect the Indian allottees through either court cases or direct settlements of debts, he asked for authority to use troops stationed at Fort Reno to evict the Indians' debtors.

In his request for permission to use troops, Shell summarized the problems he had encountered trying to protect the economic resources of the Cheyennes and Arapahoes:

... the fact remains evident that the Indians are suffering irreparable loss, and will continue to suffer until these trespassers are removed from the lands. Even should the Court render a decision favorable to the Indians, the trespassers could remove their crops before any decision is likely to be rendered. I have tried every available means to obtain relief through the Courts, but, thus far have failed. In one case, that of Wright, an attorney advised the trespasser to hold the land, as no restraining order had been issued, and that he probably would be required by the Court to pay a small rental for the use of the land. It is probable that by paying small amounts or sums to the allottees or heirs trespassers obtain possession of Indian lands and will continue to do so unless they are made to know that they can not do so without paying a severe penalty. From experience I am led to believe that before they could be removed through the Courts they would have time to mature and harvest a crop; then, if required by the courts to vacate the land, would be ready to repeat the performance upon another allotment,—and all at no cost to themselves in the way of rent or Court costs.[27]

By mid-September Shell had received permission to use troops, but he decided not to do so. Instead he planted the information in the newspapers with good results. The courts in Blaine, Kingfisher, and Canadian counties began hearing the cases which Shell had been requesting for months. The Wright case in the District Court of Blaine County was watched with particular interest by Shell, who instructed the additional farmer to bring every available fact to the attention of the judge. The case against Wright was successful. The judge issued an injunction against Wright to vacate the lands on which he had his crops within forty-eight hours, exercising care not to remove anything except his personal property; otherwise other court action would follow. For all of his work, however, Shell won only five cases against trespassers on Indian allotments either by court action or by satisfactory settlements out of court. Finally, on September 18, 1907, he informed all additional agency farmers that after that date all Indians would be able to lease their allotments in their own names.[28]

The Burke Act called for Indians to assume greater responsibility over their own financial affairs. Because of the changed policy Shell and others began submitting to the commissioner of Indian affairs lists of Indians who could lease their lands without supervision. Shell continued to look upon the policy change and its implementation as an experiment: "If it is found that the allottee is not acting wisely and becomes a loafer, and not only refused to work himself, but keeps others from doing so, the privilege will be promptly taken away from him." By late 1907, Shell had submitted a list of 252 Cheyennes and Arapahoes whom he deemed competent to manage their own leasing. From this list officials in Washington approved 140 of the people as being capable of dealing directly with white farmers or others concerning the use of allotments. The list contained in large measure intermarried people, mixed bloods, and a few full bloods educated at Carlisle and Haskell.[29]

It was also anticipated by the Burke Act that certain Indians would be identified as competent and that they would be issued patents to their allotments. For many purposes when the patent was issued, the Indian would no longer be a member of the tribal roll; thus there was considerable pressure from real estate operators to have some Indians declared competent, especially if their land was on the edges of cities or towns. It was one thing to certify that an Indian could lease his own land but quite another to cut him free from all agency supervision. At first Shell judged a few Indians competent but others clearly were still insufficiently aware of business procedures to have their property removed from the trust status.

The first applicant for a patent to his land under the Burke Act was George Frass, a Cheyenne about twenty-six years old. Shell recommended that a patent be issued to Frass because he was "an educated Indian, had been in business for himself for several years, is as shrewd as the average white man and I am satisfied is thoroughly capable of attending to his own affairs." Three months after his initial recommendation Shell changed his mind. Frass, it was learned, intended to sell his allotment or exchange his land for several town lots in El Reno. It was likely, in the opinion of the superintendent, that the young man would become "homeless." The anticipated transaction meant that Frass was no longer competent, although in the past he had taken care of his property efficiently.[30]

Shell declined to recommend other Indians for patents to their allotments. Frank R. Sweezy, an Arapaho in his early thirties, applied for a patent to his allotment early in 1907. Unfortunately Sweezy had managed to accumulate a substantial number of debts as he tried to support his wife and children. Although Sweezy had a "fair educa-

312

tion, wears short hair, dresses in citizen's clothes, speaks English, is sober and fairly industrious," and owned a good farm, his indebtedness was sufficient evidence for Shell to hold that the Arapaho was "not able to manage his own affairs." Shell feared that if Sweezy was issued his patent creditors would prevail upon him to sell his land and settle his debts. When asked to explain his negative judgment about Sweezy, Shell explained his reasons. The superintendent believed that "business ability rather than mental capacity" should be the test, because many "ignorant Indians" among the Cheyennes and Arapahoes were very shrewd in business affairs, while other Indians with greater intelligence and more education could not take care of their property. In the Darlington District of the agency real-estate men were urging Indians to obtain patents to their land, and pressure was also being brought to bear on the superintendent to make favorable recommendations so that the allotments could be sold. Shell told the commissioner of Indian affairs that the selfishness of the real-estate group caused him to take great care in making his recommendations.[31]

On at least one occasion Shell's recommendation was reversed by Washington officials. Paul Boynton, an Arapaho-Cheyenne man who had been educated at Carlisle, had a valuable allotment near the edge of El Reno, but he had a tendency to get into trouble, as in 1904, when he was arrested and jailed on a charge of adultery. For years Paul had received income from his allotment, and he had worked in the agency office as an interpreter and also as a clerk in traders' stores. In February, 1907, H. C. Bradford went to Washington to argue that Boynton should be given a patent to his trust land. Upon his return from Washington, Bradford offered to purchase the allotment for twelve thousand dollars, but Shell wanted to advertize the land for thirty days and sell it to the highest bidder, estimating that the allotment would bring at least sixteen thousand dollars. Shell wanted Boynton to agree to purchase another tract of agricultural land farther from El Reno and invest the remainder of his funds in bonds.

Boynton would not listen to Shell's plan. He wanted the cash to use as he pleased. There was no doubt, Shell said, that Boynton was an intelligent man, but he had habits that were not pleasing to the superintendent. Shell complained that for several years past Boynton had "roamed about the country much of the time living off other Indians." A white man occupied his allotment, and when he needed money, Boynton went to the man and collected some. Since no written lease was on file in the agency office, Shell initiated proceedings to eject the renter as a trespasser. The renter, rather than leave, agreed to pay his share of the court costs, execute a lease, and allow the crop growing on the allotment to be sold for Boynton's benefit. Shell recommended that Boynton's application for a patent to his allotment be denied.

El Reno real-estate and businessmen kept the pressure on Shell to approve issuance of a patent to Boynton. Shell was finally forced to hold a competency hearing in El Reno. He forwarded the papers to Washington with the comment that he could not recommend "unequivocally, that Mr. Boynton be given control of his property. While nearly all of the persons who have given testimony are reputable men, there is a selfish interest and the interests of the Indians are not considered." He hoped that the need for El Reno to grow could be reconciled with the welfare of the allottees. The superintendent argued that "nearly every allottee to whom I have recommended that a patent in fee be granted has sold or mortgaged his land and is spending the proceeds (as I look at it) in a foolish manner." In almost every instance Shell tried to pursuade the Indians to reinvest their money in other lands and in interest-bearing bonds. The Indians refused, insisting that they wanted their "money with which to have plenty to eat and wear for a season." Shell lost his battle to protect Boynton's allotment when information arrived in Darlington that a patent would be issued on December 9, 1907.[32]

Depending on his judgment about the individual and the family, Shell's recommendations varied sharply. When Minerva Burgess requested a patent for her allotment near the city limits of El Reno, Shell refused. The problem was not with Minerva but with her husband, a Sioux with whom she lived in El Reno. Both, Shell said, possessed sufficient "intelligence" to get along without the supervision of the agency, but the husband's associates assured Shell that he would use any money he could obtain for liquor and gambling. The husband was already under two indictments by a Canadian County Grand Jury for selling liquor to other Indians. But the Burgesses were, in Shell's words, "as capable as the average folks of the lower class of society." In several other cases, those of Kish Hawkins and Peter Shields, Jr., the superintendent endorsed their applications. Of the former Shell wrote, he was "thoroughly capable of managing his own affairs, I cannot recommend him as a man of good principles, but so far as I know, he has for some time been living soberly but there can be no doubt as to his intelligence and ability." Peter Shields, a mixed blood, appeared to Shell to be "sober, industrious, intelligent and able to attend to his affairs with reasonable success, as he has been doing in the past."[33]

Officials in the Washington office of the Bureau of Indian Affairs were less concerned than Shell was with the personal habits of Indians in determining competency. During a visit to Washington, Shell learned that

the policy of the Office . . . is to remove the restrictions if the allottee is capable of managing his own affairs. The question of his inclination to take care of his substance is not to be taken into account. If an Indian has enough ability to know the value of money and merchandise, even though he should buy an automobile with the proceeds, he should be given his patent in fee to his land. The Office holds that it cannot always be responsible for the operations of these Indians. The business ability of the average white man is all that is required to make an Indian eligible to have his patent.

Commissioner Leupp, however, stated that each agent or superintendent was free to establish his own criteria for competence. He noted that some used short hair and others education but that the Indian Office believed that "thrift and industry" were the safest guidelines. Regardless of the criteria employed, sixteen Cheyennes and Arapahoes were given patents to their allotments under the first year of the Burke Act. As of 1906–1907 there were two methods by which an Indian could lose his precious land, either under the competency provision of the Burke Act or under the Dead Indian Land Act of 1902.[34]

315

Why were not more Cheyennes and Arapahoes declared competent? Explanations varied, depending upon the bias or prejudice of agency officials. As the importance of the Sun Dance and the Ghost Dance declined among the Cheyennes and Arapahoes, another ceremony centering around the use of peyote gradually attracted new adherents. For more than a decade agents and superintendents and their subordinates confused peyote with mescal, but by 1907–1908 the distinctions at the Cheyenne and Arapaho agencies had become clear. In 1906 one additional farmer, Charles Ruckman, blamed peyote for Indian inefficiency, although he called the peyote ceremony a "mescal feast." The ceremony occurred every two weeks, lasting from Saturday to Monday morning, when the camp disbanded. There was no question in Ruckman's mind that the peyote rites prevented the Indians from "any kind of work for the ensuing 3 or 4 days and they naturally acquire the habit of laziness and indolence rather than one of industry." Superintendent Stouch commented in his last report that some of the young men of the tribes were using the "mescal bean" (peyote), but he took no action against it and maintained that in general the Indians of the agency had made fair progress toward civilization during his six and one-half years at Darlington.[35]

Soon after arriving at Darlington on August 1, 1906, Superintendent Shell interested himself in what he considered to be vices among the Cheyennes and Arapahoes. Two such evils were, of course, liquor and peyote; with the latter, however, he was still unfamiliar. In his correspondence of 1906 with the Indian Office and special agents, Shell was still confusing mescal with peyote. Through R. S. Connell, a special Indian agent detailed to ferret out information about the use of liquor among the Indians, Shell learned that forty-year-old Leonard Tyler (a son of Black Kettle), who had been educated at Carlisle and had previously worked in the agency office as a clerk and interpreter, was the "High Priest of the mescal eaters of this Agency." During July, 1906, five Indians from Cantonment were arrested at the Ponca Agency for conducting a "Mescal Bean conclave." They claimed to have obtained the beans from Tyler. When confronted with the charge, Tyler denied it, though admitting that he used and possessed peyote.[36]

Early in February, 1907, Shell heard that peyote was being used by Indians during weekly ceremonies. Thomas Otterby, a Cheyenne who was serving as an assistant farmer at Kingfisher, inquired of Shell, "I am wishing to know about the Mascell [mescal, but actually peyote] Bean eaters, the boys eats Mascell right near every Saturday night, I do not see them myself, and I do not go around near them, but I hear it next Sunday or Mondays." Otterby offered to draw up a list of the Cheyennes using "mescal" in the four farming districts near Kingfisher and informed Shell that a "mascell feast" was to be held by Percy Kable and Charles M. Wicks at James Red Hair's allotment, about four miles west of Okarche on Saturday night, February 9, 1907.[37]

Shell sent Indian police to prevent the peyote ceremony. Two days after the incident Reuben Taylor and twelve other Cheyennes who had been at the ceremony retained D. K. Cunningham, a lawyer in Kingfisher, to plead their case with Shell. Cunningham reported that Taylor and a number of "other good Indians who I have known for a long time, have called on me today and told me about the Indian police disturbing them while they were worshipping God last Saturday evening, a little west of Okarche and these Indians feel very sore over being interrupted in there [*sic*] services, as well as the disgrace of being told by the Police that they were under arrest." The Cheyennes asked Cunningham to tell Shell that "they are in the habit of using an herby [*sic*] known as Peyote. They all tell me that it is a valuable herby for medicinal purposes, and that there is nothing in it which is intoxicating or poisonous." One of the men, Bushy Head, claimed that peyote had cured him of a cold and chest pains following five days when he was "so poorly" that he could neither eat nor drink water. The Cheyennes maintained that peyote had been tested by Mooney, of the Bureau of American Ethnology, who found it "not dangerous but a good healthy remedy." Through Cunningham, Reuben Taylor sent Shell some peyote buttons with the information that if more were needed, he would send them to the agency office.[38]

317

Along with Cunningham's letter to Shell the Indians sent a petition. Signed by thirteen Cheyennes, only two of whom fixed their signatures with an X, the petition stated that twenty-nine people had met at Percy Kable's home, three miles west of Okarche, and had held "services to worship God and ask his assistance and to especially aid and extend his blessings on the sick grandchildren of Percy Kable." During the ceremony Indian police arrested all the participants and confiscated the drum and the gourd used to beat the drum used when the Indians were "singing praises to God, and said drum was not used in any way disrespectful to the modern way of praising God." The Cheyennes further claimed that during the ceremony they acted as "Christian Indians" and did nothing disrespectful to "civilized Christian religion." In concluding their petition, Reuben Taylor and the others requested the right "to hold similar services and worship of God according to the dictates of our own conscience, at any and all reasonable time, and that we may not be required to account to you for the worshipping of God" and asked that the order for their arrest be rescinded.[39]

Responding to Cunningham's letter, Shell took full responsibility for the order that had led to the Cheyennes' arrest. He claimed that the meeting violated Section 2652 of the Revised Statutes of Oklahoma Territory. From personal observation, Shell said, he had already drawn several conclusions. First, the herb in question, meaning peyote, was not in conformity with the teachings of the Christian religion, and, second, the identification of the peyote ceremony with Christianity was only a "cunning way" to obtain protection while using "this very injurious herb." Shell informed Cunningham that he had begun a court action against "three of the Ring leaders," expecting to prove that the statutes of the territory were being violated because he was convinced that the "use of this herb is much more injurious than the use of alcoholic drinks." Since many of the Indians arrested at Percy Kable's allotment were from Cantonment, Shell maintained that "these feasts foster the spirit of roving which we are endeavoring to break up. The followers of feasts do not seem to have time to do much of anything else."[40]

Superintendent Shell immediately began to collect information about peyote and its use by Indians. Shell wrote to James L. Mooney, asking what effect peyote had upon "generative organs" and which drug, mescal or peyote, was more dangerous to human beings. He also asked Mooney to send him samples of peyote and mescal so that he could see that they were different herbs. He asked similar information from a temperance advocate and inquired whether the minister was interested in assisting him in breaking up the use of the "Mescal Bean." Shell asked the Reverend C. C. Brannon, of Guthrie, to inform William E. Johnson, the special officer in charge of limiting the liquor among the Indians, of the problem. Because he had caught "a big bunch of these 'Mescal Bean' fiends, captured a sample, also their drum, rattle, etc.," and since the county attorney was co-operative, a trial would soon take place.[41]

George L. Bowman, the Kingfisher County attorney, warned Superintendent Shell that the Indians were "going to make a fight" over their arrest. If the prosecution of the Indians was to be successful, Bowman needed witnesses and information about mescal or the drug being used when the Indians were arrested. Thomas Otterby, the Cheyenne assistant farmer at Kingfisher, through whom Shell collected information about the Okarche peyote ceremony, gradually sent the superintendent more facts. Robe Red Wolf, Otterby's assistant, was among those arrested during the Okarche peyote meeting. Otterby asked Shell to excuse Red Wolf because he was a "good hand" and had promised not to eat "mescal" again. The Indian police apparently sympathized with those whom they had arrested because the "real Mescal drum and rattler" were not confiscated by the police; other items were substituted in their place. The "mescal eaters" also talked the police out of taking away the peyote, and the latter "did not do their duties, they told the mescal eaters that they won't do anything bad for them. So the Mescal eaters went on and eat all night anyway." The trial of the *Territory of Oklahoma* v. *Howling Wolf, Reuben Taylor and Percy Kable* was delayed until February 26, 1907. The Indians, Bowman learned, would at that time attempt to prove that "Pyota" was not mescal, and the county attorney warned Shell that, if they did, he would have not a case to prosecute.[42]

Before the trial in the probate court in Kingfisher, Shell kept his subordinates informed and searched for proper witnesses. Indians in particular were sought because, Shell pointed out, he wanted information about the "beans or button which the Indians had at their feast on the night of the 9th inst." The Cheyennes, Shell had learned from County Attorney Bowman, were going to build their defense on the assertion that peyote and mescal were not identical. The testimony of Robe Red Wolf, Shell believed, would be important, and to Otterby he wrote: "Leave no stone unturned which might help us win our case, however, I desire to say, that we want the truth in the case. While we desire to win it must be with clean hands." In addition to Red Wolf, Shell also sought the assistance of the Reverend Robert Hamilton, of Watonga, who was willing to testify against Reuben Taylor and the others. Hamilton was a personal friend of the trial judge, and he insisted that the mescal bean and peyote were similar, and he was equally certain that peyote was what former Agent Woodson had in mind when he pushed the Medicine Man and Mescal Bean Act through the territorial legislature.[43]

The trial resulted in a verdict against Taylor and the other defendants; they were fined twenty-five dollars each and sentenced to five days in jail. Shell, of course, was delighted but was concerned when the Indians appealed their conviction. In any new trial, however, Shell thought that he could add additional testimony that would conclusively prove his contention that the mescal bean mentioned in the territorial statutes was really peyote. Richard Davis, a well-educated Cheyenne and former additional farmer at the agency, had stated that the mescal bean and peyote were similar. Special Officer William Johnson advised Shell to have his policemen conduct another raid on a "mescal feast." "I am of the opinion," Johnson wrote to Shell, "that one or two affairs of this sort will discourage this thing. There is not much profit in it as there is in the whisky business."[44]

Shell was displeased by the unwillingness of the Cheyennes to testify in court against Taylor and the codefendants. When the trial was being held, Robe Red Wolf pretended to know nothing about peyote. But, Shell complained, "I am convinced that there is scarcely an Indian in this part of the country who does not know that Peyote and Mescal bean are one and the same thing. I do not care to employ men who are supporters of the mescal habit, and if he prefers to continue in the slant he seems to have taken, he cannot work for me." The superintendent was less critical of Otterby, who, at the trial of Taylor and his fellow peyote users, "did not seem to have sufficient courage to be willing to go into court and swear to what you knew." Otterby, Shell insisted, understood the identity of the two herbs, and "yet you seemed to be afraid to swear to this." Other aspects of Otterby's work pleased Shell, and he was encouraged to keep the superintendent advised of the meetings of the peyote users and to "pay no attention to what the Indians say against you, but go right ahead doing your duty. This thing will soon blow over and I think we can break the thing up."[45]

The Cheyennes quickly appealed the unfavorable verdict to the district court. As Shell assembled more evidence for the new trial, he also learned more about those connected with peyote. Otterby furnished a list of names of Indians, almost exclusively Cheyennes, who used peyote—forty-nine men and three women who came from the four farming districts of the Darlington District of the agency. Sixteen wives, though not listed by name, were also included as participants in peyote ceremonies. Not every person on the list can be identified on the agency census roll of 1900 because some Indians were known among their people by several different names or by names that did not correspond to the census or allotment list. Leonard Tyler was designated the principal leader of the Cheyenne peyote group, and Reuben Taylor and Kish Hawkins were also listed as leaders closely associated with Tyler. These three Cheyennes were well-educated Indians; Tyler and Taylor had attended Haskell, Hawkins, Carlisle and Indiana College, Fort Wayne. Thirty-five of the men pointed out by Otterby were educated, as were six of the sixteen wives. The ages of the thirty-eight identifiable men ranged from 25 to 57 years, with the median age being 36 years and the average age, 36.8. The women ranged in age from 26 to 60, with the median age being 34 and the average age being 38.7. Otterby commented that other Cheyennes had participated in the peyote ceremonies, but he did not know their names.[46]

Shell wanted to give the peyote proponents a "thorough drubbing when the case comes up again." No other agent or superintendent before Shell had made a serious attempt to prevent the peyote ceremonies, although Otterby stated that as early as 1899 he had attended meetings at Taylor's home and that he had informed his superiors about the meeting. Other Indians, knowing that Otterby was an informant, laughed at him because he could not "do anything to them." At least four Indian employees of the agency—Waldo Reed, Herbert Walker, Solomon Bearlo, and Robe Red Wolf—were among the groups using peyote.[47]

The Cheyennes and Arapahoes began collecting money for the costs of the appeal. It was also known that "Professor" James L. Mooney, of the Smithsonian Institution, was being sought by the Indians as an expert witness in their behalf. To counter Mooney's evidence, Shell sought the assistance of Special Officer W. E. Johnson, Indian Inspector Ralph S. Connell, and the Reverend C. C. Brannon to present "evidence of unquestioned quality." Appealing to their fellow tribesmen, the Indian peyote leaders collected a "considerable" amount of money for the appeal trial, but Shell proposed "to pile up a bulwark of evidence of men of known character that will settle the thing beyond the shadow of a doubt." There were other peyote groups among the Cheyennes at that time. One such group was centered among the Cheyennes living in the vicinity of Clinton and Weatherford and was led by Peter Bird Chief, also known as Standing Bird. Another peyote group living near Deer Creek in Custer County was led by Rufus Gilbert. From these and other groups Taylor and his associates could logically expect support.[48]

As Shell mustered his witnesses, the Indians continued to hold their peyote ceremonies. The Cheyennes moved their meetings to a site near Watonga, according to information received from Thomas Otterby. Shell, wanting to surprise the group, brought in a special officer from Indian Territory to assist him. A Dr. Hume, of Anadarko, was sought out as a witness through J. P. Blackman, the agent of the Kiowa, Comanche, Wichita, and Affiliated Tribes. A sample peyote button was sent to Professor H. C. Washburn, of the University of Oklahoma, for examination, with the information that, if the professor could not testify that the peyote button was not "known commonly as the Mescal Bean, his testimony would not be of much value."[49]

Before the trial, held on July 12, 1907, Shell learned that the Indians' lawyer, D. K. Cunningham, did not plan to use expert witnesses. Shell, however, insisted that Special Officer Johnson, Dr. Hume, and Professor Washburn offer their testimony before Judge C. F. Irwin in the district court. The Indians' counsel entered a demurrer to the evidence, arguing that the statute relating to the mescal bean was "class legislation and that the territory had no right to enact any such law." Judge Irwin sustained the demurrer and gave Shell thirty days to prepare a brief. The judge also remarked that although he thought the spirit of the law was good, he could not rule otherwise. After hearing the judge's statement, Shell believed that the only hope was to obtain new legislation either from Congress or from the territorial legislature. Taylor, Percy Kable and Howling Crane were thus acquitted because the case was allowed to lapse, although the Office of Indian Affairs in Washington furnished a brief for Shell's use.[50]

Despite the legal setback Shell continued his opposition to the peyote ceremony. He warned the superintendent of the Lamedeer, Montana, agency that Leonard Tyler, the "high priest" of the peyote group among the Southern Cheyennes, was visiting the northern division of the tribe. Tyler, Shell warned, should not be allowed to associate with other Indians. Shell also circulated a petition among other superintendents and agents asking Congress for legislation that would outlaw the use of peyote. After Oklahoma became a state, Shell advocated revision of the state's statutes to add peyote to the list of banned herbs and drugs. Shell encountered the opposition of William H. Murray (called by the superintendent "Cockle Burr Bill"), who told Shell that "he knew Indian Agents and knew no good of them." Murray refused to allow Shell to testify before the appropriate committee of the Oklahoma House of Representatives. As a result, Shell told Special Officer Johnson, the use of peyote was continuing to flourish and was actually increasing among the Cheyennes and Arapahoes.[51]

Why was peyote attractive to the Southern Cheyennes, especially among the educated members of the tribe? Many of those participating in the peyote ceremonies had been exposed to the teachings of Christianity in missionary, reservation, and nonreservation schools for as long as ten years. During that time they were under constant pressure to accept the whites' economic, social, religious, and political institutions, and they found that the Indian agents despised tribal ceremonies and constantly restricted the Indians' ability to attend them. The young leaders trained at Carlisle and Haskell looked, therefore, for a new ceremony that could link the old Indian ways with the new religious teachings learned in the schools. The peyote ceremony, which was held in a traditional tipi, was accompanied by drums, rattles, and songs of prayer led by a peyote leader, and appealed to a supernatural spirit for an individual's or a group's welfare was within both Indian and Christian traditions. They believed that peyote, like the Sun Dance, brought to the Cheyennes health and tribal well-being, among other benefits.

In their past Cheyennes had sought visions that guided them to correct modes of behavior. Under the influence of peyote men and women had hallucinations, during which birds, animals, and spirits spoke to them, directing them to live and act in a certain manner. The individuals enjoyed these visions without the traditional intermediaries, the medicine men or priests, who, of course, were anathemas to missionaries, agency physicians, and agents. Some of the better-educated Cheyennes were also sons and daughters of older tribal leaders. But their education, perhaps, prevented them from continuing to accept fully the older ceremonies and the powers of shamans or medicine men. As leaders of the tribe the young men used the peyote ceremony to bring more people within their influence and away from the power of the older priests and medicine men. Tyler, Taylor, and their associates, however, did not anticipate that the Indian agents and superintendents would simply shift their opposition from the older ceremonies and practices to peyote, because it did not contain all the tenets of Christianity.

With assistance from the federal government declining, it was important for the Cheyennes to manage their own funds and resources wisely. Where Indians had retained lease money or had

sold inherited land, Superintendent Shell continued to exercise supervision in the expenditure of funds. Little Chief received authorization
to spend about $1,000 that had accumulated in his account for a good
team of horses, a two-room house, a well, and a list of agricultural
implements. When Wolf Ahead was permitted to spend $360 so that
he could begin farming, Bert Frazier, the Cheyenne additional farmer
at Calumet, was directed to supervise the purchases to see that Wolf
Ahead began to break and plant in crops the forty acres of his
allotment that could not be leased to white farmers. Occasionally
a Cheyenne, such as Coyote, who had not squandered his funds, received
encouragement from Superintendent Shell. Coyote's house was "clean
and tidy," which, Shell wrote, reflected credit upon "your wife or
whoever takes care of your house." The superintendent was particularly pleased that Coyote was caring for his cattle herd. "Never sell or
kill any of the female cattle," Shell advised, but, "when you raise a
male and it is large enough, it is all right to sell or kill it but by keeping
all of the females your herd will continue to get larger and in a few
years you will have many cattle."[52]

The economic condition of the Cheyennes, however, was not changing rapidly. The amount of money earned by the Indians from the
products of their farms or from other employment remained small;
it was less than 2 per cent of the total income of the two tribes. During
the 1906–1907 fiscal year the Cheyennes and Arapahoes received an
income from all sources of $217,312.98. That figure included $50,000
from tribal interest money, $35,000 in gratuities, more than $67,000
from the sale of inherited land, and more than $60,000 from leasing
income. There well may have been other sources of income available
to the Indians during the fiscal year, but they were not listed by the
commissioner of Indian affairs. Within the three jurisdictions of the
agency, the Cheyennes and Arapahoes had a per capita income of
$78.03 for the 1906–1907 fiscal year. The income was far less than that
reported for 1904–1905, when the per capita income of the Cheyennes
and Arapahoes within the Darlington Agency had been $139.16.

The decline of Indian income was symptomatic of the decaying
and stagnating lives of the Cheyennes and the Arapahoes. Indian
farming had peaked by 1899–1900, and during the first decade of the

twentieth century the Cheyenne and Arapaho people planted fewer crops. Increasingly they, their agents, and Washington officials relied on lease money and the sale of allotments to provide the Indians with an immediate livelihood. Unable either to persuade or to coerce the Indians into agricultural pursuits, the agents and superintendents devoted much of their energy to changing the social customs and religious ceremonies of the Cheyennes and Arapahoes. With an almost fanatical fervor agency officials attempted to eradicate multiple marriages and camp life, eliminate the use of alcohol and peyote, and ban the Sun Dance and nearly all customs from which the Indians derived any human satisfaction. The Dawes and Burke acts, the keystones of the assimilation policy, were failing. Those enforcing that policy were oblivious to the misery and suffering it was causing the Indians not only in western Oklahoma but throughout the United States. Few if any individuals who were involved in the lives of the Cheyennes and the Arapahoes in 1907 realized that three decades or more would pass before any change would occur in the fortunes of the two tribes.

CHAPTER XII

Epilogue

TWENTY YEARS AFTER the passage of the 1887 Dawes Act it was incontestable that the Southern Cheyennes and the Arapahoes had not attained the status contemplated by those who had framed the statute. Philanthropists, friends of the Indians, legislators, and bureaucrats who were instrumental in the law's enactment were trapped by beliefs then current in American society. It was held almost without exception that each human being was singularly responsible for his own fate and that those who failed to reap the benefits of citizenship were dismissed as unworthy of government assistance. Aid for the unfortunate or handicapped came principally from private philanthropies, sectarian groups, or voluntary associations of well-meaning individuals. None of those organizations, however, were very influential in imposing their humanitarian views on the legislators or administrators who designed Indian policy or controlled the expenditures of public funds.

Members of Congress were nearly unanimous in their insistence that only minimal expenditures be made in behalf of the Indian people. Appropriations exceeding those specified in treaties or agreements were bitterly denounced on the floor of Congress as extravagant and needless waste of revenue. Classed as gratuities, nontreaty funds designated to educate and to provide food, medicine, farming implements, stock animals, clothing, or vocational instruction to Indians were rigorously examined by congressional committees in unceasing efforts to appropriate only the smallest subventions possible. Rarely in the last quarter of the nineteenth or the early twentieth century did Congress provide the funds needed by the Department of the Interior to care for the Indians. Gratuities were to congressmen another name for a dole, and as such they were considered an unwelcome burden on taxpaying citizens. Although members of Congress frequently stated that Indians were wards of the United States government, rarely did they manifest a desire to provide for the actual needs of the Indians by protective legislation or adequate appropriations.

These ungenerous attitudes retarded the ability of the Cheyennes and Arapahoes to acquire the knowledge, skills, and vocations that would enable them to become educated, Christian citizen-farmers. After the tribesmen were confined to their reservation in 1875, hunger, disease, despair, and lethargy dominated their lives. With buffalo and game rapidly diminishing on the Great Plains, Indian hunters could no longer feed their families. Little heed was paid to Agent Miles's almost frantic pleas that more money was imperative to provide food to replace the meat previously supplied by the men of the tribes. For a decade Miles and his successors struggled to alleviate the problems arising from inadequate food supplies for the Cheyennes and the Arapahoes. Miles's two efforts to found cattle herds sufficiently large to compensate for deficiencies in congressional appropriations ended in failure. Although Miles was not blameless for the 1885 debacle that led to the expulsion of the cattlemen from the Cheyenne and Arapaho ranges, at least his motivation to see that the Indians possessed enough meat to eat was commendable.

The mandate to transform Cheyennes and Arapahoes into farmers was impossible to fulfill because only sixteen years elapsed after the Cheyennes and Arapahoes were enclosed on their reservation when the Dawes Act was applied to the two tribes. Even under the most favorable circumstances the vast majority of the tribesmen could not have been transformed into persons capable of assuming the responsibilities of "citizenship" as the whites interpreted the term. Between 1875 and 1891 an agricultural economy failed to materialize on the Cheyenne-Arapaho Reservation. Never was the agency staffed with enough agricultural instructors to do more than assist a small number of amenable Indians. Further, agricultural labor was repugnant to

Cantonment Indian School, Cantonment, Oklahoma Territory. *Courtesy Oklahoma Historical Society.*

Young Whirlwind and Little Big Jake, Southern Cheyenne chiefs, seated in center, with Cheyenne girls and boys enrolled at Carlisle Indian School, ca. 1884. *Courtesy Oklahoma Historical Society.*

Southern Cheyenne Indian Police. *Courtesy Western History Collections, University of Oklahoma Library.*

An Arapaho winter camp near Cheyenne-Arapaho Agency. *Courtesy Western History Collections, University of Oklahoma Library.*

Beef issue to Cheyenne and Arapaho families, 1889. *Courtesy Western History Collections, University of Oklahoma Library.*

Southern Cheyenne dancers. *Courtesy Western History Collections, University of Oklahoma Library.*

Members of the Southern Cheyenne Lance Society. *Courtesy Western History Collections, University of Oklahoma Library.*

Participants in a peyote ceremony on a Sunday morning in 1912, near Clinton, Oklahoma. *Courtesy Western History Collections, University of Oklahoma Library.*

adult male Indians; crops failed; farming machinery to break the sod, cultivate, and harvest the crops was in short supply; and the climate did not permit intensive cultivation of the soil. After 1892 crop yields were too low to support even efficient white farmers on one-quarter sections of land similar to those allotted to the Indians under the Dawes Act. The quantity of land reserved for the use of the Cheyennes and Arapahoes was, therefore, an inadequate basis on which to expect them to become self-supporting.

It was quickly realized that the Cheyennes and Arapahoes could not effectively cultivate and farm their allotments. Allotments were leased to white farmers and ranchers so that the Indians could obtain some benefit from their land, but with a few exceptions the income of an Indian family did little more than prevent starvation. Nonutilization of allotments furnished the rationale in 1902 for the alienation of inherited land and in 1906 for the sale of allotments by allegedly competent Indians. Potentially, the Dead Indian Land and the Burke acts could and did destroy the already limited land base provided by the Dawes Act. While the land slipped away from the Indians by legal and fraudulent means, no other sources of money replaced the income derived from land leases. Seasonal farm labor, a limited number of agency positions, service as army scouts or Indian police, and a few clerkships in traders' stores were the only sources of employment available to Indians. Many Indian boys and girls who returned from reservation and nonreservation schools had no alternative but to join relatives in camp life.

Indian educational policy as well as land policy was a dismal failure. Those charged with educating Indian youths made no effort to blend together the Indian and white cultures. All vestiges of the Indian way of life were to be purged from the children, although later they were expected to live with and lead their relatives toward accepting the values of white men's culture. After Indian youths had completed their studies at Carlisle, Haskell, or Chilocco, they could not practice the skills and crafts they had learned. One graduating or returning class from Carlisle alone would more than fill all the agency posts to which an Indian might be appointed. Those fortunate enough to be selected as agency employees normally served for many years, while younger men and women were forced to search futilely elsewhere for a livelihood. The empty and frustrated existence of Indian youths led to the problems of alcoholism, which further blighted the lives of many Cheyennes and Arapahoes.

Despite the resiliency of Cheyenne culture, changes in tribal society were slowly occurring. Indian agents, missionaries, teachers, white friends and neighbors, and insensitive legislators made substantial inroads on the customs of the Indians. Large tribal encampments, other than those set up when the Sun Dances were held, disappeared. By 1907 the Cheyennes were living on allotments in groups no larger than those of extended families, which the Indian agents hoped to reduce even further to individual family units. Only a minority dwelled in small frame houses constructed with funds that were usually obtained from the sale of inherited land or accumulated lease money. Rarely did even the most affluent Cheyennes live more comfortably than the poorest of their white neighbors. The wants of the Indians, compared to those of whites, were few. The Indians desired only food, clothing, shelter, horses to ride to visit friends and relatives, and camping utensils. Surplus goods or bank accounts were not essential for happiness as long as the Indians could mingle with others of their tribe and participate in the tribe's traditional rites held to assure the health and spiritual satisfaction of their people.

The power of tribal chiefs, although never eliminated, had been by 1907 substantially lessened. Old village and war chiefs like Little Robe, Stone Calf, Old Whirlwind, Tall Bull, and Bull Bear were dead. Their successors, represented by Old Crow, Little Chief, Young Whirlwind, Little Big Jake, White Shield, Three Fingers, and Wolf Robe, never attained the prestige of the older generation of leaders. The Indian agents saw to that. The newer chiefs, if they were cooperative and pliable, were sometimes elevated to the tribal council by the agents. Known as "ration chiefs" among the Cheyennes, these men nonetheless shared with those chosen by traditional criteria the decisions that influenced the fate of the Cheyennes. In the eyes of an Indian agent a chief was particularly valuable if he was a member of a Christian church and if he sent his children to school, lived with only one woman, cut his hair, wore white man's clothing, labored on his allotment, did not visit for weeks with his friends and relatives, did not drink liquor, did not attend the Sun Dance, and did not spend "frivolously" his lease and interest money on feasts or presents.

After 1892 the laws of Oklahoma Territory supplemented federal statutes to force the Cheyennes and the Arapahoes to modify their ways of life. Territorial laws required Indians to abandon multiple marriages, curtailed the practices of the medicine men, and extended the authority of county officials, territorial courts, and law-enforcement officers over the new citizens. Those who violated territorial statutes were arrested, fined, and jailed for gambling, drunkenness, bigamy, vagrancy, and acts of violence. It was indeed calamitous that the territorial courts were not employed for more than punitive purposes against the Indians. Racial prejudice prevented satisfactory protection of the Cheyennes' and the Arapahoes' property. White juries with disturbing frequency ignored the clear intent of laws and substantial evidence to award verdicts that were destructive to the economic interests of the Indians. Hundreds of thousands of dollars desperately needed to sustain Indian families were lost when court cases involving unethical business practices of bankers, lawyers, merchants, loan sharks, and defaulting lessees were not prosecuted in behalf of the Indians. The Dawes Act was applied much too early to the Cheyennes and Arapahoes, who were virtually helpless to defend themselves against the cupidity of their white fellow citizens.

A people of less courage and character than the Cheyennes would have crumbled under the onslaught of the white man. When the Sun Dance, the Renewal of the Sacred Arrows, and other rites were banned, the Cheyennes found another vehicle to sustain their spirituality. A ceremony centering around the use of peyote gave them the means of combining the Christian concept of an omnipotent god with their traditional veneration of nature's elements. The spirits of the earth, air, fire, water, and the plants of the land were skillfully woven into the nightlong rituals that induced life-directing visions for the peyotist. Through peyote, God was as present among the Cheyennes as were the spirits of the sun, the land, the wind, and the animals when they lived free on the Great Plains. In another ten years the peyote ceremony would become the central ritual of the Native American Church.

339

Early in the twentieth century, despite the crushing burdens of the assimilation policy, the Cheyennes retained their identity. Chiefs were still respected, the love of earth and nature were undiminished, children and elders were cherished, friends were welcome, and food was hospitably shared. In western Oklahoma there were individuals who softly and with quiet dignity informed a new neighbor—"I am a Cheyenne."

Abbreviations Used in Notes

BIC	Board of Indian Commissioners
CS	Central Superintendency
C&A	Cheyenne and Arapaho
CCF	Central Classified Files
CF	Classified Files
Cong. Rec.	*Congressional Record*
FOF	Field Office Files
ID	Indian Division
IOHC	Indian Oral History Collection
LR	Letters Received
LS	Letters Sent
OHS	Oklahoma Historical Society
OIA	Office of Indian Affairs
OSI	Office of the Secretary of the Interior
NA	National Archives
RBIA	Records of the Bureau of Indian Affairs
Stat.	*United States Statutes at Large*
UOL	University of Oklahoma Library

Notes

CHAPTER I

1. *Annual Report of the Commissioner of Indian Affairs to the Secretary of the Interior for the Year 1875*, 269, hereafter cited as *Report, Commissioner of Indian Affairs, 1875*; Board of Indian Commissioners, *Seventh Annual Report for the Year 1875*, hereafter cited as BIC, *Report, 1875*; Donald J. Berthrong, *The Southern Cheyennes*, 403, 404–405.

2. Acting Agent J. A. Covington to E. P. Smith, Commissioner, March 19, 1875, Letters Received, Cheyenne and Arapaho Agency, Records of the Bureau of Indian Affairs, Record Group 75, National Archives Building, hereafter cited as LR-C&A-NA; *Report, Commissioner of Indian Affairs, 1875*, 269–70.

3. J. D. Miles to E. P. Smith, July 17, 1875, and Enoch Hoag's endorsement, July 27, 1875, LR-C&A-NA; *Report, Commissioner of Indian Affairs, 1875*, 270; Benjamin Williams to J. D. Miles, July 5, 1875, Nathan Davis to J. D. Miles, July 5, 1875, Letters Received, Field Office Files, Central Superintendency, Records of the Bureau of Indian Affairs, Record Group 75, National Archives Building, hereafter cited as LR-FOF-CS-NA.

4. J. Holloway, M.D. to J. A. Covington, September 1, 1875; J. A. Covington to E. P. Smith, September 14, 1875, LR-C&A-NA.

5. Enoch Hoag to J. D. Miles, September 24, 1875, Letters Sent, Field Office Files, Central Superintendency, Records of the Bureau of Indian Affairs, Record Group 75, National Archives Building, hereafter cited as LS-FOF-CS-NA; J. D. Miles to E. Hoag, October 22, 1875, LR-FOF-CS-NA; Benjamin Williams to J. D. Miles, October 22, 1875, LR-FOF-CS-NA.

6. Ammunition Permit by John D. Miles, dated November 24, 1875, J. D. Miles to E. P. Smith, December 6, 1875, LR-FOF-CS-NA; Enoch Hoag to J. D. Miles, November 18, 21, 1875, Cyrus Beede to J. D. Miles, December 8,

1875, LS-FOF-CS-NA; Major General John Pope to Enoch Hoag, November 20, 1875 (Copy), LR-C&A-NA.

7. J. D. Miles to Enoch Hoag, December 31, 1875, January 3, 1876, LR-FOF-CS-NA.

8. J. D. Miles to J. Q. Smith, Commissioner, January 31, 1876, J. D. Miles to William Nicholson, February 29, 1876, LR-FOF-CS-NA; W. Nicholson, Superintendent to Major General John Pope, February 26, 1876, W. Nicholson to J. D. Miles, LS-FOF-CS-NA; W. Nicholson to J. Q. Smith, March 4, 1876, LR-C&A-NA. William Nicholson replaced Enoch Hoag on January 19, 1876, as superintendent of the Central Superintendency.

9. J. Q. Smith to William Nicholson, April 1, 1876, Letters Sent, Office of Indian Affairs, Records of the Bureau of Indian Affairs, Record Group 75, National Archives Building, hereafter cited as LS-OIA-NA; W. Nicholson to J. Q. Smith, April 4, 1876, LS-FOF-CS-NA; J. D. Miles to W. Nicholson, April 27, 1876, W. Nicholson to J. Q. Smith, May 8, 1876, LR-C&A-NA; J. D. Miles to W. Nicholson, May 19, 1876, Letterbooks of the Cheyenne and Arapaho Agency, Vol. 1, 356, Indian Archives, Oklahoma Historical Society, Oklahoma, hereafter cited as C&A Letterbooks.

10. W. Nicholson to J. Q. Smith, May 27, 1876, LS-FOF-CS-NA; J. D. Miles to Robert Bent, June 12, 1876, J. D. Miles to W. Nicholson, June 12, 1876, July 5, 1876, 534, J. D. Miles to Colonel Bristol, Commanding Officer, Fort Reno, July 3, 1876, C&A Letterbooks, Vol. 1, 444, 446, 519–20.

11. J. M. Daugherty to J. D. Miles, February 6, 1876, LR-C&A-NA; *Report, Commissioner of Indian Affairs, 1876,* 49; J. D. Miles to E. P. Smith, July 9, 1875, LR-C&A-NA; J. D. Miles to W. Nicholson, March 6, April 4, 1876, C&A Letterbooks, Vol. 1, 168, 186–87.

12. J. D. Miles to W. Nicholson, April 10, 12, 1876, LR-FOF-CS-NA.

13. J. D. Miles to F. C. Buckley, April 18, 1876, J. D. Miles to Major J. K. Mizner, April 20, 1876, C&A Letterbooks, Vol. 1, 240–42, 252–54.

14. A. E. Wood, Second Lieut., Fourth Cavalry to Post Adjutant, Fort Reno, Indian Territory, April 22, 1876 (Copy), LR-FOF-CS-NA.

15. J. D. Miles to W. Nicholson, April 27, 1876, C&A Letterbooks, Vol. 1, 272–73.

16. E. R. Platt, Assistant Adjutant General, Headquarters, Department of the Missouri to Major J. K. Mizner, Fourth Cavalry, Commanding Fort Reno, I. T., April 29, 1876, and W. T. Sherman's endorsement, Headquarters of the Army, Washington, May 12, 1876 (Copies), LR-C&A-NA.

17. To Whom It May Concern, signed by John D. Miles, May 17, 1876, C&A Letterbooks, Vol. 1, 347, J. D. Miles to W. Nicholson, June 10, 1876, LR-FOF-CS-NA.

18. J. D. Miles to W. Nicholson, August 1, 18, 1876 (Copies), W. Nicholson to J. Q. Smith, August 5, 1876, LR-C&A-NA.

19. J. D. Miles to Colonel J. K. Mizner, Commanding Officer, Fort Reno,

August 22, 1876, C&A Letterbooks, Vol. 1, 657; J. D. Miles to W. Nicholson, September 20, 1876, LR-FOF-CS-NA; W. Nicholson to J. Q. Smith, September 25, 1876, LR-C&A-NA; S. A. Galpin to W. Nicholson, October 4, 1876, LS-OIA-NA.

20. Miles stated that 2,442 Cheyennes and Arapahoes moved to the Plains while 1,063 others, including 116 school children and old people, stayed behind. J. D. Miles to W. Nicholson, October 13, 1876, C&A Letterbooks, Vol. 1, 807–808; George Bent to J. D. Miles, November 4, 10, 15 and 26, 1876, George Bent File, Records of the Cheyenne and Arapaho Agency, Indian Archives, Oklahoma Historical Society, Oklahoma City, Oklahoma, hereafter cited as G. Bent File, C&A, OHS; J. D. Miles to W. Nicholson, January 1, 1877, LR-FOF-CS-NA.

21. J. D. Miles to W. Nicholson, January 11 and February 15, 1877, LR-FOF-CS-NA.

22. J. D. Miles to W. Nicholson, April 4, May 14, 1877, J. D. Miles to A. W. Stubbs, June 26, 1877, A. W. Stubbs to J. D. Miles, July 12, 1877, LR-FOF-CS-NA.

23. J. D. Miles to W. Nicholson, July 14, 1877, contains the full roll, LR-C&A-NA.

24. J. D. Miles to E. A. Hayt, Commissioner, October 29, 1877, LR-FOF-CS-NA; George Bent to J. D. Miles, December 20, 1877, G. Bent File, C&A, OHS; J. D. Miles to E. A. Hayt, December 20, 1877, LR-C&A-NA.

25. J. D. Miles to E. A. Hayt, December 20, 1877, S. Gunther, Captain, Fourth Cavalry to Post Adjutant, Fort Reno, I.T., December 4, 26, 1877, J. P. Hatch, Lieut. Col., Fourth Cavalry, Commanding Officer, Fort Elliott, Texas to U.S. Indian Agent, Cheyenne and Arapaho Agency, Darlington, I.T., December 8, 1877, J. D. Miles to H. A. Hambright, Major, Nineteenth Infantry, Commanding Officer, Camp Supply, I.T., December 26, 1877; J. D. Miles to Messrs. Lee and Reynolds, December 26, 1877, LR-C&A-NA.

26. J. D. Miles to J. A. Covington, December 30, 1877, January 7, 1878, J. D. Miles to E. A. Hayt, December 31, 1877, January 15, 1878, Lee & Reynolds to J. D. Miles, December 27, 1877, J. A. Covington to J. D. Miles, January 5, 7, 1878, LR-C&A-NA.

27. J. D. Miles to E. A. Hayt, July 3, 17, 1878, February 8, 1879, LR-C&A-NA; *Report, Commissioner of Indian Affairs, 1878,* 55; *ibid., 1879,* 58.

28. J. D. Miles to E. P. Smith, Commissioner, July 22, 1875, LR-FOF-CS-NA; J. D. Miles to W. Nicholson, May 25, 1876, W. Nicholson to J. Q. Smith, June 13, 1876, LR-C&A-NA.

29. J. D. Miles to W. Nicholson, January 1, March 28, 1877, James S. Weakley to J. D. Miles, March 6, 1877, LR-FOF-CS-NA; George F. Nicholson, Acting Superintendent, to Major General John Pope, March 2, 1877, LS-FOF-CS-NA.

30. W. Nicholson to J. Q. Smith, April 2, 1877, W. Nicholson to Major General John Pope, April 9, 1877, LS-FOF-CS-NA; J. D. Miles to E. A. Hayt, November 17, 1877, LR-C&A-NA.

31. John P. C. Shanks, Special Commissioner, to E. P. Smith, Commissioner, July 8, 1875, Letters Received, Central Superintendency, Records of the Bureau of Indian Affairs, Record Group 75, National Archives Building, hereafter cited as LR-CS-NA; E. P. Smith to J. D. Miles, June 4, 1875, enclosing Martin Gibbons, Acting Agent, Red Cloud Agency, to E. P. Smith, May 24, 1875, LS-OIA-NA; J. A. Covington, Acting Agent, to E. P. Smith, August 25, 1875, LR-C&A-NA.

32. J. D. Miles to E. P. Smith, November 5, December 8, 15, 1875, J. D. Miles to E. Hoag, November 10, 21, December 8, 1875, E. C. Lefebre to E. Hoag, November 15, 1875, Cyrus Beede to General John Pope, November 30, 1875, Major General John Pope to E. Hoag, December 1, 1875 (Copy), E. Hoag to General John Pope, December 4, 1875 (Copy), E. A. Carr, Lieut. Colonel, Fifth Cavalry to Assistant Adjutant General, Department of the Missouri, November 24, 1875, Major General John Pope to AAG, Department of the Missouri, January 13, 1876 (Copy), LR-C&A-NA.

33. J. D. Miles to W. Nicholson, May 15, 1876, LR-C&A-NA; W. Nicholson to J. Q. Smith, May 30, 1876, LS-FOF-CS-NA.

34. J. D. Miles to J. Q. Smith, February 11, 1876, W. Nicholson to J. Q. Smith, February 18, 1876, LR-C&A-NA; J. D. Miles to W. Nicholson, June 19, 1876, LR-FOF-CS-NA.

35. W. Nicholson to Major General John Pope, June 3, 1876, LS-FOF-CS-NA.

36. W. Nicholson to J. Q. Smith, June 8, 13, 1876, LS-FOF-CS-NA; J. D. Miles to W. Nicholson, June 27, 1876, LR-FOF-CS-NA.

37. For background see Berthrong, *Southern Cheyennes*, 372ff.

38. J. D. Miles to W. Nicholson, June 30, 1876, LR-FOF-CS-NA; W. Nicholson to Commissioner of Indian Affairs, July 12, 1876, LS-FOF-CS-NA.

39. J. D. Miles to W. Nicholson, July 11, 1876 (Copy), LR-C&A-NA.

40. General John Pope to W. Nicholson, July 28, 1876 (Telegram), LR-C&A-NA; R. S. Mackenzie to AAG, Department of the Missouri, July 29, 1876 (Telegram, Copy), J. K. Mizner to J. D. Miles, July 31, 1876 (Copy), LR-FOF-CS-NA.

41. J. D. Miles to W. Nicholson, August 4, 1876, LR-FOF-CS-NA.

42. J. D. Miles to J. K. Mizner, August 30, 1876, B. N. Miles, Chief Clerk, Cheyenne and Arapaho Agency to W. Nicholson, August 31, October 3, 1876, J. D. Miles to W. Nicholson, September 9, November 28, 1876, April 17, 1877, LR-FOF-CS-NA; George F. Nicholson, Acting Superintendent to J. Q. Smith, September 6, 1876, W. Nicholson to J. Q. Smith, May 2, 1877, W. Nicholson to J. D. Miles, May 27, 1877, LS-FOF-CS-NA.

CHAPTER II

1. W. Nicholson to J. D. Miles, May 17, 1877, LS-FOF-CS-NA; Miles's Esti-

mate, dated June 1, 1877, LR-C&A-NA; S. A. Galpin, Acting Commissioner to W. Nicholson, May 16, 1877, LS-OIA-NA.

2. P. H. Sheridan to W. T. Sherman, May 15, 1877 (Telegram, Copy), LR-C&A-NA.

3. J. D. Miles to W. Nicholson, August 8, 1877, LR-FOF-CS-NA; J. D. Miles to W. Nicholson, August 11, 1877 (Copy), enclosing census dated August 6, 1877, J. D. Miles to E. A. Hayt, November 26, 1877, LR-C&A-NA.

4. J. D. Miles to W. Nicholson, August 11, 1877, LR-FOF-CS-NA; J. D. Miles to W. Nicholson, September 1, 1877 (Copy), LR-C&A-NA; Mari Sandoz, *Cheyenne Autumn*, 6–7.

5. W. Nicholson to J. Q. Smith, September 18, 1877, LS-FOF-CS-NA.

6. H. W. Lawton to Adjutant, Fourth Cavalry, Fort Sill, Indian Territory, September 13, 1877 (Copy), LR-C&A-NA.

7. Report of an Inspection of the Condition of the Cheyenne Indians at the Cheyenne and Arapaho Agency by First Lieutenant H. W. Lawton, October 8, 1877 (Copy), LR-C&A-NA.

8. J. D. Miles to E. A. Hayt, October 31, 1877, LR-FOF-CS-NA; J. D. Miles to E. A. Hayt, November 13, 1877, LR-C&A-NA.

9. J. D. Miles to E. A. Hayt, November 23, 1877 (Copy), LR-FOF-CS-NA; R. S. Mackenzie to Assistant Adjutant General, Department of the Missouri, November 20, 1877, with endorsement by Major General John Pope, November 27, 1877 (Copy), LR-C&A-NA.

10. Philip McCusker to E. A. Hayt, March 3, 1878, LR-C&A-NA.

11. *Report, Commissioner of Indian Affairs, 1877*, 85; *Ibid., 1878*, 54, 56–57.

12. J. D. Miles to E. A. Hayt, September 10, 11, 1878, LR-C&A-NA. For another version of the causes for the flight of these Northern Cheyennes see Sandoz, *Cheyenne Autumn*, 9–24.

13. J. D. Miles to E. A. Hayt, September 19, 1878, P. H. Sheridan to General E. D. Townsend, September 19, 1878 (Telegram, Copy), LR-C&A-NA.

14. P. H. Sheridan to E. D. Townsend, September 19, 1878, P. H. Sheridan to General George Crook, September 19, 1878 (Telegrams, Copies), LR-C&A-NA.

15. Statement of Amos Chapman, Camp Supply, Indian Territory, November 28, 1878, Statement of Ben Clark, Fort Reno, Indian Territory, December 14, 1878 (Copies), LR-C&A-NA.

16. William M. Leeds to J. D. Miles, October 16, 1878, Cheyenne and Arapaho Agents and Agency File, Indian Archives, Oklahoma Historical Society, Oklahoma City, Oklahoma, hereafter cited as C&A Agents and Agency, File, OHS; J. D. Miles to E. A. Hayt, November 1, 1878, LR-C&A-NA.

17. J. D. Miles to E. A. Hayt, September 24, 1878 (Telegram), J. D. Miles to E. A. Hayt, December 2, 1878, LR-C&A-NA; *Report, Commissioner of Indian Affairs, 1879*, 58.

18. J. D. Miles to E. A. Hayt, December 10, 1878 (Telegram), LR-C&A-NA; *Report, Commissioner of Indian Affairs, 1881*, 67.

19. C. E. Campbell, Acting Agent, to E. A. Hayt, December 10, 1878 (Telegram), Ben Clark to Colonel Mizner, Fort Reno, Indian Territory, December 10, 1878 (Copy), LR-C&A-NA.

20. J. D. Miles to E. A. Hayt, January 21, 1879, Little Chief's Talk enclosed with C. E. Campbell to E. A. Hayt, March 5, 1879, J. D. Miles to E. A. Hayt, March 10, 1879, LR-C&A-NA.

21. J. K. Mizner to Assistant Adjutant General, Department of the Missouri, March 12, 1879 (Copy), C. E. Campbell to E. A. Hayt, March 14, 1879, LR-C&A-NA.

22. John Pope to P. H. Sheridan, March 19, 25, 1879 (Copies), LR-C&A-NA.

23. Almerin Gillett to J. D. Miles, enclosing a copy of the charges against the Northern Cheyennes, March 27, 1879, J. D. Miles to E. A. Hayt, April 4, 1879, LR-C&A-NA.

24. E. A. Hayt to J. D. Miles, March 3, 15, 1879, LS-OIA-NA; J. D. Miles to E. A. Hayt, July 10, 1879.

25. J. D. Miles to E. A. Hayt, September 16, 1879, J. D. Miles to Commissioner of Indian Affairs, October 13, 1879 (Telegram from Lawrence, Kansas), LR-C&A-NA; J. D. Miles to E. A. Hayt, November 11, 1879, Cheyenne and Arapaho Letterbooks, El Reno Public Library, El Reno, Oklahoma, hereafter cited as C&A Letterbooks-El Reno. The two other men were named Bushyhead and Limpy, but probably the former was previously called Big Head and Porcupine was called Limpy.

26. C. E. Campbell, Acting Agent, to E. A. Hayt, March 14, 1879, J. K. Mizner to Assistant Adjutant General, Department of the Missouri, March 21, 1879 (Copy), Special Order No. 77, Headquarters, Division of the Missouri, September 30, 1878 (Copy), H. M. Creel, Second Lieutenant, Seventh Cavalry, to Assistant Adjutant General, Division of the Missouri, April 12, 1879 (Copy), P. H. Sheridan to General E. D. Townsend, March 29, 1879 (Copy), LR-C&A-NA.

27. J. D. Miles to Commissioner of Indian Affairs, April 24, 1879, LR-C&A-NA.

28. J. D. Miles to Commissioner of Indian Affairs, May 6, 14, 1879 (Telegrams), LR-C&A-NA; *Report, Commissioner of Indian Affairs, 1879*, 58–59.

29. J. K. Mizner to Assistant Adjutant General, Department of the Missouri, June 4, 15, 18, 1879 (Copies), J. D. Miles to E. A. Hayt, June 5, 25, 1879, LR-C&A-NA.

30. The Indian police in the summer of 1879 consisted of a Captain, J. A. Covington, who was both head farmer and chief of police, and Indians who served as a lieutenant, three sergeants, and twelve privates. J. A. Covington to E. A. Hayt, June 30, 1879, J. D. Miles to E. A. Hayt, July 15, 1879, LR-C&A-NA; Richard I. Dodge, Lieutenant Colonel, Twenty-third Infantry, Commanding Cantonment, North Fork Canadian River, Indian Territory to Assistant Adjutant General, Letters Sent, Cantonment, United States Army

Commands, Records of the War Department, Record Group 98, National Archives Building, hereafter cited as LS-Cantonment-WD.

31. J. D. Miles to Commissioner of Indian Affairs, September 15, 1879 (Telegram), J. D. Miles to Commissioner of Indian Affairs, September 19, 20, 22, 1879, LR-C&A-NA.

32. R. I. Dodge to Assistant Adjutant General, Department of the Missouri, LS-Cantonment-WD.

33. Ben Clark to General N. A. Miles, January 14, 1880, and Miles's endorsement, January 20, 1880 (Copy), J. D. Miles to R. E. Trowbridge, Commissioner of Indian Affairs, April 20, 1880, LR-C&A-NA.

34. J. D. Miles to R. E. Trowbridge, August 18, 1880, LR-C&A-NA; *Cheyenne Transporter* (Darlington, Indian Territory) August 25, 1880; John H. Seger presents a different version of the incident in *Early Days Among the Southern Cheyenne and Arapahoe Indians*, 82–87.

35. J. D. Miles to Commissioner of Indian Affairs, April 14, 1881, C&A Letterbooks-El Reno; Hiram Price, Commissioner of Indian Affairs, to J. D. Miles, June 21, July 5, 1881, LS-OIA-NA.

36. J. D. Price to H. Price, June 1, 1881, C&A Letterbooks-El Reno; S. J. Kirkwood, Secretary of the Interior to Little Chief, August 25, 1881, to Secretary of War, October 6, 1881, Letters Sent, Vol. 26, Indian Division, Records of the Secretary of the Interior, Record Group 48, hereafter cited as LS-ID-OSI-NA; H. Price to J. D. Miles, September 8, 1881, LS-OIA-NA; J. D. Miles to H. Price, November 1, 1881, C&A Letterbooks, Vol. 3, 183–87; *Report, Commissioner of Indian Affairs, 1882*, lxii, 56.

37. J. D. Miles to H. Price, June 7, July 2, 1883, J. D. Miles to Major Thomas B. Dewees, Commanding Officer, Fort Reno, June 29, 1883, C&A Letterbooks-El Reno; O. J. Woodward to Commissioner of Indian Affairs, July 7, 1883 (Telegram and Letter), with roll of the Northern Cheyennes and Arapahoes, August 1, 1883, C&A Letterbooks-El Reno; *Report, Commissioner of Indian Affairs, 1883*, 62–63.

38. O. J. Woodward to H. Price, August 1, 1883, C&A Letterbooks-El Reno; *Report, Commissioner of Indian Affairs, 1883*, 62.

CHAPTER III

1. *Report, Commissioner of Indian Affairs, 1875*, 129; J. D. Miles to J. Q. Smith, February 15, 1876, J. D. Miles to W. Nicholson, April 12, 1876, C&A Letterbooks, Vol. 1, 119, 211–12.

2. 18 Stat. 449; *Report, Commissioner of Indian Affairs, 1875*, 270–71.

3. J. D. Miles to W. Nicholson, June 13, 23, 1876, C&A Letterbooks, Vol. 1, 450, 498; J. D. Miles to W. Nicholson, September 21, 1876 (Copy), LR-C&A-NA.

4. J. D. Miles to Joshua Ross, June 20, 1876, C&A Letterbooks, Vol. 1, 482–85.
5. J. D. Miles to W. Nicholson, August 31, 1876, C&A Letterbooks, Vol. 1, 670–91; *Report, Commissioner of Indian Affairs, 1876,* 47–48.
6. J. D. Miles to W. Nicholson, January 5, 1877, LR-FOF-CS-NA.
7. George F. Nicholson, Acting Superintendent, to J. Q. Smith, December 13, 1876, LR-C&A-NA; W. Nicholson to J. D. Miles, March 27, April 23, 1877, Cheyenne and Arapaho Indian Homes File, Indian Archives, Oklahoma Historical Society, Oklahoma City, Oklahoma, hereafter cited as C&A Indian Homes File, OHS; J. D. Miles to W. Nicholson, May 14, 1877, LR-FOF-CS-NA.
8. *Report, Commissioner of Indian Affairs, 1877,* 83.
9. W. Nicholson to J. D. Miles, May 15, June 16, June 25, 1877 (Telegram), LS-FOF-CS-NA; *Report, Commissioner of Indian Affairs, 1877,* 83.
10. *Report, Commissioner of Indian Affairs, 1877,* 84, 86–87.
11. J. Q. Smith to W. Nicholson, January 24, 1877, LS-OIA-NA; J. D. Miles to W. Nicholson, September 6, 1877 (Copy), LR-C&A-NA; *Report, Commissioner of Indian Affairs, 1877,* 77, 83; *Cheyenne Transporter,* May 10, 1881.
12. E. A. Hayt to J. D. Miles, November 22, 1877, LS-OIA-NA; J. D. Miles to E. A. Hayt, January 2, 1879, C&A Letterbooks-El Reno; J. D. Miles to E. A. Hayt, June 25, July 7, August 22, 1879, LR-C&A-NA.
13. *Report, Commissioner of Indian Affairs, 1877,* 27; J. D. Miles to E. A. Hayt, March 20, 1878, LR-C&A-NA; E. A. Hayt to J. D. Miles, April 4, 1878, LS-OIA-NA.
14. J. D. Miles to E. A. Hayt, March 20, April 5, June 1, 1878, C. Schurz to Commissioner of Indian Affairs, April 12, 1878, LR-C&A-NA; *Report, Commissioner of Indian Affairs, 1878,* 57–58.
15. R. I. Dodge to Assistant Adjutant General, Department of the Missouri, April 4, 1879, LS-Cantonment-WD; E. A. Hayt to J. D. Miles, July 31, 1879, LS-OIA-NA; *Report, Commissioner of Indian Affairs, 1879,* 59; BIC, *Report, 1879,* 84.
16. J. D. Miles to E. A. Hayt, December 10, 1878, C. Schurz to Commissioner of Indian Affairs, January 23, 1879, LR-C&A-NA; *Report, Commissioner of Indian Affairs, 1879,* 60.
17. *Report, Commissioner of Indian Affairs, 1880,* 69–70.
18. S. J. Kirkwood to Commissioner of Indian Affairs, October 25, 1881, LS-ID-OSI-NA, Vol. 27; J. D. Miles to H. Price, Commissioner, November 22, 1881, C&A Letterbooks, Vol. 3, 220–25.
19. *Report, Commissioner of Indian Affairs, 1880,* 68; BIC, *Report, 1880,* 78.
20. J. D. Miles to E. A. Hayt, July 1, August 1, September 1, 1879, C&A Letterbooks-El Reno; J. D. Miles to R. E. Trowbridge, Commissioner of Indian Affairs, June 3, 1880; *Report, Commissioner of Indian Affairs, 1880,* 68; *Cheyenne Transporter,* September 25, 1880.
21. *Report, Commissioner of Indian Affairs, 1880,* 68; *Cheyenne Transporter,* September 10, December 24, 1880.

22. J. D. Miles to Commissioner of Indian Affairs, May 2, 1881, C&A Letter-books-El Reno; *Report, Commissioner of Indian Affairs, 1881,* 67–68, 72, 74.

23. J. D. Miles to John [*sic.*, Joshua] Ross, September 6, 1881, C&A Letter-books, Vol. 3, 25–27; Commanding Officer, Fort Sill, Indian Territory, to J. D. Miles, July 8, 1881 (Telegram), E. L. Clark to J. D. Miles, July 14, 22, August 15, 1881, Cheyenne and Arapaho Dances File, Indian Archives, Oklahoma Historical Society, Oklahoma City, Oklahoma, hereafter cited as C&A Dances File-OHS.

24. *Cong. Rec.,* 46 Cong., 3 Sess., January 21, 1881, 816; J. D. Miles to Alex Caldwell, Leavenworth, Kansas, June 29, 1881, J. D. Miles to H. Price, July 1, September 1, 1881, C&A Letterbooks-El Reno, BIC, *Report, 1881,* 56.

25. J. D. Miles to H. Price, January 28, 1882, C&A Letterbooks, Vol. 3, 438–40.

26. J. D. Miles to H. Price, March 1, 1882, C&A Letterbooks, Vol. 4, 90.

27. J. D. Miles to P. Hunt, Indian Agent, Kiowa-Comanche Reservation, March 21, 1882 (Telegram), J. D. Miles to G. M. Randall, March 21, 1882, J. D. Miles to H. Price, March 21, 1882 (Telegram), C&A Letterbooks, Vol. 4, 195, 196–201, 209.

28. J. D. Miles to H. Price, March 21, 1882, J. D. Miles to G. M. Randall, March 23, 1882, C&A Letterbooks, Vol. 4, 212–20, 224.

29. BIC, *Report, 1882,* 40; J. D. Miles to P. B. Plumb, March 27, 1882, C&A Letterbooks, Vol. 4, 235.

30. J. D. Miles to H. Price, March 29, 1882, C&A Letterbooks, Vol. 4, 239–41.

31. J. D. Miles to P. B. Plumb, March 30, 1882, C&A Letterbooks, Vol. 4, 243–67.

32. J. D. Miles to Walker and Campbell in charge of Oburn's herd, April 3, 1882, J. D. Miles to G. M. Randall, April 3, 4, 1882 (Telegrams), to J. A. Covington, April 4, 1882, to P. Hunt, April 7, 1882 (Telegram), to John Pope, through Major G. M. Randall, April 10, 1882, C&A Letterbooks, Vol. 4, 283, 284, 301–302, 303–304, 314, 324–37; *Cheyenne Transporter,* April 10, 1882.

33. J. D. Miles to Commissioner of Indian Affairs, June 29, July 1, 1882 (Telegrams), J. D. Miles to H. Price, July 3, 1882, C&A Letterbooks, Vol. 5, 136, 145, 146–51. The statements made by the Indians in council, countersigned by George Bent, Interpreter, and witnessed by J. A. Covington and O. J. Wood-ward, are found in C&A Letterbooks, Vol. 5, 152–55.

34. J. D. Miles to Commissioner of Indian Affairs, July 1, 1882 (Telegram), J. D. Miles to H. Price, July 3, 1882, C&A Letterbooks, Vol. 5, 145, 146–51.

35. J. D. Miles to H. Price, C&A Letterbooks, July 3, 18, 20, 1882, C&A Letterbooks, Vol. 5, 146–51, 216–18, 240–43; United States Senate, "Report of the Committee on Indian Affairs, United States Senate, on the Condition of the Indians in Indian Territory and other Reservations, etc.," *Senate Report 1278,* 49 Cong., 1 Sess. (Serial 2362), Part 1, 385, hereafter cited as *SH 1278,* 49 Cong., I Sess., Part 1.

36. H. Price to J. D. Miles, July 28, 1882, H. Price to Secretary of the Interior,

August 3, 1882, *SR* 1278, 49 Cong., 1 Sess., Part 1, 387–88; G. M. Randall to John Pope, July 19, 1882 (Telegram) and General Pope's endorsement, July 21, 1882, Letters Received, Indian Division, Records of the Office of the Secretary of the Interior, Record Group 48, National Archives Building, hereafter cited as LR-ID-OSI-NA; J. D. Miles to G. M. Randall, August 3, 1882, C&A Letterbooks, Vol. 5, 312; H. M. Teller to Secretary of War, August 5, 1882, LS-ID-OSI-NA, Vol. 30.

37. J. D. Miles to G. M. Randall, July 21, August 3, 1882, J. D. Miles to W. C. Oburn, Kansas City, Missouri, July 20, 1882, C&A Letterbooks, Vol. 5, 250–52, 277, 312; H. M. Teller to Commissioner of Indian Affairs, February 13, 1883, LS-ID-OSI-NA, Vol. 31.

38. J. D. Miles to H. Price, May 3, June 1, August 5, 1882, C&A Letterbooks, Vol. 4, 406–14, Vol. 5, 1–10, 323–31.

39. BIC, *Report, 1875*, 8–9.

40. BIC, *Report, 1875*, 151; J. D. Miles to E. P. Smith, June 1, 1875, J. D. Miles to E. Hoag, October 22, 1875, LR-FOF-CS-NA; E. P. Smith to E. Hoag, October 22, 1875, E. P. Smith to J. D. Miles, LS-OIA-NA.

41. J. D. Miles to J. Q. Smith, January 1, 1876, LR-FOF-CS-NA; J. D. Miles to J. Q. Smith [January, 1876?], C&A Letterbooks, Vol. 1, 7; *Report, Commissioner of Indian Affairs, 1876*, 48.

42. Contract between J. D. Miles and John H. Seger, dated October 1, 1875, LR-CS-NA; J. D. Miles to W. Nicholson, July 31, 1876, LR-FOF-CS-NA; *Report, Commissioner of Indian Affairs, 1876*, 48.

43. *Report, Commissioner of Indian Affairs, 1877*, 84, 86–87.

44. J. D. Miles to E. A. Hayt, November 23, 1877, LR-FOF-CS-NA; BIC, *Report, 1877*, 30–31.

45. John McNeil, Inspector to E. A. Hayt, September 9, 1878, Inspector's File No. 917, Reports of the Bureau of Indian Affairs, Record Group 75, National Archives Building; J. D. Miles to E. A. Hayt, March 1, 1878, LR-C&A-NA; *Report, Commissioner of Indian Affairs, 1878*, 55–56.

46. J. D. Miles to E. A. Hayt, April 30, June 1, 1878, J. D. Mizner to Assistant Adjutant General, Department of Missouri, July 17, 1878 (Copy), LR-C&A-NA.

47. J. D. Miles to E. A. Hayt, December 9, 1878, April 10, August 26, 1879 (Telegram), LR-C&A-NA.

48. J. D. Miles to E. A. Hayt, July 1, November 11, 1879, C&A Letterbooks-El Reno; J. D. Miles to E. A. Hayt, December 10, 1879, J. D. Miles to R. E. Trowbridge, April 20, 1880, LR-C&A-NA; R. E. Trowbridge to J. D. Miles, April 12, 1880, LS-OIA-NA.

49. C. E. Campbell, Acting Agent, to Commissioner of Indian Affairs, October 7, 1879 (Telegram), J. D. Miles to E. A. Hayt, October 8, 1879, LR-C&A-NA.

50. C. E. Campbell, Acting Agent, to E. A. Hayt, October 10, 1879, LR-C&A-NA.

51. J. D. Miles to R. E. Trowbridge, May 28, July 29, 1880, LR-C&A-NA; *Cheyenne Transporter*, December 10, 1880.

52. *Report, Commissioner of Indian Affairs, 1880*, 69–70; J. D. Miles to R. E. Trowbridge, June 7, 1880, LR-C&A-NA; *Cheyenne Transporter*, January 25, 1881.

53. J. D. Miles to Captain R. H. Pratt, March 9, 1881, C&A Letterbooks-El Reno; S. J. Kirkwood to Commissioner of Indian Affairs, June 23, 1881, LS-ID-OSI-NA, Vol. 25, 478–79; *Cheyenne Transporter*, June 25, 1881; BIC, *Report, 1881*, 55–56; *Report, Commissioner of Indian Affairs*, 69, 71, 74.

54. Christian E. Krehbiel, et al. to J. D. Miles, April 14, 1880, LR-C&A-NA; J. D. Miles to H. Price, July 30, 1881, C&A Letterbooks-El Reno; *Report, Commissioner of Indian Affairs, 1882*, 57.

55. J. D. Miles to J. B. Plumb, March 30, 1882, C&A Letterbooks, Vol. 4, 243–67.

56. J. D. Miles to Dr. James E. Rhoads, July 27, 1882, C&A Letterbooks, Vol. 5, 292–96; *Report, Commissioner of Indian Affairs, 1882*, 57; BIC, *Report, 1882*, 40.

57. John H. Seger, to J. D. Miles, March 31, 1882, Cheyenne and Arapaho John H. Seger File, Indian Archives, Oklahoma Historical Society, Oklahoma City, Oklahoma, hereafter cited as Seger File, C&A, OHS.

58. *Report, Commissioner of Indian Affairs, 1883*, 63, 68–69.

59. H. Price to J. D. Miles, March 10, 1883, LS-OIA-NA.

60. H. Price to J. D. Miles, April 18, 1883, LS-OIA-NA; J. D. Miles to H. Price, June 23, 1883, J. D. Miles to Benjamin Miles, June 30, 1883, C&A Letterbooks-El Reno.

61. Harvey White Shield to J. D. Miles, April 14, 1883, Cheyenne and Arapaho Employees File, Indian Archives, Oklahoma Historical Society, Oklahoma City, Oklahoma; hereafter cited as C&A Employees File, OHS; White Shield to Rev. H. R. Voth, June 26, 1888, H. R. Voth Collection, Bethel College Library, North Newton, Kansas, hereafter cited as Voth Collection; *Congressional Record*, 47 Cong., 2 Sess., December 19, 1882, 413.

CHAPTER IV

1. *Report, Commissioner of Indian Affairs, 1883*, 60–61.

2. Council of Indian Chiefs of Cheyenne and Arapaho Tribes, Darlington, Indian Territory, December 12, 1882; J. D. Miles to H. Price, December 13, 1882, July 16, 1883, Frank C. Armstrong to Lucius Q. C. Lamar, July 17, 19, 1885, Joseph H. Potter to Adjutant General, Department of the Missouri, July 18, 1883 (Copy), Special Case 9, Records of the Bureau of Indian Affairs, Record Group 75, National Archives Building, hereafter cited as Spec. Case 9, RBIA-

NA; *SR 1278*, 49 Cong., 1 Sess., Part 1, 41, 44–45, 50, 55–56, 57, 65, 73, 398–99; Interview of Birdie Burns by Julia A. Jordan, November 9, 1967, T-162 (Typescript), 19, 22, in the Doris Duke Indian Oral History Collection in the Western History Collections, University of Oklahoma Library, Norman, Oklahoma, hereafter cited as T-162, IOHC-UOL.

3. Council of Indian Chiefs of Cheyenne and Arapaho Tribes, Darlington, Indian Territory, December 12, 1882, F. C. Armstrong to L. Q. C. Lamar, July 17, 19, 1885, J. D. Miles to H. Price, July 16, 1883, Spec. Case 9, RBIA-NA; *Cheyenne Transporter*, January 26, 1883.

4. N. K. Fairchild and others to Robert T. Lincoln, December 15, 1882, Dickey Brothers to H. Price, July 30, 1883, H. Price to Secretary of the Interior, April 21, 1883, Spec. Case 9, RBIA-NA; J. D. Miles to H. Price, May 2, 1883, C&A Letterbooks, Vol. 6, 303–304.

5. List of persons applying for grazing privileges in Indian Territory, January 18–19, 1883, B. H. Campbell to Henry Teller, January 10, 1883, LR-ID-OSI-NA; J. S. Morrison to H. Price, December 18, J. D. Miles's endorsement, December 18, 1883, B. H. Campbell to J. D. Miles, December 5, 1882, J. D. Miles to H. Price, January 13, 15, 1883, Spec. Case 9, RBIA-NA; J. D. Miles to H. Price, May 22, 1883, *SR 1278*, 49 Cong., 1 Sess., Part 1, 436-37.

6. R. D. Hunter to H. M. Teller, January 18, 1883 (Telegram), John Volz to Secretary of the Interior, May 1, 1883, John Volz to H. Price, May 29, 1883, Edwin Willets to H. M. Teller, March 8, 1883, B. H. Campbell to J. D. Miles, April 4, 1883, B. H. Campbell to John A. Logan, April 17, 1883, John A. Logan to H. M. Teller, April 20, 1883, H. Price to Secretary of the Interior, April 21, 1883, B. H. Campbell to H. Price, May 5, 1883, H. M. Teller to R. T. Lincoln, July 10, 1883, Spec. Case 9, RBIA-NA; H. M. Teller's endorsement of Willets' and Logan's Letters, *SR 1278*, 49 Cong., 1 Sess., Part 1, 411; J. D. Miles to R. D. Hunter, March 14, 1883, C&A Letterbooks, Vol. 6, 191–96.

7. J. D. Miles to A. L. Babbitt, March 23, 1883, C&A Letterbooks, Vol. 6, 219–25; Ed Fenlon to H. M. Teller, April 4, 1883, Senate Exec. Doc. 54, 48 Cong., 1 Sess. (Serial 2165), 98–99; H. M. Teller to E. Fenlon, April 25, 1883, LS-ID-OSI-NA, Vol. 31.

8. H. M. Teller to E. Fenlon, April 25, 1883, LS-ID-OSI-NA.

9. H. M. Teller to President Pro Tempore of the United States Senate, January 3, 1885, *SR 1278*, 49 Cong., 1 Sess., Part 1, 542. A distinguished historian of the range cattle industry is critical of Teller's decision not to give cattlemen any vested right to the reservation's ranges, calling it "a policy . . . little short of absurd." See Edward E. Dale, "History of the Ranch Cattle Industry in Oklahoma," *Annual Report of the American Historical Association for the Year 1920*, 315. Edward E. Dale has also written a full discussion of the grazing privileges on the Cheyenne-Arapaho Reservation in "Ranching on the Cheyenne-Arapaho Reservation, 1880–1885," *Chronicles of Oklahoma*, Vol. VI (March, 1928), 35–59.

10. H. M. Pollar to H. M. Teller [May, 1883], H. M. Teller to H. B. Denman, May 25, 1883, L. Q. C. Lamar to Commissioner of Indian Affairs, May 21, December 19, 1885, Spec. Case 9, RBIA-NA; H. M. Teller to Commissioner of the General Land Office, November 5, 1883, LS-ID-OSI-NA, Vol. 32, 282; *SR 1278*, 49 Cong., 1 Sess., Part 1, 35–36, 40, 42, 59, 61–65.

11. J. D. Miles to A. L. Babbitt, March 23, 1883, J. D. Miles to E. Fenlon, May 22, 1883, J. D. Miles to R. D. Hunter, June 4, 1883, C&A Letterbooks, Vol. 6, 219, 433, 446–53; J. D. Miles to Thomas B. Dewees, June 29, 1883, J. D. Miles to W. F. Darlington, July 5, 1883, C&A Letterbooks-El Reno; Undated Bureau of Indian Affairs Memorandum and F. C. Armstrong to L. Q. C. Lamar, July 17, 1885, Spec. Case 9, RBIA-NA.

12. *Cheyenne Transporter*, May 10, June 27, 1883, J. D. Miles to H. Price, July 2, 1883, C&A Letterbooks-El Reno; J. H. Potter to Adjutant General, Department of the Missouri, July 18, 1883 (Copy), Spec. Case 9, RBIA-NA.

13. J. D. Miles to H. Price, August 28, 1883, Report of Council, dated October 18, 1883, Cheyenne and Arapaho Agency, Indian Territory, Spec. Case 9, RBIA-NA; "Report of the Secretary of War," House Exec. Doc. 1, 49 Cong., 1 Sess. (Serial 2369), 65–71; D. B. Dyer to H. Price, October 9, 1884, C&A Letterbooks-El Reno.

14. Kansas City *Evening Star*, November 3, 1883; Robert S. Gardner to Secretary of the Interior, November 24, 1883, LR-OSI-NA; *Cong. Rec.*, 48 Cong., 1 Sess., January 20, 1885, 864, 50 Cong., 2 Sess., March 2, 1889, 2601.

15. BIC, *Report, 1884*, 51–52.

16. *Cheyenne Transporter*, June 10, 1881, June 25, 1882, May 28, 1884; D. B. Dyer to H. Price, April 5, 1883, D. B. Dyer to R. D. Hunter, April 10, 1884, C&A Letterbooks, Vol. 7, 20–24, 48–50; *Report, Commissioner of Indian Affairs, 1884*, 75, 77–78.

17. D. B. Dyer to H. Price, April 5, 1884, D. B. Dyer to E. Fenlon, April 7, 1884, D. B. Dyer to Major C. Hood, April 8, 1884, C&A Letterbooks, Vol. 7, 20–24, 34–35, 40.

18. The sources for the murder of Running Buffalo and its aftermath are: D. B. Dyer to H. Price, May 5, 6, 20, 1884, D. B. Dyer to J. F. Shearman, May 8, 1884, D. B. Dyer to T. B. Dewees, May 19, 1884, D. B. Dyer to J. H. Potter, May 28, 1884, C&A Letterbooks, Vol. 7, 147–49, 154–62, 186–90, 260–61, 262–70, 308; D. B. Dyer to H. Price, August 6, 1884, C&A Letterbooks-El Reno; David J. Gibbon to Commanding Officer, Fort Reno, May 5, 6, 1884 (Official Copies), Statement of W. T. Darlington, September 22, Ezra L. Stevens to Secretary of the Interior, May 16, 1884, LR-ID-OSI-NA; H. M. Teller to Commissioner of Indian Affairs, May 20, 1884, LS-ID-OSI-NA, Vol. 35; Potter identified Running Buffalo as a Dog Soldier leader in, J. H. Potter to Adjutant General, Department of the Missouri, July 18, 1883 (Copy), Spec. Case 9, RBIA-NA; Amos Chapman to J. H. Potter, January 25, 1885 (Copy), Statement of Stone Calf,

Fort Reno, July 17, 1885, Spec. Case 9, RBIA-NA; *Cheyenne Transporter*, May 10, 1884.

19. D. B. Dyer to H. Price, August 10, October 9, 1885, C&A Letterbooks-El Reno; *SR 1278*, 49 Cong., 1 Sess., Part 1, 7–16; BIC, *Report, 1882*, 56.

20. A transcript of the council is dated December 2, 1884, and is found in LS-ID-OSI-NA, Vol. 38.

21. *SR 1278*, 49 Cong., 1 Sess., Part 1, 7–16.

22. *Ibid.*, H. M. Teller to the President, January 2, 1885, H. M. Teller to the Secretary of War, December 24, 1884, LS-ID-OSI-NA, Vol. 38.

23. D. B. Dyer to H. Price, March 19, 1885, D. B. Dyer to John D. C. Atkins, April 8, 1885, C&A Letterbooks-El Reno; Kansas City *Evening Star*, July 10, 1885.

24. D. B. Dyer to H. Price, May 6, 8, 12, 1884, July 9, 19, 1884, C&A Letterbooks, Vol. 7, 154–62, 173–82, 233–35, 423–28, 488–95; D. B. Dyer to H. Price, July 22, 28, 1884, C&A Letterbooks-El Reno; *Report, Commissioner of Indian Affairs, 1884*, 74.

25. D. B. Dyer to H. Price, January 9, 12, 1885, D. B. Dyer to J. D. C. Atkins, May 7, 1885, C&A Letterbooks-El Reno; Kansas City *Evening Star*, July 27, 1885.

26. D. B. Dyer to J. D. C. Atkins, June 8, 15, 1885, C&A Letterbooks-El Reno; D. B. Dyer to F. T. Bennett, June 9, 1885, containing Thomas Simpson to D. B. Dyer, June 9, 1885 (Telegram), C&A Letterbooks, Vol. 8, 124–25.

27. D. B. Dyer to J. D. C. Atkins, June 17, 1885, C&A Letterbooks-El Reno; D. B. Dyer to P. B. Hunt, June 15, 1885, D. B. Dyer to Edwin V. Sumner, June 19, 1885, C&A Letterbooks, Vol. 8, 147–51, 167–68.

28. T. Simpson to J. H. Potter, June 23, 1885, J. H. Potter to C. C. Augur, June 26, 1885, Spec. Case 9, RBIA-NA.

29. D. B. Dyer to E. V. Sumner, July 2, 1885, C&A Letterbooks, Vol. 8, 184–85; Statement of Stone Calf, Fort Reno, Indian Territory, July 17, 1885, Spec. Case 9, RBIA-NA; L. Q. C. Lamar to Secretary of War, December 14, 1885, L. Q. C. Lamar to Secretary of War, to Attorney General, July 9, 1886, LS-ID-OSI-NA, Vol. 42, 49.

30. F. C. Armstrong to L. Q. C. Lamar, July 17, 19, 20, 1885 (Telegram), Spec. Case 9, RBIA-NA.

31. S. S. Baker to John A. Martin, July 7, 1885 (Telegram), Robert Anderson to J. A. Martin, July 7, 1885, C. C. Augur to J. A. Martin, June 26, July 6, 1885, A. B. Campbell to J. A. Martin, July 7, 1885, John A. Martin Papers, Kansas State Historical Society, Topeka, Kansas; J. A. Martin to Secretary of War, July 9, 1885, in Topeka (Kansas) *The Capital*, July 8, 10, 1885; Kansas City *Evening Star*, June 27, July 9, 10, 15, 1885.

32. Statement of Stone Calf at Fort Reno, Indian Territory, July 17, 1885, Spec. Case 9, RBIA-NA.

33. Statements of Little Robe, White Shield, White Horse, Spotted Horse,

Hawk, Little Magpie, and Powder Face, July 17, 1885, Fort Reno, Indian Territory; Statement of Cheyennes, July 19, 1885, Fort Reno, Indian Territory, Spec. Case 9, RBIA-NA.

34. R. D. Hunter to Secretary of the Interior, July 7, 1885, A. S. Hewitt to L. Q. C. Lamar, June 30, 1885, Spec. Case 9, RBIA-NA.

35. Statement of E. Fenlon, July [20?], 1885, before General Sheridan, J. D. Miles, and F. C. Armstrong, in General Sheridan to President Cleveland, July 24, 1885, Spec. Case 9, RBIA-NA.

36. Wichita (Kansas) *Eagle*, July 17, 31, 1885; *Barber County* (Kansas) *Index*, July 17, 1885.

37. Undated "Brief and Conclusions as to the validity of granting leases on the Cheyenne and Arapaho Reservation, Indian Territory," Spec. Case 9, RBIA-NA. The document was probably prepared by George A. Jenks, assistant secretary of the interior, for Lamar. A. H. Garland to Secretary of the Interior, July 21, 1885, *ibid.*

38. 24 *Stat.* 1023; President Cleveland to General Sheridan, July 25, 1885, in President Cleveland to L. Q. C. Lamar, August 4, 1885, F. C. Armstrong to Secretary of the Interior, July 25, 1885 (Telegram), L. Q. C. Lamar to George C. Blanchard, July 28, 1885, Spec. Case 9, RBIA-NA; *Cheyenne Transporter*, July 30, 1885.

39. F. M. Cockrell to President Cleveland, July 31, 1885, John W. Moore, *et. al.*, to President Cleveland, August 1, 1885, G. G. Best to President Cleveland, August 1, 1885, J. S. Marmaduke to President Cleveland, August 1, 1885 (Telegram), Charles W. Baker to President Cleveland, August 3, 1885, Spec. Case 9, RBIA-NA; Kansas City *Evening Star*, July 23–30, August 1, 5, 12, 1885; Caldwell (Kansas) *Journal*, July 30, August 6, 1885; Wichita *Eagle*, July 24, 31, 1885; Undated Memorial to President Grover Cleveland, Grover Cleveland Papers, Library of Congress, Washington, D.C.

40. Thomas A. Bland to President Cleveland, June 29, 1885, McCook to L. Q. C. Lamar, July 3, 1885, B. B. Richards to President Cleveland, August 10, 1885, J. B. Potterfield to President Cleveland, August 10, 1885, L. W. Forsyth to President Cleveland, August 14, 1885, Spec. Case 9, RBIA-NA.

41. General Sheridan to J. A. Martin, July 23, 1885, in Kansas City *Evening Star*, July 23, 1885.

42. L. Q. C. Lamar to Agent Dyer, July 22, 1885, LS-ID-OSI-NA, Vol. 40. General Sheridan to President Cleveland, July 24, 1885, Spec. Case 9, RBIA-NA; House Exec. Doc. 1, 49 Cong., 1 Sess., 65–71. Indian Inspector Armstrong reported on July 22, 1885, that the new census recorded 3,376 Cheyennes and Arapahoes on their reservation. See F. C. Armstrong to Secretary of the Interior, July 22, 1885, Spec. Case 9, RBIA-NA.

43. Kansas City *Evening Star*, August 1, 5, 1885; R. C. Drum to Commanding General, Department of the Missouri, August 15, 1885, Spec. Case 9, RBIA-NA; J. M. Lee to Commissioner of Indian Affairs, August 18, 22, 1885, J. M.

Lee to Commanding Officer, Fort Reno, August 24, 1885, J. M. Lee to Commanding Officer, Fort Reno, August 25, 1885 (Telegram), J. M. Lee to Manager of Foreman, Washita Cattle Company [August 23, 1885?], J. M. Lee to Commanding Officer, Fort Elliott, August 25, 1885 (Telegram), C&A Letterbooks, Vol. 8, 304–305, 337–42, 343–46, 349, 350–51, Vol. 9, 108–14, 131–33.

44. Kansas City *Evening Star*, August 20, 1885; J. M. Schofield to Adjutant General, United States Army, September 3, 1885 (Telegram), N. A. Miles to Assistant Adjutant General, Department of the Missouri, September 5, 1885 (Telegram), R. D. Hunter and A. G. Evans to L. Q. C. Lamar, January 12, 1886, J. M. Lee to Commissioner of Indian Affairs, November 16, 1885, Spec. Case 9, RBIA-NA; J. M. Lee to Commanding Officer, Fort Reno, September 3, 1885, J. M. Lee to Atkins, September 7, 1885, J. M. Lee to Adjutant General, Department of the Missouri, September 11, 1885, J. M. Lee to Manager of Dickey Cattle Company, September 12, 1885, J. M. Lee to Commissioner of Indian Affairs, November 6, 1885 (Telegram), C&A Letterbooks, Vol. 8, 454–57, Vol. 9, 168–71, 345, Vol. 10, 26, 42–44.

CHAPTER V

1. Quoted in William T. Hagan, "Private Property, the Indian's Door to Civilization," *Ethnohistory*, Vol. 3, No. 2 (Spring, 1956), 126.

2. Henry E. Fritz, *The Movement for Indian Assimilation, 1860–1890*, 206–12; William T. Hagan, *American Indians*, 139–41; *Cong. Rec.*, 49 Cong., 1 Sess., February 25, 1886, 1762.

3. 24 *Stat.*, 388–91.

4. For an excellent summary of the drive to open Indian Territory to white settlement see Arrell M. Gibson, *Oklahoma: A History of Five Centuries*, 289–93.

5. *Report, Commissioner of Indian Affairs, 1885*, 76; *Report, Commissioner of Indian Affairs, 1886*, 114; J. M. Lee to J. D. C. Atkins, August 3, 1885, C&A Letterbooks, Vol. 9, 14–15.

6. J. M. Lee to Commissioner of Indian Affairs, August 3, 22, 1885, C&A Letterbooks, Vol. 9, 14–15, 134–35.

7. J. M. Lee to Commissioner of Indian Affairs, September 2, 1885, October 14, 1885, C&A Letterbooks, Vol. 9, 155–57, 273–77.

8. J. M. Lee to Commissioner of Indian Affairs, October 26, 1885, C&A Letterbooks, Vol. 9, 301–308.

9. On May 20, 1886, Lee informed Seger that he had been appointed as an additional farmer at an annual salary of nine hundred dollars. J. M. Lee to Commissioner of Indian Affairs, May 7, 1886, Lee to J. L. Hall, May 8, 1886, J. M. Lee to Bob Tail and Little Medicine, May 19, 1886, J. M. Lee to J. H.

Seger, May 20, 1886, C&A Letterbooks, Vol. 13, 378–84, 391–93, 466, 467, 489–92. Arapahoe (Oklahoma) *Bee*, July 3, 1894; *Cheyenne Transporter*, March 4, 15, April 3, May 12, June 26, 1886; Interview of Birdie Burns by Julia A. Jordan, November 2, 1967, T-156 (Typescript), 31, IOHC-UOL.

10. J. M. Lee to Seth Clover, April 4, May 6, 1886, J. M. Lee to Commissioner of Indian Affairs, July 27, August 22, 1886, C&A Letterbooks, Vol. 13, 84–87, 374–77, Vol. 15, 102–104, 174–76.

11. J. M. Lee to Commissioner of Indian Affairs, August 24, 1885, November 11, 1885, C&A Letterbooks, Vol. 9, 136–38, 354–63.

12. J. M. Lee to Commissioner of Indian Affairs, August 25, 1885, C&A Letterbooks, Vol. 9, 125–30.

13. J. D. Miles to E. A. Hayt, July 5, 1878, January 22, 1879, LR-C&A-NA; E. A. Hayt to J. D. Miles, July 30, 1879, LS-OIA-NA.

14. Statement of Mah-minick, dated December 16, 1879, with J. D. Miles to E. A. Hayt, January 20, 1880, LR-C&A-NA.

15. J. D. Miles to Commissioner of Indian Affairs, February 24, 1880, LR-C&A-NA.

16. J. D. Miles to Commanding Officer, Cantonment, Indian Territory, March 7, 1881, J. D. Miles to C. C. Harris, August 24, 1881, C&A Letterbooks-El Reno.

17. D. B. Dyer to J. D. C. Atkins, June 2, 1885, C&A Letterbooks-El Reno; J. M. Lee to Messrs. Evans Bros., Fort Reno, December 29, 1885, J. M. Lee to Commissioner of Indian Affairs, December 31, 1885, J. M. Lee to Commissioner of Indian Affairs, March 7, 1886, C&A Letterbooks, Vol. 10, 499, Vol. 11, 4–6, 210-15.

18. "Notice," signed by J. M. Lee, dated December 27, 1885, J. M. Lee to Commissioner of Indian Affairs, February 7, 1886, C&A Letterbooks, Vol. 10, 479–80, Vol. 11, 94–112.

19. H. L. Muldrow, Acting Secretary of the Interior to the Commissioner of Indian Affairs, March 11, 1886, LS-ID-OSI-NA, Vol. 44; J. M. Lee to J. L. Hall, June 1, 1886, "Notices," signed by J. M. Lee, June 13, 1886, C&A Letterbooks, Vol. 14, 74–75, 241–43.

20. J. M. Lee to Commissioner of Indian Affairs, September 1, 1885, C&A Letterbooks, Vol. 9, 188–215.

21. J. M. Lee to S. S. Haury, November 11, 12, 1885, J. M. Lee to White Horse, May 5, 1886, C&A Letterbooks, Vol. 10, 334–35, Vol. 13, 361–65.

22. J. M. Lee to S. S. Haury, February 16, 22, 1886, J. M. Lee to J. A. Covington, [March 9?] March 9, 1886, J. M. Lee to Flying Hawk, April 29, 1886, C&A Letterbooks, Vol. 12, 242–45, 383–84, Vol. 13, 309–12.

23. J. M. Lee to E. V. Sumner, May 27, 28, June 3, 1886, A. B. Upshaw, Acting Commissioner of Indian Affairs to J. M. Lee, May 28, 29, 1886 (Telegrams), J. A. Andrews & Co. to J. M. Lee, June 2, 1886, J. M. Lee to Adjutant General, Fort Leavenworth, Kansas, June 3, 1886 (Telegram), J. M. Lee to A. H. Todd,

June 6, 1886, J. M. Lee to Lieutenant Andrus, June 15, 1886, J. M. Lee to Assistant Adjutant General, Department of the Missouri, August 24, 1886, C&A Letterbooks, Vol. 14, 52–63, 91, 92–93, 101–102, 137–38, 257–61, Vol. 15, 179–80.

24. J. M. Lee to Commissioner of Indian Affairs, March 5, 1886, April 12, 30, 1885, C&A Letterbooks, Vol. 11, 196–200, 352–53, 386–92.

25. J. M. Lee to Commissioner of Indian Affairs, May 14, 1886, C&A Letterbooks, Vol. 11, 434–38.

26. J. M. Lee to Commissioner of Indian Affairs, July 4, 1886, August 14, 22, September 2, 1886, C&A Letterbooks, Vol. 15, 51–52, 146–47, 183–84, 218.

27. *Report, Commissioner of Indian Affairs, 1886*, 119–21.

28. J. M. Lee to Commissioner of Indian Affairs, December 3, 1885, C&A Letterbooks, Vol. 9, 388–89; *Report, Commissioner of Indian Affairs, 1886*, 118–19.

29. *Report, Commissioner of Indian Affairs, 1887*, 73.

30. G. D. Williams to S. S. Haury, November 12, 1886, G. D. Williams to Commissioner of Indian Affairs, December 14, 1886, G. D. Williams to John Poisal, March 14, 1887, C&A Letterbooks, Vol. 15, 401–402, Vol. 17, 72, 361, Vol. 19, 45.

31. G. D. Williams to Commissioner of Indian Affairs, January 11, 1887, C&A Letterbooks, Vol. 15, 427–31.

32. G. D. Williams to Bull Telling Tales, February 19, 1887, G. D. Williams to T. W. Potter, March 10, 1887, C&A Letterbooks, Vol. 17, 486–87, Vol. 19, 25–26.

33. G. D. Williams to Commanding Officer, Fort Elliot, Texas, May 5, 1887, G. D. Williams to T. W. Potter, May 9, 1887, G. D. Williams to Colonel Z. R. Bliss, Commanding Officer, Fort Supply, May 21, 1887, C&A Letterbooks, Vol. 19, 298–99, 321, 365.

34. G. D. Williams to Commissioner of Indian Affairs, June 16, 1887, C&A Letterbooks, Vol. 20, 179–82.

35. *Report, Commissioner of Indian Affairs, 1887*, 73–79.

36. G. D. Williams to Eugene E. White, December 26, 1887, July 2, August 11, 1888, C&A Letterbooks, Vol. 23, 218, Vol. 25, 172–73, 222–23.

37. G. D. Williams to T. W. Potter, December 11, 1888, G. D. Williams to Commissioner of Indian Affairs, December 14, 1888, C&A Letterbooks, Vol. 25, 485, Vol. 27, 154–57; *Report, Commissioner of Indian Affairs, 1888*, 89–90, 93.

38. G. D. Williams to Commissioner of Indian Affairs, September 21, 1888, C&A Letterbooks, Vol. 27, 96; *Report, Commissioner of Indian Affairs, 1888*, 93.

39. G. D. Williams to Commanding Officer, Fort Elliott, Texas, January 17, 1889, G. D. Williams to W. T. Darlington, April 12, 1889, G. D. Williams, to T. W. Potter, April 20, 1889, Charles F. Ashley to Commissioner of Indian Affairs, May 13, 1889, C&A Letterbooks, Vol. 29, 23–24, 192, 218, Vol. 27, 218.

40. BIC, *Report, 1889*, 12–13.

41. C. F. Ashley to Commissioner of Indian Affairs, May 13, 23, June 20, September 16, October 3, 1889, C&A Letterbooks, Vol. 27, 218, 237–38, 250–51, 370–71, 394–95.

42. *Report, Commissioner of Indian Affairs, 1889*, 183–85, 186–87.

43. C. F. Ashley to Commissioner of Indian Affairs, November 4, 1889, June 6, 1890, C&A Letterbooks, Vol. 27, 446–50, Vol. 30, 186–87.

44. C. F. Ashley to Commissioner of Indian Affairs, August 4, November 25, 1890, C&A Letterbooks, Vol. 30, 237–39, 351–52; *Report, Commissioner of Indian Affairs, 1890*, 178.

45. *Report, Commissioner of Indian Affairs, 1890*, 179.

46. D. B. Dyer to H. Price, September 12, October 7, November 10, 1884, C&A Letterbooks-El Reno.

47. *Report, Commissioner of Indian Affairs, 1885*, 79; D. B. Dyer to H. Price, October 18, 1884, C&A Letterbooks-El Reno.

48. Henry Miles to H. R. Voth, September 21, October 12, 1884, Voth Collection.

49. Josiah Kelly to H. R. Voth, November 25, 1884, J. Kelly to Mother, May 4, 1885, Voth Collection.

50. *Report, Commissioner of Indian Affairs, 1885*, 81–82.

51. *Report, Commissioner of Indian Affairs, 1886*, 119.

52. *Report, Commissioner of Indian Affairs, 1886*, 78.

53. G. D. Williams to Commissioner of Indian Affairs, March 31, 1887, C&A Letterbooks, Vol. 20, 39–47.

54. G. D. Williams to S. S. Haury, June 9, 1887, G. D. Williams to Commissioner of Indian Affairs, August 10, 1887, C&A Letterbooks, Vol. 19, 439–40, Vol. 20, 236–39.

55. G. D. Williams to H. R. Voth, August 2, 5, 1887, Voth Collection.

56. C. F. Ashley to Commissioner of Indian Affairs, September 23, October 1, 1889, C&A Letterbooks, Vol. 27, 375–76, 383–85.

57. *Report, Commissioner of Indian Affairs, 1890*, 177–78.

58. *Ibid., Commissioner of Indian Affairs, 1890*, 178; C. F. Ashley to Commissioner of Indian Affairs, June 3, 1890, C&A Letterbooks, Vol. 30, 451–52.

59. *Report, Commissioner of Indian Affairs, 1890*, 181; BIC, *Report, 1890*, 29.

CHAPTER VI

1. C. C. Painter, *Cheyennes and Arapahoes Revisited and a Statement of Their Contract with Attorneys*, 38–39.

2. The Cheyenne delegation consisted of Little Chief, Cloud Chief, Cut Nose, Starved Elk, Wolf Face, and Little Bear, with Leonard Tyler, George Bent and Robert Burns serving as interpreters. The Arapahoes were represented

by Left Hand, Row-of-Lodges, White-Eyed Antelope, and Heap-of-Bears, with Jock Bull Bear acting as their interpreter. *Oklahoma Gazette* (Oklahoma City), May 23, 1893; *Evening Oklahoma Gazette* (Oklahoma City), May 24, 1893; J. W. Noble to D. B. Dyer, to M. G. Reynolds (Telegram), August 8, 1889, LS-ID-OSI-NA, Vol. 61.

3. Painter, *Cheyennes and Arapahoes Revisited*, 40–45; The *Oklahoma Evening Gazette*, August 22, 1889; J. W. Noble to Commissioner of Indian Affairs, February 5, 1890, LS-ID-OSI-NA, Vol. 63; Interview of Birdie Burns by Julia A. Jordan, May 5, 1968 (T-260), 14–15, IOHC-UOL.

4. Gibson, *Oklahoma*, 298–99, 25 *Stats*. 980, 1005.

5. *Report, Commissioner of Indian Affairs, 1891*, 341. Unless otherwise noted, the source for the councils held between the Cheyennes and Arapahoes and the Jerome Commission will be the transcript of the council proceedings, entitled "Reports of Commissioners Jerome, Sayre and Wilson on the Cheyenne and Arapaho, 1890," located in the Irregular Shaped Papers, Records of the Bureau of Indian Affairs, Record Group 75, National Archives Building.

6. J. W. Noble to D. H. Jerome, July 8, 1890, LS-ID-OSI-NA, Vol. 66.

7. Wichita *Eagle*, July 12, 1890.

8. The brief was formally submitted to the commission and was dated July 31, 1889, see Samuel J. Crawford Papers, Briefs and Private Cases File, Kansas State Historical Society, Topeka, Kansas.

9. J. W. Noble to R. H. [*sic*, C. F.] Ashley, July 13, 1890 (Telegram), LS-ID-OSI-NA, Vol. 66.

10. J. W. Noble to D. H. Jerome, July 17, 1890 (Telegram), LS-ID-OSI-NA, Vol. 66.

11. J. W. Noble to M. S. Reynolds, September 23, 1890, J. W. Noble to D. H. Jerome, September 30, 1890, LS-ID-OSI-NA, Vol. 67.

12. *Report, Commissioner of Indian Affairs, 1891*, 342.

13. Affidavit of Michael Balenti, March 14, 1892, Affidavit of Paul Boynton, undated, Jesse Bent to Captain J. M. Lee, May 17, 1892, and affidavits of Cleaver Warden, George Bent, and Leonard Tyler, LR-ID-OSI-NA; Painter, *Cheyennes and Arapahoes Revisited*, 49.

14. C. F. Ashley to Amos Chapman, November 7, 1890, C&A Letterbooks, Vol. 31, 451–53.

15. 15 *Stats.*, 593; 26 *Stats.*, 1022; *Report, Commissioner of Indian Affairs, 1890*, 177; *Senate Exec. Doc.* No. 1, Vol. 1, 51 Cong., 2 Sess. (Serial 2818), 1–24; House of Representatives Report No. 3441, 51 Cong., 1 Sess. (Serial 2885); Interview of Jess Rowlodge by Julia A. Jordan, October 24, 1967, T-144 (Typescript), 17, IOHC-UOL.

16. "Protest of Sale of Indian Lands" (Copy), January 29, 1891, Special Case 147, Records of the Bureau of Indian Affairs, Record Group 75, National Archives Building, hereafter cited as Spec. Case 147-RBIA.

17. 26 *Stats.*, 1022, 1025; *Cong. Rec.*, 51 Cong., 2 Sess., February 28, 1891, 3529.

18. *Report, Commissioner of Indian Affairs, 1891*, 342–43; C. F. Ashley to
J. H. Seger, April 17, 1891, C&A Letterbooks, Vol. 32, 228–29; William W.
Junkin to Secretary of the Interior, August 18, 1891, Spec. Case 147, RBIA;
C. F. Ashley to Commissioner of Indian Affairs, May 26, 1891 (Telegram),
C&A Letterbooks, Vol. 24, 176; Kingfisher (Oklahoma) *Free Press*, June 28,
1891.

19. M. D. Tackett to Commissioner of Indian Affairs, June 5, 1891, Spec.
Case 147-RBIA; Kingfisher *Free Press*, September 3, 1891.

20. M. D. Tackett to Commissioner of Indian Affairs, June 22, 1891, Spec.
Case 147-RBIA.

21. M. D. Tackett to Commissioner of Indian Affairs, June 22, 1891, W. W.
Junkin to Secretary of the Interior, August 18, 1891; Report of M. D. Tackett
to Secretary of the Interior [October, 1891?], Spec. Case 147, RBIA; C. F. Ashley
to Commissioner of Indian Affairs, July 8, August 31, 1891 (Telegram), C&A
Letterbooks, Vol. 24, 179, 182; El Reno (Oklahoma) *Democrat*, August 1,
8, September 19, 1891.

22. Kingfisher *Free Press*, June 25, July 2, 16, 30, September 3, 24, 1891.

23. Resolution of Mass Meeting at El Reno, Canadian County, Oklahoma
Territory, June 12, 1891, H. A. Smith, Chairman, S. W. Savage, Secretary,
Spec. Case 147-RBIA.

24. Report of the Governor for 1891, 36; C. F. Ashley to Commissioner of
Indian Affairs, October 3, 1891, C&A Letterbooks, Vol. 33, 123.

25. *Oklahoma Democrat* (El Reno), October 11, 17, 1891; Kingfisher *Free
Press*, November 21, 1891; Petition of Citizens of Canadian Co., Oklahoma
Territory to Hon. J. W. Noble, Secretary of the Interior [September 25, 1891],
M. D. Wright to George Chandler, Assistant Secretary of the Interior, September 28, 1891, Copy of Resolutions of a Statehood Convention for Oklahoma
Territory, December 15, 1891, Spec. Case 147-RBIA.

26. George Chandler to W. W. Junkins, August 10, 1891, LS-ID-OSI-NA,
Vol. 73; C. F. Ashley to Commissioner of Indian Affairs, November 21, 1891,
A. E. Woodson to Commissioner of Indian Affairs, October 24, 1894, C&A
Letterbooks, Vol. 33, 168–69, Vol. 47, 207–11, El Reno *Oklahoma Democrat*,
September 6, November 21, December 12, 1891; Kingfisher *Free Press*, July 23,
October 15, 1891.

27. M. D. Tackett to Secretary of the Interior, October 14, 1891 (Telegram),
C. F. Ashley to Secretary of the Interior, October 7, 1891, C&A Letterbooks,
Vol. 24, 185; *House Exec. Doc.* No. 10, 52 Cong., 1 Sess. (Serial 2949), 1;
Cong. Record, 52 Cong., 1 Sess., January 5, 21, 1892, Vol. 23, part 1, 123, 493.

28. C. F. Ashley to Commissioner of Indian Affairs, January 23, 1892, Commissioner of Indian Affairs to C. F. Ashley, March 23, 1892, Spec. Case
147-RBIA.

29. J. W. Noble to Members of the Cheyenne and Arapahoe Tribes of
Indians who have not taken their land in allotment, January 26, 1892, J. W.

Noble to C. F. Ashley, January 28, 1892, Spec. Case 147-RBIA; J. W. Noble to M. D. Tackett, January 28, 1892, LS-ID-OSI-NA, Vol. 74.

30. M. D. Tackett to Commissioner of Indian Affairs, February 11, 1892, Spec. Case 147-RBIA; *Report, Commissioner of Indian Affairs, 1892*, 81, 371. As finally determined, 3,294 Cheyennes and Arapahoes were allotted 529,682.06 acres of land: 231,828.55 acres were set aside as school lands, and 32,343.93 acres were reserved for military, agency, mission, and other purposes. The remaining lands from the reservations, 3,500,562.05 acres, were opened for settlement. See *Report, Commissioner of Indian Affairs, 1899*, part 1, 539.

31. J. H. Seger to T. J. Morgan, August 12, 1891, Spec. Case 147-RBIA; BIC, *Report, 1892*, 141–42.

32. A. L. McPherson to T. J. Morgan, September 1, 1891, Spec. Case 147-RBIA.

33. L. Q. C. Lamar to Commissioner of Indian Affairs, October 10, 1885, July 23, 1886, J. W. Noble to Commissioner of the General Land Office, April 10, 1889, to Secretary of War, July 16, 1890, LS-ID-OSI-NA, Vols. 41, 59, 66. H. Hauser to J. J. Coppinger, March 27, 1889; Petition of Benjamin F. Keith, Herman Hauser, John Poisal and Peter Shields to the Secretary of the Interior, March 24, 1889, Hoke Smith, Secretary of the Interior to Commissioner of Indian Affairs, "In the matter of application of Amy Hauser, *et al.* for the allotment to them of lands within the Cheyenne and Arapahoe Reservation, Motion for Review," January 21, 1895, Spec. Case 147-RBIA.

34. M. D. Tackett to Commissioner of Indian Affairs, August 19, 1891, S. J. Crawford to T. J. Morgan, December 12, 1891, March 14, 15, 1892, Spec. Case 147-RBIA.

35. G. W. Shields to Secretary of the Interior, March 23, 1892, Spec. Case 147-RBIA.

36. T. H. Carter to Commissioner of Indian Affairs, March 23, 1892, J. W. Noble to Commissioner of Indian Affairs, April 10, 1892, Spec. Case 147-RBIA; J. W. Noble to Commissioner of Indian Affairs, March 3, 1893, LS-ID-OSI-NA, Vol. 78.

37. C. F. Ashley to Commissioner of Indian Affairs, April 7, 11, 1892, Spec. Case 147-RBIA.

38. A. E. Woodson to Commissioner of Indian Affairs, November 1, 1893, March 28, 1894, C&A Letterbooks, Vol. 38, 139–41, Vol. 44, 37–39.

39. Charles Keith to D. W. Browning, Commissioner of Indian Affairs, January 29, 1895, Spec. Case 147-RBIA.

40. Hoke Smith to Commissioner of Indian Affairs, January 21, 1895, Spec. Case 147-RBIA.

41. Mary E. Keith to A. E. Woodson, February 8, 1895, Spec. Case 147-RBIA.

42. Hoke Smith to Commissioner of Indian Affairs, January 6, 1896, Spec. Case 147-RBIA.

43. C. F. Ashley to Commissioner of Indian Affairs, April 6, 1892, C&A Letterbooks, Vol. 33, 327–28.

44. *Oklahoma Democrat*, April 9, 16, 1892.

CHAPTER VII

1. Oklahoma City *Evening Gazette*, March 29, April 18, 23, 1892; *Oklahoma Democrat*, April 2, 1892; Kingfisher *Free Press*, April 21, 28, May 5, 1892; Kansas City *Star*, April 19, 20, 1892; 27 *Stat.*, 1018; *Report, Commissioner of Indian Affairs, 1892*, 370.

2. C. F. Ashley to A. J. Seay, April 11, 1892, C. F. Ashley to J. L. McCracken, April 15, 1892, C. F. Ashley to W. M. Pulling, April 15, 1892, C. F. Ashley to Commissioner of Indian Affairs, April 21, 1892, C&A Letterbooks, Vol. 35, 253, 267, 268–69, Vol. 33, 353; *Report, Commissioner of Indian Affairs, 1892*, 377; *House Exec. Doc. No.* 198, 52 Cong., 1 Sess. (Serial 2955), 2.

3. George Chandler, Acting Secretary of the Interior, to Commissioner of Indian Affairs, July 9, 1891, LS-ID-OSI-NA, Vol. 73; Kansas City *Star*, April 14, 16, 18, 1892; Virginia Cole Trenholm, *The Arapahoes: Our People*, 284-88.

4. *Report, Commissioner of Indian Affairs, 1892*, 374–75, 376; J. H. Seger to C. F. Ashley, May 2, 1892, C. F. Ashley to A. J. Seay, May 16, 1892, C&A Letterbooks, Vol. 35, 319–21, 357–59.

5. William M. Pulling to C. F. Ashley, May 8, 1892, C&A Letterbooks-Cantonment, Vol. 1, 58–59, Indian Archives, Oklahoma Historical Society, Oklahoma City, Oklahoma, hereafter cited as C&A Letterbooks-Cantonment; C. F. Ashley to J. F. Wade, C. F. Ashley to A. J. Seay, May 10, 1892, C&A Letterbooks, Vol. 35, 339–40, 341–42.

6. *Report, Commissioner of Indian Affairs, 1892*, 374–75; C. F. Ashley to W. M. Pulling, May 6, 1892, C. F. Ashley to Commissioner of Indian Affairs, May 13, 1892, C. F. Ashley to A. J. Seay, May 12, 1892, C&A Letterbooks, Vol. 35, 331–32, 349–50, Vol. 33, 408–10.

7. C. F. Ashley to A. J. Seay, May 16, 1892, A. J. Seay to C. F. Ashley, May 26, 1892, C&A Letterbooks, Vol. 35, 357–59, and in *Report, Commissioner of Indian Affairs, 1892*, 376.

8. A. E. Woodson to Red Moon and Spotted Horse, November 25, 1893, James H. Hammon to A. E. Woodson, November 21, 1893, included with A. E. Woodson to Horace Speed, November 27, 1893, A. E. Woodson to J. H. Hammon, November 29, 1893, C&A Letterbooks, Vol. 39, 147, 148–49, Vol. 40, 39–40.

9. John F. Stone to A. E. Woodson, February 13, 1894, A. E. Woodson to Commissioner of Indian Affairs, February 17, 1894, A. E. Woodson to J. F. Stone, February 17, 1894, C&A Letterbooks, Vol. 35, 357, 358, Vol. 39, 335;

Watonga (Oklahoma) *Republican*, January 17, 1894; Cheyenne (Oklahoma) *Sunbeam*, December 8, 1894; *Report, Commissioner of Indian Affairs, 1894*, 237.
10. J. H. Hammon to A. E. Woodson, April 1, 1894, J. H. Seger to A. E. Woodson, April 3, 1894, A. E. Woodson to Commissioner of Indian Affairs, April 5, 1894, C&A Letterbooks, Vol. 44, 83–84, 85–86, 93.
11. Arapahoe *Bee*, April 5, 1894; Cheyenne *Sunbeam*, April 21, 1894; A. E. Woodson to Commissioner of Indian Affairs, April 7, 1894, C&A Letterbooks, Vol. 44, 112; *Report, Commissioner of Indian Affairs, 1894*, 237.
12. Guthrie (Oklahoma) *State Capital*, April 5, 6, 12, 1894; Kingfisher (Oklahoma) *Reformer*, April 12, 1894; Watonga *Republican*, April 11, 1894.
13. A. E. Woodson to Commissioner of Indian Affairs, April 7, 1894 (Telegram), J. H. Hammon to A. E. Woodson, April 4, 7, 1894, O. C. Conway to A. E. Woodson, April 8, 1894, C&A Letterbooks, Vol. 44, 112, 113–15, 117–18, 154–56; Arapahoe *Bee*, April 12, 1894; Cheyenne *Sunbeam*, April 21, 1894; *Report, Commissioner of Indian Affairs, 1894*, 237.
14. J. H. Seger to A. E. Woodson, April 18, 1894, A. E. Woodson to Carroll Briscoe, November 13, 19, 1894, S. H. Jones to J. F. Stone, November 19, 1894, C&A Letterbooks, Vol. 44, 186–88, Vol. 47, 406, 444, 446; A. E. Woodson to Commissioner of Indian Affairs, May 2, 1893, Spec. Case 147-RBIA; Arapahoe *Bee*, May 3, 1895. An examination of the annuity rolls located in the Cheyenne and Arapaho Subagency, Concho, Oklahoma, Fort Worth Federal Records Center, Fort Worth, Texas, reveals that Roman Nose and Thunder continued to receive their payments with the Red Moon bands.
15. A. E. Woodson to Richard Davis, June 11, 12, 1895, A. E. Woodson to T. S. Shahan, June 12, 1895, C&A Letterbooks, Vol. 50, 134–35, 143–45, 158–59.
16. A. E. Woodson to J. C. Mackay, June 17, 1895, J. C. Mackay to A. E. Woodson, June 16, 1895, A. E. Woodson to Commissioner of Indian Affairs, June 24, 1895, A. E. Woodson to Wichita *Eagle* and Kansas City *Times*, June 25, 1895, A. E. Woodson to Little Man and Chief White Horse and the Indians of the Cantonment District, June 26, 1895, C&A Letterbooks, Vol. 50, 213–15, 257, 258, 259–62, 311–17, 318–20, 333–36; Richard Davis to A. E. Woodson, June 17, 1895, J. H. Seger to A. E. Woodson, June 18, 1895, Cheyenne and Arapaho Lawlessness File, Indian Archives, Oklahoma Historical Society, Oklahoma City, Oklahoma, hereafter cited as C&A Lawlessness File-OHS.
17. W. M. Pulling to C. F. Ashley, April 16, 1893, Carroll Briscoe to A. E. Woodson, June 14, July 13, 1895, C&A Letterbooks-Cantonment, Vol. 1, 305, Vol. 3, 200, 215; Hoke Smith to Commissioner of Indian Affairs, June 10, 1894, LS-ID-OSI-NA, Vol. 81.
18. C. F. Ashley to Commissioner of Indian Affairs, July 19, 1892, C. F. Ashley to M. V. Schoonover, August 1, 1892, A. E. Woodson to Commissioner of Indian Affairs, August 31, 1893, C&A Letterbooks, Vol. 24, 64, Vol. 36, 22, Vol. 38, 20–21; Carl Sweezy, *The Arapaho Way: A Memoir of an Indian Boyhood*, ed. by Althea Bass, 59.

19. Mrs. Mollie Short Teeth to A. E. Woodson, December 4, 1893, A. E. Woodson to Commissioner of Indian Affairs, December 5, 1893, C&A Letterbooks, Vol. 38, 195–98, 201–202.

20. A. E. Woodson to Commissioner of Indian Affairs, January 4, 1894, C&A Letterbooks, Vol. 38, 276–81.

21. A. E. Woodson to Whom it May Concern, September 11, 1894, January 7, 1895, A. E. Woodson to Christian Madsen, January 11, 1895, Memo of A. E. Woodson, dated January 18, 1895, A. E. Woodson to United States Marshal, January 25, 1895, C&A Letterbooks, Vol. 46, 344, Vol. 48, 314, 357, 396–97, 487–88.

22. Memo of A. E. Woodson, January 18, 1895, C&A Letterbooks, Vol. 48, 396–97.

23. *Report, Commissioner of Indian Affairs, 1895,* 246; A. E. Woodson to Commissioner of Indian Affairs, March 20, 1896, C&A Letterbooks, Vol. 60, 393–95.

24. C. F. Ashley to Commissioner of Indian Affairs, in *Report, Commissioner of Indian Affairs, 1892,* 377.

25. C. F. Ashley to J. H. Seger, May 6, 1893, C&A Letterbooks, Vol. 36, 450–52; *Report, Commissioner of Indian Affairs, 1893,* 246.

26. *Report, Commissioner of Indian Affairs, 1893,* 246; Charles Brown to P. H. Gallion, May 15, 1893, in Arapahoe *Bee,* May 18, 1893; Arapahoe *Bee,* May 25, 1893; Kingfisher *Free Press,* July 14, 1893.

27. A. E. Woodson to Commissioner of Indian Affairs, November 23, 1893, A. E. Woodson to Whom It May Concern, March 28, 1894, A. E. Woodson to Board of County Commissioners, Canadian County, April 23, 1894, C&A Letterbooks, Vol. 38, 169, Vol. 44, 36, 181–83.

28. Watonga *Republican,* May 3, 1893; A. E. Woodson to United States Attorney, July 31, C&A Letterbooks, Vol. 51, 175–76; *Report, Commissioner of Indian Affairs, 1895,* 242; Richard Davis to A. E. Woodson, May 29, 1895, Cheyenne and Arapaho Taxes File, Indian Archives, Oklahoma Historical Society, Oklahoma City, Oklahoma; hereafter cited as C&A Taxes File-OHS.

29. A. E. Woodson to Richard Davis, May 4, 1894, A. E. Woodson to T. F. McMechan, September 7, 1895, C&A Letterbooks, Vol. 55, 255, Vol. 56, 174–75.

30. A. E. Woodson to White Shield, March 30, 1896, C&A Letterbooks, Vol. 60, 488–89; *Report, Commissioner of Indian Affairs, 1896,* 248.

31. A. E. Woodson to Caleb R. Brooks, May 20, July 24, 1896, A. E. Woodson to James L. Avent, June 27, 1896, C&A Letterbooks, Vol. 62, 39–41, Vol. 63, 16, 191; A. C. Tonner, to G. W. H. Stouch, May 29, 1900, C&A Taxes File-OHS; Watonga *Republican,* December 7, 1898.

32. H. Kliewer to C. F. Ashley, August 23, 1892, in *Report, Commissioner of Indian Affairs, 1892,* 376–77; A. J. Seay to J. W. Noble, April 27, 1892, LR-ID-OSI-NA.

33. 26 *Stats.,* 795.

34. *Report, Commissioner of Indian Affairs, 1892,* 371; C. F. Ashley to Commissioner of Indian Affairs, August 20, 1892, C&A Letterbooks, Vol. 34, 116–19; C. F. Ashley to Commissioner of Indian Affairs, July 8, October 12, 1892, Special Case 191, Records of the Bureau of Indian Affairs, Record Group 75, National Archives Building, hereafter cited as Spec. Case 191–RBIA.

35. *Report, Commissioner of Indian Affairs, 1893,* 248; A. E. Woodson to G. E. Rainey, December 27, 1893, C&A Letterbooks, Vol. 39, 219.

36. A. E. Woodson to Commissioner of Indian Affairs, January 26, February 22, 1894, C&A Letterbooks, Vol. 38, 296–97, 367–69.

37. *Report, Commissioner of Indian Affairs, 1894,* 231; A. E. Woodson to Commissioner of Indian Affairs, 1894, 231; A. E. Woodson to Commissioner of Indian Affairs, May 7, 1894, C&A Letterbooks, Vol. 44, 288–89.

38. Paul Boynton to A. E. Woodson, May 15, 1894, and lease submitted with letter, Spec. Case 191–RBIA.

39. Kingfisher *Free Press,* June 21, 1894; Arapahoe *Bee,* June 28, 1894.

40. A. E. Woodson to D. T. Flynn, June 14, 1894, C&A Letterbooks, Vol. 45, 145–47; Kingfisher *Free Press,* July 5, 1894.

41. *Report, Commissioner of Indian Affairs, 1894,* 233; J. M. Lee to Assistant Inspector General, Department of the Missouri, September 14, 1894 (Copy), C&A Letterbooks, Vol. 49, 176–84; Council with the Cheyennes and Arapahoes of Oklahoma, March 19–21, 1895, Spec. Case 147–RBIA. Left Hand and Row-of-Lodges represented the Arapahoes and Cloud Chief, White Horse, Young Whirlwind, Little Coyote, and Little Chief the Cheyennes during the January, 1895 conference in Washington.

42. A. E. Woodson to Commissioner of Indian Affairs, January 23, 1895, A. E. Woodson to P. Boynton and Hoke Smith, January 23, 26, 1895, Form Letter to Lessees, January 26, 1895, C&A Letterbooks, Vol. 48, 437–38, 456–58, 493–96, 497–98; Hoke Smith to Commissioner of Indian Affairs, March 28, 1895, LS-ID-OSI-NA, Vol. 85.

43. A. E. Woodson to J. W. Thompson, June 15, 1895, A. E. Woodson to T. F. McMechan, September 25, 1895, A. E. Woodson to G. P. Pray, July 17, 1899, James Frost to Hoke Smith, September 16, 1895 (Copy), C&A Letterbooks, Vol. 50, 197–98, Vol. 57, 52, Vol. 56, 371–73, Vol. 82, 210.

44. A. E. Woodson to Commissioner of Indian Affairs, September 20, 1895, Moses Neal to D. M. Browning, January 27, 1896, Spec. Case 191–RBIA; T. P. Smith to A. E. Woodson, September 30, 1895, C&A Letterbooks, Vol. 49, 258–60; Hoke Smith to Commissioner of Indian Affairs, February 1, 1896, LS-ID-OSI-NA, Vol. 87.

45. J. O. Thompson to A. E. Woodson, August 31, 1896, R. S. Denley to A. E. Woodson, September 16, 1896, G. F. Coleman to A. E. Woodson, August 29, September 2, 1896, Spec. Case 191–RBIA.

46. A. E. Woodson to Commissioner of Indian Affairs, April 15, 1897, January 26, 1898, Spec. Case 191–RBIA.

47. *Report, Commissioner of Indian Affairs, 1898*, 1102; *Report, Commissioner of Indian Affairs, 1899*, 283.
48. A. E. Woodson to Caleb R. Brooks, April 23, 1897, A. E. Woodson to J. M. Frazier, October 25, 1898, A. E. Woodson to Mr. Oliver, October 16, 1899, A. E. Woodson to J. C. Quarles, May 17, October 14, 1899, A. E. Woodson to J. L. Avent, November 27, 1899, C&A Letterbooks, Vol. 68, 225, Vol. 77, 195, Vol. 84, 100, Vol. 80, 286, Vol. 84, 71, Vol. 85, 5–6.
49. *Report, Commissioner of Indian Affairs, 1895*, 246; A. E. Woodson to Commissioner of Indian Affairs, March 20, 1896, C&A Letterbooks, Vol. 60, 393–95.
50. A. E. Woodson to Commissioner of Indian Affairs, October 19, 1894, C&A Letterbooks, Vol. 47, 181–83.
51. Open range meant the owners of stock were not responsible for fencing in their herds. Herd law, however, required stockmen to fence their ranges or pastures, and, if their animals destroyed a farmer's crop, the rancher was liable for damages. A. E. Woodson to R. Petter, October 19, 1895, C&A Letterbooks, Vol. 57, 92–93.
52. A. E. Woodson to N. W. Butler, January 20, 1896, A. E. Woodson to Caleb R. Brooks, January 21, 1896, C&A Letterbooks, Vol. 59, 101–102, 136–37.
53. A. E. Woodson to J. W. Lawton, January 24, 27, 1896, A. E. Woodson to N. W. Butler, February 22, 1896, Woodson to C. R. Brooks, February 22, 1896, A. E. Woodson to Commissioner of Indian Affairs, March 3, 1896, C&A Letterbooks, Vol. 59, 185, 218, Vol. 60, 32, 39–40, 393–95.
54. Judson Harmon to Secretary of the Interior, April 14, 1896, Spec. Case 147–RBIA.
55. A. E. Woodson to W. C. Smoot, January 15, 1897, Assistant United States Attorney to A. E. Woodson, February 11, 1897, C&A Letterbooks, Vol. 66, 406, Vol. 67, 94–95, Vol. 69, 138.
56. A. E. Woodson to Commissioner of Indian Affairs, June 1, 1897, September 13, 1898, A. E. Woodson to J. H. Houston, September 28, 1898, C&A Letterbooks, Vol. 69, 135–37, Vol. 76, 449–50; George W. H. Stouch to Commissioner of Indian Affairs, March 24, 1900, Spec. Case 191, RBIA.

CHAPTER VIII

1. A. E. Woodson to Captain J. M. Lee, March 30, 1894, C&A Letterbooks, Vol. 49, 35–38; *Report, Commissioner of Indian Affairs, 1893*, 247, *Report, Commissioner of Indian Affairs, 1894*, 231, 235, 236.
2. A. E. Woodson to Commissioner of Indian Affairs, October 25, 1894, May 7, 1895, Orders to the Cheyenne and Arapaho tribes of Indians, October 25, 1894, C&A Letterbooks, Vol. 47, 225–26, 227–28, Vol. 55, 282.

3. Orders by A. E. Woodson, May 5, 1895, C&A Letterbooks, Vol. 49, 235–36; *Report, Commissioner of Indian Affairs, 1895,* 244.

4. A. E. Woodson to Farmers and Assistant Farmers, June 6, 1895, A. E. Woodson to the Cheyennes and Arapahoes, June 18, 1895, C&A Letterbooks, Vol. 50, 91–92, 248–50; Carroll Briscoe to A. E. Woodson, June 4, 15, 1895, Stephen Janus to Jesse Hinkle, March 6, 1896, C&A Letterbooks-Cantonment, Vol. 3, 169–70, 201–202, 428–30, *Report, Commissioner of Indian Affairs, 1895,* 244–45.

5. *Report, Commissioner of Indian Affairs, 1895,* 245.

6. A. E. Woodson to James H. Hammon, December 21, 1895, A. E. Woodson to C. Briscoe, December 5, 1895, A. E. Woodson to Commissioner of Indian Affairs, March 5, May 2, 6, 1896, A. E. Woodson to the Cheyennes and Arapahoes in camp near El Reno, May 1, 1896, A. E. Woodson to E. J. Simpson, May 1, 1896, A. E. Woodson to J. M. Lee, May 5, 1896, A. E. Woodson to Major General Wesley Merritt, May 6, 29, 1896, D. M. Browning to A. E. Woodson, May 8, 1896 (Copy), C&A Letterbooks, Vol. 52, 405–406, 163–64, Vol. 60, 185–86, Vol. 49, 316, 317, 309–15, 322–23, 318–19, 320–21, 324–28, 344–45; Stephen Janus to A. E. Woodson, February 7, 1896, C&A Letterbooks-Cantonment, Vol. 3, 409–10; *Cong., Rec.,* 53 Cong., 2 Sess., June 13, 1894, 6236.1.

7. A. E. Woodson to District Farmers, October 9, 1896, A. E. Woodson to Commissioner of Indian Affairs, May 10, 1896, D. M. Browning to A. E. Woodson, October 14, 1896, C&A Letterbooks, Vol. 49, 383, 384, 385; Stephen Janus to A. E. Woodson, August 10, September 2, 1896, C&A Letterbooks-Cantonment, Vol. 4, 25–28, 55–57; Bass, *The Arapaho Way,* 55.

8. A. E. Woodson to Colonel E. P. Pearson, Commanding Officer, Fort Reno, May 21, 1897, C&A Letterbooks, Vol. 69, 66–71; *Report, Commissioner of Indian Affairs, 1897,* 229.

9. A. E. Woodson to Commissioner of Indian Affairs, February 17, 1898, W. A. Jones to Secretary of War, April 9, 1898 (Copy), C&A Letterbooks, Vol. 74, 242–43, Vol. 69, 460.

10. A. E. Woodson to R. Petter, May 5, 1898, C&A Letterbooks, Vol. 75, 141–42.

11. A. E. Woodson to Commissioner of Indian Affairs, November 25, 1898, February 2, 1899, C&A Letterbooks, Vol. 77, 431–33, Vol. 78, 341–44.

12. Trenholm, *Arapahoes,* 283–93.

13. C. F. Ashley to Commissioner of Indian Affairs, December 23, 1891, June 28, 1892, C&A Letterbooks, Vol. 33, 202–203, Vol. 34, 27–28; *Report, Commissioner of Indian Affairs, 1892,* 383, *Report, Commissioner of Indian Affairs, 1893,* 244; BIC, *Report, 1890,* 29–30, 46; BIC, *Report, 1891,* 34, BIC, *Report, 1892,* 114; Kingfisher *Free Press,* July 16, 1891, September 17, 1891; Kansas City *Star,* April 13, 14, 16, 18, 1892; Interview of Myrtle Lincoln by Julia A. Jordan, July 30, 1970, T-613 (Typescript), 17, IOHC, UOL.

14. A. E. Woodson to Jesse Hinkle, April 24, 1894, C&A Letterbooks, Vol.

44, 192–93; *Report, Commissioner of Indian Affairs, 1895,* 244; Kingfisher *Reformer,* September 27, 1894.

15. A. E. Woodson to Andrew Tasso, April 4, 1895, C&A Letterbooks, Vol. 54, 438–39.

16. *Report, Commissioner of Indian Affairs, 1896,* 248; A. E. Woodson to Delegation of Cheyennes, June 1, 1896, A. E. Woodson to Stephen Janus, June 3, October 3, 1896, C&A Letterbooks, Vol. 62, 172–75, 207–208, Vol. 64, 425–26; El Reno *Democrat,* April 14, 1898.

17. A. E. Woodson to Chairman of the Judiciary Committee of the Council and House of Representatives of Oklahoma Territory, February 28, 1899, C&A Letterbooks, Vol. 78, 486–87.

18. George Westfall to Judiciary Committee of the House and Council, Oklahoma Territory, March 1, 1899, C&A Letterbooks, Vol. 78, 488–89.

19. A. E. Woodson to George W. Ballamy, March 2, 1899, C&A Letterbooks, Vol. 78, 490; Interview of Jess Rowlodge by Julia A. Jordan, December 12, 1967, T-172 (Typescript), 12, 18, 19, IOHC-UOL. A document written in 1912 by Jock Bull Bear, a full-blood Arapaho leader and Carlisle graduate, contains the statement that in 1884 he began using peyote. Paul Boynton, an Arapaho-Cheyenne and also a Carlisle graduate, testified in 1918 before a House of Representatives Subcommittee on Indian Affairs that in 1883 he first learned of peyote. It is reasonable to assume that the peyote ceremony was adopted at approximately the same time by the Cheyennes and Arapahoes. James A. Mooney, however, during his testimony before the same subcommittee, stated that in 1890 only one Arapaho and one Cheyenne man "knew anything about" peyote. See, *Hearings Before a Subcommittee of the Committee on Indian Affairs of the House of Representatives on H. R. 2614* [1918], *Peyote,* 65 Cong., 2 Sess., 71, 104, 181.

20. A. E. Woodson to C. M. Barnes, C&A Letterbooks, Vol. 79, 87, 135; *Report, Commissioner of Indian Affairs, 1899,* 284.

21. W. M. Pulling to C. F. Ashley, May 3, 1893, C&A Letterbooks-Cantonment, Vol. 1, 328–30.

22. *Report, Commissioner of Indian Affairs, 1893,* 247; Guthrie *State Capital,* July 6, November 20, 1893.

23. *Report, Commissioner of Indian Affairs, 1894,* 231; *Report, Commissioner of Indian Affairs, 1895,* 243; *Statutes of Oklahoma,* 669.

24. A. E. Woodson to Editor, Wichita *Eagle,* to Editor, Kansas City *Star,* May 7, 1895, W. J. A. Montgomery to A. E. Woodson, May 9, 1895, C&A Letterbooks, Vol. 55, 285–86, 287–88, 352–53.

25. A. E. Woodson to A. H. Viets, to Commissioner of Indian Affairs, September 5, 1895, C&A Letterbooks, Vol. 56, 141–42, 143–44.

26. A. E. Woodson to Roy Hoffman, Assistant United States Attorney, December 12, 1895, C&A Letterbooks, Vol. 52, 255–56.

27. A. E. Woodson to County Attorney, Canadian County, June 12, 1896, C&A Letterbooks, Vol. 62, 321–22.

28. *Report, Commissioner of Indian Affairs, 1896,* 246.

29. A. E. Woodson to Commissioner of Indian Affairs, February 9, 1897, A. E. Woodson to Herbert Welsch, February 8, 1897, A. E. Woodson to D. S. Rose, February 9, March 6, 1897, A. E. Woodson to Caleb R. Brooks, February 23, 1897, C&A Letterbooks, Vol. 67, 21–22, 37–38, 154–55, 305, 400–402.

30. Territory of Oklahoma, *Session Laws of 1897,* 212–15.

31. *Report, Commissioner of Indian Affairs, 1897,* 225; A. E. Woodson to Commissioner of Indian Affairs, April 2, August 28, 1897, A. E. Woodson to Fred S. Barde, April 3, 1897, C&A Letterbooks, Vol. 68, 71–72, 92–93, Vol. 71, 122–24.

32. Cheyenne *Sunbeam,* July 23, 1897.

33. *Report, Commissioner of Indian Affairs, 1897,* 225–26; G. W. H. Stouch to Employees, February 27, 1900, C&A Letterbooks, Vol. 86, 410.

34. *Report, Commissioner of Indian Affairs, 1893,* 246; A. E. Woodson to Reverend Charles H. Miller, September 23, 1895, A. E. Woodson to The President, El Reno Fair Association, October 14, 1895, C&A Letterbooks, Vol. 56, 239, Vol. 57, 40–41.

35. *Report, Commissioner of Indian Affairs, 1898,* 234; A. E. Woodson to Deputy U.S. Marshal Peery, February 24, 1897; A. E. Woodson to Ruben Hickox, May 23, 1898, C&A Letterbooks, Vol. 67, 169, Vol. 75, 102.

36. William Pulling to C. F. Ashley, September 15, 21, October 4, 5, 1892, C&A Letterbooks-Cantonment, Vol. 1, 116, 171, 180–81, 182–84.

37. J. S. Krehbiel to H. R. Voth, September 24, 1892, Voth Collection; *Report, Commissioner of Indian Affairs, 1893,* 373; C. F. Ashley to Commissioner of Indian Affairs, April 19, 1893, C&A Letterbooks, Vol. 34, 358–60; BIC, *Report, 1892,* 113–15.

38. *Report, Commissioner of Indian Affairs, 1893,* 243; *Report, Commissioner of Indian Affairs, 1894,* 237; BIC, *Report, 1893,* 119–21; BIC, *Report, 1894,* 26–28, 139–41. In this period less than one out of every three Indian children between the ages of six to sixteen attended schools, *Cong., Rec.,* 51 Cong., 2 Sess., February 14, 1891, 2702.

39. *Report, Commissioner of Indian Affairs, 1894,* 237; A. E. Woodson to Commissioner of Indian Affairs, September 27, 1894, C&A Letterbooks, Vol. 47, 38–40.

40. Guthrie *State Capital,* November 4, 1893, BIC, *Report, 1895,* 44–47.

41. W. H. Sims, First Assistant Secretary of the Interior, to Commissioner of Indian Affairs, January 30, 1895, LS-ID-OSI-NA, Vol. 84; *Report, Commissioner of Indian Affairs, 1895,* 242.

42. *Report, Commissioner of Indian Affairs, 1896,* 245–46.

43. A. E. Woodson to George E. Coleman, October 5, 1896, A. E. Woodson

to Commissioner of Indian Affairs, November 13, 1896, C&A Letterbooks, Vol. 64, 441–43, Vol. 65, 272–73.

44. A. E. Woodson to Commissioner of Indian Affairs, September 15, 1897, C&A Letterbooks, Vol. 71, 358–61.

45. *Report, Commissioner of Indian Affairs, 1899*, 284–85.

46. *Ibid.*, 244–45.

CHAPTER IX

1. Crawford and his associates were paid their fees based upon the Jerome Commission's estimate that the Cheyenne and Arapaho claim to the Cherokee Outlet was valued at $1,250,000, see J. W. Noble to S. K. Jones, March 17, 1892, to Secretary of War, May 6, 1892, to M. S. Reynolds, May 7, 1892, to Commissioner of Indian Affairs, May 7, 1892, LS-ID-OSI-NA, Vol. 75. A. E. Woodson to Cheyenne Chiefs at Cantonment, September 11, 1893, C&A Letterbooks, Vol. 41, 5–6.

2. A. E. Woodson to Commissioner of Indian Affairs, December 20, 1893, Spec. Case 147–RBIA; *Report, Commissioner of Indian Affairs, 1894*, 232.

3. J. H. Seger to A. E. Woodson, March 6, 1894, C&A Letterbooks, Vol. 44, 10–11.

4. A. E. Woodson to J. H. Seger, A. E. Woodson to W. M. Pulling, March 29, 1894, J. Seger to A. E. Woodson, April 4, 1894, C&A Letterbooks, Vol. 44, 50–51, 52–53, 127–28.

5. A. E. Woodson to Commissioner of Indian Affairs, April 9, 1894, C&A Letterbooks, Vol. 44, 124–26; Kingfisher *Free Press*, April 12, 1894; Arapahoe *Bee*, April 26, 1894.

6. A. E. Woodson to Commissioner of Indian Affairs, June 13, 1894, A. E. Woodson to J. H. Seger, June 20, 1894, A. E. Woodson to J. M. Lee, July 31, 1894, C&A Letterbooks, Vol. 45, 137–38, 221, Vol. 49, 162–63; BIC, *Report, 1894*, 25–26.

7. *Report, Commissioner of Indian Affairs, 1894*, 233–36.

8. J. M. Lee to Inspector General, Department of the Missouri, Spec. Case 147–RBIA.

9. *Oklahoma Democrat*, November 22, 1894; A. E. Woodson to Commissioner of Indian Affairs, October 24, November 27, 1894, A. E. Woodson to J. H. Seger, November 14, 1894, A. E. Woodson to C. C. Painter, December 28, 1894, C&A Letterbooks, Vol. 47, 207–11, Vol. 48, 19–21, 248–51.

10. "Copy of Contract," dated December 12, 1894, C&A Letterbooks, Vol. 48, 288; E. F. Mitchell to D. M. Browning, January 25, 1895, Spec. Case 147–RBIA.

11. Cheyenne *Sunbeam*, December 15, 1894; *Oklahoma Democrat*, January 3, 1895; W. H. Sims to Commissioner of Indian Affairs, January 30, 1895, LS-ID-OSI-NA, Vol. 84.

12. "Council with the Cheyennes and Arapahoes of Oklahoma," March 19–21, 1895, Washington, D.C., Spec. Case 147–RBIA; Cheyenne *Sunbeam*, March 19, 1895.

13. Orders, Cheyenne and Arapahoe Agency, May 6, 1895, T. Smith to A. E. Woodson, May 24, 1895, A. E. Woodson to T. Smith, May 30, 1895, Spec. Case 147–RBIA.

14. *Report, Commissioner of Indian Affairs, 1895*, 244.

15. *Ibid.*, 244–45.

16. W. H. Sims to Commissioner of Indian Affairs, January 16, 1896, LS-ID-OSI-NA, Vol. 87; A. E. Woodson to Commissioner of Indian Affairs, February 5, 1896, C&A Letterbooks, Vol. 59, 279–81.

17. A. E. Woodson to D. T. Flynn, February 6, 1896, A. E. Woodson to Secretary, Indian Rights Association, February 24, 1896, A. E. Woodson to Commissioner of Indian Affairs, February 5, 1896, C&A Letterbooks, Vol. 49, 289–92, Vol. 59, 278–81, Vol. 60, 45–46.

18. A. E. Woodson to Commissioner of Indian Affairs, May 29, 1896, Spec. Case 147–RBIA.

19. A. E. Woodson to Commissioner of Indian Affairs, May 29, 1896, Spec. Case 147–RBIA; *Report, Commissioner of Indian Affairs, 1896*, 251.

20. *Report, Commissioner of Indian Affairs, 1897*, 227, BIC, *Report, 1897*, 17–18.

21. A. E. Woodson to Commissioner of Indian Affairs, March 15, May 7, 1898, F. Glasbrenner, Acting Agent to Ben Road Traveler, March 23, 1898, C&A Letterbooks, Vol. 74, 426–27, 444, Vol. 75, 173–75.

22. Arapahoe (Oklahoma) *Arrow*, August 26, 1892.

23. C. F. Ashley to Commissioner of Indian Affairs, December 1, 1892, C&A Letterbooks, Vol. 34, 210–11.

24. *Report, Commissioner of Indian Affairs, 1892*, 383–84.

25. A. E. Woodson to Commissioner of Indian Affairs, December 5, 1893, October 23, 1894, C&A Letterbooks, Vol. 38, 195–98, Vol. 47, 222–24.

26. A. E. Woodson to Commissioner of Indian Affairs, May 9, July 5, 1895, C&A Letterbooks, Vol. 55, 319–20, 438–41; Arapahoe *Arrow*, August 26, 1892.

27. A. E. Woodson to Whom It May Concern, July 22, 1895, A. E. Woodson to J. J. O'Rouke, July 5, 1895, A. E. Woodson to Albert Dean, February 13, 1896, A. E. Woodson to Governor William C. Renfrow, Oklahoma Territory, April 4, 1896, J. Sterling Morton to W. C. Renfrow, April 21, 1896, A. E. Woodson to J. S. North, May 12, 1896, A. E. Woodson to Committee of Citizens, A. E. Woodson to Commissioner of Indian Affairs, May 19, 1896, C&A Letterbooks, Vol. 51, 28, Vol. 59, 276, 397, Vol. 61, 94–96, 257, 444–45, 493–96, Vol. 62, 24–26.

28. A. E. Woodson to Colonel E. P. Pearson, May 20, 1896, A. E. Woodson to Sheriffs of Blaine and G Counties, May 22, 1896, A. E. Woodson to W. C. Renfrow, May 22, 1896, W. C. Renfrow to A. E. Woodson, May 22, 1896

(Copy), A. E. Woodson to Joseph P. Murphy, May 28, 1896, C&A Letterbooks, Vol. 62, 46–47, 77, 78–80, 103, 139–40.

29. A. E. Woodson to R. Petter, September 30, 1896, A. E. Woodson to District Farmers, October 28, 1896, A. E. Woodson to Commissioner of Indian Affairs, February 12, 1899, C&A Letterbooks, Vol. 64, 371–72, Vol. 65, 71, Vol. 78, 353–54; Cheyenne *Sunbeam*, August 14, 1896.

30. A. E. Woodson to Commissioner of Indian Affairs, April 8, 1899, C&A Letterbooks, Vol. 79, 321–22.

31. *Report, Commissioner of Indian Affairs, 1893*, 244, 248.

32. A. E. Woodson to Richard Davis, August 2, 1894, C&A Letterbooks, Vol. 45, 497; W. H. Sims to Commissioner of Indian Affairs, January 30, 1895, LS-ID-OSI-NA, Vol. 84.

33. *Report, Commissioner of Indian Affairs, 1895*, 243–44; *Report, Commissioner of Indian Affairs, 1896*, 247; A. E. Woodson to Commissioner of Indian Affairs, August 27, 1896, C&A Letterbooks, Vol. 63, 441–42.

34. *Report, Commissioner of Indian Affairs, 1897*, 226; A. E. Woodson to Commissioner of Indian Affairs, January 21, 1898, C&A Letterbooks, Vol. 74, 115–17.

35. A. E. Woodson to Commissioner of Indian Affairs, October 31, 1898, A. E. Woodson to J. H. Seger, October 31, 1898, C&A Letterbooks, Vol. 77, 244–45, 246.

36. A. E. Woodson to Commissioner of Indian Affairs, January 31, 1899, C&A Letterbooks, Vol. 78, 287–89; A. E. Woodson to Merrill E. Gates, November 22, 1899, in *Report, Commissioner of Indian Affairs, 1899*, Part II, 249; *House Doc. 391*, 57 Cong., 1 Sess. (Serial 4361), 4–5.

37. *Report, Commissioner of Indian Affairs, 1892*, 370, 383.

38. C. F. Ashley to Commissioner of Indian Affairs, August 20, 1892, C&A Letterbooks, Vol. 34, 114–19.

39. C. F. Ashley to Commissioner of Indian Affairs, September 13, October 5, 1892, May 20, 1893, C&A Letterbooks, Vol. 34, 144, 153–54, 396–97.

40. *Report, Commissioner of Indian Affairs, 1893*, 245, 249–50.

41. A. E. Woodson to Commissioner of Indian Affairs, December 20, 1893, C&A Letterbooks, Vol. 38, 237–40.

42. D. M. Browning to A. E. Woodson, January 22, 1894, C&A Letterbooks, Vol. 41, 90–91.

43. A. E. Woodson to Commissioner of Indian Affairs, February 22, 1894, C&A Letterbooks, Vol. 38, 367–69.

44. A. E. Woodson to Commissioner of Indian Affairs, July 16, August 25, 1894, April 6, 1895, A. E. Woodson to R. Davis, July 19, 1894, C&A Letterbooks, Vol. 45, 357, 393, Vol. 46, 195–96, Vol. 54, 459–62.

45. A. E. Woodson to R. Davis, December 29, 1894, April 4, 1895, C&A Letterbooks, Vol. 48, 252, Vol. 54, 428–29.

46. A. E. Woodson to Commissioner of Indian Affairs, April 6, 1895, C&A Letterbooks, Vol. 54, 459–62.

47. A. E. Woodson to D. T. Flynn, February 5, 1895, A. E. Woodson to Commissioner of Indian Affairs, December 3, 1895, C&A Letterbooks, Vol. 53, 132–33, Vol. 52, 264–72.

48. A. E. Woodson to Roy Hall, July 8, 1896, A. E. Woodson to H. B. Freeman, August 29, 1896, C&A Letterbooks, Vol. 63, 86–88, 464–65.

49. A. E. Woodson to Jesse Hinkle, June 29, 1899, C&A Letterbooks, Vol. 81, 1899.

50. *Report, Commissioner of Indian Affairs, 1897*, 224, 227.

51. A. E. Woodson to Commissioner of Indian Affairs, January 25, May 7, 1895, March 4, 1898, March 7, 21, 1899; A. E. Woodson to J. H. Seger, April 23, 1895, A. E. Woodson to Cheyenne and Arapahoe Indians, May 30, 1895, A. E. Woodson to G. E. Morrow, February 27, 1899, C&A Letterbooks, Vol. 48, 475–77, Vol. 50, 5–6, Vol. 55, 134–35, Vol. 74, 366–67, Vol. 78, 457, Vol. 79, 58–59, 169.

52. A. E. Woodson to George E. Coleman, November 21, 1895, A. E. Woodson to J. T. Witcher, February 25, 1896, A. E. Woodson to Indian Traders at Darlington and Cantonment Sub-Agency, March 31, 1896, C&A Letterbooks, Vol. 52, 31–32, Vol. 60, 58–59, Vol. 61, 1–2.

53. A. E. Woodson to Additional Farmers, March 1, 30, 1897, A. E. Woodson to Commissioner of Indian Affairs, February 18, 1898, C&A Letterbooks, Vol. 67, 334, Vol. 68, 35, Vol. 74, 244; Watonga *Republican*, November 10, 1897.

54. *Report, Commissioner of Indian Affairs, 1897*, 227–28; A. E. Woodson to Commissioner of Indian Affairs, September 1, 1897, A. E. Woodson to Additional Farmers, June 10, 1898, C&A Letterbooks, Vol. 71, 223–38, Vol. 75, 325; Arapahoe *Bee*, August 27, 1897.

55. A. E. Woodson to Commissioner of Indian Affairs, October 4, 1899, C&A Letterbooks, Vol. 83, 487–96; *Report, Commissioner of Indian Affairs, 1899*, 285; Arapahoe *Bee*, March 3, April 14, May 5, 1899; BIC, *Report, 1899*, 31.

56. A. E. Woodson to Commissioner of Indian Affairs, October 4, 1899, C&A Letterbooks, Vol. 83, 487–96; *Report, Commissioner of Indian Affairs, 1899*, 285, Part II, 249–50.

CHAPTER X

1. *Report, Commissioner of Indian Affairs, 1900*, 5–8, 9–10, 326.

2. *Ibid.*, 325–26.

3. Report of Mary McCormick, Field Matron, May 1–31, 1900, Report of Mary E. Lyons, May 1–31, July 5, September 1, December 1, 1900, April 30, 1902, Cheyenne and Arapaho Field Matron File, Indian Archives, Oklahoma Historical Society, Oklahoma City, Oklahoma, hereafter cited as C&A Field Matron File-OHS.

4. Report of Mary C. Gillett, April and May, 1901, C&A Field Matron File-OHS; G. W. H. Stouch to Superintendent, Red Moon School, February 23, 1900, C&A Letterbooks, Vol. 86, 376–78.

5. G. W. H. Stouch to Commissioner of Indian Affairs, March 29, 1900, C&A Letterbooks, Vol. 92, 227–31.

6. W. A. Jones to G. W. H. Stouch, April 7, 1900, C. F. Larrabee, Acting Commissioner to G. W. H. Stouch, April 6, May 29, 1905, R. J. Eddy to Superintendents at Colony, Darlington, and Cantonment, June 18, 1907, Cheyenne and Arapaho Foreign Relations File, Indian Archives, Oklahoma Historical Society, Oklahoma City, Oklahoma, hereafter cited as C&A Foreign Relations File-OHS.

7. Horace E. Wilson to G. W. H. Stouch, June 8, 1891, C&A Letterbooks-Cantonment, Vol. 7, 415.

8. H. E. Wilson to G. W. H. Stouch, October 4, 1901, C&A Letterbooks-Cantonment, Vol. 9, 36.

9. *Report, Commissioner of Indian Affairs, 1900*, 12.

10. G. W. H. Stouch to Commissioner of Indian Affairs, January 25, 1900, C&A Letterbooks, Vol. 92, 69–72.

11. A. C. Tonner, Acting Commissioner, to A. E. Woodson, August 4, 1899, Cheyenne and Arapahoe Agency, Classified File, Land 35933–1899, Records of the Bureau of Indian Affairs, Record Group 75, United States Archives Building, hereafter Classified Files will be cited as C&A, CF and the appropriate RBIA file number; A. E. Woodson to Commissioner of Indian Affairs, December 12, 1899, G. W. H. Stouch to Commissioner of Indian Affairs, January 25, 1900, G. W. H. Stouch to Horace Speed, U.S. Attorney, July 10, 27, 1900, C&A Letterbooks, Vol. 94, 391–94, Vol. 92, 69–72, Vol. 89, 103, 212–20.

12. G. W. H. Stouch to Commissioner of Indian Affairs, January 29, 1900, G. W. H. Stouch to Farmers, August 3, 1900, C&A Letterbooks, Vol. 89, 125, Vol. 92, 73–78; A. C. Tonner, to G. W. H. Stouch, July 28, 1900, C&A, CF-Land 34570–1900, RBIA.

13. G. W. H. Stouch to Commissioner of Indian Affairs, September 8, 1900, C&A Letterbooks, Vol. 93, 280–83; Fred Winterfair to G. W. H. Stouch, September 1, 1900, C&A Letterbooks-Cantonment, Vol. 8, 41–44.

14. G. W. H. Stouch to Commissioner of Indian Affairs, January 6, 21, March 11, 1902, C&A Letterbooks, Vol. 121, 401–402, 422–24, Vol. 122, 30–32; *Report, Commissioner of Indian Affairs, 1901*, 72, 314–15; *Report, Commissioner of Indian Affairs, 1902*, 280–81; *Report, Commissioner of Indian Affairs, 1903*, 245–46.

15. Bennie Keith to Major Stouch, February 28, 1902, G. W. H. Stouch to Commissioner of Indian Affairs, March 6, 1892, C&A Letterbooks, Vol. 122, 6-10, 12–16.

16. A. C. Tonner to Secretary of the Interior, June 26, 1899, A. C. Tonner to A. E. Woodson, August 30, 1899, Cheyenne and Arapaho Guardianship File,

Indian Archives, Oklahoma Historical Society, Oklahoma City, Oklahoma, hereafter cited as C&A Guardianship File-OHS.

17. A. C. Tonner to A. E. Woodson, September 18, 1899, A. C. Tonner to G. W. H. Stouch, March 7, 1900, J. S. Krehbiel to A. E. Woodson, November 7, 1899, R. Petter to A. E. Woodson, November 15, 1899, D. A. Sanford to A. E. Woodson, November 2, 1899, C&A Guardianship File-OHS. G. W. H. Stouch to Commissioner of Indian Affairs, March 29, 1900, C&A Letterbooks, Vol. 92, 227–31.

18. W. A. Jones to G. W. H. Stouch, February 13, 1903, W. A. Jones to Baldwin & Marsh, Attorneys-at-Law, El Reno, Oklahoma, February 13, 1903, C&A Guardianship File-OHS.

19. C. F. Larrabee to Superintendent in Charge, C&A Agency, September 19, 1906, G. A. Outcelt to C. E. Shell, February 2, 1907, C&A Guardianship File-OHS.

20. G. W. H. Stouch to Commissioner of Indian Affairs, January 23, 1901, G. W. H. Stouch to James L. Avent, September 10, 1901, C&A Letterbooks, Vol. 99, 479, Vol. 102, 210–11.

21. Lee & Reynolds, Traders, Camp Supply to J. D. Miles, January 1, 1873, Cheyenne and Arapaho Romero File, Indian Archives, Oklahoma Historical Society, Oklahoma City, Oklahoma, hereafter cited as C&A Romero File-OHS. W. A. Jones to G. W. H. Stouch, January 2, 1901, Cheyenne and Arapaho Allotment File, Indian Archives, Oklahoma Historical Society, Oklahoma City, Oklahoma, hereafter cited as C&A Allotment File-OHS.

22. G. W. H. Stouch to Commissioner of Indian Affairs, January 28, 29, 1901, C&A Letterbooks, Vol. 102, 212–16, 252.

23. A. C. Tonner to G. W. H. Stouch, January 25, 1901, C&A Allotment File-OHS; G. W. H. Stouch to Commissioner of Indian Affairs, February 13, 1901, C&A Letterbooks, Vol. 102, 302–303.

24. W. A. Jones to G. W. H. Stouch, July 19, 1901, C&A Allotments File-OHS; G. W. H. Stouch to Commissioner of Indian Affairs, August 9, 1900, enclosing statement relative to affidavit made by John Washee, regarding alleged double allotment made to Ella Romero, C&A Letterbooks, Vol. 103, 242–43, 247–48.

25. G. W. H. Stouch to J. W. Scothorn, June 11, 1902, G. W. H. Stouch to Commissioner of Indian Affairs, November 25, 1902, C&A Letterbooks, Vol. 109, 279–80, Vol. 117, 118–20.

26. W. A. Jones to G. W. H. Stouch, November 10, 1902, C&A Allotments File-OHS; G. W. H. Stouch to Commissioner of Indian Affairs, March 20, 1903, C&A Letterbooks, Vol. 117, 323–27.

27. G. W. H. Stouch to Commissioner of Indian Affairs, August 12, 1901, and Statement of Nat Murphy before G. W. H. Stouch, n.d., C&A Letterbooks, Vol. 103, 267–69, 282–83.

28. 32 *Stats.*, 275; *Report, Commissioner of Indian Affairs, 1902*, 64–66; Watonga *Republican*, March 6, 1902.

29. G. W. H. Stouch to Commissioner of Indian Affairs, August 27, September 5, 1902, C&A Letterbooks, Vol. 121, 478–79, Vol. 116, 414–16.

30. G. W. H. Stouch to Ebenezer Kingsley, August 4, 1902, G. W. H. Stouch to C. H. Ruckman, August 25, 1902, C&A Letterbooks, Vol. 110, 266–67, 332.

31. G. W. H. Stouch to E. E. Blake, August 29, 1902, G. W. H. Stouch to Commissioner of Indian Affairs, October 14, 1902, G. W. H. Stouch to R. P. Carpenter, September 8, 1902, A. W. Hurley, Acting Agent to E. L. Hotchkiss, September 22, 1902, G. W. H. Stouch to J. A. LaBryer and John L. Bullen, December 16, 1902, C&A Letterbooks, Vol. 110, 391–92, 431, Vol. 111, 24, Vol. 112, 72–73, 74–75, Vol. 117, 31–32; H. Clay Willis to B. E. White, November 30, 1903, Cheyenne and Arapaho Land Sales File, Indian Archives, Oklahoma Historical Society, Oklahoma City, Oklahoma.

32. *Report, Commissioner of Indian Affairs, 1903*, 45–47.

33. G. W. H. Stouch to Commissioner of Indian Affairs, January 25, 1904; G. W. H. Stouch to J. F. Sharp, January 4, 1904, G. W. H. Stouch to J. R. Henderson, January 4, 1904, G. W. H. Stouch to G. W. Bellamy, May 24, 1904, C&A Letterbooks, Vol. 129, 440–42, Vol. 123, 215, 216, Vol. 125, 31–32; *Report, Commissioner of Indian Affairs, 1904*, 62–66.

34. G. W. H. Stouch to Governor of Oklahoma Territory, August 9, 1904, G. W. H. Stouch to Roy Caton, August 9, 1904, C&A Letterbooks, Vol. 125, 425, 428–32.

35. Stouch received the new title after the agency had been divided on November 30, 1903, into three jurisdictions. One continued at Darlington, and the other two were at Colony and Cantonment, so that the administrative responsibilities formerly controlled by Stouch were shared with two other superintendents.

36. *Report, Commissioner of Indian Affairs, 1904*, 63; W. A. Jones to Indian Agents and other Officers in Charge of Agencies, September 16, 1904, Cheyenne and Arapaho Federal Relations File, Indian Archives, Oklahoma Historical Society, Oklahoma City, Oklahoma, hereafter cited as C&A Federal Relations File-OHS; G. W. H. Stouch to Commissioner of Indian Affairs, November 29, 1904, C&A Letterbooks, Vol. 131, 15–16.

37. G. W. H. Stouch to Commissioner of Indian Affairs, November 29, December 13, 1904, C&A Letterbooks, Vol. 131, 15–16, 38–40; El Reno *Democrat*, November 24, December 1, 1904; W. A. Jones to G. W. H. Stouch, November 19, 1904, F. E. Leupp to Byron E. White, January 5, 1905, C&A Land Sales File-OHS.

38. G. W. H. Stouch to Western National Bank, Oklahoma City, Oklahoma, December 15, 1904, G. W. H. Stouch to Commissioner of Indian Affairs, February 13, 1905, C&A Letterbooks, Vol. 126, 398–400, Vol. 131, 97.

39. Byron E. White to Commissioner of Indian Affairs, January 25, 1905, C&A Letterbooks-Cantonment, Vol. 19, 275–76; C. F. Larrabee, Acting Commissioner to Superintendent, Cantonment Indian School, October 5, 1906,

Cheyenne and Arapaho Instructions to Agents File, Indian Archives, Oklahoma Historical Society, Oklahoma City, Oklahoma, hereafter cited as C&A Instructions to Agents File-OHS.

40. W. A. Jones to G. W. H. Stouch, January 6, 1902 (Copy), C&A Letterbooks, Vol. 107, 184–85.

41. W. A. Jones to U.S. Indian Agent, Cheyenne and Arapaho Agency, January 13, 1902, A. C. Tonner, Acting Commissioner to U.S. Indian Agent, Cheyenne and Arapaho Agency, March 11, 1902, C&A Federal Relations File-OHS; Report of Mary E. Lyons, February, May, 1902, C&A Field Matron File-OHS.

42. G. W. H. Stouch to those in charge of Issue Stations, January 7, 1902, Instructions to Agents File; Horace E. Wilson to G. W. H. Stouch, April 9, 1902, C&A Letterbooks-Cantonment, Vol. 9, 171–72.

43. Crow Chief to G. W. H. Stouch, June 25, 1902, C&A Allotments File-OHS; G. W. H. Stouch to Commissioner of Indian Affairs, January 2, 4, 1903, C&A Letterbooks, Vol. 115, 114–16, 119–20.

44. G. W. H. Stouch to J. M. Tyler, December 30, 1902, G. W. H. Stouch to Commissioner of Indian Affairs, March 6, 1903, C&A Letterbooks, Vol. 112, 151, Vol. 115, 307–17.

45. W. A. Jones to Superintendent, Cantonment School, August 26, 1903, C&A Farming File-OHS.

46. G. W. H. Stouch to Commissioner of Indian Affairs, September 25, 1903, C&A Letterbooks, Vol. 129, 207–208; El Reno *Democrat*, April 30, May 14, 1903.

47. G. W. H. Stouch to Agency Farmers, January 25, April 26, 1900, C&A Farming File-OHS; W. A. Jones to U.S. Indian Agent, Cheyenne and Arapaho Agency, January 4, 1902 (Copy), C&A Letterbooks, Vol. 107, 187.

48. G. W. H. Stouch to George E. Coleman, April 9, 28, 1900, C&A Letterbooks, Vol. 87, 413–14, 473–74.

49. G. W. H. Stouch to Judge Irwin, G. W. H. Stouch to G. E. Coleman, April 28, 1900, C&A Letterbooks, Vol. 87, 473–74, 475.

50. G. W. H. Stouch to Charles W. Ruckman, November 21, 1902, G. W. H. Stouch to Commissioner of Indian Affairs, December 20, 1902, C&A Letterbooks, Vol. 111, 458, Vol. 117, 156.

51. G. W. H. Stouch to Commissioner of Indian Affairs, April 9, May 7, 1903, C&A Letterbooks, Vol. 117, 357–59, 404–407.

52. *Report, Commissioner of Indian Affairs, 1903*, 251, 253–54; Thomas Otterby to Jessie T. Witcher, June 30, 1904, John M. Tyler to G. W. H. Stouch, June 28, 1904, C&A Farming File-OHS.

53. Cheyenne *Sunbeam*, December 20, 1901; *Report, Commissioner of Indian Affairs, 1901*, 316–17.

54. *Report, Commissioner of Indian Affairs, 1903*, 245–46, 253–54.

55. *Ibid., 1903*, 253–54.

56. J. H. Seger to Byron E. White, July 20, 1903, Cheyenne and Arapaho Dances File, Indian Archives, Oklahoma Historical Society, Oklahoma City,

Oklahoma, hereafter cited as C&A Dances File-OHS. Red Leggings or Red Leggins was probably allotted as Red Leg.

57. A. C. Tonner to B. E. White, August 11, 1903, J. H. Seger to B. E. White, August 6, November 18, 1903, G. W. H. Stouch to B. E. White, October 1, 31, 1903, W. A. Jones to B. E. White, November 11, 1903, C&A Dances File-OHS.

CHAPTER XI

1. *Report, Commissioner of Indian Affairs, 1905*, 1–12.

2. *Ibid.*, 30–32, 61.

3. *Ibid.*, 294–95.

4. G. W. H. Stouch to Horace Speed, August 2, 16, 23, 1905, C&A Letterbooks, Vol. 128, 329–32, 422–23, 459.

5. B. E. White to H. Speed, October 28, 1905, C&A Letterbooks-Cantonment, Vol. 20, 352–53.

6. J. W. Scothorn to G. W. H. Stouch, August 31, 1905 (Copy), C&A Letterbooks, Vol. 131, 376–80.

7. G. W. H. Stouch to James Frame, May 17, 1906, C&A Letterbooks, Vol. 137, 128–29.

8. Henry C. North and Fieldy Sweezy were Arapahoes and Thomas Otterby was a Cheyenne serving as additional farmers. John Logan to G. W. H. Stouch, July 10, 1906, Charles W. Ruckman to G. W. H. Stouch, July 10, 1906, H. C. North to G. W. H. Stouch, July 10, 1906, Fieldy Sweezy to G. W. H. Stouch, July 11, 1906, Thomas Otterby to G. W. H. Stouch, July 12, 1906, Jesse L. Witcher to G. W. H. Stouch, July 14, 1906, C&A Farming File-OHS.

9. G. W. H. Stouch to Merrill E. Gates, Secretary, United States Board of Indian Commissioners, November 20, 1905, C&A Letterbooks, Vol. 135, 372–73; *Cong. Rec.*, 58 Cong., 3 Sess., February 27, 1905, 3518.

10. *Cong. Rec.*, 59 Cong., 1 Sess., March 9, 1906, 3601.

11. *Report, Commissioner of Indian Affairs, 1906*, 1, 27–30, 38.

12. *Ibid.*, 94, 97, 104, 303.

13. C. E. Shell to Commissioner of Indian Affairs, August 13, 1906, C. E. Shell to C. C. Brannon, October 4, 1906, Homer J. Bible to C. E. Shell, October 26, 1906, C&A Letterbooks, Vol. 138, 5, 344, 468; B. E. White to William E. Johnson, September 24, 1906, C&A Letterbooks-Cantonment, Vol. 24, 341–42; W. E. Johnson to Shell, October 3, 1906, Cheyenne and Arapaho Vices File, Indian Archives, Oklahoma Historical Society, Oklahoma City, Oklahoma, hereafter cited as C&A Vices File-OHS.

14. C. E. Shell to W. E. Johnson, November 15, 1906, C. E. Shell to Friends of Temperance, Kingfisher, Oklahoma Territory, December 20, 1906, C&A Letterbooks, Vol. 139, 102, 291.

15. C. E. Shell to W. E. Johnson, January 7, 1907, C. E. Shell, to Rev. C. C. Brannon, February 15, 1907, C&A Letterbooks, Vol. 139, 402, Vol. 140, 128; J. P. Logan to C. E. Shell, April 1, 2, 1907, C&A Vices File-OHS.

16. C. E. Shell to W. E. Johnson, July 19, 1907, C&A Letterbooks, Vol. 142, 190.

17. Charles W. Ruckman to C. E. Shell, August 7, 1907, Charlie Jackson to C. E. Shell, August 10, 1907, C&A Vices File-OHS.

18. Louis E. McKnight to C. E. Shell, August 24, 1906 (Copy), October 3, 1906 (Copy), C. E. Shell to Commissioner of Indian Affairs, October 5, 1906, C&A Letterbooks, Vol. 146, 152, 153, 150–51.

19. C. E. Shell to Commissioner of Indian Affairs, October 13, 1906, C. E. Shell to Horace B. Pritner, October 19, 1906, C&A Letterbooks, Vol. 146, 163–64, Vol. 148, 59.

20. C. E. Shell to Commissioner of Indian Affairs, February 2, 1907, C&A Letterbooks, Vol. 146, 147–48.

21. C. E. Shell to George Balenti, February 9, 1907, C. E. Shell to W. L. Baxter, February 15, 1907, C&A Letterbooks, Vol. 140, 87–88, 134–35.

22. C. E. Shell to W. H. Criley, February 4, 1907, C&A Letterbooks, Vol. 140, 141–42.

23. C. E. Shell to John P. Logan, January 17, 1907, C. E. Shell to George A. Moon, January 25, 1907, C. E. Shell to Additional Farmers, January 26, 1907, C&A Letterbooks, Vol. 148, 319–20, 409, 415–16.

24. C. E. Shell to Commissioner of Indian Affairs, January 31, 1907, C&A Letterbooks, Vol. 148, 481–83.

25. C. E. Shell to Commissioner of Indian Affairs, May 10, 1907, C. E. Shell to Additional Farmers, May 10, 1907, C&A Letterbooks, Vol. 149, 490, 491–92.

26. C. E. Shell to John Embry, June 3, July 16, 27, 1907, C&A Letterbooks, Vol. 150, 118, 351, 413; John Embry to C. E. Shell, August 5, 1907, Cheyenne and Arapaho Courts File, Indian Archives, Oklahoma Historical Society, Oklahoma City, Oklahoma, hereafter cited as C&A Courts File-OHS.

27. C. E. Shell to John Embry, August 8, 1907, C. E. Shell to Commissioner of Indian Affairs, August 8, 1907, C&A Letterbooks, Vol. 150, 473–74, 489–91.

28. C. F. Larrabee, Acting Commissioner to C. E. Shell, September 16, 1907 (Telegram), Cheyenne and Arapaho Files, Sec. F., Case 1, Drawer A, Oklahoma Historical Society, Oklahoma City, Oklahoma; C. E. Shell to Major Goe, Commandant, Fort Reno, October 4, 1907, C. E. Shell to C. W. Ruckman, August 12, 1907, September 22, 1907, C. E. Shell to John Embry, September 4, 26, 1907, Homer J. Bibb, Clerk in Charge, Cheyenne and Arapaho Agency, to J. P. Logan, October 12, 1907, H. J. Bibb to C. W. Ruckman, October 25, 1907, H. J. Bibb to John Embry, October 29, 1907, C&A Letterbooks, Vol. 143, 159–60, Vol. 150, 487, Vol. 151, 8, 124, 168, 186, 202–203, 258–59, 295, 324.

29. C. E. Shell to C. W. Ruckman, June 13, 1907, and a preliminary list, C&A Letterbooks, Vol. 150, 172–73, 317; C. E. Shell to Commissioner of

Indian Affairs, December 28, 1907, C. F. Larrabee, Acting Commissioner to Superintendent in Charge, Cheyenne and Arapaho Agency, C&A–CF–6907–1908–127, 3228–1908–127, RBIA.

30. C. E. Shell to Commissioner of Indian Affairs, October 19, 1906, February 20, 1907, C&A Letterbooks, Vol. 146, 179, 345.

31. C. E. Shell to Commissioner of Indian Affairs, April 3, May 6, 1907, C&A Letterbooks, Vol. 146, 408, 463–64.

32. El Reno *Democrat*, April 21, 1904, C. E. Shell to Commissioner of Indian Affairs, February 8, 22, July 25, September 20, October 7, 1907, C&A Letterbooks, Vol. 146, 325–26, 395–96, Vol. 147, 120–21, Vol. 151, 182, 241–42; C&A-CF-96389-1907-312-RBIA.

33. C. E. Shell to Commissioner of Indian Affairs, March 26, 1907, C&A Letterbooks, Vol. 146, 395–96, Vol. 147, 137.

34. C. E. Shell to H. J. Bibb, October 17, 1907, Cheyenne and Arapaho Agents and Agency File, Indian Archives, Oklahoma Historical Society, Oklahoma City, Oklahoma, hereafter cited as C&A Agents and Agency File-OHS; *Report, Commissioner of Indian Affairs, 1907*, 63, 64.

35. C. W. Ruckman to G. W. H. Stouch, July 10, 1906, C&A Farming File-OHS; *Report, Commissioner of Indian Affairs, 1907*, 303.

36. R. S. Connell to B. E. White, July 24, 1906, C&A Vices File-OHS; C. E. Shell to R. S. Connell, August 8, 1906, C&A Letterbooks, Vol. 138, 25; Interview of Jess Rowlodge by Julia A. Jordan, December 5, 1967, T-169 (Typescript), 8, IOHC, UOL. Perhaps some of the confusion between mescal beans and peyote occurred because the former are associated with peyote ritual and are worn in strings in a bandolier fashion, see, Interview of Jess Rowlodge by David Jones, July 28, 1968, T-125 (Typescript), 37, IOHC-UOL.

37. Thomas Otterby to C. E. Shell, February 4, 6, 1907, C&A Vices File-OHS.

38. D. K. Cunningham to C. E. Shell, February 11, 1907, C&A Vices File-OHS.

39. The petition is undated and located in the C&A Vices File-OHS.

40. C. E. Shell to D. K. Cunningham, February 12, 1907, C&A Letterbooks, Vol. 140, 109–10.

41. C. E. Shell to James L. Mooney, February 12, 1907, C. E. Shell to Rev. C. C. Brannon, February 15, 1907, C&A Letterbooks, Vol. 140, 108, 128; Originals of many of the documents cited on peyote are in the Records of the Bureau of Indian Affairs, Central Classified Files 2989–1908–126, Pt. 3, Record Group 75, National Archives Building, hereafter cited as CCF–2989–1908–126, Pt. 3, RBIA.

42. Thomas Otterby to C. E. Shell, February 11, 13, 1907, George L. Bowman to C. E. Shell, February 11, 13, 15, 1907, C&A Vices File-OHS.

43. C. E. Shell to Thomas Otterby, February 15, 1907, C. E. Shell to George L. Bowman, February 16, 1907, C&A Letterbooks, Vol. 140, 129–30, 142; Robert Hamilton to C. E. Shell, February 20, 1907, C&A Vices File-OHS.

44. G. L. Bowman to C. E. Shell, March 1, 1907 (Copy), CCF–2989–1908–

126, Pt. 3, RBIA, C. E. Shell to G. L. Bowman, March 4, 1907, C&A Letterbooks, Vol. 140, 256; W. E. Johnson to C. E. Shell, March 6, 1907, C&A Vices File-OHS.

45. C. E. Shell to Thomas Otterby, March 4, 8, 1907, C&A Letterbooks, Vol. 140, 255, 287.

46. Thomas Otterby to C. E. Shell, March 1, 1907, C&A Vices File-OHS; *Cheyenne Transporter*, July 12, 1883, June 30, July 15, 1885.

47. C. E. Shell to W. E. Johnson, March 8, 1907, C&A Letterbooks, Vol. 140, 288; Thomas Otterby to C. E. Shell, March 12, 1907, C&A Vices File-OHS.

48. C. E. Shell to W. E. Johnson, March 8, April 22, 1907, C. E. Shell to R. S. Connell, May 2, 1907, C. E. Shell to Rev. C. C. Brannon, May 2, 1907, C&A Letterbooks, Vol. 140, 288, Vol. 141, 120, 185, 187; R. C. Preston to W. E. Johnson, April 13, 1907, Memorandum, unsigned, dated May 11, 1907, CCF–2989–1908–126, Pt. 3, RBIA.

49. C. E. Shell to Thomas Otterby, May 2, 1907, C. E. Shell to J. P. Blackman, July 7, 1907, C. E. Shell to Roy Hadsell, Registrar, University of Oklahoma, July 9, 1907, C&A Letterbooks, Vol. 141, 183, Vol. 142, 119–20, 123.

50. C. E. Shell to W. D. Leonard, July 13, 1907, C. E. Shell to Commissioner of Indian Affairs, July 15, 1907, C&A Letterbooks, Vol. 142, 156–57, Vol. 147, 112–13; W. E. Johnson to C. E. Shell, September 4, 1907, C&A Vices File-OHS.

51. C. E. Shell to J. R. Eddy, August 14, 1907, C. E. Shell to W. E. Johnson, June 16, 1908, C&A Letterbooks, Vol. 142, 500, Vol. 155, 313; for the petition to Congress, see undated petition, [ca. September, 1907], C&A Vices File-OHS.

52. C. E. Shell to Fieldy Sweezy, March 8, 1907, C. E. Shell to Bert Frazier, April 27, 1907, C. E. Shell to Coyote, May 4, 1907, C&A Letterbooks, Vol. 140, 286, Vol. 141, 141, 197.

Bibliography

I. ARCHIVAL MATERIALS

1. *El Reno, Oklahoma*

El Reno Public Library
  Cheyenne and Arapaho Agency, Letterbooks.

2. *Fort Worth, Texas*

Federal Records Center
  Cheyenne and Arapaho Subagency, Concho, Oklahoma.

3. *Norman, Oklahoma*

University of Oklahoma Library, Western History Collections
  The Doris Duke Indian Oral History Collection, Volumes 1–8, 23–25.
  Transcripts.

4. *North Newton, Kansas*

Bethel College Library
  H. R. Voth Collection.

5. *Oklahoma City, Oklahoma*

Oklahoma Historical Society
  Cheyenne and Arapaho Agency, Agents and Agency File.
  Cheyenne and Arapaho Agency, Allotments File.
  Cheyenne and Arapaho Agency, Courts File.
  Cheyenne and Arapaho Agency, Dances File.
  Cheyenne and Arapaho Agency, Employees File.
  Cheyenne and Arapaho Agency, Farming File.
  Cheyenne and Arapaho Agency, Federal Relations File.

Cheyenne and Arapaho Agency, Field Matron File.
Cheyenne and Arapaho Agency, Foreign Relations File.
Cheyenne and Arapaho Agency, George Bent File.
Cheyenne and Arapaho Agency, Guardianship File.
Cheyenne and Arapaho Agency, Indian Homes File.
Cheyenne and Arapaho Agency, Instructions to Agents File.
Cheyenne and Arapaho Agency, John H. Seger File.
Cheyenne and Arapaho Agency, Land Sales File.
Cheyenne and Arapaho Agency, Lawlessness File.
Cheyenne and Arapaho Agency, Letterbooks.
Cheyenne and Arapaho Agency, Letterbooks, Cantonment.
Cheyenne and Arapaho Agency, Romero File.
Cheyenne and Arapaho Agency, Schools File.
Cheyenne and Arapaho Agency, Taxes File.
Cheyenne and Arapaho Agency, Vices File.

6. Topeka, Kansas

Kansas State Historical Society
John A. Martin Papers.
Samuel J. Crawford Papers.

7. Washington, D.C.

Library of Congress
Grover Cleveland Papers.
National Archives
Records of the Department of the Interior.
Office of the Secretary of the Interior, Indian Division, Letters Received.
Office of the Secretary of the Interior, Indian Division, Letters Sent.
Records of the Bureau of Indian Affairs
Central Superintendency, Field Office Files, Letters Received.
Central Superintendency, Field Office Files, Letters Sent.
Central Superintendency, Letters Received.
Cheyenne and Arapaho Agency, Classified Files.
Cheyenne and Arapaho Agency, Letters Received.
Office of the Commissioner of Indian Affairs, Letters Sent.
Office of Indian Affairs, Central Classified Files.
Office of Indian Affairs, Inspector's Files.
Office of Indian Affairs, Irregular Shaped Papers.
Office of Indian Affairs, Letters Sent.

Office of Indian Affairs, Special Case 9.
Office of Indian Affairs, Special Case 147.
Office of Indian Affairs, Special Case 191.
Records of the War Department.
United States Army Commands, District of the Missouri, Cantonment, Letters Sent.

II. GOVERNMENT DOCUMENTS

1. *Congressional*

Report of the Board of Indian Commissioners. 1875–1907.
Report of the Commissioner of Indian Affairs. 1875–1907.
House Executive Documents: 49 Cong., 2 sess., *No. 10*; 52 Cong., 1 sess., *No. 10*; 52 Cong., 1 sess., *No. 198*; 57 Cong., 1 sess., *No. 391.*
House. *Hearings Before a Subcommittee of the Committee on Indian Affairs of House of Representatives on H. R. 2614, Peyote.* 65 Cong., 2 sess. [1918].
House Report: 51 Cong., 1 sess., *No. 3441.*
Senate Executive Documents: 48 Cong., 1 sess., *No. 13*; 48 Cong., 1 sess., *No. 54*; 48 Cong., 2 sess., *No. 16*; 48 Cong., 2 sess., *No. 17*; 51 Cong., 2 sess., *No. 1*, Vol. 1.
Senate Report: 49 Cong., 1 sess., *No. 1278.*

2. *General Documents*

Congressional Record. 1875–1907.
Kappler, Charles J., comp. and ed. *Indian Affairs: Laws and Treaties.* 4 vols. Washington, 1904, 1913, 1927.
Record of Engagements with Hostile Indians Within the Military Division of the Missouri from 1868 to 1882. Washington, 1882.
Richardson, James D., comp. *A Compilation of the Messages and Papers of the Presidents, 1789–1908.* Washington, 1909.
Statutes of Oklahoma. Guthrie, Oklahoma, 1893.
Territory of Oklahoma. *Session Laws of 1897.* Guthrie, Oklahoma, 1897.
United States Statutes at Large. Vols. 15, 18, 24, 25, 32.

III. NEWSPAPERS

Arapahoe, Oklahoma, *Arrow.*
Arapahoe, Oklahoma, *Bee.*
Caldwell, Kansas, *Barber County Index.*

Caldwell, Kansas, *Journal*.
Cheyenne, Oklahoma, *Sunbeam*.
Darlington, Indian Territory, *Cheyenne Transporter*.
El Reno, Oklahoma, *Democrat*.
El Reno, Oklahoma, *Oklahoma Democrat*.
Guthrie, Oklahoma, *State Capital*.
Kansas City, Missouri, *Evening Star*.
Kansas City, Missouri, *Star*.
Kansas City, Missouri, *Times*.
Kingfisher, Oklahoma, *Free Press*.
Kingfisher, Oklahoma, *Reformer*.
Oklahoma City, Oklahoma, *Evening Oklahoma Gazette*.
Oklahoma City, Oklahoma, *Oklahoma Gazette*.
Topeka, Kansas, *Capital*.
Watonga, Oklahoma, *Republican*.
Wichita, Kansas, *Eagle*.

IV. Theses and Dissertations

Botkin, Samuel Lee. "The Protestant Episcopal Church in Oklahoma, 1835–1941." Ph.D. dissertation, University of Oklahoma, 1957.
Chesnut, Glen Raleigh. "A History of the Ghost Dance Religion Among the Indian Tribes of Western Oklahoma." M.A. thesis, University of Oklahoma, 1960.
Cornett, Lloyd H., Jr. "Leasing and Utilization of Land of the Cheyenne and Arapaho Indians, 1891–1907." M.A. thesis, University of Oklahoma, 1954.
Wilson, Terry Paul. "Panaceas for Progress: Efforts to Educate the Southern Cheyennes and Arapahoes, 1870–1908." M.A. thesis, University of Oklahoma, 1965.
Wright, Peter Melton. "Fort Reno, Indian Territory, 1874–1885." M.A. thesis, University of Oklahoma, 1965.

V. Books and Articles

Berthrong, Donald J. "Cattlemen on the Cheyenne-Arapaho Reservation," *Arizona and the West*, Vol. XIII, No. 1 (Spring, 1971), 5–32.
———. *The Southern Cheyennes*. Norman, 1963.
———. "White Neighbors Come Among the Southern Cheyenne and Arapaho," *Kansas Quarterly*, Vol. III, No. 4 (Fall, 1971), 105–15.

Cohen, Felix S. *Handbook of Federal Indian Law*. Washington, 1945.
Cohoe. *A Cheyenne Sketchbook*. Commentary by E. Adamson Hoebel and Karen Daniels Peterson. Norman, 1964.
Dale, Edward E. "Ranching on the Cheyenne-Arapaho Reservation, 1880–1885," *Chronicles of Oklahoma*, Vol. VI (March, 1928), 38–59.
———. "History of the Ranch Cattle Industry in Oklahoma," *Annual Report of the American Historical Association for the Year 1920*, 309–22.
Debo, Angie. *A History of the Indians of the United States*. Norman, 1970.
Dorsey, George A. *The Arapaho Sun Dance: The Ceremony of the Offerings Lodge*. Field Columbian Museum *Publication No. 75, Anthropological Series*, IV. Chicago, 1903.
———. *The Cheyenne: The Sun Dance*. Field Columbian Museum *Publicaton No. 103, Anthropological Series*, Vol. IX, No. 2. Chicago, May, 1905.
Driver, Harold E. *Indians of North America*. Chicago, 1961.
Fritz, Henry E. *The Movement for Indian Assimilation, 1860–1890*. Philadelphia, 1963.
Gibson, Arrell M. *Oklahoma: A History of Five Centuries*. Norman, 1965.
Gittinger, Roy. *The Formation of the State of Oklahoma, 1803–1906*. Norman, 1939.
Hagan, William T. *American Indians*. Chicago, 1961.
———. "Private Property, the Indian's Door to Civilization," *Ethnohistory*, Vol. III, No. 2 (Spring, 1956), 126–37.
Hodge, Frederick W., ed. *Handbook of Indians North of Mexico*. Bureau of American Ethnology, *Bulletin No. 30*. 2 vols. Washington, 1910.
Josephy, Alvin M., Jr. *The Indian Heritage of America*. New York, 1968.
La Barre, Weston. *The Peyote Cult*. New edition. Hamden, Connecticut, 1964.
Llewellyn, Karl N., and E. Adamson Hoebel. *The Cheyenne Way*. Norman, 1941.
McReynolds, Edwin C. *Oklahoma: A History of the Sooner State*. Norman, 1954.
Mooney, James. *The Ghost-Dance Religion and the Sioux Outbreak of 1890. Fourteenth Annual Report of the Bureau of American Ethnology*. Washington, 1896.
Painter, C. C. *Cheyennes and Arapahoes Revisited and a Statement of Their Contract with Attorneys*. Philadelphia, 1893.

Powell, Peter J. *Sweet Medicine*. 2 vols. Norman, 1969.

Pratt, Richard A. *Battlefield and Classroom: Four Decades with the American Indian, 1867–1904.* Ed. by Robert M. Utley. New Haven, Connecticut, 1964.

Priest, Loring B. *Uncle Sam's Stepchildren: The Reformation of United States Indian Policy, 1865–1887.* New Brunswick, New Jersey, 1942.

Prucha, Francis Paul, ed. *Americanizing the American Indian: Writings by "Friends of the Indians," 1880–1900.* Cambridge, Mass., 1973.

Royce, Charles C. *Indian Land Cessions in the United States.* Bureau of American Ethnology, *Eighteenth Annual Report*, Part 2. Washington, 1899.

Sandoz, Mari. *Cheyenne Autumn.* New York, 1953.

Seger, John H. *Early Days Among the Cheyennes and Arapahoes.* Ed. by Stanley Vestal. Norman, 1934.

Slotkin, J. S. *The Peyote Religion.* Glencoe, Illinois, 1956.

Stands in Timber, John and Margot Liberty. *Cheyenne Memories.* New Haven, Connecticut, 1967.

Sweezy, Carl. *The Arapaho Way: A Memoir of an Indian Boyhood.* New York, 1966.

Trenholm, Virginia Cole. *The Arapahoes: Our People.* Norman, 1970.

Wright, Muriel H. *A Guide to the Indian Tribes of Oklahoma.* Norman, 1951.

Index

Adams, William: 179
Admire, J. V.: 200
Agriculture: 3–4, 44, 48, 57–65, 68, 100,
121, 128–31, 133–35, 141–42, 192, 265;
Indian aversion to, 48, 57–65, 68–69,
73; gardens, 58–59, 64, 66–69, 255,
300; corn, 59, 64, 120, 248, 255, 300;
hay, 62; equipment for, 64; and farm
assistants, 64, 79, 121, 251–53; and
crop failures, 69, 77–78, 248; changes
in, 71; wheat, 139–40; cotton, 255
Ah-tuck: 62
Allotments: 119, 151–52, 161–81, 194;
and dispersal of families, 121; Indian
opposition to, 137; Indians unprepared
for, 146–47; of lands, 168–81, 209; and
alloting agents, 169–76, 184; Indians on,
183; leasing of, 198–204, 266, 269–81,
289; improvement plans for, 233–34;
and farming, 248–56, 265; subleasing
of, 270–72; contested, 276–81; sales of,
281–88, 296–97, 301–302; lease money
from whites for, 305–306; and lease-
program revision, 309, 311
American Board of Commissioners for
Foreign Missions: 119
American Horse: 33
Annuities: *see* rations, annuities
Antelope, Deforest: 227
Antelope, Fenton: 172, 216
Antelope, Hugh: 224
Anti-Saloon League: 304

Arapaho Boarding School: 212, 221
Arapahoe Chief: 18
Arapaho Indians, Northern: 21–24, 46–47,
138
Arapaho Indians, Southern: 3–5, 13, 22,
43, 45, 124, 148–52, 305–306, 327;
government rations to, 4, 7, 9, 11–12,
17–19, 287; health, diseases of, 4–5, 7,
167, 209; as freighters, 11–12, 44, 62–
63, 67–70, 72, 123, 139–40; as traders,
16, 173; population of, 16–18; horse
herds of, stolen, 19–21; return to Darlington, 20–22, 25–26; at Camp Supply,
22; grievances of, 44; and farming, 48,
57–65, 68–69, 73, 91, 120, 130–31,
133–35, 141–42, 192, 248–56, 265,
300&n.; and agency schools, 48, 78–90,
140–43, 145, 228–30; and cattle herds,
59–66, 68, 74–75; houses of, 60; seek
food from Kiowas, 69; more employment sought by, 70, 74–75; and Dawes
Act, 71, 117, 119–20, 133, 146, 148,
152, 161, 182, 328, 337, 339; ration
cuts restored for, 76; and advanced
education, 81–90, 140–43; and cattlemen on reservation, 91–117; dispersal
of, 119–21; under Williams administration, 137; troubled by changes, 138–39;
search of, for Wevoka, 138–39, 150,
183, 215–16; and Ghost Dance, 138–39,
183, 215–16, 293; property of, stolen by
whites, 190–93; taxes on, 193–97; and

allotment leases, 197–204, 266, 269–81, 289; and white business practices, 199–200; voting rights of, 204–206; resistance of, to change, 209–16, 220, 241; and peyote, 216–20, 253, 282, 302–303, 316–24, 326, 339; plural marriages among, 220–25, 252, 254, 336; and whisky, 225, 282, 301–304, 316, 319; policies for, 225–30; land-sale payments, 231–40, 289, 296–97; allotment subleasing by, 270–72; and allotment sales, 281–88, 301–302; and conformity, 288–93; debts of, 297–99; law violations by, 299, 304–305; and Burke Act of 1906, 301–302, 311–15; decline of income of, 325–26

Arapaho Manual Labor and Boarding School: 85
Arbuthnot, Robert L.: 125
Arkansas City, Kans.: 69–70, 149, 163
Armstrong, Frank C.: 108, 113
Arrow, Jennie: 144–45
Ashley, Charles F.: 135–39, 145–46, 150, 163–67, 169–70, 172, 174–75, 179, 181–85, 209, 215–16, 220, 226, 245–46, 249; leasing-statute change sought by, 198
Assiniboine Agency: 44
Atkins, John D. C.: 104

Baldwin, John: 180
Balenti, Belle: 166, 307
Balenti, George: in leasing program dissent, 306–308
Balenti, John: 307–308
Balenti, Michael: 166, 199–200, 307
Balenti, William: 307
Ballamy, Sen. George W.: 219
Ballew, T. J.: 298
Barnes, C. M., territorial governor: 219
Bear Robe: 69, 106–107, 270–71
Bear Shield: 25
Beaver Creek: 5–6, 13, 17, 23
Beaver Woman: 279
Beede, Cyrus: 6
Bent, George: 13, 32, 92, 109–10, 136, 166, 204, 221, 225, 308
Bent, Jesse: 166

Bent, Julia: 221
Bent, Robert: 8, 92, 109, 122
Bent, William: 8
Bent's Fort: 8
Big Back: 58
Big Belly: 222
Big Chief: 9
Biggert, William: 179
Big Head: 40, 122
Big Horse: 60, 75, 78, 83, 85, 100, 108
Big Knee: 282–83
Big Man: 75
Big Mouth: 20, 69, 75, 94
Big White Man: 186–87
Black, Jennie: 145
Black, John F.: 136
Black, Robert: 288
Black Bear: 37
Black Bull: 222
Black Coyote: 69, 100, 138, 186
Black Horse: 33
Black Kettle: 83, 316
Black Man: 192
Blackman, J. P.: 322
Blacksmith (Buffalo Cow with Calf): 40–41
Black Wolf: 43–44, 128
Blaine County, Okla.: 196, 224, 229, 280, 311
Bland, T. A.: 113–14
Blind, Lula: 221–22
Bloom, Bernard: 307
Board of Indian Commissioners: 78, 118–19
Board of Mennonite Missions: 86
Bob Tail: 121
Bobtail Coyote: 207
Boomer movement: 119–20
Bowman, George L.: 319
Boynton, Paul: 166, 199–200, 313–14
Brannon, Rev. C. C.: 319, 322
Breeding, W. S.: 186–87
Broken Cup: 31, 80
Brooks, Caleb R. (United States attorney): 196, 206
Brown, Charles (Oklahoma territorial attorney general): 194

Browning, D. M. (Indian commissioner): 201, 212, 237, 251
Buckley, F. C.: 9, 11
Buffalo Chief: 145
Buffaloes: 3–8, 11–13, 16–18, 34, 48, 60, 69–70; last hunt for, 18–19
Buffalo Medicine Man, Kiowas': 69
Buffalo Station: 22
Bull Bear: 78, 83, 212, 338
Bull Bear, Jock: 283
Bull Coming Up: 45
Bull Telling Tales: 132
Bull Tongue: 295
Bureau of Indian Affairs: 8, 11–13, 34, 63–64, 102, 199–200, 207–208, 220, 223, 229, 231, 269–70, 273–74, 277, 281, 305, 323; and allotments, 118–19; and lease costs, 203; and farm aid, 251
Burgess, Minerva: 314–15
Burke, Rep. Charles H.: 301
Burke Act (1906): 301–302, 326, 337; and patents, 311–15
Burns, Robert: 174, 288
Burnt-All-Over: 133, 213
Butler, N. W.: 205–206

Cache Creek: 70
Caddo Indians: 13, 59, 176
Caddo Springs: 81–83, 105
Calumet, Okla.: 303–304, 307
Campbell, B. H.: 93–95
Campbell, C. E.: 38, 83
Camp Robinson: 40
Camp Supply: *see* Fort Supply
Canadian County, Okla.: 193, 196, 222, 243, 299, 311, 315
Cannon, Joseph G.: 136
Cantonment, Okla.: 39, 44, 65, 69, 82, 90–91, 94, 97–98, 100–102, 110–11, 121, 124, 128–29, 134, 162, 169, 175, 189, 211–14, 217, 220, 225, 226, 232, 244, 248, 250, 267–69, 273, 284, 286–87, 298, 318; trouble at, 107–108; Cheyenne schools at, 140–44
Cantonment Mission School: 226, 268
Carlisle Institute (Pennsylvania): 66, 81, 82–89, 106, 140, 142–43, 145–46, 188, 199, 215, 220–21, 227, 230, 232, 285,

290, 298, 306, 312, 316, 324, 337
Carr, Lieut.-Col. Eugene A.: 22
Carter, Thomas H.: 178
Carter, T. S.: 186–87
Caton, Roy: 282–83
Cattle: Arapaho herd of, 59–60, 68; for Cheyennes and Arapahoes, 59–66, 68; school (mission) herd of, 61–62, 65–66, 74, 80; and herd development, 77–78; and forage shortage, 248; *see also* cattlemen, John H. Seger, white settlers
Cattlemen: 8–9, 132–33, 185, 272, 328; cattle seized from, 9–11; and reservation grazing rights, 76–77, 176; on reservation, 91–117; and leases, 96–98, 110–13; and licensing, 98, 103–104, 114; and cattle-drive incident, 100–102; and Dog Soldiers, 102–103; herds of, plundered, 106; licensing of, ended, 108; licensees evicted, 113, 176–77; reservation free of, 118, 120–21; and open range, 204–208; *see also* white settlers
Cedar Tree: 145
Cedar Woman: 282
Central Superintendency, Lawrence, Kans.: 27, 60
Chalk (Arapaho scout): 34
Chapman, Amos: 34–35, 40–41, 44, 98, 101, 166–67, 184
Cherokee Indians: 76, 93; and land sales, 149
Cherokee Outlet: 4, 72, 75–76, 93–94, 148–51, 163–65
Chewing Gum (Indian): 33
Cheyenne and Arapaho Cattle Company: 111
Cheyenne-Arapaho Agency: *see* Cheyenne-Arapaho Reservation
Cheyenne-Arapaho Manual Training and Labor School: 61; *see also* John H. Seger
Cheyenne-Arapaho Reservation: 27–32, 47, 120, 139, 328; and cattlemen, 91–117; leases on, 96–98, 110–13; licensing, 98, 103–104, 114; and cattle-drive incident, 100–102; and license termination, 108; licensees evicted, 113; cattlemen leave, 118–21; unauthorized

persons removed from, 123–26; and "Court of Indian Offenses," 146; and Dawes Act, 148; and land sales, 148–52, 161–81; and cession-agreement protests, 167; land allotments on, 168–81; and white settlers, 182

Cheyenne-Arapaho Transportation Company: 61–62, 64

Cheyenne Boarding School: 105, 222, 227

Cheyenne Indians, Northern: 3, 16, 21, 48, 69, 73, 174, 268; and Pine Ridge Agency, 18; return south, 22–26; moved to Indian Territory, 27–32, 37; population of, 28; food distribution among, 28–29; grievances of, 29–35, 38, 42–43; illness of, 31, 35–37; and agency school, 31–32, 36–39, 42, 79–88; leave reservation, 32–34; refuse to work, 36, 39; rebellion of, 37–41; conciliation of, 41; and clashes with Southern Cheyennes, 43; war talk of, 44–45; bands of, moved north, 46–47; and advanced education, 81–88; lands ceded by, 161–81

Cheyenne Indians, Southern: 3–7, 11, 13, 28, 33, 36–37, 39, 45, 47, 148–52, 183, 305–306, 327, 340; government rations for, 4, 7–9, 11–12, 17–19, 287; health, diseases of, 4–5, 7, 31, 167, 209; as freighters, 11–12, 44, 61–63, 67–70, 123; as traders, 16, 18, 173; population of, 16–18; horse herds of, stolen, 19–21; join northern kinsmen, 21; return to Darlington, 21–26; and clashes with Northern Cheyennes, 43; grievances of, 44; and farming, 48, 57–65, 68–69, 73, 91, 120, 128–31, 133–35, 142, 192, 248–56, 265, 300&n.; and agency schools, 48, 78–90, 140–43, 145, 228–30; houses of, 60, 246–47; and cattle, 59–66, 68, 74–75; more employment sought by, 70, 74–75; and Dawes Act, 71, 117, 119–20, 133, 146, 148, 152, 161, 182, 326, 328, 337, 339; ration cuts restored for, 76; and advanced education, 81–90, 140–43; and white customs, 81; and cattlemen on reservation, 91–117; dispersal of, 119–21; factionalism among, 127–30; chiefs' influence

upon, 133, 338; under Williams administration, 136; troubled by changes, 138–39; and Ghost Dance, 138–39, 183; lands ceded by, 161–83; property of, stolen by whites, 190–93; taxes upon, 193–97; and allotment leases, 197–204, 266, 269–81, 289; and white business practices, 199–200; voting rights of, 204–206; resistance of, to change, 209–16, 220, 241; and peyote, 216–20, 253, 282, 302–303, 316–24, 326, 339; plural marriages among, 220–25, 252, 254, 339; and whisky, 225, 282, 301–304, 316, 319, 326; policies for, 225–30; land-sale payments to, 231–40, 289, 296–97; and allotment subleasing, 270–72; and allotment sales, 281–88, 301–302; and conformity, 288–93; debts of, 297–99; law violations by, 299, 304–305; and Burke Act, 301–302, 311–15, 326; income decline of, 325–26

Chickasaw Nation: 130, 168

Chief Hill camp incident: 186–88

Chilocco, Indian Territory: 140, 230, 337

Chisholm Trail: 11

Choctaw Indians: 168

Cimarron Valley: 70

Clark, Ben: 35, 37, 92, 107–109, 281

Cleveland, Pres. Grover: 112–16

Clinton, Okla.: 322

Cloud Chief: 130, 145, 151, 162–65, 169–70, 173–74, 181, 210

Clover, Seth: 122

Coates, Benjamin: 59

Cohoe's Cheyenne bands: 93

Coleman, George E.: 187, 290–91

Colony, Okla.: 121, 186, 226–27; farms near, 122, 134, 136; see also John H. Seger

Comanche Indians: 6, 96, 121, 134

Coming-in-Sight (Mrs. Rufus Gilbert): 278

Connell, R. S.: 316, 322

Convill, George O.: 273–74

Cook, Philip: 215

Coppinger, Col. J. J.: 177

Corn (Corn-e-o-tah): 276

Cottonwood Grove: 93

Council Fire: 113–14
Covington, J. A.: 5, 18, 62, 64
Crawford, Samuel J.: 148–49, 164, 166, 177–78, 232
Crazy Horse: 21, 23–26
Crazy Mule: 37, 41, 46
Creel, Heber M.: 41
Crook, Gen. George: 26, 34, 38–39
Crow Agency: 46
Crow Chief: 287
Crow Dance: 212
Crow Indian (Northern Cheyenne): 33
Cunningham, D. K.: 317–18, 323
Curley: 68
Curley Hair: 279
Custer County, Okla.: 322
Cut Finger: 69
Cut Nose: 127

Darlington, William F.: 18, 78, 96, 101, 135, 169
Darlington Agency: 3–12, 14–19, 21, 29, 31–33, 35, 38–44, 59–61, 63–64, 68–69, 74–75, 79, 81–92, 94, 100, 104, 108–109, 111, 115, 121, 125, 131, 134, 136–37, 140, 143, 148, 150, 165, 167–70, 184, 193, 196, 200–201, 215, 220–21, 225–27, 234, 241–44, 249, 271, 273, 284, 289–90, 297, 301–303, 306–307, 313, 316, 321; Indian bands move from, 13; bands return to, 18, 20–26; Northern Cheyennes moved to, 27–31, 37; conditions at, 44–45; bands leave, 46–47; Arapaho school at, 140–41
Darlington Boarding School: 269
Daugherty, J. M.: 10
Davis, Richard: 188, 251–53, 320
Dawes, Sen. Henry L.: 119
Dawes Act (1887): 71, 117, 119–20, 133, 146, 148, 152, 161–63, 177–80, 182, 198, 206, 213, 218, 224, 241, 249, 265, 280, 285, 328, 337; and allotments, 231, 270–71; objectives of, fail, 300, 327; modified by Burke Act (1906), 301
Day Woman: 290
Dead Indian Land Act (1902): 280, 295, 315, 337; and allotment sales, 301
Dead Man's Foot: 128

Deaf Woman: 279
Denman, Hampton B.: 94
Department of Indian Affairs: *see* Bureau of Indian Affairs
Department of the Interior: 9, 327; *see also* Bureau of Indian Affairs
Department of the Missouri: 28
Dickey Brothers: 93, 98, 113, 116
Dillon, John D.: 297–98
Dodge, Col. Richard I.: 44, 65
Dog Soldiers: 78, 100–105, 145, 191; decline of, 145–46
Dorsey, George A.: 292–94
Driskell, E. B.: 10
Dry Hide: 25
Dull Knife: 25, 30–31, 33–34, 37–40, 43, 46, 80, 109
Dyer, D. B.: 99, 102, 112–14, 120, 125, 140, 142; and agriculture, 100, 104–105; and grazing licenses, 103–104; and Dog Soldiers, 104–105; and Cantonment trouble, 107–108; suspended, 115–16; and Indian land contract, 148–49&n., 150, 166
Dyer, John C.: 270–71

Edson, Casper: 284
Education, Indian: 3, 225, 228–30; and agency schools, 31–32, 36–39, 42, 48, 61, 78–90, 140–43, 145; off reservation, 81–90, 140–43
Elk Horns: 124
Elk River (Indian): 184, 196
Elk Tongue: 151
El Reno, Okla.: 173, 179, 192, 225, 249, 273, 276–77, 279, 289, 308–309, 312–14
Embry, John (United States attorney): 310
Evans, A. G.: 96, 116
Everest, J. H.: 278

Fargo Wells, Kans.: 109
Fat Bull: 58
Fay, Okla.: 303–304
Feinagle, Joseph: 202
Fenlon, Ed: 62–63, 93–96, 100, 111–12
Fire (Indian): 304
Fitzpatrick, Jack: 92

Fletcher, William: 199, 288
Flying Bird: 269
Flying Hawk: 106, 128
Flynn, Dennis T. (congressional delegate):
    200, 239, 253, 267
Ford, James: 277–78
Fort Elliott: 116
Fort Keogh: 41
Fort Leavenworth: 31
Fort Marion: 81, 85
Fort Peck: 37
Fort Reno: 7–8, 10, 12, 22, 25–26, 28–30,
    33, 35, 37, 39, 42, 45, 74, 81, 101, 104,
    106–108, 115–16, 125, 165, 179, 279,
    310
Fort Sill: 6, 31
Fort Supply: 5, 7, 12–13, 18, 22, 24,
    33–34, 39, 65, 97, 106–107, 116, 166
Foster, Judge Cassius G.: 149
Frame, James: 299
Frass, George: 313
Frazier, Bert: 325
Free Press (Kingfisher): 172
Frost, James: 202, 277

Galpin, S. A.: 12
Gardner, Robert S.: 98–99
Garland, Augustus, attorney general: 112
Geary, Okla.: 297–98, 303–304
Geary, Ed (Edmund Guerrier): 109, 196
General Allotment Act: see Dawes Act
General Land Office: 178
Gentle Horse: 83
Ghost Dance: 138–39, 183, 215–16, 242,
    293
Gillett, Almerin: 40
Good Bear, Paul: 222, 268
Goodsell, William: 290–91, 304–305
Gratzer, E.: 121
Guthrie, Okla.: 173

Haag, Frederick: 308–309
Halstead, Kans.: 87, 141
Hamilton, Rev. Robert: 290, 320
Hammon, Okla.: 230, 250, 268
Hampton Institute, Va.: 81, 84–85, 309
Ha-o-ma-ista (Red Woman): 279
Hariman, Joseph: 20

Harmon, Judson: 206
Hartman, Charles S. (Montana congress-
    man): 212
Haskell Institute, Lawrence, Kans.: 140,
    145–46, 172, 199, 215, 227, 230, 285–
    86, 312, 324, 337
Hatch, Col. John P.: 17
Haury, Rev. S. S.: 86–88, 101, 106–107,
    121, 128, 141; resignation of, 144
Hauser, Amy: 179
Hauser, Annie: 178
Hauser, Herman: 122–23, 176–77
Hauser, Louise: 178
Hauser families: 176–81
Hawk (Cheyenne chief): 110, 294–95
Hawkins, Kish: 315, 321
Hayes, Pres. Rutherford B.: 42
Hayt, E. A.: 33, 40, 63
Heap-of-Birds: 25, 83, 212
Heap-of-Crows: 215
Henderson, J. P.: 149
High Wolf: 190
Hippy (Southern Cheyenne): 45
Hirshler, D. B.: 87
Hoag, Enoch: 4–6, 22
Hog (Northern Cheyenne): 18
Holloway, Jason: 4
Homestead Act: 177
Homesteaders: see white settlers
Horse Back: 106
Horse thieves: 3, 13, 17–21, 110, 129–30
Horton, E. M.: 100–101
Houston, Temple: 267
Howling Crane: 323
Howling Eagle: 25
Howling Wolf: 81, 108, 127, 137, 161,
    189–90
Hume, Dr. (of Anadarko): 322
Hunter, Robert D.: 94, 96, 110–11, 116

Indian Appropriations Act (1902): 280
Indian Marriage Law: 224
Indian Rights Association: 119, 166, 176,
    219
Indian Territory: 3, 9, 16, 18, 21, 23, 29,
    35, 38, 40, 46, 70–71, 73, 75, 140, 217,
    277, 303, 310, 322; Northern Chey-
    ennes moved to, 27, 37; Cheyenne bands

leave, 46–47; cattlemen in, 91–117; opening of, to settlers pressed, 119; and land sales, 150; and Indian Training School, West Branch, Iowa: 89
International Fair Association: 69
Iowa Indians: 150
Iron Shirt: 37, 39, 44
Irwin, Judge C. F.: 305, 323

Jackson, Charlie: 305
Jerome, David H.: 150–52, 161–66
Jerome Commission: 150, 168, 196
Johnson, George H.: 122
Johnson, William E.: 303–304, 319, 322–23
Jones, W. A. (commissioner of Indian affairs): 214, 285–86, 288
Junkin, W. W.: 170, 174

Kable, Percy: 317–18, 323
Keith, Benjamin: 273–74
Keith, Benjamin F.: 122–23, 176, 180
Keith, Charles: 178–79, 283, 308
Keith, Mary: 92, 180–81
Keith families: 176–81
Kelly, Josiah: 141
Kingfisher, Okla.: 172–73, 189, 200, 279, 303–304, 317, 319–20
Kingfisher County: 194, 311
Kiowa-Comanche Agency: 70, 96
Kiowa Dutch: 174–75
Kiowa Indians: 5–7, 69–70, 121, 134, 174, 177; and peyote, 219
Krehbiel, Rev. J. S.: 226

Laird, John W.: 27
Lamar, Lucius Q. C. (secretary of interior): 96, 108, 111, 115, 177
Lame Bull: 122
Lawton, Lieut. H. W.: 28–31, 34
Lee, Capt. J. M.: 112, 115–16, 120–23, 125–26, 132–33, 142, 201; and factionalism, 27–30; replaced, 131
Lee & Reynolds (agency traders): 11, 16, 18, 32, 112
Leeds, William M.: 35
Left Hand: 22, 40–41, 59, 61, 68–69, 75, 83, 92, 127, 149, 151, 161–65, 169,

173–75, 181, 201, 213, 215, 222, 237, 293
Left Hand, Grant: 143, 215
Left Hand Bull: 101, 105–106
Leupp, Francis E.: 283, 301–302; new policies of, 296–97, 315
Lincoln, Robert T. (secretary of war): 93
Lincoln Institute (Pennsylvania): 143
Little Big Jake: 69, 108, 127, 136, 161, 165, 167, 213, 226, 233, 338
Little Chief: 37–39, 41–46, 69–70, 81, 133, 149, 173, 215, 325, 338
Little Coyote: 45
Little Hawk: 220–21
Little Magpie: 110
Little Man: 106, 162, 189, 214, 268–69
Little Medicine: 110, 121, 127, 136, 161, 165, 226
Little Raven: 9, 18, 44, 59, 83, 105, 220
Little Robe: 25, 60, 69, 81, 93, 97, 100–102, 110–12, 116, 127–28, 136, 142, 212, 338
Little Shield: 26
Little Wolf: 33, 40–42, 45
Living Bear: 30–31, 80
Lyons, Mary E.: 267, 286

Mabry, Seth: 10, 105, 113–15
McCusker, Philip: 32
McIntyre, Maude: 220
Mackenzie, Col. Ranald S.: 6, 11, 25; Indian outbreak feared by, 31
Mackey, Capt. J. C.: 189
McKnight, Louis E.: 306
McMecham (attorney): 148
McNeil, John: 80
McPherson, A. L.: 176
Mad Wolf: 102, 161
Making Medicine: 85
Malaley, William: 20–21, 62
Man-Going-Up-Hill: 304
Man-on-a-Cloud: 192
Marsh, E. T.: 299
Martin, Gov. John A.: 109, 114
Meat (Cheyenne): 227
Medicine Bird: 219
Medicine Lodge Treaty (1867): 58, 73, 75, 146, 148, 150–52, 167, 176, 200,

213, 231, 238, 247; annuities in, 168, 174
Medicine Man (chief): 25
Medicine Pipe: 75
Medicine Rock, Rosa: 268
Medicine Woman: 278
Mescal beans: 216–20, 282, 316–20, 322; see also peyote
Mescalero Apache Indians: 70
Miles, Gen. Nelson A.: 37–38, 44, 109
Miles, Henry: 141
Miles, John D.: 3–6, 22–26, 28–33, 38–42, 45–47, 68–69, 78, 100, 103, 110, 112, 114, 122, 124, 176, 328; and food for Indians, 7–9, 11–12, 17–18, 27–28, 43–44; and Indian-property protection, 19–20; stock recovered by, 21; adminis- tration of, challenged, 31–32; criticized, 34–37; and Northern Cheyenne prison- ers, 40–41; grievances eased by, 42–43; farming urged by, 48, 57–59; transpor- tation company formed by, 61–62; ra- tion distribution changed by, 63–64; large grazing tracts projected by, 70–71; ration cut protested by, 71–75; grazing pursuits urged by, 73–74; and Indian education, 81–90; and cattlemen on reservation, 91–98; resignation of, 99; and Indian land contracts, 148–49&n., 150–52, 163, 166
Miller, Lewis H.: 252
Mills, James: 178–79, 181
Minimic: 25, 44
Missionaries: 57, 88–90, 100, 275, 287; Mennonites, 86–87, 140–41
Mitchell, E. F.: 173, 199–200; and Indian funds, 234–37
Mixed Hair, Susie: 220
Mizner, Maj. J. K.: 7, 10–11, 25–26, 29, 33, 37, 39, 42, 60, 81
Mohler, J. G.: 41
Moon Chief: 24
Mooney, James L.: 294, 319, 322
Morgan, Thomas (commissioner of Indian affairs): 173–74, 176, 182
Morrison, James S.: 94, 123
Mower: 269
Murphy, Nat: 279–80

Murray, William H. ("Cockle Burr Bill"): 323
Muskogee, Indian Territory: 69

Native American Church: 339
Neill, Lieut. Col. Thomas H.: 6
New York Times: 35
Nicholson, William: 7–9, 12, 19–20, 27, 29, 60
Noble, John W. (secretary of interior): 149–50, 164, 175, 177–78, 183
Noisy Walker: 40–41
North, Henry D.: 252
North Canadian River: 18, 59, 70, 92, 100, 121, 172

O'Conner, Washington: 40
Office of Indian Affairs: see Bureau of Indian Affairs
O'Hara, Tom (alias Red Tom): 185–86
Okarche, Okla.: 317, 319
Oklahoma City, Okla.: 148, 152, 173
Oklahoma Country: see Unassigned Lands
Oklahoma Territory: 137, 139, 150, 167, 169–70, 172–74, 178–80, 182, 191, 194, 204–208, 217, 223–24, 230, 238, 243, 253, 255, 271, 276–77, 280–82, 288, 291, 302–303, 310, 338–39
Old Bear: 18, 33
Old Crow: 18, 35, 40–41, 46, 151–52, 161, 165, 167, 169–70, 212–13, 227, 338
Old Whirlwind: 3, 9, 25, 338
Open range: 202–208
Osage Indians: 13
Otterby, John: 196, 308
Otterby, Thomas: 317, 319, 321–22

Painter, Charles C.: 119, 166, 176
Panic of 1893: 204
Parker, Quanah: 212, 219
Patents: 131, 287, 301, 307, 311–16
Pawnee (warrior): 24
Pawnee Indians: 13
Pawnee Man: 83, 105, 145–46, 191, 213
Payne, David L.: 119
Pendleton, David: see Making Medicine
Petter, Rev. Rudolf: 214, 287

Peyote: 216–20, 282, 302–303, 326, 339; ceremonies attacked, 316–24; *see also* mescal beans
Pine Ridge Agency: 46–47
Pipe Woman (Ella Romero): 276–78
Platte River: 21, 23, 35
Plumb, Sen. Preston B.: 72–73
Poisal, John: 59, 92, 122, 177, 291–92
Poisal, Mrs. John: 304
Poisal, Robert: 59
Pope, Maj. Gen. John: 5–7, 11, 22, 39–40, 76; Indian outbreak feared by, 31
Porcupine (Northern Cheyenne): 40, 46
Potawatomi Indians: 150
Potter, Col. J. H.: 97, 107, 112
Powder Face: 9, 11, 18, 22, 59, 68–69, 75, 92, 100, 102–103, 111, 127, 140
Powder Face, Clarence: 298
Powder River: 46
Prairie Chief: 188, 243
Pratt, Capt. Richard: 81, 83, 140, 143, 222
Price, Hiram: 71–72, 76–77, 88–89, 99
Pulling, W. M.: 189, 220, 226

Quakers: 78

Randall, Maj. George M.: 45, 71–73, 75–76
Rations, annuities: 7–9, 12, 16, 38, 60, 63, 70, 74–75, 109, 145, 194, 231, 235, 265, 287; beef, 4, 9–13, 19, 29–30, 35, 43, 45, 71–73, 75, 137, 163; commodities, 27–30, 35, 75; and distribution methods, 28–29, 63–64, 137–38; withholding of, threatened, 57; cuts restored, 76; funds cut for, 243–45; failure of, 296
Red Blanket: 33
Red Cloud Agency: 21–26, 29–30; Northern Cheyennes moved from, 27
Red Hair, James: 317
Red Leggings: 294–95
Red Lodge, Cosah: 188–89
Red Moon: 132–33, 170, 183–85, 205, 213, 217, 226, 230, 249
Red Moon Day School: 267
Red Wolf: 75, 128, 133
Rendlebrock, Capt. Joseph: 34
Renewal of the Sacred Arrows: 339

Revised Statutes of Oklahoma Territory: 318
Reynolds, A. E.: 65, 68
Reynolds, George E.: 98, 110–11
Reynolds, Matt: 149, 164
Rhoads, James E.: 99
Ridge Bear: 37, 39, 41, 46
Riggs, Alfred: 119
Riggs, Stacy: 251
Robe Red Wolf: 319–20
Rock, or Stone (Arapaho): 174
Roger Mills County, Okla.: 186–87, 206
Roman Nose: 107–108, 128, 187–88
Roman Nose, Henry: 85, 215, 298
Romero, Ella (Pipe Woman): 276–78
Romero, Rafael: 276–78
Romero, Rosa (Rosey): 276–77
Rose Bud, Battle of: 26
Ross, Joshua: 58, 69
Rowlodge, Jess: 219
Row-of-Lodges: 59, 161, 173, 181, 213, 215, 237
Ruckman, Charles W.: 305, 316
Running Buffalo: 100–101, 109, 115

Sac Indians: 150
Sage (Cheyenne leader): 269
San Carlos Indians: 70
Sand Hill (chief): 24–25
Sand Hill fight: 6, 17, 21, 24
Saville, J. J.: 22–23
Sayre, Warren G.: 150–52, 162, 164
Scabby (Cheyenne): 124
Scothorn, J. W.: 298–99
Schurz, Carl (secretary of interior): 64–65
Seay, A. J.: 172, 182–85, 197
Sechtem, Mrs. Anna: 279
Seger, John H.: 58–62, 65–66, 85, 88, 148, 186, 227, 233, 292–94; school run by, 61, 78–80; on Washita (Colony), 121, 136, 233, 240–42, 273; and Indian relocation, 121–22; and new farms, 122–23, 134; and wheat harvest, 139–40; allotment aid of, 175–76; and crop failure, 248; *see also* Cheyenne-Arapaho Manual Training and Labor School, cattle
Sergeant Meat: 162

Settlers, white: 148, 167, 173; lands available for, 175&n., 181; and land run of April, 1892, 182; tensions, fears of, 184–88; and Indian prejudice, 188–89, 207; and Indian crimes, 189–90; and thefts from Indians, 190–93, 207; taxes on, 193–97; resentment of, about Indian ownership, 197; and Indian allotment leases, 197–99, 269–81; business practices of, with Indians, 199–200; and open range, 202–208; Indian land sales to, 281–88; and lease-pay delinquency, 305–306
Shaking Timber: 291–92
Shanks, John P. C.: 21
Sharp Nose Woman: 174
Shawnee Indians: 150
Shell, Charles E.: Indian habits probed by, 302–304; and lease-payment problems, 305–306; and leasing-program interpretation, 306–309; and injunctions against whites, 309–11; patents assistance of, 311–15; peyote ceremonies attacked by, 316–24
Sheridan, Col. Michael: 112
Sheridan, Lieut. Gen. Philip H.: 27, 34, 37, 39, 109–11, 113–15, 117, 281
Sherman, Gen. William Tecumseh: 11, 27
Shields, G. W.: 178
Shields, Peter: 122–23, 176, 178
Shields, Peter, Jr.: 315
Shields families: 176–81
Short, O. F.: 24, 26
Short Nose: 295
Short Teeth, Jennie: 275
Short Teeth, Mrs. Mollie: 190–91
Simpson, E. J.: 212
Sioux Indians: 3, 7, 21, 24–26, 215
Sitting Bull: 26, 75
Sitting Bull (Scabby Bull): 183, 215
Sleeper, L.: 121
Sleeping Wolf: 145
Smith, Hoke (secretary of interior): 180–81
Smith, J. Q.: 7, 37
Smith, Thomas: 238
Society of Friends: 78
South Canadian River: 5, 70, 92, 121, 233

Spooner, Sen. John C.: 30
Spotted Horse: 110, 116, 161, 183–85, 196, 205, 249
Spotted Wolf: 145
Springer Amendment to Indian Bill (1889): 150
Squaw (Northern Cheyenne): 33
Standard Cattle Company: 93
Standing Bird: 255
Standing Elk: 30–31, 34, 46, 80, 165
Star, Veseva: 224
Steele, G. W.: 173
Stone Calf: 18, 38&n., 44, 97, 100–102, 106–107, 109, 112, 116, 127, 133, 136, 142, 184, 338; and grievances, 110–11; death of, 128
Stouch, George W. H.: 225, 265, 267, 271–75, 298–99, 302, 316; and allotment contests, 276–81; and allotment sales, 281–83&n., 284–88, 297; role of, in Indian conformity, 288–93
Strong Bow: 75, 128
Sumner, Col. Edwin V.: 107
Sun Dance: 81, 85, 134, 217, 292–95, 324, 336, 338–39
Sweeny, John W.: 279
Sweet Water: 269
Sweezy, Carl: 213
Sweezy, Frank R.: 312–13

Tackett, Marine D.: 169–72, 174–75
Tall Bear: 127, 151, 213
Tall Bull: 165, 215, 338
Tasso, Andrew: 199, 251
Taxes: 193–97
Taylor, Reuben: 317–24
Teller, Henry M. (secretary of interior): 76–77, 94–96, 98, 101–104, 119
Territorial Marriage Law (1897): 290
Territory of Oklahoma v. Howling Wolf, Reuben Taylor and Percy Kable: 319
Texas Panhandle: 4–5, 8, 11, 17, 35, 76, 135
Thelen, Gustav: 200
Three Fingers: 286, 338
Thunder (Cheyenne leader): 128, 187–88, 215
Thunder Bull: 213

Timber, thefts of: 192
Tongue River: 28, 37, 41
Tonner, A. C.: 247–48, 270, 274, 294
Trowbridge, Commissioner R. E.: 84
Tucker, Dan: 62, 220
Twins (Two Sons): 278
Tyler, Leonard: 89, 145, 149, 162–63, 166, 199, 215, 316–17, 321, 323–24

Unassigned Lands (Oklahoma Country): 122, 135, 150, 176–77
United States Revised Statutes: 112
Ute Indians: 26
Ute Woman: 123–24

Volz, John: 94
Voth, Rev. H.: 88–90, 141, 144–45, 148

Wade, Col. James F.: 165, 184
Wakefield, John: 271–72
Walking-in-the-Middle: 202
Warden, Cleaver: 89, 162, 166, 215
Warpath Bear: 207
Warren, Wesley: 98, 101, 124
Washburn, H. C.: 322–23
Washee: 138, 278
Washington, George (Caddo chief): 59
Washita, Okla.: 90, 169
Washita River: 4, 18, 70, 121, 128, 151, 172, 175–76, 187, 233, 279
Watonga, Okla.: 189, 192, 219, 224, 227, 229, 250, 282, 290, 298, 305, 310
Weakley, James S.: 20
Webster, Dan: 304
Weigel, E. F.: 181
Wells, W. W.: 98
Westfall, Dr. George R.: 218–19
Wevoka: 138, 150, 183, 215–16
Whirlwind: 75, 103, 108, 110
Whisky: 5, 32, 225, 282, 301–304, 316, 319, 326
White, Byron E.: 284, 294, 298
White Antelope: 25, 127, 133, 162, 165, 267
White Bird: 212
White Bear: 190, 217
White Buffalo: 69, 102

White Chief: 212
White-Eyed Antelope: 166, 213
White Fool: 284–85
White Horse: 44, 110, 128, 167, 211–14
White Shield: 75, 78, 89, 97, 100, 135, 162, 167, 170, 183–84, 205, 213, 226, 230, 245, 249, 338; on visits to northern tribes, 267–68
White Shield, Harvey: 89–90
White Shirt: 221–22
White Shirt, Mrs. Tom: 198
White Shirt, Tom: 198
White Snake: 146
Whittlesey, E.: 119
Wichita, Kans.: 61–63, 68–69
Wichita and Affiliated Bands: *see* Wichita Indians
Wichita Indians: 13, 150, 152, 176
Wichita Reservation: 93, 96, 134
Wickes, Rev. J. B.: 85
Wicks, Charles M.: 317
Wild Hog (Northern Cheyenne): 30–31, 33–34, 40–41, 46, 80
Williams, Benjamin: 5, 9–10, 19–20
Williams, Gilbert B.: 131–35, 143–45; replaced as agent, 135; and Indian land contract, 148–49&n., 150, 166
Williams, Johnny: 144–45
Willow Dance: 217
Wilson, Alfred M.: 156
Wilson, Horace E.: 268–69
Wolf Ahead: 299, 325
Wolf Chief: 145, 269
Wolf Creek: 5–6, 13, 17
Wolf Face: 133, 146, 151–52, 161, 167
Wolf Hair: 185
Wolf Robe: 131, 338
Woman-Stands-in-the-Sand-Hill: 276
Wood, Lieut. A. E.: 10
Woodson, A. E.: 179–80, 185–87, 200, 209–13, 243–45, 265, 271, 275, 320; on Indian-property protection, 190–93; and tax question, 194–97; leasing changes sought by, 198–204; and fund-distribution plan, 201; and open-range problems, 202–208; and Indian ceremonies, 217–20; policies of, for change, 220–30; and allotment pay, 231–40;

and houses for Indians, 246–47; and
  Indian agriculture, 248–56
Woodward, O. J.: 47
Woodworth, Mrs. Mary L.: 229
Woolworth, Arnold: 297–98
Wright, Will: 310–11

Yellow Bear: 65, 68, 214
Yellow Bird: 291–92

Yellow Dog: 217
Yellow Horse: 21–22, 25–26, 59; involved
  in crimes, 24&n.
Yellow Shirt: 290
Yellowstone River: 46
Yellow Woman: 124
Young Whirlwind: 133, 136, 145, 151,
  161, 165, 167, 169–70, 187, 210, 232,
  237, 338

DATE DUE

Demco, Inc. 38-293